THE BANK DIRECTOR'S HANDBOOK

The Board Member's Guide to
Banking & Bank Management

THE BANK DIRECTOR'S HANDBOOK
The Board Member's Guide to Banking & Bank Management

Benton E. Gup, Ph.D.
The University of Alabama
Tuscaloosa, Alabama

A BankLine Publication
IRWIN
Professional Publishing®
Chicago • London • Singapore

A BankLine Publication
IRWIN
Professional Publishing®

This publication is designed to provide accurate and authoritative information in regard to the subject matter covered. It is sold with the understanding that neither the author or the publisher is engaged in rendering legal, accounting, or other professional service. If legal advice or other expert assistance is required, the services of a competent professional person should be sought.

From a Declaration of Principles jointly adopted by a Committee of the American Bar Association and a Committee of Publishers.

Irwin Professional Book Team

Publisher: *Wayne McGuirt*
Acquisitions editor: *Mark Butler*
Marketing manager: *Brian Hayes*
Managing editor: *Kevin Thornton*
Project editor: *Lynne Basler*
Production supervisor: *Laurie Kersch/Carol Klein*
Assistant manager, desktop services: *Jon Christopher*
Compositor: *Precision Graphic Services, Inc.*
Jacket designer: *Palmer Design Inc.*
Typeface: *11/13 Times Roman*
Printer: *Buxton Skinner Printing Company*

◥◤ **Times Mirror**
◣◢ **Higher Education Group**

Library of Congress Cataloging-in-Publication Data

Gup, Benton E.
     The bank director's handbook : the board member's guide to banking
and bank management / Benton E. Gup.
         p.   cm.
     Includes index.
     ISBN 1-55738-792-3
     1. Bank management—Handbooks, manuals, etc.   2. Banks and
banking—United States—Handbooks, manuals, etc.   I. Title.
HG1615.G868   1996
332.1'068—dc20   95–45384

Printed in the United States of America

1 2 3 4 5 6 7 8 9 0 BS 2 1 0 9 8 7 6 5

To Jean, Lincoln, Andrew, Jeremy, and Carol

Preface

Most bank directors are successful people. They have excelled in their own fields, such as business, law, medicine, sports, or public service. They have dealt with banks as borrowers and lenders. However, they may not understand banking to the degree that is required of them as bank directors. Banking is a dynamic, complex, and regulated industry.

Banking is dynamic because banks are consolidating through mergers, acquisitions, and failures. The number of commercial banks in the United States declined from 14,147 in 1985 to about 10,000 banks in 1995. Some experts predict the number of banks will decline to about 3,000 or fewer in the years to come. Banking is dynamic because banks are offering new products to compete with nonbanking firms that offer financial services. Mutual funds, cash management services, and derivative products such as caps, collars, and floors are a few examples of new products. Banking is dynamic because of changes in technology. They are just beginning to do retail business on the internet—the worldwide communications network.

Banking is complex for a number of reasons: much technical knowledge is required to understand financial instruments such as collateralized mortgage obligations, swaps, futures, and forwards. Banking is complex because of the securitization of loans. Securitized home mortgage loans, for example, have lower risk-based capital requirements than other home mortgage loans. It is complex because of lender liability. Banks are being sued by borrowers who claim that banks loaned them too much money and by others who claim that the banks lent them too little.

Finally, banks are regulated by federal and state banking authorities. Many bankers would argue that they are overregulated. Moreover, compliance with the Community Reinvestment Act, the Home Mortgage Disclosure Act, the Truth in Lending Act, the Right to Privacy Act, and dozens of other acts is excessively costly and counterproductive.

Bank directors are expected to be familiar with all these issues and more. This book is designed to help fill that information gap. It provides an overview of selected topics that directors need to know in 11 chapters that deal with the following subjects:

1. Legal duties of directors.
2. Strategic planning.
3. Marketing strategies.
4. Analyzing banks' financial statements.
5. Bank capital.
6. Asset/liability management.
7. Managing derivatives risk.
8. Credit and lending.
9. Fraud and insider abuse.
10. Internal controls and auditing.
11. Mergers and acquisitions.

Other features include special sections titled "Think about This" found in most of the chapters and appendixes concerning loan policies and the FDIC's Red Flags warning lists for fraud.

Special thanks are due to J. Barry Mason and Gay Evans. Dr. J. Barry Mason, Dean of the College of Commerce and Business Administration, University of Alabama, wrote Chapter 3: Developing Bank Marketing Strategy. Dean Mason is the author of several leading marketing texts, and has published more than 100 articles on marketing. Gay Evans, Managing Director of Banker's Trust International, PLC (London), wrote Chapter 7: Managing Derivatives Risk. This chapter was first presented as a paper at the Federal Reserve Bank of Chicago's Bank Structure Conference in May 1995.

Benton Gup

Contents

Chapter One
BANK DIRECTORS' DUTIES   1

Accountability of Directors to Shareholders, 1
Strong Boards, Strong Banks; Weak Boards, Weak Banks, 3
The Responsibilities of Boards of Directors, 5
    Duty of Care, 6
    Business Judgment Rule, 7
    Duty of Loyalty, 8
Typical Committees, 10
    Executive Committee, 10
    Audit Committee, 11
    Asset/Liability Committee, 11
    Investment Committee, 12
    Loan Committee, 12
    Trust Committee, 12
    Personnel Committee, 13
Practices Deemed Unsafe or Unsound, 13
The SERVE Principle, 15
Conclusion, 16

Chapter Two
STRATEGIC MANAGEMENT   17

What Is Strategic Management? 17
    Strategic Management Defined, 17
    What Strategic Management Is Not, 18
Successful and Failed Strategies, 19
    Keys to Success, 19

Reasons for Failure, 20

The Complexity of Making Decisions, 21

The Reality of Performance, 23

The Major Factors That Affect Firms Are beyond Their Control, 26

The External Environment, 26

What Management Can Control, 28

Sustained Competitive Advantage, 30

Essential Ingredients, 31

Stakeholders, 32

Stakeholders Defined, 32

The Value of the Bank, 33

Operating Environment, 34

Corporate Factors, 34

Improving Communications, 35

Other Stakeholders, 36

Conclusion, 37

Appendix to Chapter Two: Criteria for Evaluating Financial Communications Efforts, 37

Chapter Three
DEVELOPING BANK MARKETING STRATEGY   43

The Tasks of Marketing Management, 43

Crafting Marketing Strategy, 44

Preconditions for Strategy Selection, 48

Situation Analysis, 48

Customer Analysis and Marketing Strategy Development, 49

The Scope of Customer Analysis, 51

Market Segmentation Strategies, 54

Mass-Market Strategy, 54

Differentiated Strategy, 55

Concentrated Strategy, 55

Defining Market Segments, 56

Positioning within Target Markets, 57
  Alternative Bases for Positioning, 57
Implementing Marketing Strategy, 58
  Services Development Strategy, 58
  Developing the Pricing Policy, 60
  Promotion Strategy, 65
  Distribution of Services, 68
Understanding the Fundamentals of Long-Term
Customer Satisfaction, 69
  The Dimensions of Customer Satisfaction, 69
  Diagnosing Customer Satisfaction Shortfalls, 70

Chapter Four
EVALUATING BANKS' FINANCIAL
PERFORMANCE   73
Four Key Steps in Analysis, 73
Bank Financial Statements, 74
  Understanding Bank Assets, 74
  Understanding Bank Liabilities and Equity, 78
  Understanding the Statement of Operations, 79
  Other Relevant Information, 82
The Directors' Point of View, 83
  Caveats about the Data, 83
  Profitability, 87
  Capital, 89
  Liquidity, 90
  Asset Quality, 91
Comparing Financial Performance, 92
  The *FDIC Quarterly Banking Profile,* 92
  Sheshunoff Information Services, 96
  Uniform Bank Performance Report, 96
Conclusion, 101
Appendix A: Bank Profile, 102
Appendix B: Uniform Bank Performance Report, 111

Chapter Five
BANK CAPITAL   126

Capital Requirements, 126
  Tier 1: Core Capital, 126
  Tier 2: Supplementary Capital, 127
  Risk-Weighted Assets, 128
  Prompt Corrective Action, 128
  Well Capitalized, but Still In Trouble, 132
The Role of Capital, 132
  Capital Facilitates Growth, 132
  Capital Absorbs Unanticipated Losses, 134
  High Financial Leverage Is Risky, 134
  Stockholders versus Regulators, 136
Conclusion, 138

Chapter Six
ASSET/LIABILITY MANAGEMENT: DEALING WITH INTEREST RATE RISK   139

What Is Asset/Liability Management? 139
  Interest Rate Risk Defined, 139
  Investment Risk, 140
  Income Risk and Interest Rate Sensitivity, 142
  Basis Risk, 143
  Options Risk, 144
  Yield Curve Risk, 144
  Trading Risk, 144
The Effects of Interest Rate Risk on Income
and Value, 144
  Gap and Net Interest Income, 144
  Managing Interest Rate Spreads, 149
Techniques for Managing Interest Rate Risk:
Strengths and Weaknesses, 150
  Gap Analysis, 151
  Duration Analysis, 156
  Simulations, 164

Hedging, 166
  The Basics of Hedging, 166
  Minimum Variance Hedge, 167
  Hedging Strategies, 168
  Puts and Calls, 170
  Effects of Hedging on NII and Value, 171
  To Hedge or Not to Hedge? 173
Swaps, 174
  Uses of Swaps, 175
  Risks of Swaps, 175
Conclusion, 176
Selected References, 177

Chapter Seven
MANAGING DERIVATIVES RISK   179
What Is Risk Management? 180
  The Conventional View, 180
  The Enlightened View, 180
  Requirements of a Risk Management System, 180
A Framework for Risk Management, 182
  Step 1. Establish Risk Categories, 182
  Step 2. Unbundle Products, 183
  Step 3. Quantify Risk Exposures, 183
  Step 4. Provide Risk-Adjusted Capital, 184
Are Derivatives Any Different? 185
Conclusion, 186

Chapter Eight
CREDIT POLICIES AND PRACTICES   187
What Is Credit? 187
Credit Policies, 187
  Lending Authority, 190
  Loan Review, 193
  The Least Directors Should Do, 195
Lending Is about Risk, 196

Seven Ways to Make Loans, 197
    1. Customer Requests, 197
    2. Solicit Loans, 197
    3. Buy Loans, 198
    4. Commitments, 198
    5. Refinancing, 198
    6. Loan Brokers, 198
    7. Overdrafts, 199
Types of Loans, 199
    Commercial and Industrial Loans, 199
    Real Estate Loans, 201
    Consumer Lending, 203
Evaluating a Loan Request, 205
    The Crucial Role of Information, 205
    The Six Cs of Credit, 207
Collateral, 209
    Characteristics of Good Collateral, 209
    Denial of Loans, 210
The Worst Cases, 211
    Charge-Off, 211
    Impact on Capital, 211
    Lender Liability, 212
Conclusion, 213

Chapter Nine
DEALING WITH FRAUD AND INSIDER ABUSE   **214**
Fraud and Insider Abuse, 214
    Fraud Defined, 214
    Insider Abuse Defined, 216
Small Banks Are the Primary Targets, 217
Common Schemes, 218
Insiders Versus Outsiders, 219
    Insiders, 219
    Outsiders, 220

Money Laundering, 221
  Organized Crime, 222
  Money-Laundering Jargon, 223
  The Process of Money Laundering, 224
  Know Your Customers! 224
  The OCC's Red Flags, 228
What Can Be Done to Deter and Detect Fraud? 230
  The Role of Directors, 230
  Bank Security Personnel, 230
  Audits, 230
  Examiners, 232
  Criminal Referral Reports, 233
  FDIC Red Flags, 233
Linked-Financing and Brokered Transactions, 234
Conclusion, 235

Chapter Ten
A DIRECTOR'S VIEW OF INTERNAL CONTROLS AND AUDITING   236

Internal Controls, 236
  What Are Internal Controls? 236
  Reasons for Using Internal Controls, 237
  Establishing Internal Controls, 240
Auditing, 243
  Closing the Expectation Gap, 243
  Internal Auditors, 251
  The Role of Bank Examiners, 252
  Security Personnel, 253
Conclusion, 263

Chapter Eleven
MERGERS AND ACQUISITIONS   254

Large Numbers of Mergers, 254
Creating Shareholder Value, 255
  Rule 1: Pure Conglomerate Mergers May Not Create New Shareholder Value, 255

Rule 2: Countercyclical Acquisitions May Not Create Value, 257

Rule 3: The Stock Market Does Not Reward Growth
due Exclusively to Acquisitions, 257

Rule 4: Related Diversification Can Create Value, 257

Rule 5: Mergers Can Be Used to Reach a Critical Size
Where Size Is a Factor, 258

Rule 6: Acquisitions Can Be Used to Defer Taxes, 258

Merger Terms, 259

Taxes, 259

Liability, 260

Market Value Exchange Ratio, 260

Price/Book Value Ratio, 261

Price/Earnings Ratio, 262

Soft Issues, 266

Offensive and Defensive Merger Tactics, 266

The Offense, 266

The Defense, 267

Accounting for Mergers, 268

Purchase Method, 268

Pooling of Interests Method, 270

Income, 270

Restrictions, 270

Conclusion, 271

Appendix A   Loan Policy for Lakeside Bank, 273

Appendix B   Loan Policy for Metropolitan Bank, 287

Appendix C   Loan Policy for County Bank, 297

Appendix D   FDIC Red Flags for Fraud and Insider Abuse, 313

Index, 335

Chapter One

Bank Directors' Duties

Management acts as agents for the shareholders who own private corporations such as commercial banks. However, management does not always have the same interests or incentives that the shareholders do. Shareholders elect directors to protect their interests. In legal jargon, directors have a fiduciary duty to the shareholders. This means directors are accountable to shareholders for their actions.[1] In the case of banks, directors are also accountable to bank regulators, the deposit insurance fund, and, to some degree, the public. This chapter provides a general overview of the duties of directors.

ACCOUNTABILITY OF DIRECTORS TO SHAREHOLDERS

In theory, directors are accountable to their shareholders. In practice, however, the theory does not always prevail. To make practice conform to theory, the Teachers Insurance Annuity Association–College Retirement Equities Fund (TIAA–CREF) produced a *Policy Statement on Corporate Governance.*[2] TIAA–CREF is one of the largest retirement systems in the United States. Although this financial organization is not a commercial bank, the role of its directors is the same. The following paragraphs dealing with boards of directors are quoted directly from its document on corporate governance. They reveal how TIAA–CREF sharpened the accountability of directors to shareholders.

---

[1] For additional discussion of this point, see Robert Monks and Nell Minow, "The Director's New Clothes (or the Myth of Corporate Accountability)," *Journal of Applied Corporate Finance,* Fall 1991, pp. 78–84.

[2] For additional information, write TIAA–CREF, 730 Third Ave., New York, NY 10107-3206.

The board should be composed of a majority of independent directors. The board committee structure should include audit, compensation, and nominating committees consisting entirely of independent directors. For this purpose, independence means no present or former employment by the company or any significant financial or personal tie to the company or its management which could interfere with the director's loyalty to the shareholders. We concur in principle with the New York Stock Exchange (NYSE) definition of independence, which excludes persons who act on a regular basis either individually or as a representative of an organization serving as a professional adviser, consultant or legal counsel to the company if the relationship is considered material. The NYSE definition would not disqualify a director from independent status due to customary commercial transactions carried on at arm's length in the ordinary course of business if, in the board's discretion, the relationship would not interfere with the individual's ability to exercise independent judgment.

The board should establish a fixed retirement policy for directors, and a requirement that all directors should own common shares in the company. A reasonable minimum ownership interest could be defined as stock holdings equal to approximately one-half of the amount of the director's annual retainer fee.

The board should be composed of qualified individuals who reflect diversity of experience, gender, race and age. Each director should represent all shareholders; therefore, TIAA–CREF opposes the nomination of specific representational directors, and the practice of cumulative voting in the election of directors.

TIAA–CREF recognizes the responsibility of the board to organize its functions and conduct its business in the manner it deems most efficient, consistent with these and similar good guidelines. Therefore, in the absence of special circumstances, ordinarily we would not support shareholder resolutions concerning separation of the positions of CEO and Chairman, the formation of shareholder advisory committees, the requirement that candidates for the board be nominated by shareholders, shareholder mandated election of directors on an annual basis, or a requirement that directors must attend a specific percentage of board meetings, unless the board supports such measures. We are also against restricting the date of the annual meeting since it is management's prerogative to set the meeting date. The corporation should be free to indemnify directors for legal expenses and judgments in connection with their service as directors and eliminate the director's liability for ordinary negligence. Directors should be held liable to the corporation for violations of their fiduciary duty involving gross or sustained and repeated negligence.

The board should have a mechanism to evaluate its performance and that of individual directors. At a minimum, there should be an annul review of performance by the board that measures results against appropriate criteria defined by the board.

While TIAA–CREF normally votes for the board's nominees, we vote for alternative candidates when our analysis indicates that those candidates will better represent shareholder interests. We may also decline to vote for unopposed candidates when their record indicates that their election to the board would not be in the interest of shareholders, or when we have requested a meeting with independent directors and have been refused.

Board independence is a key issue. The next section describes how strong, independent boards are associated with strong banks and weak boards are associated with weak banks.

STRONG BOARDS, STRONG BANKS; WEAK BOARDS, WEAK BANKS

The Office of the Comptroller of the Currency (OCC) found that deficiencies within boards of directors contributed to problem banks and bank failures.[3] The boards of such banks were frequently weak—lacking oversight responsibilities and controls—overly aggressive, or some combination of the two. In contrast, none of the consistently healthy banks the OCC examined had such deficiencies on their boards. The OCC concluded that one of the major differences between failed banks and healthy banks was the caliber of management which reflected the policies of an active and involved board of directors.

The US General Accounting Office cited passive and/or negligent directors as the major contributing factor in 90 percent of the 286 banks that failed in 1990 and 1991.[4] Passive and/or negligent means the board did not properly oversee management's operation of the bank. The failed banks had problems with insider loans, insider abuse, and fraud.[5] Small banks had the highest incidence of loan losses to insiders.

---

[3] *Bank Failure: An Evaluation of the Factors Contributing to the Failure of National Banks* (Washington, DC: Comptroller of the Currency, June 1988), pp. 5–7, 15–16.

[4] US General Accounting Office, *Bank Insider Activities,* GAO/GGD-94-88, March 1994, pp. 6, 32.

[5] Regulations pertaining to loans to insiders are covered in 12 CFR 215 (Federal Reserve Regulation O).

A study of 205 failed S&Ls came to a similar conclusion: The directors of virtually all of them failed to act prudently.[6] In another study of failed S&Ls, the boards were passive. One director said the thrift's board did not question business decisions of the former chairperson because he owned the thrift; the directors thought he could do as he pleased.[7] This chapter presents an overview of what bank boards should and should not do. By carrying out their duties correctly, bank directors can go a long way toward helping their banks flourish.

Unfortunately, weak and ineffective boards of directors are not uncommon according to management expert Peter Drucker. Drucker wrote,

> But there is one thing all boards have in common, regardless of their legal position. *They do not function.* The decline of the board is a universal phenomenon of this century. Perhaps nothing shows it as clearly as the board, which, in law, is the governing organ of a corporation, was always the last group to hear the trouble in the great business catastrophes of this century. . . . Whenever a financial scandal breaks, the board's failure is blamed on stupidity, negligence of board members, or on the failure of management to keep the board informed. But when such malfunction occurs with unfailing regularity, one must concede that it is the institution that fails to perform rather than individuals.[8]

The massive failures of banks and S&Ls in recent years are strong evidence that our institutions have a structural problem. Drucker goes on to say that boards have become a legal fiction. While that may be so de facto, de jure they are charged with certain responsibilities for which they are held liable. Not only may the banking regulators sue directors of failed institutions, but shareholders may institute class action suits, too. In a class action suit in Los Angeles against certain officers and directors of the parent company of Lincoln Savings & Loan, the share-

---

[6] Philip F. Bartholomew, financial economist, Federal Home Loan Bank Board, statement before the United States Sentencing Commission, April 7, 1989. Also see US General Accounting Office, *Failed Thrifts: Internal Control Weaknesses Create and Environment Conducive to Fraud, Insider Abuse, and Related Unsafe Practices,* statement of Frederick D. Wolf before the Subcommittee on Criminal Justice Committee on the Judiciary, House of Representatives, GAO/T-AFMD-89-4, March 22, 1989, p. 13.

[7] US General Accounting Office, *Thrift Failures: Costly Failures Resulted from Regulatory Violations and Unsafe Practices,* GAO/AFMD-89-62, June 1989, p. 18.

[8] Peter F. Drucker, *Management: Tasks, Responsibilities, Practices* (New York: Harper & Row, 1974), p. 628.

holders charged securities frauds and racketeering arising from the sale of bonds that were virtually worthless and caused their stock to decline in value.[9]

THE RESPONSIBILITIES OF BOARDS OF DIRECTORS

The stockholders of a bank elect a board of directors to oversee the bank's affairs and to ensure competent management. Competent management includes the depth and succession of management. Thus, the board has the ultimate responsibility for the success or failure of the bank. This applies whether the bank is independent or part of a holding company.

Statutes and regulations provide boards of directors with general guidelines with respect to their structure and duties. Federal banking regulations establish the minimum and maximum number of board members for national banks. National banks must have at least 5, but no more than 25, board members. S&Ls also have requirements concerning the composition of their boards. For example, no more than two directors may be from the same family or more than two lawyers from the same law firm. Moreover, participation by independent directors is essential to lend perspective and objectivity to board decisions. The intent here is to eliminate conflicts of interest and promote independent judgment.

In addition to a regular board of directors, banks may have advisory directors who bring particular expertise to the board. Advisory directors usually play a limited role in board activities and may not be liable for board decisions.

The legal duties of directors are dictated by laws and regulations. Under common law, directors are expected to carry out their functions with "duty of care" and "duty of loyalty."[10] These legal terms mean directors are required to be diligent and honest in managing the affairs of the bank and authorize bank management to do only those things that the bank is permitted to do by law and regulations. The duty of care holds directors to a standard of care equal to what a prudent person would use in

---

[9] "A Seat on the Board Is Getting Hotter," *Business Week,* July 3, 1989, p. 73.

[10] For a detailed discussion of these and other duties, see, Douglas V. Austin, *Commercial Bank Director Liabilities and Responsibilities,* 3rd ed. (Toledo, OH: Austin Financial Services, 1993).

similar circumstances.[11] In this regard, directors are expected to know what is going on at their banks. They have a "duty to investigate" existing problems or ones that may develop, and make sure that steps are taken to correct them. Failure to comply with the duty of care standard may be considered "negligence" in the eyes of the court, which said, "Directors who willingly allow others to make major decisions affecting the future of the corporation wholly without supervision or oversight may not defend their lack of knowledge, for that ignorance itself is a breach of fiduciary duty."[12]

Under Section 212 k of the Financial Institutions Reform, Recovery, and Enforcement Act of 1989 (FIRREA), directors may be held personally liable for monetary damages in civil actions brought by the Federal Deposit Insurance Corporation (FDIC) for "gross negligence, including any similar conduct or conduct that demonstrates a greater disregard of a duty of care (than gross negligence) including intentional tortious conduct, as such terms are defined and determined under applicable State law."[13]

Duty of Care

The duty of care standard does not mandate that directors guarantee the conduct of a bank's officers or the bank's profitability, and does not hold them accountable for errors in business judgment. Directors are, however, expected to act in good faith and carry out their duties diligently. This includes providing direction, oversight, and supervision of the bank's activities. More specifically, the directors must monitor the conduct of the bank's business. This includes keeping abreast of developments that may be a cause for concern for the bank. In addition, directors must use reason-

---

[11] *The Director's Book: The Role of a National Bank Director* (Washington, DC: Comptroller of the Currency, August 1987), pp. 56–57; Alan E. Grunewald and Richard B. Foster, Jr., "Bank Directors' Liability for Negligence and the Business Judgment Rule," *Journal of the Midwest Finance Association* 12 (1983), pp. 109–27; Michael Patriarca, "The Role and Responsibility of a Savings Institution Director," *Perspectives,* Federal Home Loan Bank of San Francisco, Fall 1988, pp. 2–6.

[12] *Joy* v. *North,* 692 F. 2d 880, 896 (2d Cir. 1982), cited in Federal Home Loan Bank Board Memoranda #R-62, "Directors' Responsibilities: FHLBB Guidelines; Procedures for Obtaining Information to Support Directors' Decisions," November 1988, p. 2689.

[13] The US Court of Appeals in Chicago ruled that the Resolution Trust Corporation (RTC) must prove gross negligence, rather than simple negligence, on the part of directors and officers of a failed savings and loan (*FDIC Banking Review,* Winter 1995, p. 38).

able decision-making processes and make reasonable decisions.[14] Directors' activities include

- Initiating appropriate business strategies.
- Establishing written operating policies and internal controls required by statute, regulations, and principles of safety and soundness and taking reasonable steps to ensure compliance with the policies. This requires being fully aware of the bank's operations, products, and services.
- Selecting, monitoring, and evaluating management and employees. This involves delegating authority to execute the board's policies. However, directors cannot delegate their legal accountability as fiduciaries for the care and management of the bank.
- Monitoring and assessing the progress of business operations.
- Reviewing bank examinations and audit reports and taking appropriate actions to correct deficiencies. This includes verifying that the deficiencies have been corrected.

Directors must require management to provide them with ample and timely information to enable them to fulfill their responsibilities on a fully informed basis.

Business Judgment Rule

Directors must exercise sound "business judgment" in performing their duties for the bank. The FDIC will not bring civil suits against directors who fulfill their responsibilities "and who make reasonable business judgments on a fully informed basis after proper deliberation."[15] This means

---

[14] Based on Melvin A. Eisenber, "The Duty of Care of Corporate Directors and Officers," *University of Pittsburgh Law Review* 51 (Summer 1990) appears in a statement by Clark M. Clifford before the U.S. House, *Bank of Commerce and Credit International—Part 1*, hearing before the Committee on Banking, Finance and Urban Affairs, 102nd. Cong., 1st Sess., Sept. 11, 1991, Serial No. 102-69, 815-831. Also see Robert S. Apfelberg, "The Role of Outside Directors: Recommendations for Change," *American Banker,* March 17, 1994, p. 18; "FDIC Issues Guidelines for Bank Directors, Officers," FDIC news release, PR-166-92, December 4, 1992; Stephens B. Woodrough, "How to Create a Safe Haven for Directors," *American Banker,* May 3, 1995, p. 6.

[15] See "FDIC Issues Guidelines." The most common suits brought against outside directors involve insider abuse, such as preferential loans, or the failure to implement corrective actions after being warned about problems at their banks. *FDIC v. Lowe* concerns a director held liable for a civil money penalty for a violation of the law, although there was no negligence. For further discussion, see Stephens B. Woodrough, "Director Liability: A Truly Frightening Decision," *American Banker,* February 4, 1993.

Think About This!

The Ten Commandments for Directors

1. Be honest and forthcoming in all matters related to the institution.
2. Prepare for and attend board meetings.
3. Leave your personal interests and those of your family and associates outside the boardroom.
4. Consider the impact of your actions on the institution, its owners and customers, and the surrounding community.
5. Evaluate proposals from management and other directors carefully.
6. Think independently.
7. Voice your opinion, even if it is unpopular.
8. Insist that proposals that do not make sense to you be clarified, modified, or rejected.
9. Take personal responsibility for the safety, soundness, and profitability of the institution.
10. Set an example for board management, employees, and competitors.

Source: Michael Patriarca, "The Role and Responsibilities of a Savings Institution Director," *Perspectives*, Federal Home Loan Bank of San Francisco, Fall 1988, p. 4.

---

directors must (1) act in good faith, (2) be disinterested, (3) use reasonable diligence, and (4) actually make decisions.[16] However, the business judgment rule will not protect a director from liability if he or she has a financial interest in the subject matter of the decision. This brings us to the duty of loyalty.

Duty of Loyalty

The duty of loyalty prohibits directors from putting their personal or business interests, or those of others, above the interests of the bank. Directors may not take advantage of business opportunities that they learn of as a result of their position without first offering them to the bank. Stated oth-

---

[16] Grunewald and Foster, "Bank Directors' Liability for Negligence."

erwise, directors cannot make inappropriate gains because of their connection with the bank. They can, however, do business with the bank provided the relationships are fully disclosed to the board, which must determine the fairness of those transactions to the bank and whether there are conflicts of interest. For example, the president of a thrift formed a separate corporation to receive loan referral fees for identifying borrowers to the thrift. The Federal Home Loan Bank Board (FHLBB) informed the thrift that its president was an affiliated person who could not properly accept such fees.[17] The board's guiding principle is that the bank comes first. In addition, directors may not disclose confidential information about the bank or its customers that they acquired as a result of their position on the board.

Conflicts of interest can be financial or personal, direct or indirect.[18] For example, if a director is an attorney, a real estate broker, or any other professional who would receive a fee for services rendered if a loan were approved by the board, the director should abstain from voting on that loan. Similarly, if the director sells carpeting, he or she should abstain from a vote to provide carpeting for the bank.

Some state laws give limited protection to directors with respect to "conflicting interests." The Alabama Business Corporation Act (effective January 1, 1995) contains a provision concerning "director's conflicting interest transactions." Under this provision, a court may not stop a transaction or award damages solely because a director has interest in the transaction *if* the director has followed certain procedures. Failure to follow the procedures may be interpreted as evidence of intent to self-deal in secret.

National banks and other types of financial institutions are also subject to federal and state statutes. In determining liability under certain statutory provisions, Congress has required that directors be held liable for "knowing" violations of law. This means the director knew or should have known the facts concerning the violations. Therefore, the courts presume that directors know the laws.

Finally, banks and their directors are subject to regulations by bank regulators and other government agencies. Bank regulators, such as the OCC,

---

[17] US General Accounting Office, *Failed Thrifts*, pp. 16–17.

[18] For additional discussion of conflicts of interest, see *The New Director's Primer: A Guide to Management Oversight and Bank Regulation*, Federal Reserve Bank of Atlanta, Department of Supervision and Regulation, 1993, pp. 17–20.

can take administrative actions against banks and directors that engage in unsafe or unsound practices (which will be explained shortly). The administrative actions include cease-and-desist orders, civil money penalties, and removal of individuals from office.

In summary, the board of directors is responsible for the welfare of a bank. Laws and regulations set broad limits on what bank boards may or may not do. However, the laws and regulations tell us little about how boards operate.

TYPICAL COMMITTEES

The board of directors elects its own officers, which usually consist of a chairperson, a vice-chairperson, and a secretary. Equally important, it elects the officers of the bank who are expected to carry out the plans, policies, and controls established or approved by the board. Oversight then becomes the board's primary responsibility.

The oversight functions are carried out by various committees composed of board members. It is more efficient for large boards of directors to have a few committee members deal with specific areas of concern than to encumber the entire board. Moreover, certain committees are limited to particular members of the board. Committees may make decisions on the board's behalf or report back to the full board for further consideration. In either case, the full board of directors is responsible for all committee decisions.

To avoid misunderstandings, the purposes, responsibilities, authority, and duration of all committees should be written out clearly. The committees should be given the resources and authority to discharge their responsibilities. Last but not least, they should be informed and vigilant.

The structure of committees varies from bank to bank, depending on the bank's size and needs. The typical committees found in banks and their general duties are presented next. In addition to performing its general duties, each committee must ensure that applicable laws and regulations are followed.

Executive Committee

The executive committee is usually authorized to act on behalf of the full board of directors between its regular meetings. It may review and coordinate information from other committees as well as oversee bank operations.

Audit Committee

The audit committee is a "watchdog" committee whose primary responsibility is to ensure that the bank complies with applicable laws and regulations.[19] This committee should be composed exclusively of independent directors. An independent director is one who is free from any relationship that would interfere with the exercise of his or her independent judgment. Stated otherwise, independence means no insider ties to the bank, especially no borrowing relationship.

Three is the minimum number of independent directors, and the committee should be small enough so that each member can be an active participant. The functions of the audit committee are to (1) select independent auditors and work with internal auditors, (2) review auditor's and bank examiner's reports and consider their recommendations, and (3) report to the board the committee's recommendations for the issues raised by the auditors. The audit committee may also consider the bank's internal controls. In addition, it should follow up on recommended changes to ensure that they are carried out.[20]

The audit committee should meet at least quarterly with the internal and external auditors. It should evaluate the internal audit staff and programs and review management actions to correct any weaknesses and problems outlined in internal and external audit reports and examinations. This listing of activities is not complete, but it indicates the key roles this committee plays.

Asset/Liability Committee

The asset/liability committee oversees the bank's entire balance sheet: capital, funding, and asset allocation. The major concerns of this committee include capital adequacy, interest rate sensitivity, and the quality of

---

[19] For additional details on audit committees, see *Audit Committee Guide,* Coopers & Lybrand L.L.P. (USA), 1995.

[20] See "Good Practice Guidelines for the Audit Committee," *Report of the National Commission on Fraudulent Financial Reporting,* National Commission on Fraudulent Financial Reporting, October 1987, pp. 179–82.

credit. Specific issues dealing with investments and lending are handled by other committees.

Investment Committee

The scope of the investment committee is narrower than that of the asset/liability committee. The investment committee establishes investment strategies and objectives. To provide guidelines for management, the committee must approve an investment policy that takes into account liquidity, pledging requirements, size, risk, and diversification of the portfolio.

Loan Committee

The loan committee establishes and revises lending policies to meet the changing needs of the bank. It must set standards for valid appraisals of real estate and other collateral. In some banks, the loan committee participates in credit decisions. Therefore, the committee must be knowledgeable about the economy in the market area and have a clear understanding of financial statements. Above all, it should not be a "rubber stamp" for loan officers.

The committee may also be in charge of loan review, which may be external or internal, depending on the size and needs of the bank. More will be said about loan policies and loan review in Chapter Seven.

Trust Committee

Banks with trust activities have special fiduciary responsibilities to safeguard the interests of trust customers. An important part of this duty is the establishment of a so-called "Chinese wall" to separate trust activities from the bank's other activities and to avoid conflicts of interest among the trust department, the bank, and insiders. Like the other committees, the trust committee establishes policies and fees, as well as dealing with other aspects of trust operations. A separate *trust audit committee* oversees an annual audit of trust activities. Banking regulations require that the trust audit committee consist of directors who are not bank officers. Moreover, the directors cannot serve simultaneously on the trust audit committee and the trust committee.

Personnel Committee

Quality personnel is the key to success. Thus, the board must establish policies to attract and maintain such persons. At the same time, personnel policies should be instituted that minimize the possibility of white-collar crime.[21] These policies should include periodic reviews of personnel policies, making sure that employees who handle money are adequately compensated so that they are not tempted to embezzle funds to supplement their incomes. In addition, the personnel committee should establish a written policy that adverse personal financial situations will not affect job security or promotion. This alerts the employer to potential problems and provides some measure of security to the employee. Along this line, employee education concerning white-collar crime and free and confidential financial counseling should be considered. All employees should be required to take regular vacations to make it difficult for them to cover up crimes on a continuing basis. Key financial personnel should be rotated for the same reason.

PRACTICES DEEMED UNSAFE OR UNSOUND[22]

The board of directors of a bank are responsible for establishing the bank's operating practices. We have examined what banks are expected to do in the lending area to illustrate operating practices. Now let's look at the other side of the coin and learn what they should not do. According to the FDIC, certain practices are considered "unsafe or unsound." This term refers to practices that are contrary to the generally accepted standards of prudent operation and, if continued, could result in the abnormal risk of loss to the bank, its shareholders, or the federal insurance fund. The following examples, based on the FDIC's *Manual of Examination Policies,*

---

[21] Joseph T. Wells, "White-Collar Crime: Myths and Strategies," *The Practical Accountant,* August 1985, pp. 43–45.

[22] This section is based on the FDIC *Manual of Examination Policies,* parts of which appear in US House, *Federal Response to Criminal Misconduct by Bank Officers, Directors, and Insiders, Part 2,* hearings before the Commerce, Consumer, and Monetary Affairs Subcommittee of the Committee on Government Operations, 98th Cong., 2d Sess., May 2 and 3, 1984, pp. 1383–84.

illustrate such practices. However, two caveats are in order. First, the examples do not cover every type of unsafe or unsound activity. Second, not every instance of these activities is unsafe or unsound. Each situation must be considered on its own merits.

Lack of management actions deemed unsafe or unsound

1. Failure to provide adequate supervision and direction over the bank's officers to prevent unsafe or unsound practices and the violation of laws and regulations.
2. Failure to make provision for sufficient reserves to cover possible loan losses.
3. Failure to make prompt postings to the general ledger.
4. Failure to account properly for transactions and to keep accurate books and records.
5. Failure to enforce loan repayment policies.
6. Failure to have proper documentation on the priority of liens on loans secured by real estate.

Management actions deemed unsafe or unsound

1. Operating with inadequate capital to support the quality of assets held.
2. Engaging in hazardous lending and lax collection practices. Such practices include making loans with inadequate security, extending credit without first obtaining current and complete financial information about the borrower, extending credit in the form of overdrafts without proper controls, and inadequate diversification of the loan portfolio.
3. Operating with inadequate liquidity or sources of funding.
4. Operating with inadequate internal controls on official checks and unissued CDs; failure to segregate duties of bank personnel; and failure to reconcile differences in correspondent bank accounts.
5. Engaging in speculative investment policies.
6. Paying excessive dividends relative to the bank's financial condition.
7. Paying excessive bonuses, salaries, fees, and commissions to insiders and their related interests.

Condition of a bank deemed unsafe or unsound

The overall condition of the bank may be considered unsafe or unsound as evidenced by one or more of the following conditions:

1. Maintaining very low net interest margins (interest income less interest expense divided by average earning assets).
2. Excessive overhead expenses.
3. Excessive volume of loans classified by the examiners.
4. Excessive net loan and lease losses.
5. Excessive volume of past-due loans.
6. Excessive volume of nonearning assets.
7. Excessive dependence on large-denomination liabilities.

THE SERVE PRINCIPLE

The activities of directors are summarized in the SERVE principle:[23]

- *S*elect qualified management.
- *E*stablish business goals, policies, standards, and procedures.
- *R*eview business performance.
- *V*oice opinions and questions.
- *E*nforce compliance.

Ethical behavior is the final consideration. In this context, it refers to a director's choice of courses of action that benefit the bank, its stockholders, and customers, rather than the director's own interests, without bringing harm to others. If directors cannot act in that fashion and comply with the SERVE principles, or if they have significant disagreements with other directors or management that cannot be resolved to their satisfaction, they should resign. The power of resignation is less costly for independent directors than for inside directors. Nevertheless, it is an option that should not be ignored.

Finally, but not least in importance, the directors should establish a code of ethics for all directors, officers, and employees of the organiza-

---

[23] *The Director's Guide: The Role and Responsibilities of a Savings Institution Director,* Federal Home Loan Bank of San Francisco, 1988, p. 26.

tion. The code of ethics sends a strong message from the top of the organization down to all other levels regarding how business is to be done.

CONCLUSION

This chapter presented an overview of the legal duties and responsibilities of bank directors in the United States. These include, but are not limited to, a duty of care and a duty of loyalty. Directors are expected to take an active role in the decision-making processes of their banks. This includes serving on various committees, such as the audit committee. The role and practices of directors in other countries may differ from those in the United States. For example, executives of large Japanese banks serve as outside directors on corporate boards of firms that they own and/or are large borrowers.[24] This allows the bank's directors to monitor and become involved with the bank's operating decisions. Such practices are not allowed in the United States.

---

[24] Paul Sheard, "Bank Executives on Japanese Corporate Boards," *Monetary and Economic Studies,* Bank of Japan, December 1994, pp. 85–121.

Chapter Two

Strategic Management

WHAT IS STRATEGIC MANAGEMENT?

This is the first of two chapters dealing with strategy. This chapter deals with strategic management, and the next chapter examines bank marketing strategy. There are obvious overlaps between strategic management and marketing strategies. Therefore, some issues raised in this chapter are examined in depth in Chapter Three.

Strategic Management Defined

Strategic management means different things to different people. This term is the modern version of what used to be called "strategic planning." Table 2-1 presents selected definitions of both terms. To avoid confusion, we use the term *strategic management* to refer to the process of developing, executing, and monitoring major action programs that an organization uses to achieve its missions and goals. The principal elements of this definition are as follows:

1. Strategic management begins with the development of the organization's missions and goals. The mission explains what business the firm is in, and the goals are measurable targets.
2. It requires the creation and perfection of strategies to achieve the missions and goals.
3. The strategies have to be converted into measurable targets (e.g., a return on assets of 1.2 percent for the bank, a 10 percent growth rate for consumer loans).
4. Resources must be allocated (taking actions).
5. The actions undertaken must be reviewed on a regular basis to determine the degree of their success. If they are not meeting expectations, make changes to improve their success, eliminate them to minimize losses, or change the plans.

TABLE 2–1
Selected Definitions

Alfred Chandler (1962): Strategic planning is the determination of long-term goals and objectives of an enterprise, and the adoption of courses of action and the allocation of resources necessary to carry out those actions.

George A. Steiner (1969): Strategic planning is the process of determining the major objectives of an organization, and the policies and strategies that will govern the acquisition, use, and disposition of resources to achieve those objectives.

Peter Drucker (1974): Strategic planning is the continuous process of making entrepreneurial decisions systematically, organizing the efforts to carry out the decisions, and measuring the results against the expectations.

Arthur A. Thompson, Jr., and A. J. Strickland (1995): Management's task is to craft, implement, and execute company strategies.

Sources: Based on: Alfred Chandler, Jr., *Strategy and Structure: Chapters in the History of Industrial Enterprise* (Cambridge, MA: The MIT Press, 1962), p. 13; George A. Steiner, *Top Management Planning* (London: The Macmillan Co., Arkville Press, 1969), p. 34; Peter F. Drucker, *Management: Task, Responsibilities, Practices* (New York: Harper & Row, 1974), p. 125; Arthur A. Thompson, Jr., and A. J. Strickland III, *Crafting and Implementing Strategy: What Every Manager Should Know* (Burr Ridge, IL: R. D. Irwin, 1995), pp. 1–9.

WHAT STRATEGIC MANAGEMENT IS NOT

Having defined strategic management, it is equally important to understand what is *not* strategic management.[1] This distinction is important because many firms confuse strategic management with activities that may or may not be related to it.

1. Strategic management is *not* the application of quantitative techniques to making business decisions, nor is it masses of data. It is analytical thinking and the commitment of resources to action.

2. It is *not* forecasting. In fact, the planning aspects of management are necessary because we cannot forecast beyond a short time period with any degree of precision. Changes in economic and political conditions, as well as changes in technology, can result in outcomes that were not predicted. Most political observers did not forecast the following events that affected our lives and businesses to varying degrees:

---

[1] See Peter F. Drucker, *Management: Tasks, Responsibilities, Practices* (New York: Harper & Row, 1974), pp. 123–125., Also see George A. Steiner, *Strategic Planning: What Every Manager Must Know* (New York: The Free Press, 1979), pp. 15–16.

The fall of Cuba, 1959.

The Soviet invasion of Czechoslovakia, 1968.

The Soviet invasion of Afghanistan, 1979.

The unification of Germany, 1989.

The Iraqi invasion of Kuwait, 1990.

The Soviet coup, 1991.

The Republican landslide in the 1994 elections.

3. Strategic management does *not* deal with decisions that are made in the future. It deals with decisions that affect the future that are made today.

4. Missions and strategies are *not* carved in stone. They must be flexible and responsive to meet changing conditions.

5. Strategic management does *not* eliminate risk. It helps management assess the risks it must take.

SUCCESSFUL AND FAILED STRATEGIES

Keys to Success

Now that we know what strategic management means, let's examine why some strategies succeed and others fail. According to Robert M. Grant, author of *Contemporary Strategy Analysis,* successful strategies usually have four key ingredients:[2]

1. They are directed toward unambiguous long-term goals.

2. They are based on insightful understanding of the external environment.

3. They are based on intimate self-knowledge of the organization and its internal capabilities.

4. They are implemented with resolution and with the coordination and efforts of the entire organization.

Obviously not all strategies are successful. Some strategies fail. Worse yet, failed strategies may contribute to failing firms and banks.

---

[2] Robert M. Grant, *Contemporary Strategy Analysis: Concepts, Techniques, Applications* (Cambridge, MA: Blackwell Publishers, 1991), p. 30.

Reasons for Failure

"Why Companies Fail" was the cover story in *Fortune* (November 14, 1994). The article deals with major mistakes that contributed to the failure or distress of nonfinancial firms. However, some of the mistakes described provide insights for bank operations.

1. *What business are you in?* Some firms lack an understanding of the fundamentals of their core expertise. What core products and services should banks provide (1) to survive and (2) to grow? Banks used to be the sole experts in lending to businesses, but that is no longer the case. General Electric Credit and Commercial Credit are two examples of competitors in business lending. General Motors, Ford, and Sears are examples of competitors for consumer loans. Nonbank firms also compete in the payments system. So what's a bank to do?

2. *Management shortsightedness.* Some firms are unable or unwilling to establish contingency plans for unexpected events. When interest rates were 5 percent in the late 1970s, few banks thought rates would soar to 18 percent. As a result, some banks and many savings and loan associations made long-term, fixed-rate home mortgage loans and funded them with short-term deposits. When rates rose to record levels and interest costs exceeded interest incomes, thousands of financial institutions failed.

3. *Complacency.* Some firms fail because managers were complacent. Bill Gates, chairman of Microsoft, argues that Lotus (spreadsheet) "fell prey to complacency that is fatal in the software industry. The marketplace soon showed that it is more powerful than any single company and Microsoft Excel filled the void . . . created for an innovative Windows spreadsheet."[3] Now Gates is getting ready to use Microsoft's resources and the information superhighway to enter banking. Is your bank complacent?

There is a tendency to believe that what worked in the past will work in the future. For example, the practice of borrowing short and lending long led to many of the bank failures in the 1970s. As another example, many banks built costly branch offices to acquire deposits and provide other services. Is that a strategy for the past or for the future? Consider money market mutual funds. They have no branch offices; nevertheless, their deposits grew dramatically in recent years, while demand and savings deposits at banks grew at a slow pace.

---

[3] Bill Gates, "They're Talking, We're Selling," *The Wall Street Journal*, March 16, 1995, p. A22.

A lead article in *The Wall Street Journal* (January 9, 1991) was headlined "Costly Strategy: Southeast Bank Got into Trouble by Sticking to Its Stodgy Ways." The article explained how trying to do "business as usual" was as risky as jumping on the latest industry bandwagon. Instead of joining the consumer boom or the merger mania of the mid-1980s, Southeast concentrated on highly profitable corporate lending in Florida. As its competitors grew, it was forced to become more adventuresome in its lending, and gradually became swamped with bad loans. Southeast Bank no longer exists.

4. *Understand customers' needs and satisfy them.* Smart managers pay special attention to customers who no longer want their products and services. Business concerns that are able to do so borrow in the capital markets, and individual investors (depositors) make extensive use of mutual funds. There may be more to be learned from an exit poll of dissatisfied customers than from basking in the glory of current successes.

5. *Avoid managerial malpractice.* Do not teach the importance of teamwork and then reward individuals whose work stands out from the crowd. Do not announce a preference for workers with broad experience and then select someone who does not have it. Do not encourage risk taking and then punish good-faith failures.

The Complexity of Making Decisions

Making management decisions is a complex process. Figure 2–1 provides some insights into the decision-making process. Today, at time period 0 ($T = 0$), it is necessary to make a decision about expanding into a new market, adding a new product, or some similar issue. The outcome of that decision can be good or bad. When the outcome is reviewed in time period 1 ($T = 1$), additional decisions must be made. If the original decision resulted in a good outcome, we must now decide whether to continue on the same course of action or to change it. If the original decision had a bad outcome, we must now decide to abandon the project or to make changes to improve the outcome. In subsequent time periods, we must make additional decisions about the success or failure of past decisions. This example illustrates how one decision made today inevitably leads to additional decisions in the future.

Figure 2–1 does not reveal the true complexity of the decision-making process. For example, suppose a banker must make five decisions today

FIGURE 2–1
Real Decisions for Finance, Production, Labor, etc.

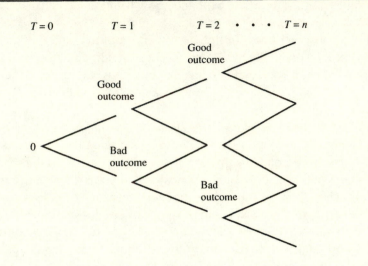

and has only five choices from which to select.[4] Only one possible combination of choices and decisions can be made. However, if there are 10 choices from which to select, 252 possible combinations exist. If there are 100 choices, more than 75 million combinations are possible!

	Number of Choices			
	5	*10*	*50*	*100*
Decisions to be made (5)	1	252	2,118,759	75,287,520

In reality, bankers make hundreds of decisions every day. The probability that the banker will select the "best" out of millions of available combinations is very small. Nevertheless, most banks are profitable. In the first quarter of 1995, the average return on assets, or ROA (net income/total assets), was 1.1 percent, which is reasonably good.

_____

[4] The combination C of n decisions taken x at a time can be determined by:

$$C_x^n = \frac{n!}{x!(n-x)!}$$

The Reality of Performance

Suppose that your bank does everything right in terms of strategic management: using the four keys to successful strategies and avoiding the five mistakes that contribute to failures. Does this mean your bank will have persistently high profits? Unfortunately, the answer is "probably not." Two studies found that banks with formal strategic planning processes were no more profitable than banks that did no formal strategic planning.[5] Other studies suggest that some banks have persistently high returns on assets year after year.[6]

Theory. Why is it that planning does not seem to have a big payoff, yet some banks have high ROAs year after year? According to economic theory, the answer is that the market is working the way it is supposed to work. Economic theory tells us that if firms earn abnormally high profits, other firms will be attracted into that industry. The effect of the increased competition will reduce the profits of all of the firms to a normal level. However, it takes time for this to occur. During that time, the abnormally high returns will be eroded unless there are barriers to entry in the industry, patents to keep others out, or some other sustainable competitive advantage. The barriers to entry, such as laws prohibiting branch banking, are now history. Most banks do not have patents on their products. That leaves us with a sustainable competitive advantage. More will be said about this shortly.

Chance. Historical chance is the second reason some firms do better than others. It is virtually impossible to make decisions that will result in positive outcomes all of the time. Chance plays an important role in the success or failure. Consider how being in the right place at the right time affected bank profitability in 1995. Although the US economy grew during the first quarter, the rate of growth varied widely across different

---

[5] Benton E. Gup and David Whitehead, "Bank and Thrift Profitability: Does Strategic Planning Really Pay?" *Economic Review,* Federal Reserve Bank of Atlanta, October 1985, pp. 14–25; Benton E. Gup and David Whitehead, "Strategic Planning in Banks—Does it Pay?" *Long Range Planning,* February 1989, pp. 124–30.

[6] Benton E. Gup and John R. Walter, "Top Performing Small Banks: Making Money the Old Fashioned Way," *Economic Review,* Federal Reserve Bank of Richmond, 75, no. 6 (1989), pp. 22–33; Mark E. Levonian, "The Persistence of Bank Profits: What the Stock Market Implies," *Economic Review,* Federal Reserve Bank of San Francisco, no. 2 (1994), pp. 3–17.

economic regions. These differences in growth rates were reflected in bank profitability. The average ROA was 1.12 percent for banks located in the Northeast, 1.23 percent for banks in the Southeast, and 1.42 percent for banks in the Midwest.[7]

Growth is a stochastic process.   Many economists who have studied the growth of large numbers of firms believe their growth can be represented by a stochastic process.[8] A *stochastic process* can be thought of as an indexed collection of random variables. Daily stock prices are one example. The Standard and Poor's Composite Index may be advancing, but the prices of the stocks that make up the index may be moving up and down in a random fashion. Similarly, the profitability of 10,241 banks may be increasing on average. However, we saw that there are regional differences in profitability. Within each region, some banks were very profitable while others had losses.

Chance does not imply a random outcome of the success or failure of management decisions. Management decisions affect the success or failure of their banks. However, when observing the behavior of all 10,241 banks, none of which has perfect foresight, their collective behavior appears stochastic.

One consequence of stochastic growth is the tendency for a few large firms to dominate the industry. As Table 2–2 shows, 63 large banks out of a total of 10,241 control 50.07 percent of total assets.[9] At the other end of the size spectrum, 7,122 small banks control only 7.54 percent of total assets.

This distribution of assets suggests three principal types of banking organizations: A few very large banks operating on a national and international basis, a larger number of large regional banks serving various geo-

---

[7] The FDIC Quarterly Banking Profile, first quarter 1995.

[8] Research supporting this view includes F. M. Scherer, *Industrial Market Structure and Economic Performance,* 2d ed. (Boston: Houghton Mifflin, 1980), pp. 145–50; Armen A. Alchain, "Uncertainty, Evolution, and Economic Theory," *Journal of Political Economy,* June 1950, pp. 211–21; Joseph Steindl, *Random Processes and the Growth of Firms* (New York: Hafner Publishing Co., 1965); Dennis C. Mueller, *The Modern Corporation: Profits, Power, Growth and Performance* (Sussex England: Wheatsheaf Books, Ltd., 1986); Thomas Gilovich, Robert Vallone, and Amos Tversky, "The Hot Hand in Basketball: On the Misperception of Random Sequences," *Cognitive Psychology* 17 (1985), pp. 295–314; Robin Marris, *The Theory and Future of the Corporate Economy and Society* (Amsterdam: North-Holland, 1979), Chapter 3.

[9] *The FDIC Quarterly Banking Profile,* first quarter 1995.

TABLE 2–2
Selected Banking Statistics

All Banks	Less Than $100 Million	$100 Million to $1 Billion	$1 Billion to $10 Billion	Greater Than $10 Billion
Number of banks (10,241)	7,122	2,725	331	63
Total assets ($4116.1 billion)	$310.3	$667.8	$1,077.0	$2,061.0
Percentage of total (100%)	7.54%	16.22%	26.17%	50.07%

Source: FDIC.

graphic regions, and a very large number of community banks serving both local urban and rural needs. A recent survey by the Federal Reserve Bank of Kansas revealed that 60 percent of the community banks were the dominant financial institution, or the only financial institution, in their communities.[10]

The fact that growth is a stochastic process is not something managers or directors want to hear. In essence, the theory suggests that managers' decisions may have less impact on the growth and survival of their firms than they would like. Some of the reasons for the lack of performance and failure were explained previously. Another reason is that most (but not all) banks lack a sustainable competitive advantage. Anything that one bank does another can copy quickly and at relatively low cost. For example, if bank A offers a new product, bank B can offer a similar product. Equally important, by waiting to evaluate the success of a bank A's new product, bank B may be able to offer an improved product at lower cost because it did not incur the same developmental or marketing costs.

Geographic location, which was a sustainable competitive advantage in the days of restricted branch banking, may no longer be a sustainable advantage. Changes in banking technology and competition, including automatic teller machines, home banking, the Internet, and mutual funds purchased by phone or fax, have reduced the advantage of geographic location.

---

[10] Catherine M. Lemieux, "Meeting the Challenges: Community Bankers' View," *Financial Industry Perspectives,* October 1994, pp. 7–20.

There are other reasons strategic planning did not seem to pay off. First, the planning was done at top levels of the organization, but it was not carried out at all levels. As noted in the discussion of keys to success, the plans must be carried out throughout the organization. If the president wants one thing and the loan officers and others have different goals, the plan will not succeed. Second, banks continued to implement losing strategies as though they were carved in stone. They did not respond to changing conditions. The large number of bank failures in the early 1980s, when interest rates soared, is one example of a lack of response to changing conditions. Banks lagging other firms in the use of computer technology for delivering financial services to customers may be another. Finally, many banks did not begin to plan until they were already in trouble, and by that time they were no longer profitable.

THE MAJOR FACTORS THAT AFFECT FIRMS ARE BEYOND THEIR CONTROL

The External Environment

The major factors affecting the success or failure of firms is beyond the firms' control. This concept means that management must have a clear understanding of the environment within which the organization operates and must react appropriately to threats or opportunities. The manager of a leasing department did not realize that the success of her department depended on tax laws favorable to leasing and a strong market for used equipment.[11] Following the Tax Recovery Act of 1986, the law was less favorable to leasing, and the department was not prepared to deal with the equipment when it came off lease. Equally important, because of rapid changes in technology, large amounts of used equipment were available at low prices. The board rubber-stamped management's plans because it overlooked two major external factors: tax laws and technological changes.

What other external factors affect banks? Some of them are easy to identify; others are not. The easy ones include changes in laws and regu-

---

[11] Stephen F. Cooper et. al., "When to Hold, When to Fold," *Financial Executive,* November–December, 1994, p. 42.

lations, innovations by competitors, and natural disasters (e.g., floods and earthquakes). Changes in banking laws and regulations obviously affect banks. The Community Reinvestment Act (CRA) of 1977 is one example of a banking law that affects the way banks do business. The CRA is designed to encourage banks to meet local credit needs, especially those of low- and moderate-income neighborhoods. Risk-based capital guidelines are another example of changed regulations. In the past, capital adequacy did not take risk into account. Today, bank regulators use risk-based capital guidelines to evaluate the capital adequacy of banks. The guidelines are based on the possibility that a bank will incur a loss if certain obligors or counterparties default on a transaction. The risk weights are minimal for US Treasury securities and are highest for commercial transactions. Banks that do not have sufficient capital must get it, or be closed.

Changes in competition also affect banks. Three major nonbank credit card issuers (Discover, GM, and American Express) are planning to join forces with mortgage companies to make home loans.[12] Commercial banks are currently the largest lenders of home mortgage loans, and real estate loans account for about 42 percent of total loans and leases.

Other changes in the operating environment are not as obvious. Consider the effects of demographics on the financial industry.[13] First, the population is aging. The number of retired persons relative to the active work force is expected to increase dramatically in the years to come. Second, the aging population is expected to put substantial pressure on state-funded pension plans; as a result, more funding will be done in the private sector. Third, the retirement funding will result in more funds being invested in stocks, bonds, and other long-term investments. The share of household assets invested in stocks and bonds increased from 60 percent in 1982 to 75 percent in 1993. Fourth, there will be a tremendous transfer of wealth as the parents of the baby boomers pass on the more than $12 trillion they have accumulated to their children. How should commercial banks react to these predictable changes?

---

[12] Jonathan S. Hornblass, "Discover, GM, American Express Planning to Offer Home Loans," *American Banker,* October 28, 1994, pp. 1, 10.

[13] See Alger B. Chapman, "Future of Derivatives Markets: Products, Technology and Participants," presentation before the Financial Management Association, St. Louis, Missouri, October 14, 1994.

Think about This!

Companies without Walls

Companies without walls are called *virtual companies*. These are stripped down, "lean and mean" companies that use computer networks, phones, and fax machines to link the various parts of their business together. The basic idea is that it is not necessary for all employees to be located in the same place to run a business. Much of what was formerly done by one company in one place can be subcontracted or "outsourced." Consider a book publisher located in Los Angeles. The author of the book, who lives in New Orleans, delivers the manuscript to the publisher via computer. The administrative and editorial services necessary to prepare the book for publication are done in Chicago via computers. The final manuscript is sent over computer lines to the printer in St. Paul, Minnesota, for typesetting. Finally, the marketing is handled by a firm in Austin, Texas. Based on this type of model, how can banks be businesses without walls?

Next, consider Chase Manhattan Corporation, one of the nation's largest banking organizations. Chase built a $130 million center in Bournemouth, England, to process trillions of dollars' worth of financial transactions from around the world.[1] A satellite network connects the center to offices in New York, Hong Kong, Luxembourg, and Tokyo.

[1] Kelley Hollard, Paula Dwyer, and Gail Edmonson, "Technobanking Takes Off," *Business Week, 21st Century Capitalism,* (special issue) 1994, 52–53.

What Management Can Control

Management can control certain internal and external aspects of their business.

Internal factors. The major internal items management can control include, but are not limited to,

- The amount of capital held in addition to the regulatory minimums.
- The interest rates it is willing to pay to attract deposits (above, at, or below market rates).
- The bank's loan policy with respect to the types of loans it is willing to make.
- The limits of the geographic market it will serve when making loans.

Think about This!

Banking in an Electronic Age

The electronic information superhighway is another threat or opportunity, depending on your point of view. The interactive computer/television/telephone services affect retail banking. Exactly how it will affect retail banking is an issue that planners and managers must address now, before it affects their markets. Consider the Quicken program for personal computers. There are about 30 million PCs in homes, and many of them have modems. In 1994, an estimated 7 million PCs were sold. The Quicken program is the forerunner of home electronic banking. BankAmerica and Nations Bank agreed to jointly acquire Meca Software, a competitor of Quicken.[1]

Another aspect of electronic banking deals with digital money. When someone buys goods and services via the Internet, the payments may be made by using digital money. Digital money will involve the transfer of funds in both domestic and foreign markets. Finally, there is the "electronic purse," a multipurpose, prepaid card that researchers at the Federal Reserve Bank of New York believe may replace currency in many routine transactions.[2] Banks are going to play a role in the new payments system as it evolves. What will it be?

[1] Jerry Kutler and Valerie Block, "NationsBank, B of A Buying A Rival to Quicken Software," *American Banker,* May 11, 1995, 1, 18.

[2] John Wenniger and David Laster, "The Electronic Purse," *Current Issues in Economics and Finance,* Federal Reserve Bank of New York, April 1995.

- Asset/liability management policies.
- Risk management policies.
- Dividend policy.
- Personnel policies.

External factors.   Management must also make decisions about growing the bank externally. The bank can grow by acquiring another bank or an affiliate. For example, Mellon Bank Corporation acquired Dreyfus Corporation, a mutual fund manager. Banks may form strategic alliances with other firms, such as cobranding credit cards. The Aadvantage card, for instance, cobrands Citibank's Visa with American Airlines. Banks can do more outsourcing and be more like "virtual" companies that buy the services they need rather than having them in-house. Many banks have reduced their back office operations by using external data processing services.

Sustained Competitive Advantage

Management must try to gain a sustainable competitive advantage. How can it do so when all banks offer similar products and services? The answer is that banks can gain some competitive advantages, but the advantages may not be sustainable. For example, a bank's size and the scope of its services can be a competitive advantage—or a disadvantage. Big banks offer a wider variety of services than small banks. These services include the capacity to make very large commercial loans, international banking, trust services, derivatives, and more. For example, Citibank, the largest bank in the United States, offers global banking services that a small local bank cannot offer directly. However, the small local bank has intimate knowledge of the small and mid-size firms in its local market area that Citibank may lack. Moreover, the small local bank can make lending decisions quickly and has a degree of flexibility that may not be possible in a large organization that requires standardized procedures for its operations.

Specialization can be a competitive advantage. Some banks specialize in particular lines of business. For example, a large regional bank has a reputation for helping small commercial borrowers meet their financial needs for growth. This bank places considerable emphasis on building long-term financial relationships with small, growing firms. In contrast, another large bank focuses on retail lending and is a major player in the credit card market. At the other end of the size spectrum, a community bank goes after "upscale" clientele. Instead of having teller counters, each "client representative" sits at a desk to give the customers individualized service. The bank actively courts wealthy depositors and borrowers. To meet its CRA responsibilities, it takes a leading role in financing low-income public housing programs.

Location is a competitive advantage. Despite the fact that computer technology will provide an increasing share of banking services in the years to come, some customers like going to the bank to transact their business.

A study of market leaders by Michael Treacy and Fred Wiersema revealed that their organizations were built around one of three value disciplines.[14] The first value discipline is *operational excellence*. This means the company has a core business that provides middle-of-the-market products at the best prices and greatest convenience. Wal-Mart Stores and Dell Computer are examples of such companies. Such organizations have strong central authorities maintaining standard operating procedures. Their corporate culture can be characterized as "one size fits all." *Product leadership* is the second value discipline. Firms that are product leaders, such as Johnson & Johnson and Nike, concentrate on offering quality products that push performance. They are innovators, continuously introducing new products. Their organizations tend to be more ad hoc, changing to meet new innovations. Finally, there is *customer intimacy*. Its adherents focus on customer needs. They specialize in satisfying unique needs to build strong customer relationships. They have the best solutions for their customers and will provide whatever support is needed. Such organizations push empowerment very close to the customer and have a corporate culture that fosters flexibility.

Other methods for developing competitive advantages are examined in Chapter Three.

Essential Ingredients

Successful firms and banks have three essential ingredients. First, they must have *sufficient capital* to finance expansion and continued operations. Commercial banks are required to have a minimum of 8 percent capital. More important, however, studies have shown a positive relationship between capital and profitability; that is, high capital tends to be associated with high profitability.

Second, organizations must have *sufficient technology* to provide a continuous stream of state-of-the-art products and services. The technology of tomorrow will make increasing use of home computers to provide banking services.

Finally, organizations must have *sufficient scale* or size to mass-produce and manage products at the lowest possible cost. Some businesses, such as credit cards and servicing mortgage loan portfolios, must be large to be profitable.

---

[14] Michael Treacy and Fred Wiersema, "How Market Leaders Keep Their Edge," *Fortune*, February 6, 1995, pp. 88–98.

STAKEHOLDERS

Richard Terrlink, chief executive officer of Harley-Davidson, Inc., describes his company's commitment to its stakeholders: "Our vision is simple: Continuous improvement activities to continuously improve the quality of profitable relationships with all of our stakeholders. That's what we are in business to do."[15]

Stakeholders Defined

In finance, we teach that the objective of firms is to maximize stockholders' wealth. While that objective is correct, it does not explicitly deal with other stakeholders. The term *stakeholders* refers to those who benefit from the success of the firm. For convenience, they are divided into primary, secondary, and tertiary stakeholders. The composition of each group is arbitrary, but useful for purposes of our discussion. The extent to which any of the stakeholders benefit depends on the *survival* of the firm or bank. If the bank fails, the attorneys involved with the closure will be the only ones who benefit. Survival, in turn, may depend on growth. More will be said about survival and growth in Chapter 3.

Primary stakeholders.   The primary stakeholders include stockholders, managers, and employees who receive incentive pay. If the bank is profitable and growing, the price of its stock will appreciate and pay cash dividends. Managers are rewarded on the basis of the bank's profitability and asset size. A big bank and a small bank can each have an ROA of 1.5 percent, but the managers of the big bank will be paid more for their efforts. Finally, employees who receive incentive pay, such as loan or investment officers, have incentives to *profitably* grow the portfolios they manage. The word *profitable* is highlighted because incentive compensation leads some managers to increase the dollar value of their portfolios without regard to risk.

Secondary stakeholders.   The secondary stakeholders include employees who do not receive incentive pay, creditors, and those who

---

[15] Henry A. Davis and Frederick C. Miletello, *The Empowered Organization: Redefining the Roles and Practices of Finance* (Morristown, NJ.: Financial Executives Research Foundation, Executive Report, June 1994), p. 12.

have contractual obligations. The employees gain from the wages and benefits they earn now and in the future, as well as from their working conditions. Thus, they have a strong incentive for the bank to succeed.

Creditors want the bank to succeed because they want to be repaid. In this regard, the FDIC can be considered a guarantor for some creditors (depositors). Creditors monitor the behavior of the bank to reduce the likelihood that they will have to pay off the depositors if the bank fails.

Customers and suppliers with contractual obligations also have a stake in the bank's success. Borrowers, for example, want an assured source of funds for their continued operations. Suppliers, such as a data processing firm used by the bank, is dependent on the bank as a source of revenue.

Tertiary stakeholders. Customers depend on the bank to provide continuous service. In a collective sense, the customers are the community in which the bank is located. The community has a vital interest in the success of the bank. In fact, the Community Reinvestment Act (CRA) mandates that banks play an active role in providing credit to low- and moderate-income elements of their communities. On the other side of the coin, some community groups are actively going after banks. For example, a lead article in the *American Banker* (October 14, 1994) was "Civil Rights Groups Planning Suits to Spur Minority, Low-Income Loans."

Banks go far beyond what the law mandates. Their success is directly linked to the growth and health of the communities they serve. What's good for the community is good for the bank. That is why bankers are leaders in many community activities.

Government is another stakeholder. For example, the state of Alabama gave Mercedes Benz an incentive package of more than $250 million to build a plant near Tuscaloosa, Alabama. Their logic was that the employment and other business associated with the plant will, over time, generate tax revenues far in excess of the investment.

THE VALUE OF THE BANK

Table 2–3 illustrates the broad categories of information stock analysts, stockholders, and creditors use to determine the fair market value of a bank. These categories include the operating environment, corporate factors, and stakeholders. This is the same information directors should consider when making decisions about managing their banks.

TABLE 2–3
The Value Matrix

Shareholder and Creditor Value	Operating Environment	Corporation	Other Stakeholders
Information	Trends (e.g., population)	Past (e.g., past financial data)	Employees
Information	Technology (e.g., information highway)	Present (e.g., current performance)	Customers
Information	International (e.g., foreign exchange)	Future (e.g., projections)	Community
Information	Competition		

Operating Environment

The *operating environment* includes any trends, technology, domestic or international factors, and competition that affect the bank. They may represent threats or opportunities. Some of these factors take a long time to develop, while others occur overnight. For example, population trends are reasonably predictable, and information about such trends is readily available. However, information about what a competitor is going to do may be neither public nor predictable. Recall that the major factors that affect banks are beyond their control.

Corporate Factors

Directors, customers, and financial analysts require information about the bank's performance. Information from the bank and other sources affects investors' expectations about performance. Those expectations are reflected in the bank's stock price, the rates the bank pays for uninsured borrowed funds, and customers' willingness to do business with the bank. If a bank does not perform as well as expected or has other negative outcomes, lower stock prices and/or higher costs of funds will result. Consider L.M. Ericsson Telephone AB, a Swedish telecommunications company. Ericsson reported that pretax profits jumped 88 percent for the first nine months of 1994 and earnings increased to $1.38 per share, up from $0.56

per share in the previous year.[16] However, the stock price plunged $4 5/8 to $59 per share because stock analysts expected higher earnings.

High-quality information increases investors' and customers' certainty about the bank's operations and future. Stated otherwise, high-quality information reduces the risk of investing in or doing business with the bank.

Improving Communications

Information about a bank and its performance is available in annual and quarterly financial statements. However, the usefulness of financial reports varies widely from bank to bank. The Association for Investment Management and Research (AIMR) publishes an annual Corporate Information Committee Report that aims to improve communications between publicly held companies and the investment community. The appendix at the end of the chapter presents a checklist of criteria for evaluating financial data communications; the items listed apply to all industries. Good investor relations are important because they affect the bank's stock price, borrowers, and lenders who evaluate the bank's performance.

Financial reports are important, but they do not tell the whole story. The complete story includes corporate strategies, market share, and other information. It is necessary to determine "where" the bank is today before projecting where it is going tomorrow. That is an important part of strategic management.

Management provides information about the bank through meetings with analysts, media releases, and other means. According to Ted Blood, vice president for General Mills, "The key is to be open at all times, and be as communicative in bad times as in good times. We have to maintain credibility."[17] However, there is a thin line between maintaining effective communications and saying too much. Here are a few general guidelines for communications:[18]

---

[16] "Ericsson Posts Big Profit Rise, But Stock Falls," *The Wall Street Journal*, November 18, 1994, p. A14.

[17] John W. Kensinger and John Martin, *New Realities for Stockholder-Management Relations* (Morristown, NJ.: Financial Executives Research Association, Executive Report, May 1994), p. 11.

[18] For further discussion of these points, see Tower C. Snow, Jr., "Stock Crash Needn't Lead to Legal Hash," *The Wall Street Journal*, November 8, 1993, p. A14.

- Avoid surprising the market. Let analysts and others know what's going on.
- Stick to the facts. Don't use adjectives such as "strong" or "extraordinary earnings" to describe company performance.
- Refrain from making projections or trying to "hype" the stock. In a case involving Time Warner, Inc., the Second US Court of Appeals of New York found that companies have a duty to update optimistic projections of business plans whenever secret information renders prior public statements materially misleading.[19]
- Include risk factors in most documents and releases.
- Do not permit insiders to trade the stock before good or bad news is about to be announced. For example, two Continental Bank directors bought stock before BankAmerica announced its acquisition of Continental.[20] SEC guidelines prohibit insider trading when investors have material nonpublic information. *Material* means the information will affect the price of the stock. The price of Continental stock jumped 22 percent on news of the friendly merger. *Nonpublic* means information that has not been publicly disclosed. Insiders have a duty not to trade when they have such information, or they can disclose the information to the public and then trade.[21]

Other Stakeholders

The role other stakeholders play in the organization varies widely. Bank customers, for example, can impede bank mergers and acquisitions by asserting that under the CRA, their interests will not be served. Bank regulators, another stakeholder group, contributed to the "credit crunch" of the early 1990s.[22] They have also contributed to a costly burden of regulatory compliance and paperwork that adversely affects bank profitability.

---

[19] Margaret A. Jacobs, "Court Limits Companies' Liability for Overly Optimistic Forecasts," *The Wall Street Journal,* December 1, 1993, p. B5; also see Edward Felsenthal, "Disclosure Issues Top Survey of Lawsuits," *The Wall Street Journal,* March 1, 1994, p. B7.

[20] Warren Gettler and Steven Lipin, "Continental Bank Insiders Bought during Talks," *The Wall Street Journal,* February 2, 1994.

[21] Paul G. Haaga, Jr., "Compliance Guidelines: The Securities Firm," *Good Ethics: The Essential Element of a Firm's Success* (Charlottesville, VA: Association for Investment Management and Research, 1994), pp. 51–55.

[22] For various views concerning the credit crunch, see Edward J. Green and Soo Nam Oh, "Can a 'Credit Crunch' be Efficient?" *Quarterly Review,* Federal Reserve Bank of Minneapolis, Fall 1991, pp. 3–17.

CONCLUSION

The challenge of strategic management is to find ways to survive and grow profitably in a dynamic environment. The only constant in the dynamic business environment is change. Changes present threats or opportunities. In either case, banks have to be proactive to take advantage of the opportunities or mitigate the threats.

This chapter presented factors common in both successful and failed strategies. To a significant degree, the outcomes of the strategies implemented by banks are affected by factors beyond their control. In some cases the strategies will be profitable, and in other cases they won't. The profitable strategies may be copied by competitors, thereby reducing their benefits over time. Banks have no sustainable competitive advantage because whatever they do can be copied by competitors. Thus, when viewed collectively, the growth and survival of banks appear to be stochastic. While that may be true, well-managed banks stand the best chance of being the industry leaders and survivors. The next chapter explains marketing techniques for survival and growth.

Appendix to Chapter 2
CRITERIA FOR EVALUATING FINANCIAL COMMUNICATIONS EFFORTS[1]

This appendix presents the criteria financial analysts use to assess a firm's communications efforts with them. The analysts use information from the firm and other sources in forming their opinions about valuation, creditworthiness, timeliness of investments, and so on.

Qualification Questions

1. To your knowledge, during the past year has the management of this company suppressed or misrepresented material facts adverse to the company and/or its operations or outlook?

---

[1] *Corporate Information Committee Report, 1992–1993* (Charlottesville, VA.: Association for Investment Management and Research, 1994), pp. 95–97.

2. In your opinion, are any accounting or other managerial practices of this company materially misleading?

3. In your opinion, is this company unduly dilatory with respect to its press releases and/or earnings statements?

If you have answered any of these questions in the affirmative, do not proceed with the rating of this company, but contact the subcommittee chairperson. An affirmative answer to one of the questions by two or more subcommittee members will disqualify the company from being considered in this year's rating.

Note: The percentage weights appearing after each major category title (below) can be distributed to subcategories in whatever manner seems appropriate to each subcommittee.

Annual Published Information

(40 to 50 percent of total weight)

A. Annual Report

1. Financial Highlights: Are they clear and unambiguous?

2. President's Letter Review: Does it hit the highlights of the year in an objective manner? Is it relevant to the company's results and candid in appraising problems? It should include

   a. Review of the year

   b. Insights into operating rates, unit production levels, and selling prices

   c. Acquisitions and divestments, if any

   d. Government business, if material

   e. Capital expenditures program; start-up expenses

   f. Research and development efforts

   g. Employment costs, labor relations, union contracts

   h. Energy cost and availability

   i. Environmental and OSHA costs

   j. Backlogs

   k. New products

   l. Legislative and regulatory developments

   m. Outlook

   n. Unusual income or expense

3. Officers and Directors
   a. Age, background, and responsibilities
   b. Description of company organization
   c. Outside affiliations of directors
   d. Principal personnel changes
4. Statement of Corporate Goals: What are the short-term and long-term corporate goals, and how and when does management expect to achieve them? (This section could be included in several areas of the report, but separate treatment is preferred.)
5. Discussions of Divisional and/or Segment Operations
   a. How complete is the breakdown of sales materials, costs, overhead, and earnings?
   b. Are the segments logical for analytical purposes? Do they parallel lines of business?
   c. Are unusual developments explained, and do the explanations include management's response?
   d. Comparisons with relevant industry developments should include
      i. Market size and growth
      ii. Market penetration
      iii. Geographical divergencies
   e. Foreign operations
      i. Revenues, including export sales
      ii. Consolidated foreign earnings versus equity interest
      iii. Market and/or regional trends
      iv. Tax status
6. Financial Summary and Footnotes
   a. Statement of accounting principles, including explanation of changes and their effects
   b. Adjustments to EPS for dilution
   c. Affiliates' operating information
   d. Consolidated finance subsidiary's disclosure of separate balance sheet information and operating results
   e. Cash flows statement (FAS No. 95)
   f. Tax accounting investment tax credits identified; breakdown of current and deferred taxes for US and non-US tax jurisdictions;

reconciliation of effective and statutory tax rates; impact of changes in tax law; early application of FAS No. 96

g. Clarity of explanation of currency exchange rate accounting

   i. Impact on earnings from balance sheet translation, if any

   ii. Indication of "operating" or income statement effect of exchange rate fluctuations

h. Property accounts and depreciation policies

   i. Methods and asset lives used for tax and for financial reporting

   ii. Quantification of effect on reported earnings of use of different method and/or asset lives for tax purposes

i. Investments: composition and market values disclosed

j. Inventories: method of valuation and identifying different methods for various product or geographic segments

k. Leases and rentals: terms and liability

l. Debt repayment schedules

m. Pension funds: costs charged to income, interest rate, and wage inflation assumptions; amount of any unfunded past service liability; amortization period for unfunded liability (FAS No. 87)

n. Other post-employment benefits: pay-as-you-go amount, discussion of potential liability, and impact of FAS No. 106, including plans to fund or amend plans, and FAS No. 112

o. Capital expenditure programs and forecasts, including costs for environmental purposes

p. Acquisitions and divestitures (if material)

   i. Description of activity and operating results

   ii. Type of financial transaction

   iii. Effect on reported sales and earnings

   iv. Quantification of purchase acquisitions or small pooling that do not require restatement of prior years' results (when restating for pooling, both old and new data are useful for comparison)

q. Year-end adjustments

r. Restatement of quarterly reports to year-end accounting basis

s. Research and development and new products; amounts and types of outlays and forecasts

t. Contingent liabilities, particularly environmental

      u. Derivation of number of shares used for calculating primary and fully diluted earnings per share

      v. Disclosures of the fair values of financial instruments (FAS No. 107)

      w. Goodwill amount being amortized and number of years

      x. Ten-year statistical summary:

          i. Adequacy of income statement and balance sheet detail

          ii. Helpfulness of "nonstatement" data (e.g., number of employees, adjusted number of shares, price of stock, capital expenditures)

B. 10-Ks, 10-Qs, and Other Required Published Information

Quarterly and Other Published Information Not Required

(30 to 40 percent of total weight)

A. Quarterly Reports

    1. Depth of commentary on operating results and developments

    2. Discussion of new products, management changes, and problem areas

    3. Degree of detail of profit and loss statement, including divisional or segmental breakdown

    4. Inclusion of a balance sheet and cash flow statement

    5. Restatement of all prior- and current-year quarters for major pooling acquisitions and quantification of effect of purchase acquisitions and/or disposals

    6. Breakout of nonrecurring or exceptional income or expense items, including effects from inventory valuation and foreign currency translation factors

    7. Explicit statement of accounting principles underlying quarterly statements

    8. Timeliness of reports

    9. Separate fourth-quarter report

B. Other Published Material

    1. Availability of proxy statements (even though this is required public information)

    2. Annual meeting report: available with questions and identity of those posing questions

3. Addresses to analysts' groups: available with questions and answers

4. Statistical supplements and fact books

5. Company magazines, newsletters, and explanatory pamphlets

6. Press releases: Are they sent to shareholders and analysts? Are they timely? Do they include earnings numbers?

7. How are documents filed with public agencies (SEC, Federal Trade Commission, Department of Labor, court cases, etc.) made available? Does the company disseminate all material information in 10-K, 10-Q, and similar reports?

Other Aspects

(20 to 30 percent of total weight)

A. Is there a designated and advertised individual(s) for shareholder and analyst contacts?

B. Interviews

1. Knowledgeability and responsiveness of company contact

2. Access to policymakers and operational people

3. Candor in discussing negative developments

C. Presentations to analyst groups: frequency and content

D. Company-sponsored field trips and meetings

E. Annual meetings

1. Accessibility

2. Worthwhile to shareholders and analysts

Chapter Three

Developing Bank Marketing Strategy[1]

Marketing is a way of thinking about the problems of exchanges between buyers and sellers. Marketing strategists approach the issue of exchange from the perspective of existing or potential customers and then create services to fill an identified need. The American Marketing Association thus defines marketing as the performance of all activities necessary for the conception, pricing, promotion, and distribution of services to create exchanges that satisfy individual and organizational objectives.

THE TASKS OF MARKETING MANAGEMENT

In the context of the above definition, marketing management is management of the level, timing, and character of demand in facilitating the exchange process.[2] The task of bank marketing management is to develop and execute plans for creating customer satisfaction by facilitating exchanges. Marketing management tasks thus require decisions about

1. The services to be offered.
2. The types of promotional programs needed to create consumer awareness.
3. The prices to be charged that reflect acceptable values to consumers and to the bank.

---

[1] This chapter was written by J. Barry Mason, Russell Professor of Business Administration and Dean, College of Commerce, University of Alabama. Mason has served as a consultant in bank marketing strategy for more than 20 years. Since 1978, he has served on the city board of directors of a bank in his local community.

[2] Philip Kotler, *Marketing Management* (Englewood Cliffs, NJ: Prentice Hall, 1988), p. 12.

4. The distribution systems needed to make the services available to customers at the time and in the form that appeals to them.

Marketing plans must be developed in the context of the larger strategic plans for the organization. Otherwise, the plans will be developed in isolation, and results will be less than satisfactory. Individuals at all levels of the bank will be more valuable employees when they understand the pervasive role of marketing from the perspective of upper-level management.

Crafting Marketing Strategy

Marketing strategy requires an equal emphasis on consumers and competitors, as shown in Figure 3–1. Marketers typically tend to place the consumer at the heart of all of their actions. Strategists normally focus primarily on competitors. However, each concept by itself is insufficient.[3] Focusing entirely on consumers, for example, allows competitors to outmaneuver a bank in the marketplace.

Equal attention to customers and competitors results in a more viable concept of competitive advantage. In today's markets, "strategy is a way

FIGURE 3–1
Marketing Strategy Essentials

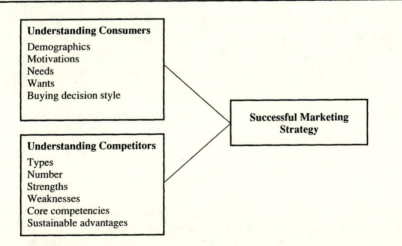

---

[3] J. Barry Mason and Hazel F. Ezell, *Marketing Management* (New York: Macmillan, 1993), p. 4.

of thinking about consumers, competitors, and competitive advantage that is inculcated into every member of the organization."[4]

No two banks have the same marketing strategy, although many similarities may exist. Some banks may choose to compete by establishing market power through market share dominance or finding and dominating a special niche in a market. Others may obtain operating cost efficiencies through innovation or establish strong consumer loyalty through superior service. Regardless of the strategy chosen, no strategy will succeed unless it helps to create significant customer value and sets the bank apart from the competition. Also, no strategy will succeed indefinitely because each instance of success provides a model for new competitors. The focus must always be on where we want to position the bank in the future and how we will get there.

The centerpiece of the marketing strategy followed by all organizations can be analyzed in terms of the three strategies presented in Figure 3–2:

FIGURE 3–2
Marketing Strategy Options

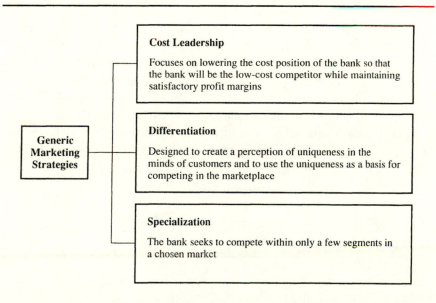

Cost Leadership

Focuses on lowering the cost position of the bank so that the bank will be the low-cost competitor while maintaining satisfactory profit margins

Differentiation

Designed to create a perception of uniqueness in the minds of customers and to use the uniqueness as a basis for competing in the marketplace

Specialization

The bank seeks to compete within only a few segments in a chosen market

Generic Marketing Strategies

---

[4] Steven P. Schnaars, *Marketing Strategy: A Customer Driven Approach* (New York: The Free Press, 1991), p. 27.

strategies based on cost leadership, strategies based on differentiation, and strategies based on focus or specialization. Regardless of the strategy chosen, the focus should always be on the key success factors necessary to achieve a sustainable competitive advantage (SCA).

Low cost, differentiation, and specialization should not be viewed as mutually exclusive choices. For example, successful banks strive to lower their costs while at the same time providing excellent customer service that ideally results in a price premium because of added value. Excellent quality results in strong customer satisfaction, which can more than offset the costs of offering higher quality. Higher quality, in turn, can lead to a larger market share. A large market share can help reduce costs by spreading overhead across a higher volume of sales.

Thus, in essence, successful banks continually emphasize ways to increase customer value and reduce costs. These dimensions are interactive. Still, the core business strategy is typically anchored on one of the three fundamental strategy options so that the bank is not in an unduly vulnerable position.

Low-cost strategies.   A low-cost strategy focuses on lowering the bank's cost position so that the bank will be the low-cost competitor while maintaining satisfactory profit margins. However, low cost is not necessarily equivalent to low price. Banks competing on the basis of cost leadership strive for efficient-scale facilities, avoid marginally profitable lines and small customer accounts, and minimize their investment in sales expense and service. They give careful attention to the budget and overall cost control. Figure 3–3 highlights some approaches banks use to control costs.

A cost leadership strategy is especially effective when consumers are sensitive to price, competition is primarily on the basis of price, differentiation (identifying distinguishing service features) is difficult to achieve, and most customers use the service in the same way.

FIGURE 3–3
Illustrative Ways to Lower Cost Structures

• Efficient use of labor	• Minimizing overhead
• No-frills service	• Services innovation
• Services design	• New methods of delivery

Differentiation strategies.   Marketing strategies based on differentiation are designed to create a perception of uniqueness in the minds of customers and to use the uniqueness as a basis for competing in the marketplace. The differentiation may be achieved on numerous bases, such as image or special customer services.

A strategy of differentiation can be particularly effective when the bank can distinguish itself from competitors in ways that are valuable to customers, consumer needs and uses are numerous, and the number of competitors using a differentiation strategy is smaller than the number of meaningful ways to differentiate the service.

In contrast to cost leadership, a bank can use more than one differentiation strategy successfully if a number of attributes are widely valued by consumers. Sustainability is what is important. The sources of sustainability must remain valuable to the customer and not be imitated easily by competitors.

Specialization strategies.   Specialization is a marketing strategy whereby a bank competes within only one or a few segments in a chosen market. In essence, a specialization strategy rests on the choice of a narrow competitive scope within an industry. A bank following a specialization strategy strives to achieve a competitive advantage in the target segment(s) even though it does not have a competitive advantage overall. A specialization strategy may emerge as the only viable option for a bank with narrowly focused strengths or limited resources in an environment characterized by larger and stronger competitors.

Specialization strategies can be driven by either low cost or differentiation. The strategy can be most effective when

- Management can identify strategic clusters of easily accessible buyers who have unique needs for the service and are sufficiently large in number to make the effort profitable.
- Competitors tend to appeal to a broad market rather than targeting a limited number of segments.
- A bank lacks the resources to appeal to all segments of the market.

The most attractive segments in a specialization strategy share one or more of the following characteristics:

1. The segment has good growth potential.
2. The segment is not crucial to the success of major competitors.

3. The bank can defend the segment against challengers because of its superior ability to serve buyers in the segment.
4. The bank has the skills and resources needed to effectively serve the segment.

Opportunities for a specialization strategy include focusing on the services line, targeting a particular segment, or serving a limited geographic area.

PRECONDITIONS FOR STRATEGY SELECTION

Before making decisions about marketing strategy, management must explore the full range of environmental factors as part of a comprehensive situation assessment. Key factors affecting the choice of competitive strategy include understanding aggregate driving forces in the industry, the bank's internal strengths and weaknesses, its position in the industry, and prevailing industry and competitive conditions.

The goal of management should be to capitalize on the bank's strengths when responding to prevailing industry norms and competitor profiles. Management must understand the economics of the industry, the forces effecting change in the industry, the nature and strength of competition, the distinctive competencies of competitors, their likely moves and countermoves, and the bank's own internal strengths and weaknesses.

Development of strategy is not solely a creative exercise. It is based on a careful assessment of all available information sources. The strategy options chosen for consideration should reflect the full range of situations the bank faces.

Situation Analysis

A careful situation analysis can identify the strategic window of opportunity as the linchpin for a bank's marketing strategy. Management is always seeking to identify the few critical factors that hold the key to strategic success. The search for the strategic window of opportunity begins with an assessment of market conditions (see Figure 3–4), followed by an assessment of the industry and competitors and an internal assessment of the bank. Such an analysis must occur before management can do a good job of beginning the process of marketing strategy development and implementation.

Clearly, sustained competitive advantage does not result from a fixed stock of competencies; rather, continual accumulation of competencies is

FIGURE 3–4
Preconditions for Marketing Strategy Selection

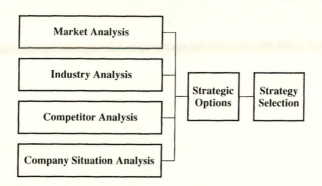

necessary to permit sustainability of advantage over rivals. Also, the greater the ambiguity of the sources of competitive advantage, the more sustainable they will be because ambiguity creates barriers to imitation by competitors. The most effective barriers to imitation are achieved when competitors do not fully understand the competencies on which the advantage is based.

Table 3–1 provides a summary format for conducting the types of analyses that form the preliminary steps to marketing strategy development. The analysis cannot be reduced to a simple mechanical process. Various opinions may exist about the importance and impact of each factor and the possible synergies among the factors. It is important to know the questions to ask, where to find the answers, and how to interpret the data that become available.

The changes suggested as a result of the analysis are likely to be ongoing as opposed to sweeping and revolutionary. Information emerges over time as management becomes more astute at assessing the environment. Sweeping analyses are necessary periodically, but continuous monitoring as outlined here can help management make the marginal adjustments that are important in fine-tuning current strategies.

Customer Analysis and Marketing Strategy Development

The end result of marketing strategy development, regardless of the plan followed, is the creation of customer satisfaction. Marketing strategy thus must

TABLE 3–1
Analytical Checklist for Bank Marketing Strategy Development

Market factors	*Profile*
	• Size
	• Growth rate
	• Life cycle stage
	• Profitability
	Environmental factors
	• Regulatory
	• Economic
	• Technological
	• Political
	• Social
Industry factors	*Key factors*
	• Marketing
	• Technology
	• Others
Competition analysis	• Threat of new competitors
	• Power of buyers
	• Threat of substitutes
	• Power of customers
	• Extent of rivalry
	• Likely competitor moves and countermoves
Company situation analysis	• Internal strengths
	• Internal weaknesses
	• External threats
	• External opportunities
	• Relative costs

also carefully consider the customer in crafting marketing strategy. Management writer Theodore Levitt reminds us of the importance of understanding customers in shaping marketing strategy: "What should be done can be defined only with reference to what customers do, can do, or might do in the marketplace."[5] Similarly, Peter Drucker notes, "Any serious attempt to 'state what business is' must start with the customer, his realities, his situation, his behavior, his expectations, and his values."[6] We are reminded, however, that

---

[5] Theodore Levitt, *The Marketing Imagination* (New York: The Free Press, 1983), p. 135.

[6] Peter Drucker, *Management: Tasks, Responsibilities, Practices* (New York: Harper & Row, 1984), p. 61.

target markets are always moving targets because of continuous changes in demographics, buying behavior, technologies, and the strategies of competitors. Marketing strategy, as noted earlier, thus evolves out of continuous attention to understanding how buyers view and shop for services in conjunction with understanding competitors.[7]

Marketers' interest in consumers arises primarily from a search for competitive advantage. Marketers have long known that customer satisfaction translates into higher long-term profitability as management becomes more aware of customer needs and how to meet those needs. Customers are loyal to high-quality services and are likely to be repeat buyers. In addition, satisfied customers are not easily lured away by competitors; they are less inclined to try each new bank that comes along to save a few pennies. Banks with excellent services quality have superior financial performance. High quality is closely related to strong customer satisfaction.

The Scope of Customer Analysis

Understanding buyers and creating buyer satisfaction require answers to the following set of questions:

1. Who are the buyers?
2. What are buyer motivations?
3. How does the bank compare with the competition?
4. What are the sources of customer-perceived differences between competitors?[8]

Buyer characteristics can be grouped in almost limitless ways to help marketers understand differences important in developing marketing strategy. Generally, the characteristics can be grouped according to whether they identify customers or describe how customers behave toward a service. Identifiers, as Figure 3–5 shows, are the generic and stable descriptions of consumer or organizational markets targeted in marketing.

Buyer motivations reflect the values sought in bank services and underlie buyer behavior decisions. Understanding buyer motivations can help

---

[7] "Market-Driven Culture, Customer Orientation, and Innovation All Required for Success," *Tuck Forum* 1, no. 1 (1994), p. 1.

[8] George S. Day, *Market Driven Strategy* (New York: The Free Press, 1990), p. 39.

FIGURE 3–5
Typical Bank Customer Identifiers and Benefits Profile Variables

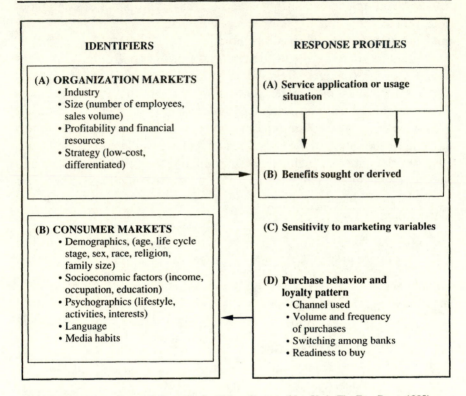

Source: Adapted from George S. Day, *Market Driven Strategy* (New York: The Free Press, 1990), p. 102.

management develop the assets or skills that can provide a sustainable competitive advantage in the marketplace, illustrated as follows:[9]

Customer   →   Key Relevant   →   Sustainable
Motivations   Assets and Skills   Competitive Advantage

The attributes important to homogeneous groups of buyers can be understood by an analysis of usage patterns and decision processes. Focus

---

[9] David Aaker, *Developing Business Strategies* (New York: John Wiley & Sons, 1988), p. 61.

groups, consumer surveys, and other ways of ensuring continuing close contact with customers can help identify important attributes.

Analysis of consumers should go beyond current users and also look at the customers of competitors, as well as individuals who are not users of the bank's services. Management needs specific information about current and potential customers of the bank and its competitors: who they are, what they do with the service, where they buy it, when they buy, why they buy, how they buy, and the benefits sought, as illustrated in Table 3–2.

TABLE 3–2
Information Needed on Current and Potential Bank Customers

Current and Potential Customer Information Needed	Bank	Competitors	
		A	*B*
1. Who they are: Who is the purchaser? Who is the user?			
2. How do they use it: What they buy What they do with it			
3. Where they buy it: Information services location Purchase location			
4. When they buy: Time of the year On versus off promotion			
5. Why they buy: Basic need Specific attributes			
6. How they buy: Amount Terms Selection procedure			
7. Benefits: Currently obtained Desired			

Source: Adapted from Donald R. Lehmann and Russell S. Winer, *Analysis for Marketing Planning* (Homewood, IL: Richard D. Irwin, 1991), p. 109.

MARKET SEGMENTATION STRATEGIES

Given its chosen competitive strategy and an understanding of consumer and organizational markets, a bank must then determine those people or organizations to whom it will direct its marketing efforts. As such, banks must determine the segmentation strategy that it will follow.

Table 3–3 shows that banks may choose from one of three segmentation strategies: a mass-market strategy, a differentiated strategy, or a concentrated strategy.

Mass-Market Strategy

A mass-market strategy assumes most consumers are alike in their needs and wants. The differences that do exist among consumers are not thought to be important influences on bank patronage. Marketers who follow such a strategy treat the market as if it were one homogeneous segment and develop a single marketing program to serve potential consumers within the market. Cost economies result for banks that follow a mass-market strategy.

Although a mass-market strategy may be appropriate in markets where homogeneity exists, such homogeneous markets rarely exist today, especially in economies such as that of the United States. Thus, most banks segment the market and follow either a differentiated or a concentrated strategy.

TABLE 3–3
Bank Segmentation Strategy Options

Mass-Market Strategy

Assumes most consumers are alike in their needs and wants. The market is treated as if it were one homogeneous segment, and a single marketing program is developed to serve potential consumers in the market.

Differentiated Strategy

An attempt is made to appeal to several segments of consumers by designing a separate marketing program for each segment.

Concentrated Strategy

A bank selects one or a relatively few segments on which to focus its marketing efforts.

Differentiated Strategy

A differentiated strategy attempts to appeal to several segments of consumers by designing a separate marketing program for each segment. Even though a multiple-segment strategy leads to higher marketing costs, total sales are also usually higher.

Some banks following a multiple-coverage segmentation strategy cover all segments of the market. Alternatively, a bank might target some, but not all, of the segments that make up the market. In such situations, the bank often focuses on the largest segments, believing that serving smaller segments may not be worth the effort.

Concentrated Strategy

A bank follows a concentrated strategy when it selects a single segment of the market on which to focus its marketing efforts. Such an approach allows the bank to obtain greater knowledge of customer needs, thereby giving it a strong competitive advantage in meeting those needs. The bank is likely to acquire a special reputation and strong customer loyalty. Further, specialization results in marketing cost economies. Such a strategy is especially appealing to banks that have limited resources and are unable to compete in a large number of market segments. A disadvantage of the strategy is the risk that demand will decline in the focused segment.

In selecting the segment on which to focus, a number of strategic alternatives are available. For example, a bank might focus on the largest segment because large segments usually have a higher volume of potential sales, making them more attractive than smaller segments. Such a strategy is appealing if the bank has the resources to be successful. Alternatively, a bank might elect to focus on a smaller segment and build a dominant position in a niche where it can exploit its competitive advantage. Large sales are traded for a defendable market position. Often the intent of such a strategy is to avoid competition rather than directly confront large, powerful competitors. Another alternative is to target a segment of the market that is experiencing faster growth than other segments. The objective of this strategy is to build a strong position in an increasingly attractive segment.

This discussion does not include all of the strategic options available, but it does underscore the fact that a variety of approaches are available to banks in selecting a target segment when following a single-segment segmentation strategy.

Defining Market Segments

An effective segmentation process defines market segments that meet certain criteria. As Table 3–4 shows, these criteria are differential response, substantiality, measurability, accessibility, and reliability.

Differential response.   The most important criterion of effective market segmentation is that the process establishes groups of consumers who respond differently to some aspect of the marketing strategy. Consumers within a segment, however, should be as much alike as possible in their responses to some marketing variable.

Substantiality.   When segmentation is carried too far, the resulting segments are so narrowly defined that the costs of serving each segment are greater than the generated revenues. Therefore, the segmentation variable must be shared by enough potential customers to justify the expense and effort of focusing marketing attention on the segment.

Measurability.   Segments must be identifiable and measurable. One reason demographic variables are often used to segment markets is that a great deal of such information is available from secondary sources. It is relatively easy, for example, for marketers to determine the number of consumers in different age and income groups who reside in various geographical areas.

Accessibility.   The variables used to segment a market must provide direction on how to reach the segments. For example, knowing that

TABLE 3–4
Requirements for Effective Bank Market Segmentation

Differential response	The process must create groups of consumers who respond differently to some aspect of the marketing strategy.
Substantiality	The segmentation variable must be shared by enough potential customers to justify the expense and effort of focusing marketing attention there.
Measurability	Segments must be identifiable and measurable.
Accessibility	The variable(s) used to segment a market must provide direction as to how to reach the segments.

consumers in a particular segment live in a certain geographical area provides the marketer with information that is useful in developing a strategy to reach the segment.

Reliability. Markets must be segmented in such a way that the resulting segments exhibit adequate stability over time. If not, the marketing efforts may not have enough time to elicit the desired response from targeted segments.

POSITIONING WITHIN TARGET MARKETS

Once market segments have been selected, management must develop a positioning strategy for its offering in each target segment. Positioning simply means determining how to differentiate one's offering from those of competitors in the minds of consumers. Developing a positioning strategy requires that managers know how important various attributes are to consumers in making choices and how well consumers think the bank and competitors are doing with respect to those attributes.

Alternative Bases for Positioning

A number of bases can be used for positioning bank services. Management must decide which of the alternative positioning bases to use. In making this decision, management should consider the following:[10]

1. The bank's market position—is the service a leader?
2. The positioning used by competitors.
3. The compatibility of the desired positioning with consumers' needs, wants, and current perceptions of the offering's positioning versus its competitors.
4. The newness of the considered basis for positioning and its departure from the current practice in the market.
5. The resources available to communicate the positioning effectively and the compatibility of the positioning with the bank's marketing strategy.
6. The bank's desire for an innovative versus a "me-too" image.

---

[10] Yoram Wind, *Product Policy: Concepts, Methods, and Strategy* (Reading, MA: Addison-Wesley, 1982), p. 81.

7. The ability to develop an effective, creative execution for the chosen positioning.
8. The legal environment, that is, likely legal action against the proposed positioning.

Positioning options include

1. Positioning on specific service features. Positioning on the basis of price or performance on specific service attributes is a common approach to positioning.
2. Positioning on benefits, problem solution, or needs. Stressing benefits rather than attributes is often a more effective positioning approach.
3. Positioning for specific usage occasions.
4. Positioning for user category, that is, the retail customer versus the commercial customer.
5. Positioning against another service.

IMPLEMENTING MARKETING STRATEGY

Decisions about how to implement the marketing strategy developed are made in the context of what are known as the *marketing mix variables*. The mix includes the elements of marketing strategy under the control of management. The marketing mix variables include

1. Services: the mix of services and the breadth and depth of the service lines.
2. Distribution: how to make the services accessible to the buyer.
3. Promotion: making the buyer aware of the offering, persuading the individual to buy, and instilling customer loyalty.
4. Price: the value the bank attaches to the services it offers.

Services Development Strategy

A steady stream of new services is critical to a bank's growth and success even after decisions are made about segmentation and positioning. Intense competition, rapid technological change, the maturing or stagnation of certain markets, deregulation, and demographic and lifestyle changes have drastically altered the nature of markets, competition, and consumer needs. Such changes cut two ways, creating opportunities for new services and profits and threatening the survival of established ones.

New service introductions are critical to the long-term growth and success of organizations. While new service launches offer considerable rewards, they also present risks. The failure rate is high, and the costs of failure can be extremely high. Numerous reasons exist for new service failures. Some of the major reasons include a lack of superior benefits over existing services, problems in market research, a poor strategic match between the service and the bank's unique skills, a target market that is too small to serve profitability, technical problems with the service, a poor positioning strategy, and managerial problems.

If new services programs are to succeed, they must be backed by top management. New services are long-term, high-risk, and costly projects. Established services compete with new services for resources. Only top-level managers have the power and authority to allocate resources to new services and accept the risks and costs of new services programs.

Proactive versus reactive strategy. Generally, new services development strategies may be classified as either proactive or reactive. Banks following a proactive strategy are technologically innovative and take the lead in developing new services and markets. As such, proactive strategies lead to the development of "revolutionary" new services and are based on preempting competition by being first in the market with a new service.

A reactive strategy suggests that a bank is responsive to change rather than being an initiator of change. The goal is not the introduction of revolutionary new services and the creation of new markets. Instead, new service development activities focus on either modifying existing services, expanding the services, or developing services to enter markets not currently served by the bank.

Selecting a strategy. In selecting an appropriate new service development strategy, banks must consider a number of factors, including growth opportunities, the probable protection for innovation, the scale of the market, and the strength of the competition.

Certainly not all banks choose a proactive new service development strategy, but many banks are in a good position to innovate. Table 3–5 lists the characteristics of banks that often follow proactive strategies. Alternatively, for some organizations, innovation may be too great a risk. Such banks elect

TABLE 3–5
Organizational Characteristics Affecting New Bank Service Development
Strategy Selection

Proactive Strategies May Be Best for Banks That
- Follow an overall policy of growth
- Are willing to enter new services and markets
- Are capable of achieving market protection
- Are able to enter high-volume or high-margin markets
- Have the resources and time necessary to develop new services
- Are not vulnerable to imitation by competitors

Reactive Strategies May Be Best for Banks That
- Require concentration on existing services or markets
- Can obtain little protection for innovation
- Are in markets too small to allow them to recover development costs
- Are in danger of being overwhelmed by competitive imitation

Source: Adapted from Glen L. Urban and John R. Hauser, *Design and Marketing of New Products*
(Englewood Cliffs, NJ: Prentice Hall, 1980), p. 25.

to implement reactive new service development strategies. Table 3–5 also
presents characteristics of banks that tend to follow such strategies.

Developing the Pricing Policy

Price is one of the most powerful weapons available to bank managers in
developing marketing strategy. Managers must develop pricing strategies
in the context of competition, market segments in which the bank competes, consumer value perceptions, cost considerations, and the overall
marketing plan.

To set prices, a bank must establish pricing objectives, which must be
consistent with the organization's overall purpose or mission. The objectives must also be consistent with what the bank has decided to accomplish with the service offered, given a selected target market and
positioning strategy. Numerous pricing objectives exist, including profit,
return on investment, market share, cash flow, and survival.

Profit.   Some banks set profit maximization as their goal, which
means they develop a marketing plan to enable management to achieve
the greatest profit per unit of the service sold. Demand and cost estimates

associated with different output and price alternatives are determined, and a price is chosen that will enable the bank to maximize current profits.

The goal of profit maximization does not necessarily lead to high prices. Some banks attempt to maximize current profits by charging relatively low prices if competitors offer good substitutes and if demand is elastic. The low prices may lead to market expansion, which, in turn, leads to lower costs, higher revenues, and greater profits.

Profit maximization is often a short-term strategy that requires the bank to minimize investment in equipment and facilities and in developing human resources skills as a means of increasing the level of corporate earnings. As a result, banks often pursue an objective of earning a satisfactory profit rather than attempting to maximize profits. Earning a satisfactory profit means achieving a target rate of return. Earning a satisfactory profit is often perceived as being more socially responsible. It also may be easier to implement a satisfactory profit goal because organizations often do not have all the revenue and cost information necessary to determine at what price profit will actually be maximized.

Return on investment. Management may seek a target rate of return on internally generated and borrowed funds. A variety of factors influence the choice of a target rate of return on investment. For example, the current and impending competitive picture is a factor. If a bank wishes to discourage competitors from entering a market, it may set a low target return goal. A high target return goal may be set if there is little threat of impending competition.

Market share. The purpose of a market share objective is to gain market share in a growth market, take market share from competitors, or retain an existing share. In such situations, management expects to sacrifice short-run profits in return for an acceptable level of market share. Once the bank obtains an acceptable market share, prices can be raised and profits returned to normal levels.

A strategy of price reductions to gain market share is not without disadvantages. Once consumers see a service offered at a low price, they may not want to pay more and the bank may encounter problems initiating price increases.[11]

---

[11] Walter K. Levy, "Beware, the Pricing Genie is Out of the Bottle," *Arthur Andersen Retailing Issues Newsletter,* November 1994, pp. 1–4.

Cash flow. A bank may set price to recover cash as rapidly as possible. Such an objective may be especially relevant when introducing a new service. An early cash recovery objective does not necessarily mean the bank should set a high rather than a low price on its product. The price that results in the largest cash flow may be high or low, depending on such variables as price elasticity of demand and whether the bank can achieve economies of scale. Constant unit costs and low elasticity of demand suggest that cash flow will be maximized through a high price; falling unit costs and high elasticity of demand are conditions that indicate the bank can maximize cash flow by setting a low price on its offering.

Pricing strategy options. Organizations follow one of three broad types of pricing strategies to support the marketing plan and the objectives to be achieved through pricing decisions: cost-oriented pricing, demand-based pricing, and competitive pricing. Several options are available under each strategy (see Figure 3–6).

Cost-oriented pricing. *Cost-plus pricing* is the most common approach to establishing prices. Management simply adds a specified amount to its cost of producing and marketing the service.

FIGURE 3–6
Pricing Strategies Available to Bank Management

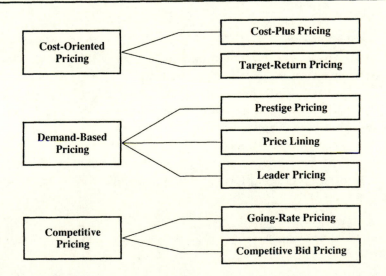

The strength of cost-plus pricing is its simplicity. Management simply needs a schedule of costs. The approach, however, does require an accurate understanding of costs, which is often not an easy task, especially in times of changing technology or inflation. There are several weaknesses to cost-plus pricing. First, the approach ignores current consumer demand and competition. Also, it assumes a level of sales before the price is set. If fewer sales occur, fixed costs would be spread over fewer units and the realized markup would be less than desired. Therefore, cost-plus pricing may be used effectively only when the expected level of sales actually materializes. For this reason, cost-plus pricing is more often used for services that have a stable, predictable demand and a predictable set of competitors.

A variation of cost-plus pricing used by some banks operating in rapidly growing markets is experience-curve pricing. In this approach, the average unit cost used as the base in determining price is an estimate of future average costs. Experience-curve pricing is based on the assumption that over time costs decline as a bank gains experience in producing and marketing a service. Therefore, the bank sets price in relation to where costs will be when the service is to be sold in the future, not where costs actually are when the bank develops the strategy for the service.

Target-return pricing is another cost-oriented approach to price setting, but the price is set to yield a target rate of return on investment. Assume the bank invested $5 million in the business and wants to set price to earn a 10 percent return, or $500,000. The price is determined by using the following formula:

$$\text{Price} = \text{Unit Cost} + \frac{\text{Desired Dollar Return}}{\text{Unit Sales}}$$

$$= \$150 + \frac{\$500,000}{10,000}$$

$$= \$200$$

While target-return pricing is a more sophisticated approach to pricing than cost-plus pricing, it ignores competitors' prices and demand considerations, just as cost-plus pricing does. In addition, the bank will realize its desired return only if the estimated cost and sales figures prove to be accurate.

Demand-based pricing. Demand-based pricing suggests that prices be set based on consumer perceptions of value. Using this approach, pricing is no longer a technical issue solved by applying a formula. Instead, prices are based on the marketing executive's understanding of buyer motivations. Banks may implement a variety of demand-oriented approaches to pricing, including prestige pricing, price lining, and leader pricing.

Prestige pricing means setting a premium price for the service in the belief that consumers will associate the high price with high quality. Because of a variety of environmental (primarily demographic and economic) trends, increasing attention is being paid to the development and marketing of premium services targeted at the upper end of the price pyramid. The premium segment can exist in almost any service category. Consumers who are willing to pay higher prices for premium services typically view them as status symbols. An example is personal banking services.

Banks practicing *price lining* feature services at a limited number of price levels. Each price level is aimed at a different market segment. Management limits service offerings to two or three price points that reflect varying service levels.

In *leader pricing* a bank offers unusually low prices on a few items to attract customers who may then purchase additional, regularly priced services. The assumption is that a positive cross-elasticity of demand exists between the leaders and other offered services. By stimulating demand for the leaders, the bank will also increase sales of complementary services.

Competitive pricing.   Demand-based and cost-oriented pricing do not always explicitly recognize the effects of competition on pricing. Pricing policies are, however, often established primarily with a view toward competition. Examples include going-rate (competitive-parity) pricing, customary pricing, and competitive-bid pricing.

In adopting *going-rate* or *competitive-parity pricing,* banks set prices equal to those of one or more major competitors. This practice is common in industries, such as banking, characterized by a few firms with large market shares and little services differentiation. A price leader takes the first step in either raising or lowering prices in the industry, and other banks typically follow. Competitors know that a price increase on their part will not be followed and can result in a substantial loss of sales. On the other hand, a price decrease will quickly be met, which can mean less revenue for all parties.

Prices for some services, such as the purchase of high-denomination certificates of deposit, are established through *competitive-bid pricing.* Bidders know only their own prices, not those of competitors. Typically, the contract is awarded to the high-priced bidder. Banks attempting to sell through sealed bids must consider demand, competition, and costs when developing price. Demand is known because it is stated in the bid specifications, and the bank may have a good understanding of its own cost situation. The difficulty arises in understanding the cost structures and probable bidding strategies of competitors.

Promotion Strategy

Promotional efforts play a key role in communicating the bank's positioning strategy to the target market. As such, promotional plans must be designed to support the overall competitive strategy and must be consistent with decisions about pricing and other elements of the marketing mix.

Promotion is the communication function of marketing. Communication, however, is more than the sending of information. Effective communication occurs only when individuals understand and respond to the message sent.

Promotion strategy is implemented through advertising, publicity and public relations, personal selling, and sales promotion (see Table 3–6).

TABLE 3–6
Principal Forms of Bank Promotion

Advertising

Advertising includes all sponsored and paid forms of nonpersonal mass media communication by an identified sponsor. Examples include the use of radio, television, newspapers, magazines, outdoor billboards, and similar forms of communication.

Publicity and Public Relations

Publicity is any news item or editorial comment about services, business activities, or organizations communicated through the mass media that is not paid for by the organization named in the publicity. Examples include news releases, speeches, and press conferences. Public relations consists of programs and activities designed to obtain public understanding, acceptance, and goodwill for the organization. Examples include entertainment, education, and community service programs.

Personal Selling

Personal selling involves the use of person-to-person communication to assist and persuade a prospect to buy a service. Types of salespersons include order generators, order takers, and support personnel.

Sales Promotion

Sales promotion includes all promotional activities other than advertising, publicity and public relations, and personal selling designed to achieve short-term sales results through stimulation of consumer purchasing or dealer effectiveness. Examples include coupons, contests, and sweepstakes.

Promotion objectives. The market response management seeks from its largest audience determines the objectives for a promotion plan. After determining whom the bank wants to reach, management must decide what it wishes to accomplish through its promotional strategy. One perspective from which to discuss objectives is whether they are expressed primarily in communication terms or in sales terms. The objective to be achieved often depends on the stages of the consumer decision-making process in targeted segments. The stages of this model, as shown in Figure 3–7 in the context of the hierarchy of effects model, are awareness, knowledge, liking, preference, conviction, and purchase.

The hierarchy of effects is basically a model of consumer response to promotional activity. Promotion stimulates awareness, which leads to attitude change, which leads to behavior change. Therefore, different promotion objectives exist at the various stages of the model. Individuals who are in the earlier stages of the model (for example, awareness or knowledge) are not likely to make a purchase simply by being exposed to some type of promotion. The objective of the promotion might be to stimulate awareness or initial interest and thus is stated in communication terms. Sales response as a promotion objective would be more appropriate for individuals in the latter stages of the model.

The model presented in Figure 3–7 is more relevant in certain situations than in others. For example, consumers are most likely to move through the stages when purchasing strongly differentiated services. Movement through each stage is also likely when consumers are highly

FIGURE 3–7
The Hierarchy of Effects Model

Awareness ↓	The ability of the consumer to recall the name of a bank's service either with or without prompting
Knowledge ↓	The ability of the consumer to describe the important attributes of a service
Liking ↓	The favorable attitude of the consumer toward a bank service
Preference ↓	The degree to which the consumer feels more positive about a service relative to other offerings
Conviction ↓	The likelihood that the consumer will purchase the service
Purchase	The acquisition of a bank service

involved with the service. Such buying situations result in extended decision making, in which the buyer proceeds through various stages (problem recognition, information search, alternative evaluation) until a purchase decision is made. A consumer in the early stages of problem recognition will not likely be motivated to make a purchase by being exposed to an advertisement; this is especially true when the planning period for purchasing is relatively long.

At the problem recognition stage, all advertising can hope to accomplish is to affect the propensity to buy and to move the consumer closer to a purchase at some future point. If the consumer has already decided to buy and is engaging in search, however, an advertisement or other promotional stimulus may trigger a sale. In this case, a sales objective would be appropriate. Similarly, an objective stated in sales terms would be acceptable when the planning period for a purchase is relatively short.

Another perspective from which to view objectives is whether the promotional strategy is designed to inform, persuade, or remind. Consumers must know something about a service before they can buy it; therefore, in some instances, the purpose of promotion is to inform. For example, when a revolutionary new service is introduced into the marketplace, consumers must be informed of what the service is, what its benefits are, why they should want the service, and how the service differs from existing services.

In competitive market situations, the purpose of promotion is often to persuade consumers to buy a particular service rather than a competitive one. This is accomplished by pointing out how the service excels in attributes important to consumers.

In some instances, a reminding objective may be appropriate. Even consumers who are loyal buyers are targets for threats of competitors. They need to be reminded of their satisfaction with a service to keep them from switching to a competitive one.

Formulating an appropriate promotion mix.   The promotion mix is the combination of the forms of promotion to be used. This decision is essential in that promotion campaigns for most services involve the use of several forms of promotion. The promotion mix and the emphasis on the various forms of promotion depend on several factors, including the use of a push or pull strategy, the amount of money available, service features, characteristics of the target market, and the stage of the service in the service life cycle.

Banks following a push strategy rely heavily on personal selling in their promotion mix. In contrast, advertising aimed at ultimate consumers is emphasized in the promotion mix when management follows a pull strategy to stimulate consumer demand.

Many banks are too small to engage in heavy advertising programs. Such banks must rely instead on various forms of short-term sales promotion and on their personnel to stimulate demand. They may design the sales promotion programs around various incentives. Many services are supported rarely, if at all, by advertising simply because the bank does not have the funds for such an effort.

Some services are promoted primarily through advertising, while others rely primarily on personal selling. Advertising tends to be a dominant part of the promotion mix under the following conditions:

1. Hidden qualities exist.
2. Emotional buying motives exist.
3. Services are in the earlier stages of the service life cycle when consumer information needs are high.
4. The buyer perceives little risk to be associated with buying the service.

In contrast, personal selling tends to dominate when the service

1. Has a high unit value.
2. Is technical in nature.
3. Must be tailored to the needs of a specific company or group.
4. Is used infrequently.

Distribution of Services

Bank management has the option of using intensive, selective, or exclusive distribution in planning market coverage.

Intensive distribution. Intensive distribution is designed to make the services of the bank available to as many markets and outlets as possible. High sales volume and wide market coverage are the goals of banks using intensive distribution. Such a mass-market strategy works especially well for standardized, low-cost services such as those provided by automatic teller machines.

Selective distribution. In selective distribution, the availability of a service in a given market is restricted to a limited number of outlets. Selective distribution enables banks to maintain a reasonable degree of control in protecting the integrity of their services. An example of selective distribution is commercial loan services, which are often not available in all area branch offices of a bank. Selective distribution depends on the quality of sales personnel and their level of service knowledge at the individual outlet level.

Exclusive distribution. Exclusive distribution tightly limits the available services in a market to a particular location. An example is trust services. Typically, such services are available only in the central office of the bank. Such an arrangement is the only way a bank can maintain a high degree of control over the service.

UNDERSTANDING THE FUNDAMENTALS OF LONG-TERM CUSTOMER SATISFACTION

The driving purpose of marketing strategy development, as noted earlier, is to create satisfied customers. Customer satisfaction thus is the end result of successful marketing strategy implementation. Understanding the dimensions of customer satisfaction and how to diagnose customer satisfaction shortfalls are therefore key elements in assessing the success of a bank's marketing strategy.

Banks with strong customer satisfaction ratings share the following attributes:

1. They set themselves "impossibly high" standards.
2. They are obsessive about knowing what the customers want even better than the customers themselves.
3. They create and manage customers' expectations.
4. They design services to maximize customer satisfaction.
5. They focus resources to meet their commitment to customers, virtually regardless of the cost.
6. They make customer satisfaction everybody's business.

The Dimensions of Customer Satisfaction

Customer-focused banks realize that every dimension of the organization must be structured from the customer's point of view. As Table 3–7

TABLE 3–7
Fundamental Components of Customer Satisfaction

Service	*Design*
	• Messages
	• Sales and support effectiveness
	Feedback and incentives
	• Customer contact
	• Quality
	• Cost
Sales activity	*Messages*
	• Overt
	• Covert
	Attitudes
	• Sales force training
	• Sales force rewards
After-sales support	*Support services*
	• Quality and performance
	• Responsiveness
Organization culture	*Formal symbols and systems*
	• Mission statements
	• Performance standards
	• Compensation
	Informal symbols and systems
	• Beliefs
	• Values

Source: Melind Lele, *The Customer Is the Key: Gaining an Unbeatable Advantage Through Customer Satisfaction* (New York: John Wiley & Sons, 1987), p. 84.

shows, long-term customer satisfaction results from the interaction of four distinct variables—the service, sales activity, after-sales support, and the culture of the organization. Building long-term customer satisfaction is a costly proposition.

Diagnosing Customer Satisfaction Shortfalls[12]

Management cannot address the issue of customer satisfaction unless it understands of the dimensions of customer expectations as they permeate

---

[12] Melind Lele, *The Customer is the Key: Gaining an Unbeatable Advantage Through Customer Satisfaction* (New York: John Wiley & Sons, 1987), p. 55.

the bank.[13] Customer expectations can be understood in the context of five dimensions:

- Tangibles: visible facilities and equipment.
- Reliability: ability to perform dependably and accurately.
- Responsiveness: willingness to provide strong customer satisfaction.
- Assurance: knowledge and courteousness of employees and their ability to inspire trust and confidence.
- Empathy: sharing and individualized attention to customers.

Differences between customer expectations and perceptions result from four organizational gaps in the bank:

1. Not knowing what customers expect.
2. The wrong customer satisfaction standards.
3. An expectations–performance gap.
4. Promises that do not match delivery.

To varying degrees, each of the four internal organizational gaps is caused by inadequate performance at one or more of the five dimensions of tangibles, reliability, responsiveness, assurance, and empathy.

The reasons management does not know what customers expect are diverse, but they often occur because of a lack of research-based findings in structuring customer support programs. In addition, failure to interact with customers on a continuing basis can contribute to the gap, as can a lack of intense, ongoing communication between customer contact personnel and management. Excessive layers of bureaucracy often separate customer contact personnel from top management.

Progress in closing the gap is achieved by making strategic use of customer complaints. Top management needs to review customer complaints on a regular, perhaps daily basis and help customer contact personnel learn how to resolve issues. Use of customer panels chosen from target markets can help identify opportunities for improvement, as can assessing customer satisfaction with individual purchases. A service satisfaction research process is needed, not just an occasional study.

---

[13] Based on Valarie Ziethaml, A. Parasuraman, and Leonard Berry, *Delivering Quality Service* (New York: The Free Press, 1990).

TABLE 3–8
Research-Based Customer Satisfaction Assessments

Type of Research	Frequency
Customer complaint solicitation	Continuous
Post-transaction follow-up surveys	Continuous
Managers telephoning customers for informal feedback	Weekly
Customer focus groups	Monthly
"Mystery shopping" of service providers	Quarterly
Employee surveys	Quarterly
Total market service quality surveys	3 times/year
Special-purpose research	As needed

Source: A. Parasuraman, Leonard L. Berry, and Valarie Zeithaml, "Guidelines for Conducting Service Quality Research," *Marketing Research: A Magazine of Management and Applications* 2 (December 1990), p. 43.

Snapshots at one point in time are not sufficient; continuing assessments over time are necessary. The types and frequency of research appropriate in assessing customer satisfaction in a continuous context are shown in Table 3–8.

Chapter Four

Evaluating Banks' Financial Performance

FOUR KEY STEPS IN ANALYSIS

Bank directors are responsible for monitoring the financial condition of their banks. The directors are responsible to the shareholders, whose primary interests are profitability and growth, but they are also responsible for the bank's safety, soundness, and compliance with laws and regulations. Bank regulators provide bank management with CAMEL and BOPEC ratings, which provide some information about a bank's financial condition. CAMEL and BOPEC are acronyms for the risk-rating systems used by bank regulators. CAMEL stands for *c*apital, *a*sset quality, *m*anagement, *e*arnings, and *l*iquidity and is used for banks. BOPEC stands for *b*ank, *o*ther subsidiaries, *p*arent company, *e*arnings, and *c*apital and is used for bank holding companies. These ratings are not discussed in this chapter, because the focus is on analyzing banks' financial statements.

The process of evaluating the financial performance of a bank involves four steps. First, one must be able to interpret bank financial statements, which differ significantly from the financial statements of nonfinancial corporations. Common terms such as *inventories* and *accounts receivable* do not appear on a bank's balance sheets. Similarly, the provision for loan losses does not appear on the income statements of most nonfinancial corporations. Therefore, we will define only the major items on bank balance sheets and income statements.

Second, it is necessary to determine the objectives of the financial analysis to establish which financial measures to examine. Security analysts, for example, have a different focus than bank examiners do. Security analysts want information about expected earnings, dividends, or mergers that may affect the stock price. Bank examiners want minute details on every aspect of the bank. Our perspective is that of a director, who is interested in the overall financial condition of the bank. Directors don't need to know every detail.

Hundreds of measures can be used to evaluate banks, but only a small number of them may be necessary for measuring, say, profitability. By establishing measurement objectives, we can avoid "not seeing the forest through the trees." In this case, the trees represent the huge amount of available data and financial measures that make no sense when viewed collectively or without a particular objective in mind.

Third, data must be analyzed over a sufficiently long period of time to evaluate trends. As a general rule, four to five years of annual data are sufficient. A caveat: Because a balance sheet represents one day of the year (e.g., December 31), it may not accurately reflect the banks' activities. This is especially true if large year-end adjustments (window dressing) were made to the balance sheet. Some banks show both year-end and average balance sheet figures to deal with this problem.

Finally, data for the bank being examined must be compared to peer organizations. Peer banks are banks that are of similar asset size and located in the same geographic area.

BANK FINANCIAL STATEMENTS

Table 4–1 shows the consolidated balance sheet for BankAmerica Corporation and subsidiaries for 1992–1993. At the end of 1993, BankAmerica Corporation was the second largest bank holding company in the United States, with total assets of $186.9 billion. BankAmerica Corporation is used to explain the principal components found in bank financial statements; therefore, not every item will be mentioned.

The presentation of bank statements varies from bank to bank in annual reports and elsewhere. Typically, the balance sheet summarizes a bank's major activities. For example, total loans are shown in the balance sheet, but details of the loans appear elsewhere.

The financial statements show year-end figures. Although not shown in Table 4–1, the annual report also shows average balances.

Understanding Bank Assets

Cash and due from banks.   When people think of banks, they think of cash. However, cash due from banks represents only 5.6 percent of total assets. The term *cash* means coins and currency held in the bank's vaults to meet customers' demands. The term *due from banks* means deposits at the Federal Reserve bank, deposits in other banks, and items in the process of collection from other banks (the float). Deposits at the Federal Reserve bank are part of the reserve requirement. The Monetary Control Act of 1980 requires all depository institutions offering transaction accounts to maintain reserves with the Federal Reserve or as vault cash. Institutions that are not members of the Federal Reserve can hold their reserves with certain approved institutions. Reserve requirements are 3 percent of net transaction accounts for amounts up to $51.9 million and 10 percent above that amount.[1]

Because cash is a nonearning asset, banks try to minimize the size of this account. The amount of cash required largely depends on weekly and seasonal needs.

Interest-bearing deposits in banks.   Commercial banks have correspondent relationships with other banks, and they may maintain interest-bearing deposits in those banks. BankAmerica has deposits in foreign offices.

Federal funds sold.   Federal funds are short-term, immediately available funds that are sold to increase income. From the bank's point of view, they are excess funds in the reserve account, which earns no interest. Securities are sold overnight (or over longer periods) with the agreement to repurchase them (*repurchase agreements, repos, RPs*), and securities are purchased under agreements to resell them at a different price (*reverse repos*). The difference between the purchase and sale price represents the interest rate (*repo rate*).

Securities.   Banks hold securities for liquidity and for income. They hold US government, US government agency, and state and local government (*municipal*) securities. Also, they may hold corporate debt and equity securities. State laws in California, New York, and other states, permit state banks to hold equity securities.

Interest income from state and local government securities issued prior to August 1986 is exempt from federal income taxes and, in some cases,

---

[1] Reserve requirements of depository institutions are published in the *Federal Reserve Bulletin.*

TABLE 4-1
Consolidated Balance Sheet

(dollar amounts in millions)	December 31	
	1993	1992
Assets		
Cash and due from banks	$ 10,482	$ 11,848
Interest-bearing deposits in banks	2,988	2,866
Federal funds sold	2,050	1,070
Securities purchased under resale agreements	3,549	2,840
Trading account assets	6,866	3,474
Securities available for sale (market value: 1993 — $3,405; 1992 — $2,831)	3,282	2,661
Securities held for investment (market value: 1993 — $16,802; 1992 — $12,937)	16,415	12,593
Loans	126,379	$125,709
Less: Allowance for credit losses	3,508	3,921
Net loans	122,871	121,788
Premises and equipment, net	3,631	3,310
Customers' acceptance liability	851	1,443
Accrued interest receivable	982	992
Real estate acquired in satisfaction of debt	517	652
Assets pending disposition	1,345	4,240
Goodwill, net	3,973	3,929
Identifiable intangibles, net	2,191	1,640
Other assets	4,940	5,300
Total Assets	$186,933	$180,646

Liabilities and Stockholders' Equity

Deposits in domestic offices:

Interest-bearing	$ 89,134	$ 91,571
Noninterest-bearing	31,578	32,139
Deposits in foreign offices:		
Interest-bearing	19,608	12,443
Noninterest-bearing	1,298	1,730
Total deposits	141,618	137,883
Federal funds purchased	220	417
Securities sold under repurchase agreements	4,229	926
Other short-term borrowings	3,523	2,092
Acceptances outstanding	851	1,443
Accrued interest payable	505	498
Other liabilities	4,728	5,504
Long-term debt	13,508	14,326
Subordinated capital notes	607	2,069
Total liabilities	169,789	165,158

Stockholders' Equity

Preferred stock	2,979	2,979
Common stock, par value $1.5625 (authorized: 1993 and 1992 — 700,000,000 shares; issued: 1993 — 358,498,930 shares; 1992 — 349,054,862 shares)	560	545
Additional paid-in capital	7,118	6,690
Retained earnings	6,502	5,283
Common stock in treasury, at cost (1993 — $86,760 shares; 1992 — 451,886 shares)	(15)	(9)
Total stockholders' equity	17,144	15,488
Total Liabilities and Stockholders' Equity	$186,933	$180,646

See notes to consolidated financial statements.

from state income taxes. The Tax Reform Act of 1986 reduced the tax benefits from industrial development bonds and eliminated the deduction of interest on borrowing costs to finance most purchases of municipal securities.

Under FAS 115 (Accounting for Certain Investments in Debt and Equity Securities), securities are divided into three groups: trading account, available-for-sale, and held-to-maturity (investment account). *Trading account* securities are actively traded. They are reported at fair value. *Available-for-sale* securities cannot be held to maturity, but can be traded actively as part of the trading account. They too are reported at fair value.[2] National banks must report unrealized net gains or losses in Reports of Condition and Income (call reports), but those amounts are excluded from calculations of Tier 1 capital. Finally, *investment account* securities are recorded at amortized cost.

Loans. Banks are in business to lend funds. For BankAmerica, loans accounted for 68 percent of total assets. Although not shown on the balance sheet, there are three major categories of loans: loans to businesses (commercial and industrial loans), real estate loans, and consumer loans (loans to individuals for personal expenditures). Other categories include loans to other banks, governments, agricultural concerns, and so on.

The *allowance for credit losses* is deducted from loans to avoid overstating the value of the loans, and to establish a reserve for expected losses. More will be said about this reserve account later and in the next chapter.

All other assets. These include buildings, equipment, and other items not included above. Buildings and equipment accounted for about 2 percent of total assets for BankAmerica.

Understanding Bank Liabilities and Equity

Deposits. Deposits are the major source of funds. Demand deposits are non-interest-bearing checking accounts of individuals, partner-

---

[2] See *OCC Bulletin*, OCC 94-68, Regulatory Capital Treatment under FAS 115, Final Rule, December 22, 1994. National banks will deduct unrealized losses on equity securities from Tier 1 capital. Moreover, bank regulators will consider unrealized gains and losses when evaluating bank capital.

ships, and corporations (IPCs) and other holders, including governments. Most deposits bear interest. BankAmerica's total deposits accounted for 76 percent of total liabilities.

Other sources of funds include federal funds purchased, securities sold under repurchase agreements (repos), and other debt instruments.

Stockholders' equity. Stockholders' equity and bank capital are the subject of the next chapter; therefore, they are not discussed here. Notice in Table 4–1 that total stockholders' equity amounted to 9 percent of total assets. Relative to other lines of business, that percentage is small; relative to other banks, it is quite large.

Understanding the Statement of Operations

Interest income. The statement of operations is sometimes called the *statement of income and expenses*. It reveals income and expenses. As Table 4-2 shows, the principal sources of income are interest income and noninterest income. Interest income comes primarily from loans and secondarily from securities. *Interest expense,* mainly interest on deposits, is deducted from interest income to give *net interest income.*

Provision for credit losses. The provision for credit (loan) losses is deducted from net interest income. The provision for credit losses is the amount charged against earnings as a reserve for expected credit losses. Part of this provision appears on the balance sheet as the allowance for credit losses that was deducted from loans; it also appears in the bank's equity as a reserve account. More will be said about this account in the next chapter.

Noninterest income. Noninterest income is the second major source of bank income. It comes mainly from fees earned on deposits and other banking activities. Noninterest income accounted for 27 percent of total income, and is becoming an increasingly important part of bank income.

Expenses. The two major categories of expense are interest expense and noninterest expense. Interest expense was mentioned previously. Employee expenses (salaries and benefits) are the largest variable noninterest expense items. Occupancy expense is the largest fixed expense

TABLE 4-2
Consolidated Statement of Operations

(dollar amounts in millions, except per share data)	Year Ended December 31		
	1993	1992	1991
Interest Income			
Loans, including fees	$ 9,463	$ 9,729	$8,349
Interest-bearing deposits in banks	194	283	341
Federal funds sold	35	61	120
Securities purchased under resale agreements	174	163	107
Trading account assets	372	297	277
Securities available for sale and securities held for investment	1,389	1,080	666
Total interest income	11,627	11,613	9,860
Interest Expense			
Deposits	2,971	3,769	4,645
Federal funds purchased	16	20	23
Securities sold under repurchase agreements	158	108	132
Other short-term borrowings	201	270	236
Long-term debt	727	614	255
Subordinated capital notes	113	114	97
Total interest expense	4,186	4,895	5,388
Net interest income	7,441	6,718	4,472
Provision for credit losses	803	1,009	805
Net interest income after provision for credit losses	6,638	5,709	3,667
Noninterest Income			
Deposit account fees	1,198	1,049	645
Credit card fees	354	350	308
Trust fees	294	222	68
Other fees and commissions	1,083	922	686
Trading income	569	463	326
Net securities gains	61	11	33
Net gain on sales of subsidiaries and operations	—	155	3
Net gain on sales of assets	106	117	135
Other income	608	360	204
Total noninterest income	4,273	3,649	2,408

Noninterest Expense

Salaries	2,886	2,557	1,847
Employee benefits	573	491	339
Occupancy	684	561	465
Equipment	610	523	372
Amortization of intangibles	421	248	48
Communications	330	305	215
Regulatory fees and related expenses	309	265	160
Professional services	268	201	135
Merger-related restructuring expense	9	449	—
Other expense	1,393	1,076	621
Total noninterest expense	7,483	6,676	4,202
Income before income taxes	3,428	2,682	1,873
Provision for income taxes	1,474	1,190	749
Net Income	$ 1,954	$ 1,492	$ 1,124
Net income applicable to common stock	$ 1,713	$ 1,323	$ 1,063
Average number of common shares outstanding (number of shares in thousands)	355,107	308,191	215,846
Earnings per common and common equivalent share	$ 4.79	$ 4.24	$ 4.81
Earnings per common share — assuming full dilution	4.76	4.21	4.78
Dividends declared per common share	1.40	1.30	1.20

See notes to consolidated financial statements.

item. Banks that wish to trim expenses can do so only by reducing interest expense or by cutting employees.

Net income.   The bottom line is that the bank's net income was $1.9 billion, or $4.76 per share (fully diluted). Of that amount, the bank paid cash dividends of $1.40 and retained the remainder.

Other Relevant Information

Allowance for credit losses.   As previously noted, the allowance for credit losses is deducted from loans. The amount deducted from loans takes into account credit loss recoveries, the provision for credit losses, and other adjustments. For example, BankAmerica had total credit losses of $1,599 million, credit loss recoveries of $484 million, and a provision for credit losses of $803 million. Other adjustments amounted to a negative $101 million. Thus, the total *change* in the allowance for credit losses for 1993 was a negative $413 million:

Total credit losses	$1,599
– Recoveries	484
– Provision for losses	803
– Other adjustments	(101)
Total	$ 413

The total allowance at the end of 1993 was $3,508 million, which amounted to 2.78 percent of loans outstanding, compared to 3.12 percent in the previous year. The allowance is established by bank credit officers responsible for those loans.

Information about problem loans, restructured loans, and other credit problems should be examined too.

Interest rate sensitivity.   BankAmerica reports its interest rate sensitivity in terms of a gap between its interest rate–sensitive assets and liabilities for various time periods. For example, for 0 to 3 months, it had $9 billion more rate-sensitive liabilities than assets; for 3 to 0 months, it had $7 billion more rate-sensitive assets than liabilities; and so on. The implications of these figures are explained in connection with asset/liability management in Chapter Six. Therefore, we do not cover interest rate risk in this chapter.

Risk-based capital.   The amount of stockholders' equity does not reveal the degree of capital adequacy for a bank because bank capital requirements include more than equity, and they are based on certain risk-based assets. As noted earlier, total stockholders' equity amounts to 9 percent of total assets for BankAmerica. However, the total risk-based capital ratio for the bank is 12 percent. This is a well-capitalized bank. These and other terms dealing with bank capital are explained in Chapter Five.

Off–balance sheet activities.   Many banks have extensive off–balance sheet activities that involve credit-related financial instruments (e.g., letters of credit, loan commitments), derivatives (e.g., swaps, options), foreign exchange, and other contingencies. These activities are subject to varying degrees of credit and market risk and capital requirements. They are usually reported in the notes to the financial statements.

THE DIRECTORS' POINT OF VIEW

Bank directors are interested in the overall financial performance of the bank. For convenience, financial performance is divided into four broad categories: profitability, capital, liquidity, and asset quality. Selected measures in each category are examined next.

This listing of categories is not complete. For example, it does not include interest rate risk. It requires more explanation than we can give here and is examined in Chapter Six. Nevertheless, the information presented here is sufficient to provide directors with a good starting point to review the performance of their banks.

Caveats about the Data

The measures presented here involving data from both the balance sheet and the income statement use average balance sheet data. The logic behind using average balance sheet data is that the balance sheet measures the condition of a firm on one day (e.g., December 31), whereas the income statement covers 365 days. To equate the time periods covered by both statements, average balance sheet data (data covering the entire year) are used. BankAmerica obtained its averages from daily, weekly, or monthly data. Averages computed using such data may differ from averages computed from two balance sheets. For example, in Table 4–3,

TABLE 4-3
Average Balances and Rates

(dollar amounts in millions)	Year Ended December 31					
	1993		1992		1991	
	Balance[a]	Rate[b]	Balance[a]	Rate[b]	Balance[a]	Rate[b]
Assets						
Interest-bearing deposits in banks[c]	$ 2,642	7.36%	$ 4,055	6.97%	$ 3,938	8.64%
Federal funds sold	1,131	3.12	1,617	3.76	2,086	5.76
Securities purchased under resale agreements	3,903	4.46	4,400	3.70	1,828	5.86
Trading account assets	6,341	5.91	4,234	7.08	3,066	9.08
Securities available for sale	4,118	6.79	1,401	8.79	—	—
Securities held for investment:						
U.S. Treasury securities	3,554	5.28	3,036	6.06	1,050	8.33
U.S. federal agency securities	10,784	7.28	6,341	9.27	4,981	9.17
State, county, and municipal securities	553	7.93	549	8.34	184	7.95
Other domestic securities	740	13.01	797	15.13	469	8.63
Foreign securities	128	7.61	369	9.17	722	9.96
Total securities held for investment	15,759	7.13	11,092	8.76	7,406	9.06
Domestic loans:[c]						
Consumer—secured by first mortgages on residential properties	29,083	6.39	25,231	7.83	17,247	9.61
Consumer—credit card	7,499	16.26	7,963	16.70	7,271	17.21
Other consumer	24,659	9.04	23,149	9.82	16,053	10.97
Commercial and industrial	20,580	6.32	19,640	6.25	13,927	8.13
Commercial loans secured by real estate	9,707	7.51	8,735	7.98	5,532	9.51
Construction and development loans secured by real estate	5,718	5.17	6,700	5.21	4,133	7.57
Loans for purchasing or carrying securities	1,447	4.05	1,049	4.38	297	7.50
Financial institutions	1,948	3.48	1,821	3.85	1,447	5.92
Lease financing	1,773	12.36	1,669	14.40	748	6.19
Agricultural	1,605	7.62	1,554	7.81	1,110	9.70
Other	1,099	5.03	830	5.10	428	5.28
Total domestic loans	105,118	7.76	98,341	8.51	68,193	10.15
Foreign loans[c]	19,531	6.72	17,492	7.80	16,312	8.75
Total loans	124,649	7.60	115,833	8.40	84,505	9.88
Total earning assets	158,543	7.35	142,632	8.16	102,829	9.60
Nonearning assets	30,609		26,984		13,747	
Less: Allowance for credit losses	3,826		3,764		2,606	
Total Assets	$185,326		$165,852		$113,970	

Liabilities and Stockholders' Equity

	Balance	Rate	Balance	Rate	Balance	Rate
Domestic interest-bearing deposits:						
Transaction	$ 13,469	1.34%	$ 11,368	1.95%	$ 6,276	3.83%
Savings	13,977	2.23	13,454	2.96	8,266	4.83
Money market	34,182	2.49	27,504	3.26	16,753	5.31
Time	30,939	2.50	31,925	3.79	28,268	6.49
Total domestic interest-bearing deposits	92,567	2.29	84,251	3.24	59,563	5.65
Foreign interest-bearing deposits	15,549	5.50	15,544	6.71	16,093	7.96
Total interest-bearing deposits	108,116	2.75	99,795	3.78	75,656	6.14
Federal funds purchased	570	2.78	626	3.24	409	5.66
Securities sold under repurchase agreements	2,837	5.58	2,015	5.35	1,929	6.84
Other short-term borrowings	3,088	6.52	3,913	6.90	2,327	10.12
Long-term debt	14,090	5.16	10,158	6.04	3,035	8.40
Subordinated capital notes	1,499	7.52	1,836	6.22	1,280	7.58
Total interest-bearing liabilities	130,200	3.22	118,343	4.14	84,636	6.37
Domestic noninterest-bearing deposits	30,688		26,029		15,709	
Foreign noninterest-bearing deposits	1,425		1,521		1,232	
Other noninterest-bearing liabilities	6,728		7,360		5,274	
Total liabilities	169,041		153,253		106,851	
Stockholders' equity	16,285		12,599		7,119	
Total Liabilities and Stockholders' Equity	$185,326		$165,852		$113,970	
Interest income as a percentage of average earning assets		7.35%		8.16%		9.60%
Interest expense as a percentage of average earning assets		(2.64)		(3.43)		(5.24)
Net Interest Margin		4.71%		4.73%		4.36%

a Average balances are obtained from the best available daily, weekly, or monthly data.

b Average rates are presented on a taxable-equivalent basis. The taxable-equivalent basis adjustments are based on a marginal tax rate of 40 percent for 1993 and 39 percent for 1992 and 1991.

c Average balances include nonaccrual assets.

BankAmerica lists average total assets as $185,326 million. The average computed from total assets for 1993 and 1992, shown in Table 4–1 ($186,933 + $180,646 = $367,579/2 = $183,789), is $183,789 million. The difference between the two measures is $1,537 million. That difference is larger than the asset size of most banks in the United States! Be aware that calculating the averages in different ways gives different results.

Equally important, when using average data computed from, say, monthly data, some ratios (e.g., the leverage multiplier) may not be consistent with measures computed from year-end averages. For purposes of illustration, we use the average figures shown in Table 4–3 and point out inconsistencies so that you will be aware of such measurement problems.

Finally, a financial ratio, such as the "efficiency ratio," may be computed differently by different sources of financial information. For example, the efficiency ratio in its most general form is defined as operating expense divided by operating income:[3]

Efficiency Ratio = Operating Expense/Operating Income   (4–1)

Operating expense is defined as noninterest expense. It excludes interest expense and the provision for loan losses. In addition, it should exclude noncash charges, such as amortization of purchased intangibles and expenses related to other real estate owned.

Operating income is defined as net interest income plus nonrecurring noninterest income. The net interest income may be "grossed up" to adjust for tax-exempt income for municipals. Trading income should be "normalized" to avoid peaks and valleys that can distort the ratio. Noninterest income should exclude securities gains/losses and other one-time gains/losses.

Various purveyors of financial data use different definitions for the financial measures. Thus, an efficiency ratio of 60 percent or less, which may be considered desirable for a particular bank, could be substantially higher if the ratio is defined differently. For BankAmerica, the efficiency ratio (noninterest expense/(net interest income + noninterest income) was 64 percent in 1993:

Efficiency Ratio = $7,483/($7,441 + $4,212) = 64%.

---

[3] For additional discussion of this ratio, see David C. Cates, "A Safety Guide to Efficiency Ratios: Use Them Only with Special Caution," *American Banker*, December 29, 1993.

The bottom line is that caution must be used in interpreting financial data, especially if one is comparing the same measures that are computed in different ways. Banks, bank regulators, and bank information providers may calculate measures differently.

No single measure provides complete information. Some commonly used measures are misleading. Therefore, one must consider a variety of measures to gauge the overall condition of the bank.

Finally, no interpretation of BankAmerica's measures is presented here; the measures are shown only to illustrate calculations. Interpretation of financial ratios requires an analysis of historical trends and comparisons with peers. Equally important, interpretation must be done within the context of the bank's strategy.

Profitability

Return on equity.   Return on equity (ROE) measures the rate of return on stockholders' investment in the corporation. It is calculated by dividing net income by average total stockholders' equity. Using data from BankAmerica's financial statements for 1993, the ROE is computed as follows:

$$\text{Return on Equity} = \frac{\text{Net Income}}{\text{Average Total Stockholders' Equity}} \qquad (4\text{--}2)$$

$$= \frac{\text{NI}}{\text{E}} = \frac{\$1,954}{\$16,285} = 12.00\%$$

Return on assets.   Return on assets (ROA) is the broadest measure of profitability. It measures the productivity for both shareholders and creditors. ROA is calculated by dividing net income by average total assets. Here we have our first look at the ROA. It is shown in greater detail in connection with Uniform Bank Performance Reports, which we examine later in this chapter. The ROA for BankAmerica is

$$\text{Return on Assets} = \frac{\text{Net Income}}{\text{Average Total Assets}} \qquad (4\text{--}3)$$

$$= \frac{\text{NI}}{\text{A}} = \frac{\$1,954}{\$185,326} = 1.05\%$$

The relationship between ROE and ROA can be seen in equation 4–4. The ROE is equal to the ROA times a multiplier, M. The multiplier reflects the degree of financial leverage and is computed by dividing ROE by ROA or by dividing average total assets by average total equity. The multiplier for BankAmerica is 11.43; it was determined by dividing ROE by ROA (12.00%/1.05 = 11.43). Here is one of the inconsistencies. Dividing average total assets by average total equity amounts to 11.38 percent (185,326/$16,285 = 11.38).

$$\text{Return on Equity} = \text{Return on Assets} \times \text{Multiplier} \qquad (4\text{–}4)$$

$$\text{ROE} = \text{ROA} \times \text{M}$$

$$\frac{\text{Net Income}}{\text{Average Total Equity}} = \frac{\text{Net Income}}{\text{Average Total Assets}} \times \frac{\text{Average Total Equity}}{\text{Average Total Assets}}$$

$$12.00\% = 1.05 \times 11.43$$

Core capital leverage ratio.   The significance of the multiplier is that the reciprocal of M (1/M or E/A) is the *gross core (Tier 1) capital leverage ratio* (1/M). The reciprocal is 8.75 percent. This measure must be used with caution because it differs from that used by bank regulators. They deduct goodwill, intangibles, mortgage servicing rights, and other items from shareholders' equity (Tier 1 equity capital). If a bank did not have such deductions, the two measures would be the same. For BankAmerica, these deductions were $5,125 million. Equally important, the regulators consider risk-based assets rather than total assets. When these factors are taken into account, the ratio is 6.64 percent. Despite the differences between the two measures, the multiplier (and its reciprocal) provide useful insights into a bank's capital position.

Net interest margin.   The net interest margin (NIM) is computed by dividing net interest income (interest income – interest expense) by earning assets. It measures the rate of return on earning assets. Earning assets are loans and investments that earn interest and dividend income. Cash, bank premises, and other nonearning assets are deducted from total assets. For BankAmerica, the net interest margin is 4.69 percent.[4] No

---

[4] This figure differs slightly from the NIM shown in Table 4–3 because of an error in the table. Interest income as a percentage of average earning assets is 7.33 percent, not 7.35 percent. When the error is corrected, the results are the same.

adjustment was made to gross up the interest income to take tax-free income into account.

$$\text{Net Interest Margin} = \frac{\text{Net Interest Income}}{\text{Average Earning Assets}} \qquad (4\text{--}5)$$

$$= \frac{\$7,441}{\$158,543} = 4.69\%$$

Capital

The core capital leverage ratio was mentioned previously. Other measures of capital are explained in Chapter Five.

Dividend payout ratio.   The dividend payout ratio is the percentage of net income paid to shareholders in the form of cash dividends. It is computed by dividing cash dividends by net income:

$$\text{Dividend Payout Ratio} = \frac{\text{Cash Dividends}}{\text{Net Income}} \qquad (4\text{--}6)$$

BankAmerica paid $497 million in cash dividends to common stockholders and $241 million in cash dividends to preferred stockholders for a total of $738 million. Net income was $1,954 million. The dividend payout ratio for both classes of stock was 37.8 percent.

Some analysts argue that the preferred stock is similar to debt because the dividends on preferreds are usually fixed. Therefore, only common stock should be considered in the dividend payout ratio. When only common stock is considered, BankAmerica's ratio is 25.4 percent.

When using total cash dividends paid, net income gives a different payout ratio than would be obtained using cash dividends *per share*. When per share data are used, the data may reflect shares outstanding at year-end, average shares outstanding during the year, common equivalent shares, fully diluted shares, or some other figure.

Growth rate of equity less growth rate of assets.   This measure shows the extent to which equity is growing relative to assets. It is computed by subtracting the growth rate of assets (percentage change) from the growth rate of equity (percentage change):

$$\text{Equity Growth} = \$17,144 - \$15,488 = \$1,656$$
$$\$1,656/\$15,488 = 10.69\%$$

$$\text{Asset Growth} = \$186,933 - \$180,646 = \$6,287 \qquad (4\text{--}7)$$
$$\$6,287/\$180,646 = 3.48\%$$

$$\text{Difference} = 10.69\% - 3.48\% = 7.21\%$$

Liquidity

Liquidity means having sufficient funds to meet the needs of borrowers and depositors. Banks meet these needs through two types of liquidity: asset and liability liquidity. *Asset liquidity* refers to the fact that assets such as short-term Treasury securities can be liquidated to meet customer needs. *Liability liquidity* means the bank can borrow funds to meet customer needs. Liability liquidity is available to profitable, sound banks, but not to weak or failing banks. Liquidity is an elusive concept and thus difficult to measure accurately. Two measures of liquidity and their limitations are presented next.

Net loans and leases to deposits. This ratio reveals the extent to which the bank has lent its current deposits. Public deposits should be subtracted from total deposits because they cannot be lent (this figure for BankAmerica is not available). BankAmerica's net loans to deposits was 86.76 percent:

$$\text{Net Loans to Deposits} = \$122,871/\$141,618 = 86.76\% \qquad (4\text{--}8)$$

This measure does not reveal other sources of funds, the extent to which the bank can raise additional funds, the fact that loans can be sold. While this is a widely used measure of liquidity, it is not precise.

Liquid assets to total liabilities. Liquid assets are securities and deposits in other banks divided by total liabilities. For BankAmerica,

$$\text{Liquid Assets to Liabilities} = \$31,601/\$169,789 = 18.61\% \qquad (4\text{--}9)$$

Liquid assets include securities pledged against public deposits. These securities cannot be sold to meet liquidity needs. Also, some longer-term securities may be carried at book value, even if their fair value is higher or lower than book. This measure, like other measures of liquidity, provides no insights about hedges, derivatives, or other devices used to affect liquidity.

Asset Quality

Asset quality refers to the probable losses of a bank's assets. The losses usually come from the loan portfolio. However, some banks have other credit products, such as swaps. Finally, securities held by banks may decline in value. Therefore, asset quality is a broader concept than loan quality.

Allowance for credit losses to total loans.   The allowance measures losses that are expected to occur in the loan portfolio over time. The measure includes significant credits classified as "doubtful" as well as projections by credit officers and models used by the bank. (*Doubtful* means the loan is a probable loss, but the amount may not be readily determinable.) The ratio is computed by dividing the allowance for credit losses by total loans. For BankAmerica,

Allowance for
Credit Losses to Total Loans = $3,508/$126,379 = 2.78%   (4–10)

Nonperforming loans to total loans.   Nonperforming loans include loans that are on a nonaccrual basis, restructured loans, and loans that are 90 days or more past due and still accruing interest. BankAmerica's ratio is

Nonperforming
Loans to Total Loans = $2,886/$126,379 = 2.28%   (4–11)

Net charge-offs to average loans and leases.   Net charge-offs are credit losses less credit recoveries. This is the net amount of credit that the bank lost. It is typically compared to average loans and leases. For BankAmerica,

Net Charge-Offs
to Average Loans and Leases = $1,115/$124,649 = 0.89%   (4–12)

Examiner classifications.   Bank examiners classify credits that they think are excessively risky or that may have collection problems into the following four categories:[5]

---

[5] These definitions are based on Kenneth Spong, *Banking Regulation: Its Purposes, Implementation, and Effect*, 4th ed., Federal Reserve Bank of Kansas City, 1994, p. 61.

- *Substandard*. These credits involve abnormal risks due to their performance, financial condition, collateral, or other factors that require more than normal servicing and supervision.
- *Doubtful*. Doubtful loans have a probable loss, but the amount of the loss is not readily determinable.
- *Loss*. The loans are charged off.
- *Other loans especially mentioned* (OLEMs). OLEMs have a potential weakness and require management's attention. If the problems are not corrected, the loan can deteriorate in quality.

COMPARING FINANCIAL PERFORMANCE

In this section, we examine three sources of data for evaluating bank performance over time and in comparison with peers. The first source, the *FDIC Quarterly Banking Profile*, is useful for examining national and regional trends. The second source, *Sheshunoff Information Services*, is a private vendor that provides information about financial institutions. The federal *Uniform Bank Performance Report* is the third source of information.

The FDIC Quarterly Banking Profile[6]

The *FDIC Quarterly Banking Profile* provides data concerning national and regional trends for FDIC-insured commercial banks and savings institutions. To illustrate, let's examine two tables from the first quarter 1995 issue of the *Banking Profile*. Table 4–4 shows the historical trends of selected indicators of FDIC-insured commercial banks. The data reveal that the return on assets ranged from a low of 0.48 percent in 1990 to a high of 1.20 percent in 1993. The core capital leverage ratio increased from 6.17 percent in 1990 to 7.67 in the first quarter of 1995. Net charge-offs to loans has been declining, and so on. Now that you understand the general trends, let's get more specific.

Table 4–5 contains financial data for all institutions, by asset size distribution and geographic distribution. Both asset size and geographic distribution are important factors influencing financial performance. To illustrate the use of this table, consider the return on assets (shown under

---

[6] For copies and subscriptions, contact the FDIC's Office of Corporate Communications, 550 17th St. NW, Washington, DC 20429; telephone: 202-898-6996.

TABLE 4–4
Selected Indicators, FDIC-Insured Commercial Banks

	1995*	1994*	1994	1993	1992	1991	1990
Return on assets (%)	1.10	1.17	1.15	1.20	0.93	0.53	0.48
Return on equity (%)	14.00	14.81	14.61	15.34	12.98	7.94	7.45
Core capital (leverage) ratio (%)	7.67	7.62	7.64	7.65	7.20	6.48	6.17
Noncurrent assets plus other real estate owned to assets (%)	0.99	1.46	1.01	1.61	2.54	3.02	2.94
Net charge-offs to loans	0.38	0.48	0.50	0.85	1.27	1.59	1.43
Asset growth rate (%)	7.10	9.38	8.21	5.72	2.19	1.21	2.73
Net interest margin (%)	4.31	4.27	4.36	4.40	4.41	4.11	3.94
Net operating income growth (%)	4.23	28.90	16.14	35.44	92.41	-0.63	2.53
Number of institutions reporting	10,241	10,839	10,450	10.958	11,462	11,921	12,343
Percentage of unprofitable institutions	3.47	4.22	3.88	4.87	6.85	11.60	13.44
Number of problem institutions	215	383	247	426	787	1,016	1,012
Assets of problem institutions (in billions)	$27	$53	$33	$242	$408	$528	$342
Number of failed/assisted institutions	3	0	11	42	100	108	159

* Through March 31, ratios annualized where appropriate. Asset growth rates are for 12 months ending March 31.

93

TABLE 4-5
First Quarter 1995, FDIC-Insured Commercial Banks

FIRST QUARTER Preliminary (The way it is . . .)	All Institutions	Asset Size Distribution				Geographic Distribution by Region					
		Less than $100 Million	$100 Million to $1 Billion	$1 Billion to $10 Billion	Greater than $10 Billion	East			West		
						North-east	South-east	Central	Mid-west	South-west	West
Number of institutions reporting	10,241	7,122	2,725	331	63	830	1,696	2,237	2,586	1,828	1,084
Total assets (in billions)	$4,116.1	$310.3	$667.8	$1,077.0	$2,061.0	$1,597.9	$682.0	$665.0	$261.3	$306.8	$603.3
Total deposits (in billions)	2,862.6	270.1	559.0	763.6	1,269.8	979.2	503.0	484.3	198.1	248.4	449.6
Net income (in millions)	11,132	905	2,053	3,471	4,704	3,624	1,884	1,911	916	829	1,969
% of unprofitable institutions	3.5	4.0	2.1	2.4	4.8	4.9	3.1	3.8	2.3	2.0	7.7
% of institutions with earnings gains	59.8	58.6	63.2	55.0	83.5	63.3	65.9	60.3	52.5	57.5	67.4
Performance Ratios (annualized, %)											
Yield on earning assets	8.28	8.16	8.24	8.49	8.20	8.48	8.05	8.11	8.35	7.70	8.55
Cost of funding earning assets	3.97	3.36	3.42	3.83	4.36	4.52	3.77	3.93	3.76	3.35	3.32
Net interest margin	4.31	4.80	4.82	4.66	3.84	3.96	4.28	4.19	4.60	4.35	5.23
Noninterest income to earning assets	2.19	1.18	1.47	2.45	2.49	2.68	1.69	1.56	2.45	1.73	2.43
Noninterest expense to earning assets	4.24	3.95	3.99	4.37	4.30	4.47	3.90	3.58	4.36	4.20	4.77
Net operating income to assets	1.10	1.20	1.25	1.31	0.92	0.91	1.13	1.17	1.43	1.12	1.34
Return on assets	1.10	1.17	1.23	1.29	0.94	0.93	1.12	1.15	1.40	1.09	1.32
Return on equity	14.00	11.63	13.86	15.82	13.53	12.73	14.15	14.41	16.34	13.11	15.69
Net charge-offs to loans and leases	0.38	0.15	0.31	0.50	0.37	0.59	0.23	0.21	0.41	0.16	0.37
Loan loss provision to net charge-offs	117.62	180.11	130.95	140.36	90.72	110.22	112.94	157.11	110.93	116.97	125.19
Condition Ratios (%)											
Loss allowance to:											
Loans and leases	2.18	1.67	1.71	2.11	2.46	2.62	1.77	1.73	1.84	1.62	2.50
Noncurrent loans and leases	163.28	147.68	155.19	183.61	157.83	137.56	201.68	200.39	216.84	182.03	169.26
Noncurrent assets plus other real estate owned to assets	0.99	0.88	0.91	0.90	1.07	1.24	0.73	0.65	0.67	0.66	1.28
Equity capital ratio	7.88	10.23	9.22	8.32	6.86	7.25	7.97	8.14	8.75	8.45	8.46
Core capital (leverage) ratio	7.67	10.35	9.19	7.98	6.58	7.16	7.72	7.99	8.70	8.23	7.85
Net loans and leases to deposits	82.82	62.99	70.79	90.12	87.94	84.28	83.82	84.02	80.13	65.21	88.13
Growth Rates (year-to-year, %)											
Assets	7.1					6.7	12.1	6.3	4.3	3.3	6.9
Equity capital	7.8					8.6	11.9	7.2	4.6	5.0	5.3
Net interest income	7.1					5.5	10.6	4.9	4.8	7.0	10.2
Net income	0.7					-10.6	4.6	6.7	2.7	-8.5	21.9
Noncurrent assets plus other real estate owned	-27.6					-31.0	-16.5	-20.9	-28.1	-18.4	-30.2
Net charge-offs	-12.0					-14.6	13.7	-16.2	10.2	171.5	-28.5
Loan loss provision	-1.2					-7.4	14.0	-8.2	1.5	203.2	3.8

(The way it was . . .)

Number of institutions 1994	10,839	7,673	2,787	325	54	870	1,806	2,383	2,686	1,920	1,174
1992	11,805	8,659	2,777	318	51	967	1,914	2,612	2,859	2,088	1,365
1990	12,596	9,613	2,613	327	43	1,084	1,960	2,808	2,987	2,285	1,472
Total assets (in billions) 1994	$3,843.3	$330.6	$682.2	$1,062.5	$1,767.9	$1,497.3	$608.3	$625.9	$250.6	$296.8	$564.4
1992	3,435.8	350.5	676.6	1,031.0	1,377.8	1,267.5	528.4	559.7	235.3	272.8	552.1
1990	3,317.9	363.4	627.6	1,044.7	1,282.2	1,307.6	490.9	531.9	211.6	263.2	512.8
Return on assets (%) 1994	1.17	1.14	1.19	1.43	1.01	1.12	1.20	1.16	1.42	1.23	1.16
1992	0.87	1.08	1.02	1.01	0.65	0.76	0.96	1.06	1.28	1.09	0.60
1990	0.76	0.80	0.88	0.69	0.74	0.50	0.75	0.87	1.16	0.44	1.30
Net charge-offs to loans & leases (%) 1994	0.48	0.13	0.27	0.68	0.50	0.74	0.24	0.28	0.41	0.07	0.58
1992	1.24	0.42	0.61	1.50	1.52	1.77	0.84	0.75	0.75	0.77	1.28
1990	1.30	0.48	0.60	1.41	1.75	1.93	0.71	1.10	0.91	1.19	0.71
Noncurrent assets plus OREO to assets (%) 1994	1.46	1.02	1.24	1.36	1.69	1.91	0.98	0.87	0.97	0.84	1.96
1992	3.03	1.67	2.09	2.78	4.02	4.15	2.16	1.68	1.56	2.28	3.59
1990	2.37	1.81	1.91	1.95	3.10	3.10	1.43	1.29	1.47	3.23	2.48
Equity capital ratio (%) 1994	7.83	9.85	8.87	8.27	6.78	7.12	7.99	8.07	8.72	8.31	8.60
1992	6.96	9.23	7.94	7.24	5.69	6.28	7.26	7.59	8.21	7.04	7.04
1990	6.38	8.99	7.63	6.50	4.94	5.57	7.10	7.02	7.84	6.36	6.50

REGIONS: *Northeast* — Connecticut, Delaware, District of Columbia, Maine, Maryland, Massachusetts, New Hampshire, New Jersey, New York, Pennsylvania, Puerto Rico, Rhode Island, Vermont, U.S. Virgin Islands
Southeast — Alabama, Florida, Georgia, Mississippi, North Carolina, South Carolina, Tennessee, Virginia, West Virginia
Central — Illinois, Indiana, Kentucky, Michigan, Ohio, Wisconsin
Midwest — Iowa, Kansas, Minnesota, Missouri, Nebraska, North Dakota, South Dakota
Southwest — Arkansas, Louisiana, New Mexico, Oklahoma, Texas
West — Alaska, Arizona, California, Colorado, Hawaii, Idaho, Montana, Nevada, Oregon, Pacific Islands, Utah, Washington, Wyoming

Performance Ratios and Prior First Quarters). ROAs are frequently, but not always, higher for small banks than for large banks. The table shows that banks with assets of more than $10 billion had ROAs lower than those of small banks.

The geographic data are important because not all sectors of the economy grow at the same rate. A bank's performance is linked to the geographic areas it serves; thus, it makes sense that bank performance will vary geographically. Therefore, on average, banks in the Midwest had higher ROAs than banks in the Northeast and West. The fewest unprofitable institutions were in the Midwest, and the most were in the West and Northeast.

Sheshunoff Information Services[7]

Sheshunoff is one of several private vendors of data concerning financial institutions. It provides financial data for banks, bank holding companies, savings banks, and savings and loan associations.

A Sheshunoff report for an individual bank is provided in Appendix A to this chapter. The report is one of many products Sheshunoff offers. It shows balance sheet and income statement data for prior periods, as well as key financial ratios and measures. The data are compared to peer banks and then evaluated by Sheshunoff Rating Guidelines. The major advantages of this report are that it is up to date, condensed, and easy to understand.

Uniform Bank Performance Report[8]

Uniform Bank Performance Reports (UPBRs) are produced by the Financial Institutions Examination Council and are designed to be used by bank examiners and management to evaluate the financial condition of banks. The UPBR presents three types of data: individual bank data, peer group data, and percentile rankings.

Four UPBR products may be of interest to directors.

---

[7] For information, contact Sheshunoff Information Services, One Texas Center, 505 Barton Springs Rd., Austin, TX 78704; telephone: 512-472-2244, 1-800-456-2340.

[8] For information about UBPRs, contact the Federal Financial Institutions Examination Council, 2100 Pennsylvania Ave. NW, # 200, Washington, DC 20037; or the FDIC Disclosure Group, 1-800-945-2186, or John Smullen, 202-634-6526.

Bank report.   Bank reports are about 13 pages long and are prepared for each FDIC-insured bank in the United States. An example of a bank report appears in Appendix B to this chapter. The report contains detailed financial information, measures, and peer group comparisons. Both annual and quarterly data are examined. The UPBR has 25 peer groups for banks and 4 peer groups for savings banks to show how banks with similar characteristics have performed. Banks are then ranked by percentiles within their peer groups. Each bank ratio is ranked in an ascending order from 0 to 99. A bank with a rating of 99 percentile is at the top of its peer group. Sheshunoff has a total of 11 peer groups for banks.

Unfortunately, the bank reports are less user friendly than the Sheshunoff report; however, they provide much greater detail.

UPBR User's Guide.   The *UPBR User's Guide* is required to interpret the wide number of financial measures and terms presented in the bank report. For example, terms such as "volatile liability dependence" and "I ENC-Loans to total loans" may not be familiar to some readers. Finally, some measures in the bank report may have been computed differently than those in Sheshunoff or those provided by your bank.

Peer group data, and state average data.   These two sources provide additional information that may be used for detailed comparisons with peer banks and with banks in the same state. The volume of data is overwhelming.

Figure 4–1 shows a breakdown of return on assets (ROA). It reveals how all of a bank's income and expenses relate to that measure.

Financial Institutions Monitoring System (FIMS).   FIMS was developed by the Federal Reserve to identify troubled banking institutions.[9] It is an off-site surveillance system that uses data from quarterly Reports of Condition and Income (call reports) to estimate a bank's financial condition and the probability that a bank will fail or become "critically undercapitalized" within the next two years. If it is estimated that a bank will be in such a condition within the next two years, the information is reported to the bank. However, such information is not made available to the public.

---

[9] Rebel A. Cole, Barbara G. Cornyn, and Jeffery W. Gunter, "FIMS: A New Monitoring System for Banking Institutions," *Federal Reserve Bulletin,* January 1995, pp. 1–15.

FIGURE 4-1
Return on Assets

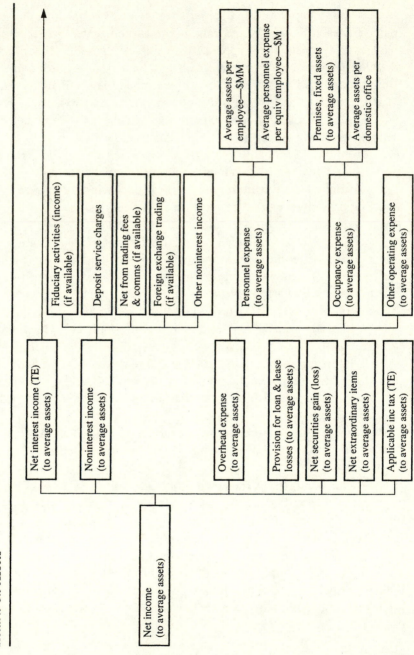

FIGURE 4–1
(continued)

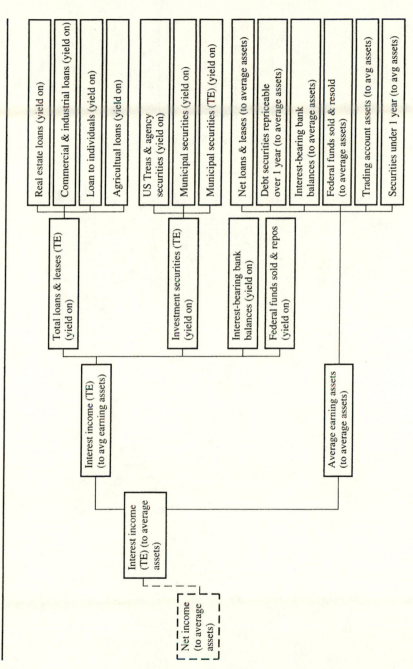

100

FIGURE 4–1
(concluded)

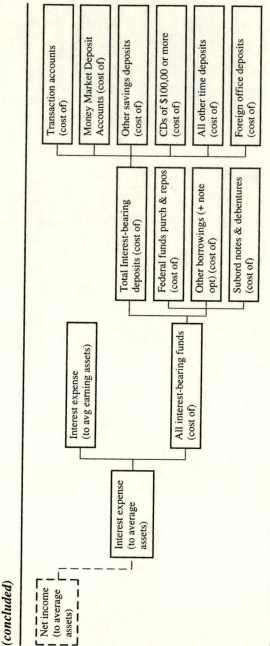

Source: *UBPR User's Guide,* June 1988, pp. I-4–I-5.

> **Think about This!**
>
> *No Bank Is a Mirror Image of Its Peers*
>
> Each bank has unique operating characteristics, and no bank is a mirror image of its peers. A bank's significant divergence from its peer group should not automatically be a concern. Suppose a bank's net interest income to average assets is 3.03 percent compared to the peer group average of 3.97 percent, placing the bank in the 15th percentile. This may suggest that the bank is having profit margin difficulties. However, the bank's temporary investments are 49 percent compared to a peer group average of 18 percent, and its large CDs and federal funds purchased are 43 percent compared to 20 percent for the peer group. Thus, it is clear that the composition of the bank's assets and liabilities differs significantly from those of the peers. Therefore, strict comparisons with peer group percentile ratings may be misleading. Look at the whole picture, not just a small part of it.
>
> Source: Based on the *UBPR User's Guide,* June 1988, p. I-1.

CONCLUSION

Directors are responsible for monitoring the financial performance of their banks. The process involves comparing the bank's financial performance over time and relative to its peers. Unfortunately, most financial data are not up-to-the-minute, which adds an element of uncertainty to the analysis. The chapter explained how to interpret bank financial statements, which differ significantly from the financial statements of nonfinancial firms. It also explained selected key financial ratios dealing with profitability, financial leverage, liquidity, and asset quality. Finally, the chapter presented various private and government sources of data that can be used for comparisons.

APPENDIX 4A
Bank Profile

BANK PROFILE

BALANCE SHEET $(000)	6/94	6/93	12/93	12/92	12/91
Assets					
Interest-Bearing Assets:					
Total Loans	66,596	63,673	62,913	63,880	81,114
Securities	30,150	26,325	25,718	25,034	30,490
Other Interest-Bearing Assets	1,907	3,867	7,076	10,250	0
Total Interest-Bearing Assets	98,653	93,865	95,707	99,164	111,604
Noninterest-Bearing Assets:					
Premises and Fixed Assets	1,869	1,756	1,785	1,785	1,811
Other Noninterest-Bearing Assets	6,050	6,664	5,622	5,905	5,574
Total Assets	105,601	101,255	102,117	105,990	117,989
Memo: Nonperforming Loans	102	198	135	258	1,435
Allowance for Losses	971	1,030	997	864	1,000
Net Charge-Offs	130	164	317	966	926
Other Real Estate Owned	399	925	399	1,209	441

Source: Financial Institutions Examination Council.

APPENDIX 4A
(continued)

Liabilities

Interest-Bearing:					
Domestic Interest-Bearing Deposits	75,694	74,453	74,726	78,976	84,342
Federal Funds Purchased	2,000	2,000	2,000	2,000	11,700
All Other Interest-Bearing Liabilities	496	804	746	600	319
Total Interest-Bearing Liabilities	78,190	77,257	77,472	81,576	96,361
Noninterest-Bearing:					
Demand Deposits	17,404	14,589	14,762	15,097	12,890
All Other Noninterest-Bearing	539	542	567	721	802
Foreign Deposits	0	0	0	0	0
Total Liabilities	96,133	92,388	92,801	97,394	110,053
Memo: Total Deposits	93,098	89,042	89,488	94,073	97,232
Limited Life Preferred Stock	0	0	0	0	0
Capital					
Total Equity	9,468	8,867	9,316	8,596	7,936
Total Liabilities & Equity	105,601	101,255	102,117	105,990	117,989

APPENDIX 4A
(continued)

INCOME STATEMENT $(000)	6/94	6/93	12/93	12/92	12/91
Interest Income and Expenses					
Interest Income	3,677	3,845	7,557	9,358	11,349
Interest Expense	1,360	1,429	2,795	3,767	6,206
Net Interest Margin	2,317	2,416	4,762	5,591	5,143
Provision for Loan & Lease Losses	105	330	450	830	1,062
Noninterest Income and Expenses					
Noninterest Income	610	584	1,193	1,158	994
Noninterest Expense	1,881	1,778	3,585	3,889	3,708
Income and Dividends					
Income Before Extra Items	675	649	1,386	1,490	1,138
Net Income	675	649	1,386	1,490	1,138
Dividends	372	401	752	864	682

APPENDIX 4A
(continued)

BALANCE SHEET ANALYSIS (%)	6/94	6/93	12/93	12/92	12/91
Assets					
Total Loans as a % of Deposits less Pub Funds	83.45	91.40	81.91	83.03	101.95
Loan Losses:					
Net Charge-offs as a % of Avg Loans	0.20	0.26	0.50	1.33	1.10
Nonperforming Loans as a % of Gross Loans	0.15	0.30	0.21	0.39	1.69
Loan Loss Reserve as a % of Total Loans	1.46	1.62	1.58	1.35	1.23
Liabilities					
Source of Deposits as a % of Domestic Deposits:					
Demand IPC	18.16	15.95	15.97	14.74	12.13
All Other Noninterest-Bearing Deposits	0.54	0.43	0.53	1.31	1.13
$100,000 Time	17.50	19.05	18.50	21.53	22.23
All Other Interest-Bearing	63.81	64.57	65.01	62.42	64.51
Public Funds	14.28	21.76	14.17	18.22	18.17
Capital					
Core Cap & Ln Loss Reserve / Total Loans	15.81	15.54	16.39	14.81	11.02
Core Capital / Adj Tot Assets (Leverage Ratio)	8.99	8.91	9.03	8.38	6.72
Core Capital / Risk-Weighted Assets	13.74	12.73	14.12	11.64	8.92
Risk-Adjusted Capital Ratio	14.99	13.98	15.37	12.81	10.04

APPENDIX 4A
(*continued*)

INCOME STATEMENT ANALYSIS (%)	6/94	6/93	12/93	12/92	12/91
Rate of Return					
Return on Average Assets	1.29	1.27	1.35	1.33	0.94
Return on Average Equity	14.38	14.86	15.55	18.03	14.91
Spread					
Yield on Avg Earning Assets (Tax Adj)	7.74	8.35	8.18	9.20	10.18
Rate on Funds	2.77	3.00	2.92	3.57	5.40
Net Interest Spread	4.97	5.35	5.26	5.62	4.78
Expenses & Profits / Tot Oper Income Minus Int Exp					
Salaries and Benefits	25.31	24.88	23.87	22.57	23.80
Occupancy & Furniture	5.64	5.48	5.64	5.11	5.28
Other Operating Expense	30.72	26.29	28.08	27.24	28.04
Total Overhead	61.67	56.65	57.60	54.92	57.12
Provision for Loan Losses	3.44	10.51	7.23	11.72	16.36
Profits Before Taxes & Extra Items	30.85	28.68	30.99	28.92	21.64
Effective Tax Rate	28.27	27.89	28.15	27.25	19.00
Dividends					
Dividend Payout	55.11	61.79	54.26	57.99	59.93
Internal Growth Rate of Equity	3.25	2.89	7.38	7.89	6.22

APPENDIX 4A
(continued)

PEER GROUP COMPARISON

Ratios and Percentile Rankings within National Peer Group, Asset Size:
100 - 299 Million, non-MSA. There are 904 banks in this peer group.

PEER GROUP ANALYSIS (% / Rank)	6/94	6/93	12/93	12/92	12/91
Profitability					
Return on Average Assets	1.29/51	1.27/43	1.35/55	1.33/56	0.94/35
Return on Average Equity	14.38/55	14.86/50	15.55/61	18.03/74	14.91/69
Net Interest Spread (Tax Adj) (Adj for Mtg Indebt)	4.97/73	5.35/83	5.26/81	5.62/91	4.78/71
Noninterest Income / Average Assets	1.16/88	1.14/89	1.16/88	1.03/85	0.82/75
Overhead (incl Mtg Debt) / Average Assets *	3.59/14	3.47/18	3.50/21	3.47/18	3.06/34
Net Overhead Exp / Average Assets *	2.42/31	2.33/35	2.33/41	2.44/30	2.24/42
Asset Quality					
Adj Nonperf Assets & Repossessed RE / Tot Assets *	0.47/52	1.11/30	0.52/51	1.38/24	1.59/26
Nonperforming Loans / Gross Loans *	0.15/89	0.30/82	0.21/85	0.39/79	1.69/35
Nonperforming Assets / Core Cap & Ln Loss Rsrve *	0.97/86	2.00/79	1.31/82	2.73/75	16.06/18
Earnings Coverage of Net Charge-Offs	8.05/18	7.45/21	7.48/22	2.96/10	2.62/16
Net Charge-Offs / Average Loans *	0.20/12	0.26/13	0.50/16	1.33/6	1.10/14
Loan Loss Reserve / Total Loans	1.46/47	1.62/57	1.58/56	1.35/38	1.23/36

107

APPENDIX 4A
(continued)

Liquidity

Liquid Assets / Total Liabilities	17.41/60	13.34/29	14.79/33	17.40/39	5.74/1
$100M+ Time Deposits / Total Assets *	15.43/6	16.75/5	16.21/5	19.11/2	18.32/6
Borrowing & Foreign Deposits / Total Assets *	0.47/34	0.79/20	0.73/24	0.57/25	0.27/30
Liquid Assets - Lg Liab / Total Assets	-1.94/24	-7.34/4	-5.46/8	-5.57/5	-23.15/0
Net Fed Funds Purch (Sold) / Total Assets *	0.09/50	-1.83/60	-3.01/68	-7.78/89	9.92/1
Brokered Deposits / Total Assets *	0.00/N/A	0.00/N/A	0.00/N/A	0.00/N/A	0.00/N/A
Total Loans / Deposits less Public Funds *	83.45/23	91.40/5	81.91/19	83.03/10	101.95/0

Capital

Core Capital / Adj Tot Assets (Leverage Ratio)	8.99/50	8.91/52	9.03/52	8.38/48	6.72/14
Core Cap & Ln Loss Reserve / Total Loans	15.81/41	15.54/35	16.39/44	14.81/31	11.02/7
Risk-Adjusted Capital Ratio	14.99/39	13.98/28	15.37/42	12.81/20	10.04/3
Core Capital / Risk-Weighted Assets	13.74/39	12.73/28	14.12/42	11.64/20	8.92/4
Annual % Change in Core Capital (Tier 1)	7.82/48	N/A/N/A	8.38/39	8.32/43	8.28/58
Annual % Change in Total Assets	4.29/50	N/A/N/A	-3.65/8	-10.17/1	-5.30/4
Dividend Payout *	55.11/30	61.79/21	54.26/31	57.99/25	59.93/30

* Indicates the percentile ranking is subtracted from 99 to associate a
numerically higher percentile ranking with "better" performance within
the peer group.

SHESHUNOFF RATING GUIDELINES & PERFORMANCE EVALUATIONS

For the Sheshunoff Bank Rating Guidelines, banks are divided into ten peer groups based on total asset size. There is a seperate peer group for new banks. A new bank is defined as one with total assets of less than $50 million that was established in the past three years. The same peer group classifications are used to derive the percentile rankings, with the exception of banks between $10 million and $300 million in assets. These are assigned to their respective asset size peer groups based on metropolitan versus nonmetropolitan location using the U.S. Department of Commerce as geographical areas which encompass either a city with a population of at least 50,000 or a Bureau of Census urbanized area of at least 50,000 and a total population of at least 100,000. MSAs may also include outlying counties that have close economic and social relationships with the area's main population concentration.

Peer Group Number	Performance Profiles by National Asset Size Group
1	$10 Billion and over
2	$5 Billion to $9.999 Billion
3	$1 Billion to $4.999 Billion
4	$500 Million to $999 Million
5	$300 Million to $499 Million
6	$100 Million to $299 Million
7	$50 Million to $99 Million
8	$25 Million to $49 Million
9	$10 Million to $24 Million
10	$0 to $9 Million
11	Less than 3 years old and less than $50 Million

The Sheshunoff Rating Guidelines can be converted into grades using the following table:

A+ = 90 - 99
A = 70 - 89
B+ = 50 - 69
B = 30 - 49
C+ = 20 - 29
C = 10 - 19
NR = 0 - 9

APPENDIX 4A
(concluded)

SHESHUNOFF RATING GUIDELINES & PERFORMANCE EVALS	6/94	6/93	12/93	12/92	12/91
Total Assets $(000)	105,601	101,255	102,117	105,990	117,989
Asset Size Peer Group	6	6	6	6	6
Bank Presidents' Weighting					
All Banks In State	43	27	46	33	9
All Banks In Nation	58	34	54	37	17
Asset Peer Group	64	40	62	42	16
Equal Weighting					
Asset Peer Group	66	37	57	44	10
Loan Quality (%)					
Net Charge-Offs / Average Loans	0.20	0.26	0.50	1.33	1.10
Loan Growth	4.59	N/A	-1.51	-21.25	-6.43
Nonperforming Assets / Core Cap & Ln Loss Reserve	0.97	2.00	1.31	2.73	16.06

CAMEL Ratings (% / Rank)	6/94	6/93	12/93	12/92	12/91
Core Capital / Adj Total Assets (Leverage Ratio)	8.99/57	8.91/61	9.03/61	8.38/56	6.72/22
Adj Nonperf Assets & Repossessed RE / Tot Assets *	0.47/56	1.11/39	0.52/58	1.38/33	1.59/35
Management					
Return on Average Assets	1.29/59	1.27/50	1.35/61	1.33/64	0.94/45
Liquid Assets / Total Liabilities	17.41/54	13.34/25	14.79/31	17.40/38	5.74/2

APPENDIX 4B

June 30, 1994 Uniform Bank Performance Report

CERT # _____ DSB # _____
CHARTER # _____
FPU # _____

June 30, 1994 UNIFORM BANK PERFORMANCE REPORT

INFORMATION

TABLE OF CONTENTS

SECTIONS	PAGE NUMBER
SUMMARY RATIOS	01
INCOME INFORMATION:	
INCOME STATEMENT - REVENUES AND EXPENSES ($000)	02
NONINTEREST INCOME AND EXPENSES ($000) AND YIELDS	03
BALANCE SHEET INFORMATION:	
BALANCE SHEET - ASSETS, LIABILITIES & CAPITAL ($000)	04
OFF-BALANCE SHEET ITEMS	05
BALANCE SHEET - % COMPOSITION OF ASSETS & LIABILITIES	06
ANALYSIS OF LOAN & LEASE ALLOWANCE AND LOAN MIX	07
ANALYSIS OF PAST DUE, NONACCRUAL & RESTRUCTURED LNS&LS	08
MATURITY AND REPRICING DISTRIBUTION	09
LIQUIDITY AND INVESTMENT PORTFOLIO	10
CAPITAL ANALYSIS	11
LAST-FOUR-QUARTERS INCOME ANALYSIS	12

FOR ORDERING ASSISTANCE PHONE: (800) 945-2186
(IN THE WASHINGTON, DC AREA; (202) 898-7108)

QUESTIONS REGARDING CONTENT OF REPORTS: (202) 634-6526

BANK AND BANK HOLDING COMPANY INFORMATION

CERTIFICATE # _____ BANK # _____ CHARTER # _____ NA

(HOLDING CO. # _____ NA)

(HOLDING COMPANY REFERS TO TOP HOLDER)

INTRODUCTION

THIS UNIFORM BANK PERFORMANCE REPORT COVERS THE OPERATIONS OF YOUR BANK AND THAT OF A COMPARABLE GROUP OF PEER BANKS. IT IS PROVIDED FOR YOUR USE AS A MANAGEMENT TOOL BY THE FEDERAL FINANCIAL INSTITUTIONS EXAMINATION COUNCIL. DETAILED INFORMATION CONCERNING THIS REPORT IS PROVIDED IN "A USER'S GUIDE FOR THE UNIFORM BANK PERFORMANCE REPORT" FORWARDED TO YOUR BANK UNDER SEPARATE COVER. TO OBTAIN ADDITIONAL USER'S GUIDE OR OTHER UBPR MATERIALS, CALL THE NUMBER INDICATED AT RIGHT FOR ORDERING ASSISTANCE.

AS OF THE DATE OF PREPARATION OF THIS REPORT, YOUR BANK'S FEDERAL REGULATOR WAS THE FEDERAL DEPOSIT INSURANCE CORPORATION.

YOUR CURRENT PEER GROUP # 07
INCLUDES ALL INSURED COMMERCIAL BANKS HAVING ASSETS BETWEEN $100 MILLION AND $300 MILLION WITH 3 OR MORE BANKING OFFICES, AND LOCATED IN A METROPOLITAN AREA.

FOR THE DEFINITION OF OTHER UBPR PEER GROUPS, REFER TO THE UBPR USER'S GUIDE.

ADDRESSEE
_____ CHIEF EXECUTIVE OFFICER

NOTE

111

APPENDIX 4B
(continued)

CERT # ___ DSB # ___
CHARTER # ___ MA COUNTY: ___

SUMMARY RATIOS — PAGE 01

	06/30/94 BANK	PEER 07	PCT	06/30/93 BANK	PEER 07	PCT	12/31/93 BANK	PEER 07	PCT	12/31/92 BANK	PEER 07	12/31/91 BANK	PEER 07
AVERAGE ASSETS ($000)	294728			243452			262907			231796		221797	
NET INCOME ($000)	2970			2015			5802			4200		3714	
NUMBER OF BANKS IN PEER GROUP	932			938			945			963		924	
EARNINGS AND PROFITABILITY													
PERCENT OF AVERAGE ASSETS:													
INTEREST INCOME (TE)	7.76	6.91	90	8.37	7.26	94	8.06	7.14	89	8.58	7.68	10.11	9.08
- INTEREST EXPENSE	2.68	2.39	74	3.06	2.65	85	2.88	2.56	74	3.54	3.32	4.95	4.74
NET INTEREST INCOME (TE)	5.08	4.48	81	5.31	4.55	85	5.18	4.54	71	5.04	4.34	5.16	4.33
+ NONINTEREST INCOME	1.76	0.90	89	1.77	0.92	87	2.07	0.96	90	1.06	0.91	1.57	0.85
MEMO: FEE INCOME	0.75	0.20	94	0.77	0.19	94	0.83	0.20	94	0.71	0.18	0.49	0.17
- NON-INTEREST EXPENSE	3.14	3.58	32	3.85	3.58	52	3.69	3.67	52	4.08	3.62	3.68	3.36
- PROVISION: LOAN & LEASE LOSSES	0.31	0.13	92	0.41	0.21	76	0.32	0.20	71	0.19	0.34	0.51	0.38
= PRETAX OPERATING INCOME (TE)	3.18	1.72	69	2.06	1.74	71	3.25	1.69	97	2.63	1.56	2.34	1.33
+ REALIZED GAINS/LOSSES SECS	0.00	1.00	69	2.80	1.02	89	0.03	0.02	63	0.07	0.04	0.00	0.02
= PRETAX NET OPERATING INC(TE)	3.18	1.74	96	1.76	1.61	84	3.27	1.73	96	2.70	1.65	2.34	1.39
NET OPERATING INCOME	2.02	1.19	96	1.78	1.26	88	2.33	1.18	97	1.85	1.06	1.67	0.89
ADJUSTED NET OPERATING INCOME	2.47	1.19	98	1.99	1.31	84	2.25	1.19	97	1.85	1.13	1.72	0.97
ADJUSTED NET INCOME	2.40	1.11	97	1.99	1.21	81	2.25	1.19	97	1.81	1.13	1.72	0.96
NET INCOME	2.02	1.11	95	1.66	1.21	81	2.21	1.17	97	1.81	1.07	1.67	0.90
MARGIN ANALYSIS:													
AVG EARNING ASSETS TO AVG ASSETS	92.01	92.66	38	92.93	92.54	53	92.11	92.44	43	89.89	92.43	92.59	92.49
AVG INT-BEARING FUNDS TO AVG AST	74.70	75.99	40	74.16	77.22	30	73.56	76.56	30	71.02	77.65	75.57	76.56
INT INC (TE) TO AVG EARN ASSETS	8.43	7.48	89	9.00	7.87	89	8.75	7.75	89	9.54	8.55	10.92	9.81
INT EXPENSE TO AVG EARN ASSETS	2.91	2.59	75	3.13	2.87	75	3.13	2.78	76	3.93	3.60	5.35	5.13
NET INT INC-TE TO AVG EARN ASSET	5.52	4.85	80	5.71	4.94	84	5.62	4.92	80	5.61	4.92	5.57	4.68
LOAN & LEASE ANALYSIS													
NET LOSS TO AVERAGE TOTAL LN&LS	0.08	0.12	49	0.38	0.21	68	0.27	0.26	56	0.21	0.44	0.62	0.50
EARNINGS COVERAGE OF NET LOSS(X)	60.07	22.34	68	11.13	16.18	46	18.10	13.81	61	18.69	8.80	6.55	6.74
LN&LS ALLOWANCE TO NET LOSS(X)	16.69	10.68	68	3.17	7.78	29	4.55	6.77	41	5.84	4.32	1.87	3.54
LN&LS ALLOWANCE TO TOTAL LN&LS	1.38	1.56	39	1.10	1.61	16	1.09	1.57	41	1.25	1.58	1.28	1.45
NON-CURRENT LN&LS TO GROSS LN&LS	1.11	0.93		0.35	1.26	16	0.25	1.09	16	0.88	1.35	0.52	1.61
LIQUIDITY													
VOLATILE LIABILITY DEPENDENCE	2.10	-2.48	63	0.64	-4.91	66	7.91	-5.13	85	-9.29	-5.82	-9.62	-2.88
NET LOANS & LEASES TO ASSETS	74.22	59.19	92	67.62	57.98	79	73.90	58.07	93	64.95	57.55	63.18	59.48
CAPITALIZATION													
TIER ONE LEVERAGE CAPITAL(***)	12.24	8.36	94	11.72	8.07	94	11.52	8.10	92	11.35	7.77	10.52	7.48
CASH DIVIDENDS TO NET INCOME	11.89	24.91	35	14.44	21.53	40	10.60	29.07	26	9.71	26.98	7.05	37.19
RETAIN EARNS TO AVG TOTAL EQUITY	15.33	8.48	89	12.11	9.88	63	17.36	8.46	92	14.98	8.24	15.68	5.85
GROWTH RATES													
ASSETS	3.87	5.84	41	16.95	5.10	88	18.20	5.51	86	3.77	6.00	9.12	5.74
TIER ONE CAPITAL(***)	20.69	9.68	86	16.84	10.69	76	21.01	7.10	92	16.34	10.50	-17.88	7.43
NET LOANS & LEASES	14.00	9.53	69	17.43	5.18	83	34.50	5.66	92	6.68	4.22	-14.38	2.84
TEMPORARY INVESTMENTS	-24.81	-4.50	08	31.03	16.98	62	-15.25	6.44	32	-4.57	11.18	144.35	5.50
VOLATILE LIABILITIES	-45.63	8.03	04	75.98	-2.03	93	104.98	6.44	93	-8.56	-10.19	-20.25	-10.09

(***) TIER ONE CAPITAL FOR 12/31/93 EXCLUDES FASB 115 NET UNREALIZED HOLDING GAIN ON AVAILABLE-FOR-SALE SECURITIES.

APPENDIX 4B
(continued)

CERT #   DSB #
CHARTER #   NA   COUNTY:

INCOME STATEMENT - REVENUES AND EXPENSES ($000)

	06/30/94	06/30/93	12/31/93	12/31/92	12/31/91	PERCENT CHANGE 1 YEAR
INTEREST AND FEES ON LOANS	10360	9066	18981	17705	19863	14.27
INCOME FROM LEASE FINANCING	0	0	0	0	7	NA
FULLY TAXABLE	10360	9066	18981	17705	19869	14.27
TAX-EXEMPT	0	0	0	0	1	NA
ESTIMATED TAX BENEFIT	0	0	0	0	0	
INCOME ON LOANS & LEASES (TE)	10360	9066	18981	17705	19870	14.27
U.S. TREAS & AGENCY SECURITIES	382	268	490	391	247	42.54
TAX-EXEMPT SECURITIES INCOME	38	88	168	197	132	-11.36
ESTIMATED TAX BENEFIT	38	44	80	93	59	
OTHER SECURITIES INCOME	257	315	607	499	310	-18.41
INVESTMT INTEREST INCOME (TE)	755	715	1345	1180	748	5.63
INTEREST ON DUE FROM BANKS	90	2	2	15	0	+ ##
INT ON FED FUNDS SOLD & RESALES	231	400	865	982	1801	-42.25
TRADING ACCOUNT INCOME	0	0	0	0	0	NA
TOTAL INTEREST INCOME (TE)	11436	10183	21193	19882	22419	12.31
INTEREST ON CD'S OVER $100M	480	464	959	1239	2229	-0.83
INTEREST ON ALL OTHER DEPOSITS	2697	2815	5601	6784	8640	-4.19
INT ON FED FUNDS PURCH & REPOS	0	0	0	0	0	NA
INT BORROWED MONEY (+NOTE OPT)	771	422	1008	171	34	82.70
INT ON MORTGAGES & LEASES	0	0	0	0	82	NA
INT ON SUB NOTES & DEBENTURES	0	0	0	0	0	NA
TOTAL INTEREST EXPENSE	3948	3721	7568	8194	10985	6.10
NET INTEREST INCOME (TE)	7488	6462	13625	11688	11434	15.88
NONINTEREST INCOME	2589	2066	5453	4301	3478	25.31
ADJUSTED OPERATING INC (TE)	10077	8528	19078	15989	14912	18.17
NON-INTEREST EXPENSE	4633	4688	9696	9465	8155	-1.17
PROVISION: LOAN & LEASE LOSSES	755	495	845	435	1125	52.53
PROV: ALLOCATED TRANSFER RISK	0	0	0	0	0	
PRETAX OPERATING INCOME (TE)	4689	3345	8537	6089	5632	40.19
REALIZED G/L HLD-TO-MATURITY SEC	0	67	67	161	0	-100.00
REALIZED G/L AVAIL-FOR-SALE SEC	0	NA	NA	NA	NA	NA
PRETAX NET OPERATING INC (TE)	4689	3412	8604	6250	5632	37.43
APPLICABLE INCOME TAXES	1681	1353	2722	1957	1859	
CURRENT TAX EQUIV ADJUSTMENT	38	44	80	93	59	
OTHER TAX EQUIV ADJUSTMENTS	0	0	0	0	0	
APPLICABLE INCOME TAXES (TE)	1719	1397	2802	2050	1918	
NET OPERATING INCOME	2970	2015	5802	4200	3714	47.39
NET EXTRAORDINARY ITEMS	0	0	0	0	0	
NET INCOME	2970	2015	5802	4200	3714	47.39
CASH DIVIDENDS DECLARED	353	291	615	408	262	21.31
RETAINED EARNINGS	2617	1724	5187	3792	3452	51.80

113

CERT #   **CHARTER #** NA **COUNTY:** DSB

NONINTEREST INCOME AND EXPENSE ($000) AND YIELDS   PAGE 03

NONINTEREST INCOME & EXPENSES ($000)

	06/30/94	06/30/93	12/31/93	12/31/92	12/31/91
FIDUCIARY ACTIVITIES	524	572	1135	1212	1182
DEPOSIT SERVICE CHARGES	0	0	0	0	0
TRADING COMMISSIONS & FEES	0	0	0	0	0
FOREIGN EXCHANGE TRADING	0	0	0	0	0
OTHER FOREIGN TRANSACTIONS	0	0	0	0	0
OTHER NONINTEREST INCOME	2065	1494	4318	3089	2296
NONINTEREST INCOME	2509	2066	5453	4301	3478
MEMO: FEE INCOME	1107	939	2193	1647	1331
PERSONNEL EXPENSE	1864	1878	3673	3943	3326
OCCUPANCY EXPENSE	597	642	1268	1208	997
OTHER OPER EXP(INCL INTANGIBLES)	2172	2168	4755	4714	3832
TOTAL OVERHEAD EXPENSE	4633	4688	9696	9465	8155
O/H & INTEREST ON MORTG & LEASES	4633	4688	9696	9465	8237
DOMESTIC BANKING OFFICES (#)	8	8	8	8	8
FOREIGN BRANCHES (#)	0	0	0	0	0
ASSETS PER DOMESTIC OFFICE	36253	34903	36019	30471	29363
NUMBER OF EQUIVALENT EMPLOYEES	142	133	136	121	114

PERCENT OF AVERAGE ASSETS

	06/30/94 BANK	PEER 07	PCT	06/30/93 BANK	PEER 07	PCT	12/31/93 BANK	PEER 07	PCT	12/31/92 BANK	PEER 07	12/31/91 BANK	PEER 07
PERSONNEL EXPENSE	1.26	1.71	16	1.54	1.69	38	1.40	1.71	27	1.53	1.66	1.50	1.63
OCCUPANCY EXPENSE	0.41	0.52	16	0.51	0.51	56	0.48	0.52	45	0.52	0.52	0.49	0.52
OTHER OPER EXP(INCL INTANGIBLES)	1.47	1.31	65	1.78	1.33	76	1.81	1.37	78	2.03	1.36	1.73	1.33
TOTAL OVERHEAD EXPENSE	3.14	3.58	32	3.85	3.58	62	3.69	3.67	52	4.08	3.62	3.68	3.54
O/H & INTEREST ON MORTG & LEASES	3.14	3.59	32	3.85	3.58	62	3.69	3.67	52	4.08	3.62	3.71	3.54
OVERHEAD LESS NONINTEREST INCOME	1.39	2.60	02	2.15	2.56	26	1.61	2.61	04	2.23	2.62	2.11	2.59
OTHER INCOME & EXPENSE RATIOS:													
AVG PERSONNEL EXP PER EMPL($000)	26.25	31.53	15	28.24	30.41	34	27.01	30.80	24	29.28	29.73	29.18	28.28
ASSETS PER EMPLOYEE ($MILLION)	2.04	1.90	62	2.10	1.86	69	2.12	1.90	67	2.01	1.88	2.06	1.83
MARGINAL TAX RATE	36.67	36.42	54	40.95	35.56	69	32.57	35.60	19	32.80	36.03	34.06	36.28

YIELD ON OR COST OF:

	06/30/94 BANK	PEER 07	PCT	06/30/93 BANK	PEER 07	PCT	12/31/93 BANK	PEER 07	PCT	12/31/92 BANK	PEER 07	12/31/91 BANK	PEER 07
TOTAL LOANS & LEASES (TE)	9.20	8.58	78	10.17	8.93	91	9.87	8.88	87	10.92	9.56	10.75	10.75
TOTAL LOANS	9.20	8.55	75	10.17	8.90	91	9.87	8.85	87	10.92	9.53	12.12	10.70
REAL ESTATE**	8.02	8.60	25	10.72	9.01	92	9.58	8.95	72	10.32	8.69	12.12	10.65
COMMERCIAL TIME, DEMAND ,OTH**	9.08	8.21	68	9.85	8.19	90	9.88	8.22	89	10.29	10.78	11.54	10.23
INSTALLMENT**	9.84	9.17	68	11.03	10.00	76	10.77	9.82	74	11.63	10.78	12.01	11.54
CREDIT CARD PLANS	12.12	13.93	33	12.63	12.92	52	12.42	14.01	35	14.82	14.68	15.81	15.04
MEMO: AGRICULTURAL LNS IN ABOVE	NA	8.40		NA	6.42		NA	6.40		NA	9.04	NA	10.44
TOTAL INVESTMENT SECURITIES (TE)	5.51	5.67	21	7.09	6.51	73	6.63	5.98	65	6.96	7.34	7.86	8.16
U.S. TREASURIES & AGENCIES	5.12	5.67	32	6.12	6.16	30	5.47	5.98	33	5.85	6.55	6.57	6.95
STATE & POLITICAL SUB (BOOK)	7.65	6.13	37	8.42	8.96	96	8.08	6.45	36	8.62	9.54	9.52	10.09
STATE & POLITICAL SUB (TE)	7.65	6.13	44	12.48	5.15	96	6.21	5.15	44	6.95	7.35	8.60	8.23
OTHER DEBT SECURITIES	5.78	5.13	89	6.51	6.66	96	12.27	6.45	97	7.23	5.47	0.00	5.89
EQUITY SECURITIES	7.32	3.83	89	4.00	5.15	56	4.00	3.85	57	4.25	5.24	5.51	7.31
INTEREST-BEARING BANK BALANCES	3.87	3.43	84	2.88	1.91	84	2.92	2.97	24	3.96	3.23	5.26	5.04
FEDERAL FUNDS SOLD & RESALES	3.60	2.03	84	2.98	2.34	82	3.65	2.35	84	4.50	2.98	4.28	5.17
TOTAL INTEREST-BEARING DEPOSITS	2.56	2.57	76	3.11	2.39	84	3.02	2.73	92	3.85	3.44	5.30	4.95
TRANSACTION ACCOUNTS	2.79	2.56	66	3.14	2.85	78	3.08	2.78	78	3.85	3.51	4.97	6.71
MONEY MARKET DEPOSIT ACCOUNTS	2.98	3.75	83	4.12	3.93	61	3.87	3.87	60	4.98	4.60	7.09	6.71
OTHER SAVINGS DEPOSITS	3.95	3.99	71	4.71	4.34	70	4.61	4.25	69	5.67	5.29	7.35	6.97
LARGE CERTIFICATES OF DEPOSIT													
ALL OTHER TIME DEPOSITS													
FEDERAL FUNDS PURCHASED & REPOS	0.00	3.35	05	NA	2.91	83	NA	2.94	73	NA	3.55	NA	5.60
OTHER BORROWED MONEY	3.53	3.11	57	5.75	2.41		4.32	2.50		5.74	2.54	2.08	4.04
SUBORDINATED NOTES & DEBENTURES	NA	7.53		NA	7.65		NA	7.73		NA	8.19	NA	9.24
ALL INTEREST-BEARING FUNDS	3.59	3.15	84	4.12	3.43	89	3.91	3.35	86	4.98	4.26	6.50	6.03

**BANKS UNDER $100 MILLION IN TOTAL ASSETS REPORT THIS LOAN DETAIL (BY TYPE) USING THEIR OWN INTERNAL CATEGORIZATION SYSTEMS.

APPENDIX 4B
(continued)

CERT #   DSB #   CHARTER #   NA   COUNTY:

BALANCE SHEET - ASSETS, LIABILITIES AND CAPITAL ($000)

	06/30/94	06/30/93	12/31/93	12/31/92	12/31/91	PERCENT CHANGE 1 QTR	PERCENT CHANGE 1 YEAR
ASSETS:							
REAL ESTATE LOANS	159766	132117	160490	112450	102359	-5.34	20.93
COMMERCIAL LOANS	51103	51412	47614	40354	40105	-4.69	-0.60
INDIVIDUAL LOANS	7216	6826	6825	7164	7783	9.77	5.71
AGRICULTURAL LOANS	0	0	0	0	0	NA	NA
OTHER LNS & LS IN DOMESTIC OFFICES	168	630	359	362	78	-51.86	-73.33
LNS&LS IN FOREIGN OFFICES	NA	NA	NA	NA	NA	NA	NA
GROSS LOANS & LEASES	218253	190985	215288	160330	150325	-4.83	14.28
LESS: UNEARNED INCOME	0	0	0	0	0		
LNS&LS ALLOWANCE & ATRR	3004	2162	2339	2008	1917	9.00	38.95
NET LOANS & LEASES	215249	188823	212949	158322	148008	39.04	14.00
U.S. TREASURY & AGENCY SECURITIES	20587	10985	10979	10998	3011	-1.66	81.41
MUNICIPAL SECURITIES	3015	3425	2775	3760	2805		-11.97
FOREIGN DEBT SECURITIES							
ALL OTHER SECURITIES	9565	8501	7567	8930	4568	25.07	12.52
INTEREST-BEARING BANK BALANCES	8049	0	0	1000	0	NA	NA
FEDERAL FUNDS SOLD & RESALES	9000	36300	29700	32400	43800	NA	NA
TRADING ACCOUNT ASSETS	0	0	0	0	0		
TOTAL INVESTMENTS	50216	59211	51021	57088	54184		
TOTAL EARNING ASSETS	265465	248034	263970	215410	202592		
NON-INT CASH & DUE FROM BANKS	10571	16954	10115	14017	14325	-9.46	-37.65
ACCEPTANCES	0	0	0	0	0		
PREMISES, FIX ASSTS, CAP LEASES	6121	6317	6179	6426	5837	0.16	-3.10
OTHER REAL ESTATE OWNED	5173	5967	5714	5869	10155	-10.58	-13.31
INV IN UNCONSOLIDATED SUBS	0	0	0	0	0		
OTHER ASSETS	2699	1952	2175	2052	1899	7.66	38.27
TOTAL ASSETS	290029	279224	288153	243774	234908	-5.27	3.87
AVERAGE ASSETS DURING QUARTER	291163	251802	286638	240359	222969	-2.39	15.63
LIABILITIES:							
DEMAND DEPOSITS	36450	52806	47434	44217	45237	-15.04	-30.97
ALL NOW & ATS ACCOUNTS	24358	23784	26176	25987	22841	-3.11	-2.41
MONEY MARKET DEPOSIT ACCOUNTS	21078	19898	20814	20828	17609	9.01	5.93
OTHER SAVINGS DEPOSITS	31067	27943	29671	25854	13885	-4.81	15.91
TIME DEP UNDER $100M	73101	73949	74148	70989	81089	-0.50	-1.15
CORE DEPOSITS	186854	197930	198243	187875	180221	-3.84	-5.60
TIME DEP OVER $100M	26500	25276	23087	24236	28786	3.31	4.84
DEPOSITS IN FOREIGN OFFICES	NA	NA	NA	NA	NA		
TOTAL DEPOSITS	211335	223206	221330	212111	209007	-3.01	-4.41
FEDERAL FUNDS PURCHASED & RESALE	591	25096	32191	2732	707	-6.93	-97.65
OTHER BORROWINGS INCL MAT < 1 YR	27388	50372	55278	26968	29993	3.02	-45.63
VOLATILE LIABILITIES	39175			NA	NA	-20.19	
OTHER BORROWINGS WITH MAT > 1 YR	1532	1800	1620	1650	1745	-6.43	9.43
ACCEPTANCES & OTHER LIABILITIES	254652	249702	255141	216493	211859		1.98
TOTAL LIABILITIES (INCL MORTG)							
SUBORDINATED NOTES & DEBENTURES	35377	29522	33012	2728	0		
ALL COMMON & PREFERRED CAPITAL	290029	279224	288153	243774	234908	-5.27	19.83
TOTAL LIABILITIES & PREFERRED CAPITAL							3.87
MEMORANDA:							
OFFICER, SHAREHOLDER LOANS (#)	274	147	186	0	125	87.67	86.39
OFFICER, SHAREHOLDER LOANS ($)	5173	5967	5714	5869	10155	-10.58	-13.31
NON-INVESTMENT ORE							
HELD-TO-MATURITY SECURITIES	3015	22911	21321	23668	10388	-1.66	-86.04
AVAILABLE-FOR-SALE-SECURITIES	30152	NA	0	NA	NA	34.28	NA
ALL BROKERED DEPOSITS	2797	0	0	0	0	0.00	NA

115

APPENDIX 4B
(continued)

OFF-BALANCE SHEET ITEMS

	06/30/94	12/31/93	06/30/93	12/31/92	12/31/91	PERCENT CHANGE 1 QTR	PAGE 05 PERCENT CHANGE 1 YEAR
UNUSED COMMITMENTS							
HOME EQUITY (1-4 FAMILY)	0	0	0	0	0	NA	NA
CREDIT CARD	4515	4896	4252	4663	4404	0.76	-7.78
COMMERCL RE SECURED BY RE	29225	20527	25660	16945	16737	-3.44	42.37
COMMERCL RE NOT SECURED BY RE	0	0	0	0	0	NA	NA
ALL OTHER	15223	14150	15075	16032	13684	-6.82	7.58
SECURITIES UNDERWRITING	0	0	0	0	0	NA	NA
MEMO:UNUSED COMMIT W/MAT GT 1 YR	5010	5763	5390	6636	6806	-6.58	-13.07
STANDBY LETTERS OF CREDIT	452	301	282	796	0	23.16	50.17
AMOUNT CONVEYED TO OTHERS	0	0	0	0	0	NA	NA
COMMERCIAL LETTERS OF CREDIT	0	0	0	42	302	NA	NA
INTEREST RATE CONTRACTS							
NOTIONAL VAL OF INT RATE SWAPS	0	0	0	0	0	NA	NA
FUTURES AND FORWARD CONTRACTS	0	0	0	0	0	NA	NA
OPTION CONTRACTS	0	0	0	0	0	NA	NA
FOREIGN EXCHANGE RATE CONTRACTS							
NOTIONAL VAL OF EXCHANGE SWAPS	0	0	0	0	0		
COMMITMENTS TO PUR FOREIGN CUR	0	400	483	202	743	-100.00	-100.00
OPTION CONTRACTS	0	0	0	0	0	NA	NA
PRINCIPAL BALANCE OF MTG POOLS	0	0	0	0	0	NA	NA
AMOUNT OF RECOURSE EXPOSURE	2000	0	0	0	0	NA	NA
ALL OTH OFF-BALANCE SHEET ITEMS	0	0	0	0	0	NA	NA
GROSS OFF-BALANCE SHEET ITEMS	51415	40274	45752	38680	35870	-0.61	27.66

PERCENT OF TOTAL ASSETS

	06/30/94 BANK	PEER 07	PCT	06/30/93 BANK	PEER 07	PCT	12/31/93 BANK	PEER 07	PCT	12/31/92 BANK	PEER 07	12/31/91 BANK	PEER 07
UNUSED COMMITMENTS													
HOME EQUITY (1-4 FAMILY)	0.00	1.01	21	0.00	0.92	23	0.00	0.95	22	0.00	0.94	0.00	0.84
CREDIT CARD	1.56	0.30	82	1.75	0.27	84	1.48	0.26	83	1.91	0.26	1.87	0.26
COMMERCL RE SECURED BY RE	10.08	1.66	96	7.35	1.27	96	8.90	1.40	96	6.95	1.14	7.12	1.00
COMMERCL RE NOT SECURED BY RE	0.00	0.00	51	0.00	0.00	82	0.00	0.00	81	0.00	0.00	0.00	0.00
ALL OTHER	5.25	4.56	84	5.07	4.22	81	5.23	4.30	81	6.58	3.99	5.83	3.92
TOTAL LN&LS COMMITMENTS	16.88	9.58	89	14.17	8.49	89	15.61	8.76	89	15.44	8.18	14.82	8.18
SECURITIES UNDERWRITING	0.00	0.00	99	0.00	0.00	99	0.00	0.00	99	0.00	0.00	0.00	0.00
STANDBY LETTERS OF CREDIT	0.16	0.44	25	0.11	0.44	20	0.10	0.44	19	0.33	0.44	0.00	0.47
AMOUNT CONVEYED TO OTHERS	0.00	0.00	94	0.00	0.00	94	0.00	0.00	95	0.00	0.00	0.00	0.00
COMMERCIAL LETTERS OF CREDIT	0.00	0.00	78	0.00	0.00	76	0.00	0.00	78	0.02	0.00	0.13	0.00
INTEREST RATE CONTRACTS													
NOTIONAL VAL OF INT RATE SWAPS	0.00	0.00	94	0.00	0.00	95	0.00	0.00	95	0.00	0.00	0.00	0.00
FUTURES AND FORWARD CONTRACTS	0.00	0.00	98	0.00	0.00	99	0.00	0.00	98	0.00	0.00	0.00	0.00
OPTION CONTRACTS	0.00	0.00	99	0.00	0.00	99	0.00	0.00	97	0.00	0.00	0.00	0.00
FOREIGN EXCHANGE RATE CONTRACTS													
NOTIONAL VAL OF EXCHANGE SWAPS	0.00	0.00	99	0.00	0.00	99	0.00	0.00	99	0.00	0.00	0.00	0.00
COMMITMENTS TO PUR FOREIGN CUR	0.00	0.00	98	0.14	0.00	98	0.17	0.00	98	0.08	0.00	0.32	0.00
OPTION CONTRACTS	0.00	0.00	95	0.00	0.00	88	0.00	0.00	90	0.00	0.00	0.00	0.00
PRINCIPAL BALANCE OF MTG POOLS	0.00	0.00	98	0.00	0.00	98	0.00	0.00	98	0.00	0.00	0.00	0.00
AMOUNT OF RECOURSE EXPOSURE	0.00	0.00	98	0.00	0.00	98	0.00	0.00	98	0.00	0.00	0.00	0.00
ALL OTH OFF-BALANCE SHEET ITEMS	0.69	0.00	95	0.00	0.00	88	0.00	0.00	90	0.00	0.00	0.00	0.00
GROSS OFF-BALANCE SHEET ITEMS	17.73	10.67	80	14.42	9.77	73	15.88	10.00	77	15.87	9.39	15.27	9.06

116

APPENDIX 4B
(continued)

CERT # DSB #
CHARTER # NA COUNTY:

BALANCE SHEET - PERCENTAGE COMPOSITION OF ASSETS AND LIABILITIES

	06/30/94 BANK	06/30/94 PEER 07	06/30/94 PCT	06/30/93 BANK	06/30/93 PEER 07	06/30/93 PCT	12/31/93 BANK	12/31/93 PEER 07	12/31/93 PCT	12/31/92 BANK	12/31/92 PEER 07	12/31/92 PCT	12/31/91 BANK	12/31/91 PEER 07
ASSETS, PERCENT OF AVG ASSETS														
TOTAL LOANS	74.96	59.36	93	67.96	58.43	77	69.92	58.76	83	66.45	59.22	79	72.19	61.23
LEASE FINANCING RECEIVABLES	0.00	0.90	79	0.80	0.00	80	0.00	0.00	79	0.00	0.00	38	0.01	0.00
LESS: LN&LS ALLOWANCE & ATRR	0.92		54	0.60	0.91	40	0.79	0.91	38	0.80	0.88	18	0.85	0.83
NET LOANS & LEASES	74.04	58.56	93	67.16	57.52	78	69.12	58.01	65	65.66	58.46	93	71.36	60.54
INTEREST-BEARING BANK BALANCES	0.91	0.06	86	0.13	0.07	67	0.07	0.09	60	0.22	0.16		0.00	0.25
FEDERAL FUNDS SOLD & RESALES	7.54	2.76	88	13.20	3.59	95	12.61	3.56	95	14.64	3.63		14.73	4.05
TRADING ACCOUNT ASSETS	0.00	0.00	97	0.00	0.00	96	0.00	0.00	95	0.00	0.00		0.00	0.00
HELD-TO-MATURITY SECURITIES	3.10	18.51	02	8.27	28.23	05	7.77	28.21	05	7.07	26.89		3.85	24.30
AVAILABLE-FOR-SALE SECURITIES	5.95	8.44	38	NA	NA		NA	NA		NA	NA		NA	NA
TOTAL EARNING ASSETS	91.54	91.63	46	88.76	91.29	21	89.57	91.39	26	87.59	91.13		89.94	90.91
NONINT CASH & DUE FROM BANKS	3.66	4.31	33	5.69	4.47	76	5.14	4.42	65	5.54	4.56		5.53	4.72
PREMISES, FIX ASSTS & CAP LEASES	2.08	1.80	64	2.35	1.78	76	2.31	1.80	71	2.64	1.75		2.28	1.80
OTHER REAL ESTATE OWNED	1.89	0.22	91	2.32	0.39	91	2.78	0.34	91	3.38	0.42		1.21	0.35
ACCEPTANCES & OTHER ASSETS	0.83	1.48	02	0.78	1.45	01	0.19	1.46	01	0.86	1.50		1.03	1.59
SUBTOTAL	8.46	8.16	53	11.24	8.71	78	10.42	8.61	73	12.41	8.67		10.06	9.09
TOTAL ASSETS	100.00	100.00		100.00	100.00		99.99	100.00		100.00	100.00		100.00	100.00
STANDBY LETTERS OF CREDIT	0.12	0.45	20	0.19	0.45	28	0.15	0.45	22	0.24	0.45		0.00	0.51
LIABILITIES, PERCENT OF AVG ASST														
DEMAND DEPOSITS	14.34	14.79	50	18.65	14.06	76	18.24	14.44	73	18.61	13.48		15.93	13.12
ALL NOW & ATS ACCOUNTS	8.56	12.21	22	9.55	12.09	30	9.19	12.10	26	9.91	11.38		9.48	10.03
MONEY MARKET DEPOSIT ACCOUNTS	6.92	12.20	17	7.64	12.91	19	7.52	12.89	18	8.32	13.03		7.07	12.14
OTHER SAVINGS DEPOSITS	10.96	12.78	40	10.19	12.14	42	10.12	12.29	41	8.61	10.73		5.83	8.81
TIME DEP < $100M	24.96	24.89	52	24.25	25.65	53	26.91	32.48	52	31.64	29.07		35.99	32.28
CORE DEPOSITS	65.52	81.69	03	74.25	82.16	12	71.99	82.07	71	77.09	81.77		74.29	79.75
TIME DEP OVER $100M	8.51	6.14	69	9.39	6.39	72	8.96	6.24	71	10.78	7.13		14.30	9.23
DEPOSITS IN FOREIGN OFFICES	NA	2.43	01	NA	2.89		NA	0.68		NA	2.06		NA	1.17
TOTAL DEPOSITS	74.91	88.78	39	83.64	89.40	10	80.95	89.20	05	87.87	89.74		88.59	89.82
FEDERAL FUNDS PURCH & REPOS	0.00	0.19	96	4.81	0.59	43	0.00	0.62	90	0.00	0.65		0.00	0.70
OTHER BORROWINGS INCL < 1 YR	3.78	8.70	72		8.73		7.51	0.22	98	0.91	0.16		0.41	0.15
VOLATILE LIABILITIES	12.35			14.20		79	16.47	8.74	87	11.69	9.34		14.72	11.39
OTHER BORROWINGS > 1 YR	10.02	0.00	99	NA	NA		NA	0.67	41	NA	0.75		NA	NA
ACCEPTANCES & OTHER LIABILITIES	0.59	0.63	85	0.61	0.67	45	0.59	0.67	10	0.71	0.75		1.27	0.91
TOTAL LIABILITIES(INCL MORTG)	88.42	91.64	08	89.06	91.94		89.04	91.85		89.49	92.26		90.28	92.45
SUBORDINATED NOTES & DEBENTURES	0.00	0.00	94	0.00	0.00	94	0.00	0.00	94	0.00	0.00		0.00	0.00
ALL COMMON & PREFERRED CAPITAL	11.58	8.32	91	10.94	8.02	90	10.96	8.10	89	10.51	7.70		9.72	0.50
TOTAL LIABILITIES & CAPITAL	100.00	100.00		100.00	100.00		100.01	100.00		100.00	100.00		99.99	100.00
MEMO: ALL BROKERED DEPOSITS	0.63	0.00	93	0.00	0.00	89	0.00	0.00	88	0.00	0.00		0.00	0.00
INSURED BROKERED DEP	0.63	0.00	93	0.00	0.00	89	0.00	0.00	88	0.00	0.00		0.00	0.00

117

APPENDIX 4B
(continued)

CERT # DSB #
CHARTER # NA COUNTY:

ANALYSIS OF LOAN & LEASE ALLOWANCE AND LOAN MIX

CHANGE: LNWLS ALLOWANCE ($000)	06/30/94			06/30/93			12/31/93			12/31/92		12/31/91	
	BANK	PEER 07	PCT	BANK	PEER 07	PCT	BANK	PEER 07	PCT	BANK	PEER 07	BANK	PEER 07
BEGINNING BALANCE	2339			2008			2008			1917		1815	
GROSS LOAN & LEASE LOSSES	96			352			530			371		1045	
RECOVERIES	6			11			16			27		22	
NET LOAN & LEASE LOSSES	90			341			514			344		1023	
PROVISION FOR LOAN & LEASE LOSS	755			495			845			435		1125	
OTHER ADJUSTMENTS	0			0			0			0		0	
ENDING BALANCE	3004			2162			2339			2008		1917	
NET ATRR CHARGE-OFFS	NA			NA			NA			NA		NA	
OTHER ATRR CHANGES (NET)	NA			NA			NA			NA		NA	
AVERAGE TOTAL LOANS & LEASES	225221			178243			192309			162096		163912	

ANALYSIS RATIOS

	BANK	PEER 07	PCT	BANK	PEER 07	PCT	BANK	PEER 07	PCT	BANK	PEER 07	BANK	PEER 07
LOSS PROVISION TO AVERAGE ASSETS	0.51	0.13	92	0.41	0.21	76	0.32	0.20	71	0.19	0.34	0.51	0.38
LOSS PROVISION TO AVG TOT LNWLS	0.67	0.23	88	0.56	0.37	70	0.44	0.35	71	0.27	0.59	0.69	0.63
NET LOSS TO AVERAGE TOTAL LNWLS	0.08	0.12	49	0.38	0.21	68	0.27	0.26	56	0.21	0.44	0.62	0.50
GROSS LOSS TO AVERAGE TOT LNWLS	0.09	0.24	28	0.39	0.35	58	0.28	0.42	39	0.23	0.59	0.64	0.71
RECOVERIES TO AVERAGE TOT LNWLS	0.01	0.10	10	0.01	0.11	16	0.01	0.12	08	0.02	0.12	0.01	0.11
RECOVERIES TO PRIOR PERIOD LOSS	2.26	31.23	05	5.93	21.60	16	4.31	24.87	08	2.58	21.76	10.53	22.60
LNWLS ALLOWANCE TO TOTAL LNWLS	1.38	1.56	39	1.13	1.61	16	1.09	1.57	16	1.25	1.58	1.28	1.45
LNWLS ALLOWANCE TO NET LOSSES(X)	16.69	10.64	64	3.17	7.78	29	4.55	6.77	27	5.84	4.21	1.87	3.34
LNWLS ALL TO NONACCRUAL LNWLS(X)	1.57	2.98		5.27	2.25		29.24	2.43		5.35	2.11	4.65	1.71
EARN COVERAGE OF NET LOSSES (X)	60.07	22.34	79	11.13	16.18	46	18.10	13.81	63	18.69	8.80	6.55	6.74

NET LOSSES BY TYPE OF LNWLS

	BANK	PEER 07	PCT	BANK	PEER 07	PCT	BANK	PEER 07	PCT	BANK	PEER 07	BANK	PEER 07
REAL ESTATE LOANS	0.00	0.02	58	0.00	0.05	52	0.36	0.07	39	0.44	0.15	1.46	0.11
COMMERCIAL AND INDUSTRIAL LOANS	0.11	0.09	62	0.55	0.32	62	0.31	0.31	59	0.10	0.56	0.23	0.62
INSTALLMENT LOANS	0.33	0.23	62	0.19	0.00	41	0.52	0.40	62	0.46	0.61	0.28	0.73
LEASE FINANCING	NA	0.00		NA	0.00		NA	0.00		0.00	0.00	-5.16	0.00

MEMORANDA:

	BANK	PEER 07	PCT	BANK	PEER 07	PCT	BANK	PEER 07	PCT	BANK	PEER 07	BANK	PEER 07
CREDIT CARD PLANS	1.02	0.57	64	1.58	0.78	68	2.30	1.05	78	2.22	1.39	0.99	1.90
LOANS TO FINANCE COMML REAL EST	0.00	0.00	96	0.00	0.00	92	0.00	0.00	86	0.42	0.00	1.40	0.23
CONSTRUCTION & LAND DEV	0.00	0.00	93	0.00	0.00	91	0.00	0.00	85	0.00	0.06	0.00	0.63
SECURED BY FARMLAND	0.00	0.01	97	0.00	0.02	96	0.00	0.03	95	0.00	0.06	0.00	0.04
MULTIFAMILY MORTGAGE	NA	0.00	69	NA	0.02	62	0.00	0.03	51	0.00	0.06	0.00	0.04
HOME EQUITY LOANS	NA			NA			NA			NA		NA	
1-4 FAMILY NON-REVOLVING	0.00	0.00	72	0.00	0.01	67	0.00	0.02	55	0.00	0.05	0.00	0.03
MULTIFAMILY LOANS	0.00	0.00	97	0.00	0.00	95	0.00	0.00	92	0.00	0.08	0.00	0.04
NON-FARM NON-RESIDENTIAL MTG	0.00	0.00	80	0.00	0.00	75	0.00	0.02	66	0.00	0.08	0.00	0.04
BANKS W/AGRI LOANS OVER 5%:													
AGRICULTURAL LOANS	NA	0.00		NA	0.00		NA	0.00		NA	0.05	NA	-0.02

APPENDIX 4B
(continued)

CERT # DSB #
CHARTER # NA COUNTY:

ANALYSIS OF LOAN & LEASE ALLOWANCE AND LOAN MIX

LOAN MIX, % AVERAGE GROSS LN&LS	BANK	PEER 07	PCT	BANK	PEER 07	PCT	BANK	PEER 07	PCT	BANK	PEER 07	BANK	PEER 07
CONSTRUCTION & DEVELOPMENT	23.43	3.71	97	22.66	3.37	98	22.65	3.53	97	24.48	3.33	32.89	3.67
1-4 FAMILY RESIDENTIAL	30.45	29.69	52	26.12	30.72	39	28.47	30.49	44	24.63	30.71	24.37	29.26
HOME EQUITY LOANS	0.00	2.34	20	0.00	2.33	21	0.00	2.42	19	0.00	2.39	0.00	2.12
OTHER REAL ESTATE LOANS	19.90	23.21	33	21.10	23.98	31	20.08	24.17	30	17.92	22.47	13.86	20.54
FARMLAND	0.06	0.44	36	0.10	0.41	41	0.09	0.40	40	0.09	0.39	0.04	0.36
MULTIFAMILY	1.84	1.42	60	1.23	1.21	53	1.60	1.28	59	0.61	1.09	0.23	0.97
NON-FARM NON-RESIDENTIAL	17.99	21.52	39	19.76	20.54	48	18.39	20.76	43	17.22	19.37	13.60	17.68
TOTAL REAL ESTATE	73.78	63.81	72	69.88	62.72	66	71.20	62.97	68	67.02	60.85	71.13	57.79
FINANCIAL INSTITUTION LOANS	0.00	0.00	89	0.00	0.00	88	0.00	0.00	86	0.00	0.00	0.00	0.00
AGRICULTURAL LOANS	0.00	0.21	45	0.00	0.20	45	0.00	0.18	45	0.00	0.18	0.00	0.19
COMMERCIAL & INDUSTRIAL LOANS	22.83	16.42	71	26.00	16.44	76	24.79	16.78	73	28.20	17.24	23.82	18.61
LOANS TO INDIVIDUALS	3.11	12.28	09	3.89	12.79	10	3.69	12.70	09	4.43	13.56	4.98	15.15
CREDIT CARD LOANS	0.76	0.50	63	1.00	0.52	70	0.91	0.52	69	1.13	0.56	1.04	0.54
MUNICIPAL LOANS	0.00	0.34	40	0.00	0.43	38	0.00	0.39	38	0.00	0.48	0.04	0.61
ACCEPTANCES OF OTHER BANKS	0.15	0.00	97	0.00	0.00	94	0.21	0.00	95	0.00	0.00	0.00	0.00
FOREIGN OFFICE LOANS & LEASES	0.00	0.00	00	0.00	0.00	00	0.00	0.00	00	0.00	0.00	0.00	0.00
ALL OTHER LOANS	0.13	0.28	40	0.24	0.13	53	0.21	0.33	48	0.15	0.36	0.06	0.40
LEASE FINANCING RECEIVABLES	0.00	0.00	79	0.00	0.00	79	0.00	0.00	79	0.00	0.00	0.02	0.00
SUPPLEMENTAL:													
LOANS TO FOREIGN GOVERNMENTS	0.00	0.00	99	0.00	0.00	98	0.00	0.00	98	0.00	0.00	0.00	0.00
LOANS TO FINANCE COMML REAL EST	0.23	0.01	81	0.28	0.61	80	0.26	0.02	79	0.31	0.04	0.31	0.04
MEMORANDUM (% OF AVG TOT LOANS):													
COMMERCIAL PAPER IN LOANS	0.00	0.00	97	0.00	0.00	98	0.00	0.00	96	0.00	0.00	NA	NA
LOAN & LEASE COMMITMENTS	22.10	16.91	69	20.97	15.16	71	21.09	15.60	70	22.86	14.49	22.03	13.55
LOANS SOLD DURING THE QUARTER	NA			0.84	0.13	78	2.60	0.18	87	0.95	0.13	0.08	0.09
OFFICER, SHAREHOLDER LOANS	0.12	1.85	09	0.84	1.77	69	1.84	1.84	11	0.03	0.25	0.08	0.28
OFFICER, SHAREH LOANS TO ASSETS	0.09	1.04	12	0.05	0.97	12	0.06	1.01	11	0.02	0.13	0.05	0.16
OTHER REAL ESTATE OWNED % ASSETS													
CONSTRUCTION & LAND DEVELOPMENT	1.33	0.00	97	1.57	0.01	97	1.49	0.01	97	1.89	0.02	NA	NA
FARMLAND	0.35	0.04	91	0.00	0.07	87	0.46	0.06	87	0.95	0.00	NA	NA
1-4 FAMILY	0.23	0.05	95	0.49	0.08	88	0.23	0.06	90	0.32	0.08	NA	NA
MULTIFAMILY	0.00	0.04	91	0.25	0.15	85	0.23	0.16	94	0.32	0.16	NA	NA
NON-FARM-NON-RESID.	NA	0.08	40	NA	0.00	30	NA	0.00	28	NA	0.00	NA	NA
FOREIGN OFFICES													
SUBTOTAL	1.89	0.21	92	2.32	0.38	91	2.18	0.33	92	3.38	0.41	NA	NA
DIRECT AND INDIRECT INV.	0.00	0.00	96	0.00	0.00	96	0.00	0.00	96	0.00	0.00	NA	NA
TOTAL	1.89	0.22	91	2.32	0.39	91	2.18	0.34	91	3.38	0.42	NA	NA
MORTGAGE SERVICING % ASSETS													
MORTGAGES SERV. UNDER GNMA	0.00	0.00	98	0.00	0.00	98	0.00	0.00	98	0.00	0.00	NA	NA
MORTGAGES SERVICED UNDER FHLMC	0.00	0.00	81	0.00	0.00	81	0.00	0.00	80	0.00	0.00	NA	NA
MORTGAGES SERVICED UNDER FNMA	0.00	0.00	85	0.00	0.00	89	0.00	0.00	87	0.00	0.00	NA	NA
OTHER MORTGAGE SERVICING	0.00	0.00	75	0.00	0.00	84	0.00	0.00	83	0.00	0.00	NA	NA
TOTAL	0.00	0.14	71	0.00	0.10	72	0.00	0.15	70	0.00	0.09	NA	NA

119

(continued)

ANALYSIS OF PAST DUE, NONACCRUAL & RESTRUCTURED LOANS & LEASES PAGE 08

CERT # DSB #
CHARTER # NA COUNTY:

NON-CURRENT LNMLS ($000)	06/30/94	06/30/93	12/31/93	12/31/92	12/31/91
90 DAYS AND OVER PAST DUE	516	267	452	1036	368
TOTAL NONACCRUAL LNMLS	1914	410	80	375	412
TOTAL NON-CURRENT LNMLS	2430	677	532	1411	780
RESTRUCTURED LNMLS 90+ DAYS P/D	0	0	0	0	0
RESTRUCTURED LNMLS NONACCRUAL	0	0	0	0	0
CURRENT RESTRUCTURED LNMLS	0	0	0	0	0
ALL OTHER REAL ESTATE OWNED	5173	5967	5714	5869	10155

% OF NON-CURR LNMLS BY LN TYPE*

	06/30/94 BANK	PEER 07	PCT	06/30/93 BANK	PEER 07	PCT	12/31/93 BANK	PEER 07	PCT	12/31/92 BANK	PEER 07	12/31/91 BANK	PEER 07
REAL ESTATE LNS-90+ DAYS P/D	0.00	0.11	42	0.00	0.16	39	0.00	0.13	39	1.51	0.20	0.41	0.31
-NONACCRUAL	2.03	0.66	80	0.00	0.88	17	0.00	0.82	18	1.51	0.90	0.45	0.98
-TOTAL	2.03	0.96	76	0.00	1.28	08	0.00	1.17	09	1.51	1.37	0.86	1.61
COML, OTHER LNS-90+ DAYS P/D	0.19	0.05	82	0.33	0.09	68	0.33	0.06	79	0.41	0.09	0.16	0.16
-NONACCRUAL	0.33	0.53	39	0.06	0.83	38	0.06	0.64	29	0.33	0.89	0.18	1.10
-TOTAL	0.52	0.77	31	0.39	1.14	38	0.39	0.90	40	0.74	1.24	0.34	1.55
INSTALLMENT LNS-90+ DAYS P/D	0.00	0.09	34	0.06	0.12	46	0.25	0.10	72	0.02	0.15	0.08	0.23
-NONACCRUAL	0.00	0.10	42	0.00	0.12	42	0.00	0.10	44	0.02	0.13	0.28	0.15
-TOTAL	0.00	0.31	15	0.06	0.39	22	0.25	0.34	49	0.02	0.45	0.36	0.57
CREDIT CARD PLANS-90+ DAYS P/D	0.85	0.13	82	1.22	0.14	86	0.17	0.13	62	0.69	0.14	1.46	0.22
-NONACCRUAL	0.00	0.00	92	0.00	0.00	88	0.00	0.00	92	0.00	0.00	0.00	0.00
-TOTAL	0.85	0.17	80	1.22	0.20	83	0.17	0.17	59	0.69	0.20	1.46	0.29
LEASE FINANCING-90+ DAYS P/D	NA	0.00		NA	0.00		NA	0.00		NA	0.00	NA	0.00
-NONACCRUAL	NA	0.00		NA	0.00		NA	0.00		NA	0.00	NA	0.00
-TOTAL	NA	0.00		NA	0.00		NA	0.00		NA	0.00	NA	0.00
GROSS LNMLS-90+ DAYS P/D	0.24	0.15	66	0.14	0.20	48	0.21	0.16	62	0.65	0.24	0.24	0.34
-NONACCRUAL	0.88	0.66	62	0.21	0.90	19	0.04	0.79	09	0.23	0.94	0.27	1.08
-TOTAL	1.11	0.93	59	0.35	1.26	17	0.25	1.09	15	0.88	1.35	0.52	1.61

SUPPLEMENTAL:
BANKS WITH AGRI LOANS OVER 5%:

	06/30/94 BANK	PEER 07	PCT	06/30/93 BANK	PEER 07	PCT	12/31/93 BANK	PEER 07	PCT	12/31/92 BANK	PEER 07	12/31/91 BANK	PEER 07
$NON-CURR AGRI LNS-90+ DAYS P/D	NA	0.02		NA	0.03		NA	0.01		NA	0.03	NA	0.01
-NONACCRUAL	NA	0.13		NA	0.30		NA	0.31		NA	0.39	NA	0.37
-TOTAL	NA	0.39		NA	0.54		NA	0.48		NA	0.64	NA	0.58

*BANKS UNDER $300 MILLION IN TOTAL ASSETS REPORT THIS LOAN DETAIL (BY TYPE) USING THEIR OWN INTERNAL CATEGORIZATION SYSTEMS.

APPENDIX 4B
(continued)

CERT #   DSB #
CHARTER #   NA COUNTY:

ANALYSIS OF PAST DUE, NONACCRUAL & RESTRUCTURED LOANS & LEASES
MEMORANDA INFORMATION

NON-CURR LN&LS BY LN TYPE ($000)

	06/30/94	06/30/93	12/31/93	12/31/92	12/31/91
LNS FIN COML RE-90+ DAYS P/D					
-NONACCRUAL	0	0	0	0	0
-TOTAL	0	0	0	0	0
CONST & LAND DEV-90+ DAYS P/D					172
-NONACCRUAL	1688	0	0	557	192
-TOTAL	1688	0	0	557	364
SINGLE & MULTI MTG-90+ DAYS P/D					
-NONACCRUAL	0	0	0	0	0
-TOTAL	0	0	0	0	0
NON-FARM/RESI MTG-90+ DAYS P/D					
-NONACCRUAL	0	0	0	0	0
-TOTAL	0	0	0	0	0

% NON-CURRENT LN&LS BY LN TYPE

	06/30/94 BANK	PEER 07	PCT	06/30/93 BANK	PEER 07	PCT	12/31/93 BANK	PEER 07	PCT	12/31/92 BANK	PEER 07	12/31/91 BANK	PEER 07
LNS FIN COML RE-90+ DAY P/D	0.00	0.00	97	0.00	0.00	96	0.00	0.00	97	0.00	0.00	0.00	0.00
-NONACCRUAL	0.00	0.00	95	0.00	0.00	96	0.00	0.00	92	0.00	0.00	0.00	0.00
-TOTAL	0.00	0.00	94	0.00	0.00	88	0.00	0.00	90	0.00	0.00	0.00	0.00
CONST & LAND DEV-90+ DAYS P/D	0.00	0.00	94	0.00	0.00	92	0.00	0.00	92	1.48	0.00	0.44	0.00
-NONACCRUAL	3.30	0.00	89	0.00	0.00	81	0.00	0.00	82	0.00	0.00	0.49	0.03
-TOTAL	3.30	0.00	88	0.00	0.01	77	0.00	0.00	79	1.48	0.02	0.93	0.20
SINGLE & MULTI MTG-90+ DAYS P/D	0.00	0.08	51	0.00	0.09	48	0.00	0.10	47	0.00	0.12	0.00	0.20
-NONACCRUAL	0.00	0.32	31	0.00	0.37	28	0.00	0.36	29	0.00	0.34	0.00	0.39
-TOTAL	0.00	0.57	19	0.00	0.65	17	0.00	0.63	17	0.00	0.66	0.00	0.81
NON-FARM/RESI MTG-90+ DAYS P/D	0.00	0.00	79	0.00	0.01	75	0.00	0.00	79	0.00	0.02	0.00	0.03
-NONACCRUAL	0.00	0.38	50	0.00	0.66	45	0.00	0.55	47	0.00	0.71	0.00	0.64
-TOTAL	0.00	0.56	44	0.00	0.95	37	0.00	0.73	41	0.00	1.05	0.00	1.05

OTHER PERTINENT RATIOS:

	06/30/94 BANK	PEER 07	PCT	06/30/93 BANK	PEER 07	PCT	12/31/93 BANK	PEER 07	PCT	12/31/92 BANK	PEER 07	12/31/91 BANK	PEER 07
IENC-LOANS TO TOTAL LOANS	0.44	0.60	08	0.47	0.61	13	0.46	0.57	20	0.57	0.63	0.73	0.76

% CURRENT RESTRUCT LN&LS BY TYPE:

	06/30/94 BANK	PEER 07	PCT	06/30/93 BANK	PEER 07	PCT	12/31/93 BANK	PEER 07	PCT	12/31/92 BANK	PEER 07	12/31/91 BANK	PEER 07
REAL ESTATE LOANS	0.00	0.00	72	0.00	0.01	74	0.00	0.01	73	0.00	0.01	0.00	0.00
INSTALLMENT LOANS	0.00	0.00	92	0.00	0.00	92	0.00	0.00	92	0.00	0.00	0.00	0.00
CREDIT CARD AND RELATED PLANS	0.00	0.00	99	0.00	0.00	99	0.00	0.00	99	0.00	0.01	0.00	0.03
COMMERCIAL AND ALL OTHER LOANS	0.00	0.00	78	0.00	0.00	76	0.00	0.00	77	0.00	0.01	0.00	0.01
LEASE FINANCING RECEIVABLES	NA	0.00		NA	0.00		NA	0.00		NA	0.00	NA	0.00
AGRI LOANS INCLUDED ABOVE	0.00	0.00		0.00	0.00		0.00	0.00		0.00	0.00	0.00	0.00

121

APPENDIX 4B
(*continued*)

CUMULATIVE AMOUNT AS A PERCENT OF ASSETS

	TOTAL			PERCENT REPRICED WITHIN 3 MONTHS			PERCENT REPRICED WITHIN 12 MONTHS		
ASSETS	BANK	PEER 07	PCT	BANK	PEER 07	PCT	BANK	PEER 07	PCT
LOANS AND LEASES (EXCL NONACC)	74.59	59.73	92	43.90	21.96	90	49.20	33.25	83
FIXED RATE BY MATURITY	33.16	29.35	90	2.47	2.67	50	7.77	6.74	59
FLOATING RATE BY REP INTERVAL	41.43	26.83	79	41.43	18.55	90	41.43	26.08	83
DEBT SECURITIES	10.74	28.23	06	0.68	2.56	19	1.77	7.40	08
FIXED RATE BY MATURITY	10.40	24.44	09	0.35	0.84	36	1.43	3.93	24
FLOATING RATE BY REP INTERVAL	0.33	1.95	34	0.33	1.00	44	0.33	1.89	35
FEDERAL FUNDS SOLD(OVERNIGHT)*	3.10	1.68	69	3.10	1.68	69	3.10	1.68	69
SECURITIES PURCHASED UNDER AGREEMENT TO RESELL*	0.00	0.00	97	0.00	0.00	97	0.00	0.00	97
INTEREST-BEARING BANK BALANCES**	2.78	0.03	94	0.00	0.00	98	2.78	0.00	94
TRADING ACCOUNT ASSETS*	0.00	0.00	98	0.00	0.00	98	0.00	0.00	98
TOTAL INT-BEARING ASSETS(IBA)	91.21	91.88	39	47.68	28.62	86	56.85	45.39	77
LIABILITIES									
DEPOSITS IN FOREIGN OFFICES**	NA	2.65							
CD'S OF $100,000 OR MORE	9.14	5.92	75	3.77	2.48	69	7.83	4.76	76
FIXED RATE BY MATURITY	9.14	5.78	75	3.77	2.37	71	7.83	4.63	76
FLOATING RATE BY REP INTERVAL	0.00	0.00	84	0.00	2.00	85	0.00	4.00	84
OTHER TIME DEPOSITS	25.20	25.00	51	6.05	6.65	42	19.33	17.03	63
MONEY MARKET DEPOSIT ACCOUNTS*	7.27	11.94	21	7.27	11.94	21	7.27	11.94	21
OTHER SAVINGS DEP (EXCL MMDA)**	10.99	12.97	23						
NOW ACCOUNTS*	8.40	11.97	22	8.40	11.97	22	8.40	11.97	22
FEDERAL FUNDS PURCH(OVERNIGHT)*	0.00	0.16	66	0.00	0.16	66	0.00	0.16	66
SECURITIES SOLD UNDER AGREEMENT TO REPURCHASE*	0.00	0.19	62	0.00	0.19	62	0.00	0.19	62
OTHER BORROWED MONEY**	13.51	0.04	98						
SUB NOTES & DEBENTURES**	0.00	0.00	95						
TREASURY NOTES*	0.20	0.02	77	0.20	0.02	77	0.20	0.02	77
TOTAL INT-BEARING LIABS (IBL)	74.71	75.79	41	25.68	38.22	08	43.03	51.77	19
NET POSITION (IBA - IBL)	16.50	15.90	55	22.00	-9.02	96	13.81	-5.92	90

*INDICATES ITEMS THAT ARE NOT REPORTED BY MATURITY/REPRICING INTERVAL; HOWEVER, REPRICING ASSUMPTIONS WERE MADE.
**INDICATES ITEMS THAT ARE NOT REPORTED BY MATURITY/REPRICING INTERVAL; HOWEVER, NO REPRICING ASSUMPTIONS WERE MADE.

APPENDIX 4B
(continued)

CERT #   DSB #
CHARTER #   NA   COUNTY:

LIQUIDITY AND INVESTMENT PORTFOLIO

	06/30/94	06/30/93	12/31/93	12/31/92	12/31/91
TEMPORARY INVESTMENTS	22172	490069	36650	43492	45573
CORE DEPOSITS	186854	197930	190243	187875	180221
VOLATILE LIABILITIES	27388	50372	55278	26968	29493
NON-CUR DEBT SECURITIES & OTH ASSETS:					
-90+ DAYS P/D	0	0	0	0	0
-NONACCRUAL	0	0	0	0	0
CURRENT-RESTRUCTURED DEBT SEC	0	0	0	0	0

	06/30/94 BANK	PEER 07	PCT	06/30/93 BANK	PEER 07	PCT	12/31/93 BANK	PEER 07	PCT	12/31/92 BANK	PEER 07	12/31/91 BANK	PEER 07
PERCENT OF TOTAL ASSETS													
TEMPORARY INVESTMENTS	7.64	10.90	33	17.57	12.51	73	12.79	12.60	53	17.84	12.99	19.40	12.31
CORE DEPOSITS	64.63	81.40	04	70.89	82.01	07	68.80	82.19	04	77.07	82.61	76.72	81.09
VOLATILE LIABILITIES	9.44	8.83	56	16.04	8.76	89	19.18	8.51	92	11.06	8.56	12.56	10.06
LIQUIDITY RATIOS													
VOLATILE LIABILITY DEPENDENCE	2.10	-2.48	63	0.64	-4.91	66	7.91	-5.13	85	-9.29	-5.82	-9.62	-2.88
BROKERED DEPOSITS TO DEPOSITS	1.31	0.00	95	0.00	0.00	90	0.00	0.00	91	0.00	0.00	0.00	0.00
TEMP INV TO VOLATILE LIABILITIES	80.96	137.85	35	97.41	162.38	34	66.68	167.99	09	161.27	172.74	154.52	132.78
TEMP INV LESS VOL LIAB TO ASSETS	-1.80	-1.85	35	-0.47	-1.54	34	-6.39	-3.90	14	6.78	4.40	6.85	2.13
NET LOANS & LEASES TO DEPOSITS	100.89	67.31	98	84.60	65.34	93	65.21	65.78	47	74.64	64.62	71.01	66.73
NET LN&LS TO CORE DEPOSITS	115.20	73.30	97	95.40	71.05	91	107.42	65.26	97	84.27	57.15	82.35	73.63
NET LOANS & LEASES TO ASSETS	74.22	59.19	92	67.62	57.98	79	73.90	58.07	93	64.95	57.55	62.35	59.48
NET LN&LS & SBLC TO ASSETS	74.37	59.80	91	67.73	58.61	76	74.00	58.70	92	65.27	58.18	63.18	60.14
SECURITIES MIX													
HELD-TO-MATURITY % TOTAL SECS													
U.S.TREAS & GOVT AGENCIES	0.00	20.84	27	47.95	51.66	45	51.49	53.13	47	46.43	53.06	29.00	50.44
MUNICIPAL SECURITIES	9.09	9.14	51	14.95	11.82	58	13.02	11.22	56	15.87	11.11	27.01	12.97
PASS-THROUGH MTG BACKED SECS	0.00	2.03	50	0.00	9.64	24	0.00	9.19	25	0.00	9.15	0.00	9.63
CMO & REMIC MTG BACKED SECS	0.00	0.64	70	0.00	5.52	44	0.00	5.03	44	0.00	4.72	43.87	2.71
OTHER DOMESTIC DEBT SECS	0.00	0.07	89	28.91	1.46	87	24.24	0.97	86	32.31	2.02	0.00	3.69
FOREIGN DEBT SECURITIES	NA	NA		0.00	0.00	83	0.00	0.00	84	0.00	0.00	0.00	0.00
INVESTMENTS IN MUTUAL FUNDS	NA	NA		0.00	0.00	97	0.00	0.00	98	0.00	0.00	0.00	0.00
OTHER EQUITY SECURITIES	NA	NA		8.20	0.41	94	9.25	0.54	95	5.39	0.35	0.13	0.24
LESS: UNREALIZED LOSS (MBS)	NA	NA		0.00	0.00	99	0.00	0.00	99	0.00	0.00	0.00	12.97
TOTAL HELD-TO-MATURITY	9.09	52.87	12	100.00	100.00		100.00	100.00		100.00	100.00	100.00	100.00
AVAILABLE-FOR-SALE % TOTAL SECS													
U.S.TREASURY & GOVT AGENCIES	62.07	24.46	88	NA	NA		NA	NA		NA	NA	NA	NA
MUNICIPAL SECURITIES	0.00	0.03	75	NA	NA		NA	NA		NA	NA	NA	NA
PASS-THROUGH MTG BACKED SECS	0.00	2.49	50	NA	NA		NA	NA		NA	NA	NA	NA
CMO & REMIC MTG BACKED SECS	0.00	1.44	59	NA	NA		NA	NA		NA	NA	NA	NA
OTHER DOMESTIC DEBT SECURITIES	22.72	0.90	98	NA	NA		NA	NA		NA	NA	NA	NA
FOREIGN DEBT SECURITIES	0.00	0.00	83	NA	NA		NA	NA		NA	NA	NA	NA
INVESTMENTS IN MUTUAL FUNDS	0.00	0.00	97	NA	NA		NA	NA		NA	NA	NA	NA
OTHER EQUITY SECURITIES	6.12	0.66	87	NA	NA		NA	NA		NA	NA	NA	NA
TOTAL AVAILABLE-FOR-SALE	90.91	47.13	87	NA	NA		NA	NA		NA	NA	NA	NA
DEBT SECURITIES UNDER 1 YEAR	16.45	27.82	25	41.74	28.93	73	31.84	28.95	57	45.03	29.13	17.10	27.63
DEBT SECURITIES 1 TO 5 YEARS	78.44	45.17	95	51.84	41.40	69	61.15	42.38	81	52.16	41.45	73.59	40.83
DEBT SECURITIES OVER 5 YEARS	5.11	21.24	19	6.42	24.19	22	7.00	22.98	23	2.81	23.29	9.31	24.67
OTHER SECURITIES RATIOS:													
APP(DEP) IN HTM SEC TO HTM SEC	-0.77	-1.08	56	1.27	2.26	23	1.24	1.24	48	0.63	1.79	2.41	2.94
APP(DEP) IN HTM SEC TO LQY CAP	-0.07	-1.62	56	0.99	2.73	07	0.71	4.00	20	0.55	6.05	1.07	9.72
PLEDGED SECURITIES TO TOT SEC	11.71	27.73	24	16.67	26.79	34	18.47	26.31	38	11.88	26.81	31.23	29.02

APPENDIX 4B
(continued)

CERT # ___ DSB # ___
CHARTER # NA

RISK-BASED CAPITAL ANALYSIS

PAGE 11A

RISK-BASED CAPITAL ($000)	06/30/94	06/30/93	12/31/93	12/31/92	12/31/91
TIER ONE CAPITAL					
+ COMMON EQUITY	35629	29522	33012	27281	23449
+ NONCUMULATIVE PERP PREFD STOCK	0	0	0	0	0
+ MINORITY INTEREST UNCONS SUBS	0	0	0	0	0
- INELIGIBLE DEF TAX ASSETS	0	0	0	NA	NA
- INELIGIBLE INTANGIBLES	0	0	0	0	0
NET TIER ONE	35629	29522	33012	27281	23449
TIER TWO CAPITAL					
+ ALLOWABLE SUB DEBT & LTD LIFE	0	0	0	0	0
+ CUMULATIVE PREFERRED STOCK	0	0	0	0	0
+ MANDATORY CONVERTIBLE DEBT	0	0	0	0	0
+ ALLOWABLE LN&LS LOSS ALLOWANCE	3004	2162	2339	2008	1917
+ AGRICULTURAL LOSS DEFERRAL	0	0	0	0	0
+ NET WORTH CERTIFICATES	0	0	0	0	0
NET ELIGIBLE TIER TWO*	3004	2162	2339	2008	1917
TOTAL RBC BEFORE DEDUCTIONS	38633	31684	35351	29289	25366
- TIER ONE & TIER TWO HOLDINGS	0	0	0	0	0
- RECIPROCAL CAPITAL HOLDINGS	0	0	0	0	0
TOTAL RISK-BASED CAPITAL	38633	31684	35351	29289	25366
RISK-WEIGHTED ASSETS(**)					
ON-BALANCE SHEET					
CATEGORY TWO - 20%	7266	11043	8532	9790	11577
CATEGORY THREE - 50%	9502	7028	8912	6114	4140
CATEGORY FOUR - 100%	223154	200605	218440	172418	165228
TOTAL ON-BALANCE SHEET	239923	218676	235884	188323	180945
MEMO: CATEGORY ONE - 0%	14923	11508	11567	12182	5432
OFF-BALANCE SHEET					
CATEGORY TWO - 20%	0	0	0	0	0
CATEGORY THREE - 50%	0	0	0	0	0
CATEGORY FOUR - 100%	2863	3173	2977	4082	3463
TOTAL OFF-BALANCE SHEET	2863	3173	2977	4082	3463
MEMO: CATEGORY ONE - 0%	0	0	0	0	0
ADJUSTMENTS TO RISK-WEIGHTED ASSETS					
RISK-WEIGHTED ASSET BEFORE DED	242786	221849	238661	192405	184408
- INELIGIBLE DEF. TAX ASSETS	0	0	0	NA	NA
- INELIGIBLE INTANGIBLES	0	0	0	0	0
- RECIPROCAL CAPITAL HOLDINGS	0	0	0	0	0
- EXCESS ALLOWABLE LN&LS LOSS AL	0	0	0	0	0
- ALLOCATED TRANSFER RISK RESERV	0	0	0	0	0
TOTAL RISK-WEIGHTED ASSETS	242786	221849	238661	192405	184408

RISK-BASED CAPITAL(***)	BANK	PEER 07	PCT	BANK	PEER 07	PCT	BANK	PEER 07	PCT	BANK	PEER 07	BANK	PEER 07
TIER ONE RBC TO RISK-WGT ASSETS	15.68	13.24	64	13.61	13.03	56	13.82	13.02	52	14.18	12.49	12.72	11.72
TOTAL RBC TO RISK-WEIGHT ASSETS	15.91	14.46	64	14.31	14.28	56	14.80	14.24	58	15.22	13.69	13.76	12.90
TIER ONE LEVERAGE CAPITAL	12.24	8.36	94	11.72	8.07	94	11.52	8.10	92	11.35	7.77	10.52	7.48
OTHER CAPITAL RATIO:													
DEF TAX ASSET TO T1 CAP	3.34	2.95	55	1.66	1.98	46	2.17	1.66	54	NA		NA	

*NET ELIGIBLE TIER TWO RISK-BASED CAPITAL CANNOT EXCEED NET TIER ONE RISK-BASED CAPITAL.
**BANK DID NOT REPORT ALL SCHEDULE RC-R DATA, THEREFORE, RISK-WEIGHTED ASSETS ARE ESTIMATED.
(***) TIER ONE CAPITAL AFTER 12/31/93 EXCLUDES FASB 115 NET UNREALIZED HOLDING GAIN/LOSS ON AVAILABLE-FOR-SALE SECURITIES.

APPENDIX 4B
(concluded)

CERT # ____ DSB # ____
CHARTER # ____ NA COUNTY: ____

EARNINGS AND PROFITABILITY

INCOME ANALYSIS (JULY 1ST THROUGH JUNE 30TH)

Period groups: LAST-FOUR-QUARTERS 1993-1994 · 1992 · 1991-1992 · 1990-1991 · 1989-1990. Each period reports BANK, PEER 07 and PCT; the 1989-1990 group reports BANK and PEER 07 only. Middle-period PEER/PCT columns are too faint to read reliably and are left blank.

PERCENT OF AVERAGE ASSETS

Item	93-94 BANK	93-94 PEER 07	93-94 PCT	1992 BANK	91-92 BANK	90-91 BANK	89-90 BANK	89-90 PEER 07
INTEREST INCOME (TE)	7.76	6.97	66	8.39	9.12	11.24	12.11	9.90
− INTEREST EXPENSE	2.70	2.43	75	3.14	4.24	5.32	5.35	5.50
NET INTEREST INCOME (TE)	5.08	4.50	79	5.25	4.88	5.91	6.76	4.40
+ NONINTEREST INCOME	2.07	0.94	92	1.77	1.74	1.63	1.62	0.80
− MEMO: FEE INCOME	0.82	0.20	93	0.76	0.72	NA	NA	NA
− NONINTEREST EXPENSE	3.38	3.63	40	3.62	3.90	3.87	4.30	3.43
= PROVISION: LOAN/LEASE LOSSES	0.33	0.16	61	0.73	0.47	0.35	0.31	0.31
= PRETAX OPERATING INCOME (TE)	3.42	1.70	97	2.67	2.25	3.33	3.77	1.54
+ REALIZED GAINS/LOSSES SECS	0.00	−0.01		0.07	0.00	0.01	0.02	0.00
= PRETAX NET OPERATING INC(TE)	3.42	1.73	97	2.74	2.27	3.34	3.78	1.56
NET OPERATING INCOME	2.34	1.12	98	1.89	1.50	2.37	2.44	0.99
ADJUSTED NET OPERATING INCOME	2.63	1.17	98	1.85	1.47	2.34	2.71	1.08
NET INCOME	2.34	1.13	97	1.75	1.50	2.17	2.68	1.00

MARGIN ANALYSIS

Item	93-94 BANK	93-94 PEER 07	93-94 PCT	1992 BANK	91-92 BANK	90-91 BANK	89-90 BANK	89-90 PEER 07
INT INC (TE) TO AVG EARN ASSETS	8.48	7.56	88	9.15	10.09	12.18	13.29	10.72
INT EXPENSE TO AVG EARN ASSETS	2.94	2.64	73	3.42	4.69	5.77	5.87	5.96
NET INT INC-TE TO AVG EARN ASST	5.54	4.88	79	5.73	5.40	6.41	7.42	4.76

LOAN & LEASE ANALYSIS

Item	93-94 BANK	93-94 PEER 07	93-94 PCT	1992 BANK	91-92 BANK	90-91 BANK	89-90 BANK	89-90 PEER 07
NET LOSS TO AVERAGE TOTAL LN&LS	0.12	0.20	42	0.25	0.71	0.18	0.05	0.37
EARNINGS COVERAGE OF NET LOSS(X)	41.49	17.47	77	16.20	5.35	25.50	63.70	9.10
LN&LS ALLOWANCE TO NET LOSSES(X)	11.42	8.62	64	4.99	1.69	6.41	17.64	4.32

CAPITALIZATION

Item	93-94 BANK	93-94 PEER 07	93-94 PCT	1992 BANK	91-92 BANK	90-91 BANK	89-90 BANK	89-90 PEER 07
CASH DIVIDENDS TO NET INCOME	10.02	31.72	24	12.50	9.55	4.73	4.11	39.71
RETAIN EARNS TO AVG TOTAL EQUITY	18.67	7.88	96	13.36	12.85	22.28	27.53	6.53

YIELD ON OR COST OF (1993-1994)

Item	BANK	PEER 07	PCT
TOTAL LOANS & LEASES (TE)	9.40	8.70	79
TOTAL LOANS	9.40	8.67	79
REAL ESTATE**	8.37	8.74	36
COMMERCIAL TIME, DEMAND, OTH**	9.89	8.23	86
INSTALLMENT**	10.18	9.42	69
CREDIT CARD PLANS	12.17	13.85	34
MEMO: AGRICULTURAL LNS IN ABOVE	NA		
TOTAL INVESTMENT SECURITIES (TE)	5.79	5.88	45
U.S. TREASURIES & AGENCIES	4.72	5.45	33
STATE & POLITICAL SUB (BOOK)	5.22	5.77	35
STATE & POLITICAL SUB (TE)	7.68	8.39	35
OTHER SECURITIES	5.83	6.24	42
INTEREST-BEARING BANK BALANCES	7.32	5.10	95
FEDERAL FUNDS SOLD & RESALES	2.93	3.82	88
FEDERAL INT-BEARING DEPOSITS	3.61	3.19	08
TOTAL INT-BEARING DEPOSITS	2.66	NA	87
TRANSACTION ACCOUNTS	2.84	2.10	75
MONEY MARKET DEPOSIT ACCOUNTS	3.00	2.62	81
OTHER SAVINGS DEPOSITS	3.43	2.65	81
LARGE CERTIFICATES OF DEPOSIT	4.33	3.36	61
ALL OTHER TIME DEPOSITS	5.00	4.07	71
FEDERAL FUNDS PURCH & REPOS	0.00	3.21	05
OTHER BORROWED MONEY	3.59	2.89	62
SUBORDINATED NOTES & DEBENTURES	NA	7.22	
ALL INTEREST-BEARING FUNDS	3.66	3.22	83

**BANKS UNDER $100 MILLION IN TOTAL ASSETS REPORT THIS LOAN DETAIL (BY TYPE) USING THEIR OWN INTERNAL CATEGORIZATION SYSTEMS.

Chapter Five

Bank Capital

CAPITAL REQUIREMENTS

Bank regulators require commercial banks to maintain a minimum amount of capital relative to the risky assets they hold. Failure to do so may result in closure of the bank. Thus, at the minimum, capital is important because bank regulators say it is important. It is also important to bank creditors and stockholders, who also have an interest in the bank's safety, soundness, and prosperity.

What is capital? The Canada Deposit Insurance Corporation provides a general definition of capital: "the investment in, or contribution to, the business of a member institution that ranks behind depositors and other creditors as to the entitlement to repayment or return on investment."[1] That's a starting point; a more detailed definition follows.

Tier 1: Core Capital

The capital requirements for commercial banks are shown in Table 5–1. They fall into two categories, Tier 1 and Tier 2 capital. Tier 1 capital is called *core capital*. It includes the owner's equity less goodwill and other intangibles.[2] This is the equivalent of net worth in nonbank organizations. Core capital must equal or exceed 4 percent of risk-weighted assets, which will be defined shortly.

---

[1] Canada Deposit Insurance Corporation, *Standards of Sound Business and Financial Practices: Capital Management,* 1993, p. 3.

[2] Net unrealized losses of equity securities are deducted from Tier 1 capital, but net unrealized losses of debt securities deemed available-for-sale are not deducted. National bank regulators consider unrealized securities gains and losses of the entire investment portfolio when evaluating capital adequacy. See *OCC Bulletin,* OCC 94-68, Regulatory Treatment under FAS 115, Final Rule, December 22, 1994.

TABLE 5–1
Capital Requirements

Tier 1 Capital (core capital)

Tier 1 capital must equal or exceed 4 percent of risk-weighted assets

Common stockholders' equity
Noncumulative perpetual preferred stock
Minority interest in consolidated subsidiaries
Less goodwill and other ineligible intangibles (including mortgage servicing rights)
Less net unrealized losses on marketable securities*

Tier 2 Capital (supplementary capital)

Tier 2 capital is limited to 100 percent of Tier 1 capital†

Allowance (reserve) for loan losses
Limited-life preferred stock
Hybrid capital instruments
Subordinated debt
Revaluation reserves
Less investments in unconsolidated subsidiaries, reciprocal holdings of banking organizations' capital securities, other deductions

Total Capital

Tier 1 + Tier 2 less deductions must equal 8 percent of risk-weighted assets

---

* Effective December 31, 1994 (Federal Reserve Board), 59 *Federal Register,* 63241-5, 66662-6 (FDIC), 60552-5 (OCC).

† Amounts in excess of Tier 1 do not qualify as capital.

Tier 2: Supplementary Capital

Tier 2 capital supplements the owner's equity. It includes subordinated long-term debt, hybrid debt instruments, and limited-life preferred stock. Bank regulators believe that holders of long-term debt and equity securities provide a form of capital and that their claims are inferior to those of depositors.

Reserve for loan losses.   Tier 2 capital also includes the *allowance for loan losses,* also known as the *reserve for loan losses.*[3] It repre-

---

[3] For an excellent discussion of this topic, see John R. Walter, "Loan Loss Reserves," *Economic Review,* Federal Reserve Bank of Richmond, July/August 1991, pp. 20–30; For simplicity, we ignore leases.

sents the amount of loans the bank believes it will be unable to collect. The reserve appears on the asset side of the balance sheet as a deduction from total loans. Total loans less the reserve for loan losses is called *net loans*. We ignored the reserve account In the previous example, which illustrated the effect of loan losses on capital. The deduction of the reserve for loan losses helps to avoid overstating the true value of the loans.

The reserve for loan losses can be as high as 1.25 percent of risk-weighted assets for computing capital requirements. The actual ratio of the reserve to total loans and leases is somewhat higher. In the first quarter of 1995, the ratio was 2.18 percent for FDIC-insured commercial banks.[4] Because of regional differences in the economy, it ranged from a high of 2.62 percent in the Northeast to a low of 1.62 percent in the Southwest.

The reserve for loan losses is maintained by making periodic charges against earnings, which appear in the *provision for loan losses (PLL)* in the income statement. Banks periodically increase the PLL, which reduces their earnings but increases their reserves for loan losses. The charges to the PLL are made when the bank believes certain loans are likely to be uncollectible, when the loan portfolio increases, or when an unexpected charge-off occurs for which funds were not set aside. During periods of high earnings, some banks use the PLL to "smooth" earnings, lower taxes, or boost the reserve account.

Tier 2 capital is limited to 100 percent of Tier 1 capital. Banks can have more than the required amount of subordinated debt, preferred stock, and so on, but the amount that will be counted toward the capital requirement is limited. In total, Tier 1 plus Tier 2 capital equals 8 percent or more of risk-adjusted assets.

Risk-Weighted Assets

Table 5–2 shows the risk weights assigned to various categories of assets. The assets are divided into four categories, ranging from 0 percent risk weights for the least risky assets to 100 percent weights for the riskiest assets. Simply stated, cash has the least risk and loans have the greatest risk.

To some extent, banks have shifted their loan portfolios to take advantage of the lower weights. For example, banks may shift from high-yield loans to lower-yielding government securities, which will lower the

---

[4] *FDIC Quarterly Banking Profile*, First Quarter 1995, Table 1-III-A.

TABLE 5–2
Risk-Based Capital Asset Classification*

Balance Sheet

Category 1: 0% Risk Weight

Cash and balances due from Federal Reserve banks

Treasury and government agency securities,

GNMA mortgage-backed securities

Federal Reserve stock

OECD government unconditionally guaranteed securities

Repurchase agreements, securities lending, certain collateralized letters of credit, and other collateralized on– and off–balance sheet credit exposures.†

Category 2: 20% Risk Weight

Cash items in the process of collection

FNMA, FHLMC mortgage-backed securities

State and local government general obligation bonds

Claims on other banks

US government, its agencies, and OECD government conditionally guaranteed loans and claims

Category 3: 50% Risk Weight

State and local government revenue bonds

Selected private mortgage-backed securities

Mortgage loans on 1–4 family residential property

Category 4: 100% Risk Weight

All other private loans not previously mentioned (commercial and industrial, commercial mortgage, LDC, etc.)

Bank premises

Industrial development bonds

Certain intangible assets

Off–Balance Sheet

Category 1: 0% Risk Weight

Loan commitments with less than 1 year to maturity

Category 2: 20% Risk Weight

Commercial letters of credit and other trade-related claims

Category 3: 50% Risk Weight

Loan commitments with maturities of 1 year or more, revolving credit facilities, etc.

Category 4: 100% Risk Weight

Standby letters of credit, assets sold with recourse, counterparty credit risk exposure in derivatives contracts

---

* This listing is not complete. Only selected assets and off–balance sheet items are shown.

† Effective December 31, 1994, 59 *Federal Register,* pp. 66642–5.

required capital. Similarly, conventional mortgage loans have a 100 percent weight, while FNMA securitized mortgage loans have a 20 percent weight. Thus, banks may shift from originating mortgages to buying collateralized mortgage loans. If risk-weighted capital requirements were the only factors to consider, banks would shift their portfolios in favor of securitized loans. However, yields, servicing fees, and other factors must be taken into account.

Collateralized transactions, such as securities lending, repurchase agreements, and collateralized letters of credit, differ from other transactions in that the collateral reduces the bank's credit risk. The extent to which the credit risk is reduced depends on the quality of the collateral and the effectiveness of the pledge,[5] for example, transactions collateralized by cash or government securities issued by the Organization of Economic Cooperation and Development (OECD) or US government agencies.

The mechanics of dealing with the weights and portfolio decisions are complex. For example, in December 1994, the FDIC issued a final ruling concerning *Financial Accounting Standard 115*, which requires institutions to recognize as a separate component of stockholders' equity net gains or losses on securities that are deemed available-for-sale. These are securities that the bank does not have a positive intent and ability to hold until maturity, but also does not intend to actively trade. The final rule is that net unrealized holding losses on available-for-sale *equity* securities (but not debt securities) with readily determinable fair values will be deducted from elements that determine Tier 1 capital. All other unrealized holding gains or losses on available-for-sale securities will be excluded from the elements that determine Tier 1 capital. However, they will be included as a factor that examiners consider in their assessment of an institution's capital adequacy.[6] Note that banks are required to report FAS 115 (Accounting for Certain Investments in Debt and Equity Securities) on their quarterly Reports of Condition and Income (*Call Reports*).

Many banks have substantial off–balance sheet claims. These include loan commitments, letters of credit, derivatives, and more. These claims have also been assigned risk weights by the bank regulators and must be backed by bank capital.

---

[5] See 12 CFR, Part 3, for the OCC's ruling on risk-based capital guidelines: collateralized transactions.

[6] "FDIC Adopts Capital Rule for Unrealized Gains and Losses on Securities," *FDIC News Release*, PR-85-94, December 20, 1994.

Prompt Corrective Action

Bank regulators monitor the level of banks' capital to reduce the chances of bank failure and protect the FDIC insurance fund. Bank regulators are required to take *prompt corrective action* when a bank falls below specified "tripwires." For example, banks with a total risk-based ratio (qualifying total capital to risk-weighted assets) of 10 percent or more, Tier 1 capital of 6 percent or more, and a leverage ratio (Tier 1 capital to average consolidated assets) of 5 percent or more are considered *well capitalized.* The definitions for the other capital zones (*adequately capitalized* to *critically undercapitalized*) are presented in Table 5–3.[7]

Table 5–3 does not show the sanctions for the banks in each capital zone. Well-capitalized and adequately capitalized banks may not make

TABLE 5–3
Prompt Corrective Action Capital Zones

Capital Zones	Total Risk-Based Ratio*		Tier 1 Risk-Based Ratio†		Leverage Ratio‡
Well capitalized	10% or above	and	6% or above	and	5% or above
Adequately capitalized	8% or above	and	4% or above	and	4% or above§
Undercapitalized	Under 8%	or	Under 4%	or	Under 4%¶
Significantly undercapitalized	Under 6%	or	Under 3%	or	Under 3%
Critically undercapitalized#					

* Ratio of qualifying total capital to risk-weighted assets.

† Ratio of Tier 1 capital to risk-weighted assets.

‡ Ratio of Tier 1 capital to average total consolidated assets.

§,¶ The standard is 3 percent or above for a bank with a CAMEL rating of 1 in its most recent examination report.

The only criterion is a tangible equity to total assets ratio that is equal to or less than 2 percent. Tangible equity includes core capital, plus outstanding perpetual preferred stock, minus all intangible assets except purchased mortgage servicing rights.

Source: Catherine Lemieux, "FDICIA Mandated Capital Zones and the Banking Industry," *Financial Industry Trends, Annual 1993*, Federal Reserve Bank of Kansas City, 1993.

---

[7] For additional details about prompt corrective actions, see Kenneth Spong, *Banking Regulation: Its Purposes, Implementation, and Effects,* 4th ed., Federal Reserve Bank of Kansas City, 1994, Chapter 5.

capital distributions to managers or individuals with controlling interests that would impair the capital of the institution.

Undercapitalized banks are subject to the previously stated conditions. In addition, they must cease paying dividends, restore their capital, restrict their growth, and get regulatory approval for acquisitions, branches, and new activities. They may not solicit deposits at rates that are significantly higher than prevailing rates.

Significantly undercapitalized banks are subject to the previously stated conditions. In addition, they must raise capital or arrange for a merger. They may be required to reduce their assets (e.g., divest affiliates), elect a new board of directors, and fire certain officers. They cannot pay bonuses or raises, or cash dividends without regulatory approval.

Critically undercapitalized banks are subject to all of the conditions stated above. In addition, they must be placed in receivership within 90 days unless bank regulators determine that other measures will better achieve prompt corrective action. Such banks are prohibited from paying interest or principal on subordinated debt without regulatory approval. Still other restrictions apply.

Well Capitalized, but Still in Trouble

A bank can be well capitalized and still be in trouble. The capital zones pertain only to capital accounts; they do not provide information about the quality of loans or other aspects of safety and soundness that bank examiners consider. Accordingly, a bank can be well capitalized but have a significant number of problem loans and weak management that could result in a poor CAMEL rating.

THE ROLE OF CAPITAL

Capital Facilitates Growth

Initial source of funds.   Bank capital serves two primary functions: It is a source of funds that facilitates growth, and it absorbs unanticipated losses. Anticipated losses are recognized in the reserve for loan losses described previously.

As a condition for organizing a *de novo* (new) bank, bank regulators require a minimum amount of capital to finance the organization. The minimum amount of capital varies from state to state and depending on the location of the bank. For example, the minimum capital may be $3 million in rural areas and $5 million or more in metropolitan areas. The initial capital, usually in the form of common stock, provides part of the funds used to acquire resources (premises, equipment, and personnel), loans, and investments. Other funding comes primarily from deposits. The capital absorbs the start-up expenses and losses until the bank becomes profitable. That process may take two years or more.

Constrains growth.   As banks prosper, they retain earnings that become part of their equity capital. The periodic injections of retained earnings are used to support the bank's growth. For example, capital must be at least 8 percent of selected loans and investments. If the bank's capital, including retained earnings, is not sufficient to meet regulatory minimums, the bank will have to raise new capital. The alternative is for the bank to shrink in size. Thus, growth and capital go hand in hand. The amount of capital available constrains bank growth to limits that bank regulators believe are consistent with safety and soundness of the banking system.

In summary, the previous example demonstrates that capital can come from external sources, such as sales of stock, and from internal sources, such as retained earnings. Banks can also improve their capital position by selling assets and reducing liabilities.[8] However, the sale of loans, for example, may result in the loss of loan customers to those who bought the loans. In addition, it may leave the bank with poorer-quality, less liquid assets because the purchasers want only high-quality, marketable loans. Banks can sell other assets, too. To illustrate, AmSouth Bancorp sold its mortgage subsidiary and "spun off" its bond department.[9]

Loan limits.   Capital also limits the size of loans that banks can make to a single borrower. In the case of national banks, the limit is 15 percent of unimpaired capital and surplus for unsecured loans and 25 percent for loans fully secured by marketable collateral. Few banks, however, would lend that much to one borrower or to a group acting together. Nevertheless, it is clear that a bank with $10 million in capital is limited to

---

[8] For additional discussion of this point, see Forest E. Myers, *Basics for Bank Directors,* Federal Reserve Bank of Kansas City, December 1993, pp. 23–24.

[9] Kenneth Cline, "AmSouth Spinning Off its Bond Department to Morgan Keegan in Deal Termed 'Alliance,' " *American Banker,* May 17, 1995, p. 6; Kenneth Cline, "AmSouth to Eliminate 44 Branches, 1,000 Jobs," American Banker, April 25, 1995, pp. 1, 20.

a loan of $1.5 million, while a bank with $100 million in capital can make a $15 million loan. Banks can get around this limit by selling participations in loans that exceed their lending limits.

FDIC deposit insurance premiums.   The FDIC proposed risk-based deposit insurance premiums based on a bank's capitalization and the quality of its management.[10] Premiums will range from $0.04 per $100 of deposits for well-capitalized, well-managed banks to $0.31 per $100 of deposits for undercapitalized banks with weak management.

Capital Absorbs Unanticipated Losses

Once the bank is in operation, the primary role of capital from the bank regulator's point of view is to absorb unanticipated losses before they endanger the bank's insured deposits and to protect against failure. Anticipated losses are provided for in the allowance (reserve) for loan losses. If there is sufficient capital, uninsured depositors may be protected too. Recall that the Federal Deposit Insurance Corporation (FDIC) insures selected deposits. Deposits of state and local governments, for example, are not covered by the FDIC. The FDIC wants to minimize the likelihood that it will have to pay insured depositors in the event a bank fails. Therefore, the more capital the banks hold, the less risk the FDIC bears. Recall that in the 1980s, when the Federal Savings and Loan Insurance Corporation (FSLIC) did not have sufficient funds to pay depositors of failed savings and loan associations, the taxpayers footed the bill. As a result of that fiasco, the deposit insurance system was restructured into the system we have today. The current system of deposit insurance is predicated on the twin beliefs that banks should have a predetermined minimum amount of capital to absorb losses and the capital requirements should be based on the degree of risk of the assets held.

High Financial Leverage Is Risky

On average, corporations in the United States have 28 percent equity capital.[11] In the extreme, some firms have negative equity capital. Georgia Gulf Corporation, a chemical company that is listed on the New York

---

[10] "FDIC Proposes Cuts in Deposit Insurance Payments for Most Banks, No Changes Yet in Rates for Savings Associations," FDIC news release, PR-6-95, January 31, 1995.

[11] *Statistical Abstract of the United States, 1994*, Table 840; data are for 1991.

Stock Exchange, had a negative 23 percent equity capital as a result of restructuring in a leveraged buyout (LBO).[12] Negative equity is not uncommon in LBOs. In contrast, FDIC-insured commercial banks had only 7.7 percent (core) equity capital in 1995.[13] Stated otherwise, on average, corporations were financed by 72 percent debt and banks were financed by 92.3 percent debt! Banks have a substantially smaller cushion to absorb losses than other types of corporations.

Let's examine the implications of the high degree of financial leverage. Suppose a bank has $100 million in total assets and $10 million in capital. This a well-capitalized bank that has adequate capital for expansion. The bank is profitable, and the stockholders, managers, and employees want it to grow. The stockholders want higher stock prices and larger dividends. The managers and employees want the higher incomes that come with bank growth. Everyone wants growth, including the community served by the bank.

Bank with $100 Million in Assets, $10 Million in Capital

Assets ($ millions)		Liabilities and Equity ($ millions)	
Securities	$20	Deposits	$80
Loans	70	Borrowed funds	10
Other assets	10	Capital	10
Total	$100	Total	$100

In order to grow, the bank raises an additional $10 million in deposits and makes five loans of $2 million each. As shown below, total assets are $110 million and the bank has loans of $80 million. The bank is adequately capitalized to support the growth.

Bank with Additional $10 Million in Loans

Assets ($ millions)		Liabilities and Equity ($ millions)	
Securities	$20	Deposits	$90
Loans	80	Borrowed funds	10
Other assets	10	Capital	10
Total	$110	Total	$110

---

[12] For details about Georgia Gulf, see *The Value Line Investment Survey,* November 4, 1994, p. 1251. For a discussion of LBOs, see William D. Samson and Benton E. Gup, "The Hidden Side of Corporate Restructuring," *Tax Notes,* November 13, 1989, pp. 877–884.

[13] *FDIC Quarterly Banking Profile,* First Quarter, 1995, Table 1-A. Data represent the core capital (leverage) ratio for the first quarter of 1995.

Unfortunately, four of the $2 million loans became bad loans, and they are declared losses and charged off. The term *charged off* means the bank will not be able to collect anything from the loan, and the loan is not of sufficient quality to remain as assets on the bank's balance sheet. Therefore, the assets are reduced by $8 million, the capital is reduced by the same amount in our simplified example.

Bank after $8 Million in Losses

Assets ($ millions)		Liabilities and Equity ($ millions)	
Securities	$20	Deposits	$80
Loans	72	Borrowed funds	10
Other assets	10	Capital	2
Total	$102	Total	$102

Now the bank is critically undercapitalized, with only $2 million in capital. As a consequence, the bank must be placed in receivership within 90 days unless regulators decide to allow other actions. For all practical purposes, the bank has failed.

This simplified example highlights the point that even well-capitalized banks are thinly capitalized, and it does not take much in terms of unexpected losses to undermine a bank.

Stockholders versus Regulators

Bank regulators are interested in the safety and soundness of the banks they regulate. In contrast, stockholders are interested in the bank's profitability, and they are willing to take more risks than bank regulators. By definition, owning stocks is risky, and banking is the management of risk.

The relationship between bank equity capital and returns to stockholders can be seen in equation 5–1, which was introduced in Chapter Four (equation 4–4). The equation states that the return on equity (ROE) is equal to the return on assets (ROA) times a multiplier (M). The ROE is computed by dividing net income by total equity, which is Tier 1 (core) capital in our previous example. ROA is computed by dividing net income by average total assets. M is computed by dividing total assets by average total equity. The reciprocal of M is the core capital leverage ratio (1/M). Accordingly, a high multiplier, M, means a low core capital leverage ratio, 1/M. We will use equation 5–1 to show that the higher the equity capital, the lower the ROE to stockholders.

$$\text{Return on Equity} = \text{Return on Assets} \times \text{Multiplier}$$

$$\text{ROE} = \text{ROA} \times \text{M}$$

$$\frac{\text{Net Income}}{\text{Average Total Equity}} = \frac{\text{Net Income}}{\text{Average Total Assets}} \times \frac{\text{Total Assets}}{\text{Average Total Equity}}$$

$$(5\text{--}1)$$

For simplicity, assume a bank has total assets of $100 million and a net income of $1 million. Also assume total assets consist of risky loans and investments. The ROA is 1 percent, which is considered a good return for banks. In 1994, the average ROA for FDIC-insured commercial banks was 1.17 percent; in contrast, the average was 0.48 percent in 1990. In this example, the bank's net income and the ROA do not change (see Table 5–4). Only the amount of equity capital changes. If our hypothetical bank has $10 million in equity capital (the gross core capital leverage ratio 1/M is 10 percent), the ROE will be 10 percent.[14] If the bank had less capital— say, $7 million—the ROE would be 14.3 percent. Table 5–4 shows that

TABLE 5–4
Bank Equity vs. ROE

ROE *Net Income/Total Equity*	ROA *Net Income/Total Assets*	M *Total Assets/Total Equity*	1/M
$1/$10 = 10%	$1/$100 = 1%	$100/$10 = 10; 1/10	= 10%
$1/$9 = 11.1%	$1/$100 = 1%	$100/$9 = 11.1 1/11.1	= 9%
$1/$8 = 12.5%	$1/$100 = 1%	$100/$8 = 12.5 1/12.5	= 8%
$1/$7 = 14.3%	$1/$100 = 1%	$100/$7 = 14.3 1/14.3	= 7%
$1/$6 = 16.7%	$1/$100 = 1%	$100/$6 = 16.7 1/16.7	= 6%
$1/$5 = 20%	$1/$100 = 1%	$100/$5 = 20 1/20	= 5%
$1/$4 = 25%	$1/$100 = 1%	$100/$4 = 25 1/25	= 4%

---

[14] As mentioned in the previous chapter, this "gross" measure of core capital does not take into account deductions for goodwill, intangibles, or other factors.

Think about This!

Heads, the Stockholders Win; Tails, the Taxpayers Lose

It is well documented in the finance literature that stockholders have a general incentive to increase risk once debt has been issued.[1] This is especially true if the debt has an implicit government guarantee, such as FDIC-insured deposits. If the bank takes big risks and wins, the stockholders make a lot of money. If the bank loses, the stockholders have much less to lose than the depositors, who provide about 92 percent of the funds to operate the bank. To protect the insured deposits, bank regulators routinely monitor banks' behavior.

One solution to the problem is to restrict the investment of insured deposits to safe government securities. Risky investments in loans could be backed by funds raised in the capital markets that are not guaranteed by the government. This concept is called *narrow banking*.

[1] For a discussion of this point, see Michael Jensen and William Meckling, "Theory of the Firm: Managerial Behavior, Agency Costs and Ownership Structure," *Journal of Financial Economics*, October 1976, pp. 305–60.

the smaller the amount of capital, the higher the ROE for a given ROA. Accordingly, stockholders who want to increase ROE without a commensurate increase in net income, or ROA, prefer less capital to more. In reality, most banks strive to increase their ROAs. Recall that banks in the United States had a capital ratio 7.7 percent, which is a multiplier of 13.

CONCLUSION

The directors are responsible for ensuring that the quantity and quality of capital are sufficient to meet regulatory capital requirements and to foster the safe and sound growth of their banks. Banks require capital to ensure their growth and to serve as a cushion against unexpected losses.

Directors usually charge management with developing capital management policies, subject to their approval. The policies and the adequacy of capital should be reviewed periodically, but no less than once each year. Such reviews are imperative, because changes in regulations or accounting standards, such as FAS 115, may affect banks' capital requirements.

Chapter Six

Asset/Liability Management: Dealing with Interest Rate Risk

WHAT IS ASSET/LIABILITY MANAGEMENT?

The term *asset/liability management (ALM)* was first used in the late 1970s when bankers began to recognize the importance of managing both assets and liabilities simultaneously for the purposes of mitigating interest rate risk, providing liquidity, and enhancing the market value of their banks.[1] ALM is usually considered "short-term" in nature, focusing on near-term financial goals. Nevertheless, it is an integral part of a bank's overall planning process.

Interest Rate Risk Defined

The last thing a referee says to boxers before they begin their bout is "Gentlemen, defend yourselves at all times!" That is the basic theme of this chapter: Try your best to win, but defend yourself at all times. "Defend against what?" you may ask. The answer is: defend against interest rate risk. The Office of the Comptroller of the Currency defines *interest rate risk* as "the risk to earnings or capital arising from the movement of interest rates."[2] *Capital* refers to the economic value of equity, which is the present value of the assets less the present value of the liabilities, with adjustments for off–balance sheet activities.

---

[1] Banks face other risks, including credit risk, foreign exchange risk, business risk, and other risks that are important in terms of risk-based capital adequacy standards. For a discussion of these risks and capital standards, see United States General Accounting Office, *International Banking: Implementation of Risk-Based Capital Adequacy Standards*, GAO/NSIAD-91-80, 1991.

[2] "Q's & A's Clarify OCC Policy on Interest Rate Risk Management," OCC news release NR 95-63, June 20, 1995; *Interest Rate Risk Management*, OCC Bulletin 95-28, June 20, 1995.

The Canada Deposit Insurance Corporation defines interest rate risk as follows:

> Interest rate risk is the potential impact on a member's earnings and net asset values of changes in interest rates. Interest rate risk arises when an institution's principal and interest cash flows (including final maturities), both on– and off–balance sheet, have mismatched pricing dates. The amount of risk is a function of the magnitude and direction of interest rate changes and the size and maturity of the mismatch positions.[3]

These definitions provide a starting point for examining the effects of interest rate risk on banks and our discussion of ALM. In this chapter, we examine various techniques for defending against the *adverse consequences* of interest rate risk. The adverse consequences are losses in earnings and reductions in the bank's capital. However, not all interest rate risk is bad. In fact, you can take advantage of desirable interest rate changes to increase the income and value of your bank.

Figure 6–1 shows the levels of market rates of interest in recent years. Notice that Treasury bill rates peaked in 1989 at about 9 percent, declined to about 3 percent in 1993, and then increased sharply in 1994. The figure reveals that change is the only constant with respect to interest rates. Banks must predict the changes correctly in order to profit. That is easier said than done.

Investment Risk

Let's return to the definition of interest rate risk. The Bank for International Settlements (BIS)/Committee on Banking Regulations and Supervisory Practices states that interest rate risk has two elements: investment risk and income risk.[4]

Investment risk, sometimes called *price risk,* arises when changes in interest rates cause changes in the market value of fixed-rate and off–balance sheet items. An inverse relationship exists between changes in interest rates and the price of fixed-rate assets. In other words, when interest rates go up, the market value (price) of the fixed-rate assets goes down. In

---

[3] Canada Deposit Insurance Corporation, *Standards of Sound Business and Financial Practices: Interest Rate Risk Management,* n.d.

[4] Committee on Banking Regulations and Supervisory Practices, *Report on International Developments in Banking Supervision,* Report No. 6 (Basle, Switzerland: Bank for International Settlements, September 1988), Chapter VII.

FIGURE 6–1
Interest Rates and Bond Yields (Interest Rates Fell in April)

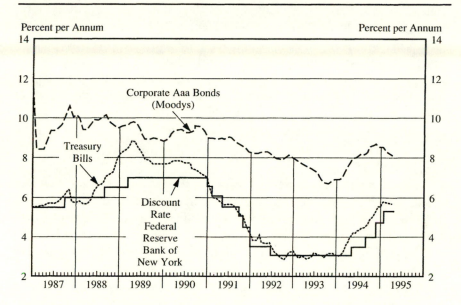

1994, the three-month Treasury bill rate increased from 3 percent to almost 6 percent. Some banks did not foresee the increase in interest rates and held securities portfolios that had large unrealized after-tax losses. Selected examples of such losses follow:[5]

Bank	Loss ($ millions)
PNC Bank	$699
Bank of America	610
Chemical Bank	517
Nations Bank	407
Keycorp	313
Fleet Financial	249
Wells Fargo	246
Banc One	184

The BIS argues that investment risk should be considered an opportunity cost rather than exposure to actual losses, except in the case of a

---

[5] Kelley Holland and Zachary Schiller, "Fixed Income, Broken Balance Sheets," *Business Week,* December 19, 1994, p. 103.

forced sale. In theory, when interest rates increase, low-yielding bonds are sold at a loss. The proceeds are then invested at current rates. The present value of the stream of income derived from investing at current rates will offset the loss. Therefore, in perfect markets, the impact on the bank's net worth should be neutral in the long term. However, accounting practices in most countries do not recognize this long-term neutrality, and trading portfolios are marked to market, which affects the bank's published net worth. The published net worth differs from the stock market valuation of the bank. Stock market values include attributes beyond balance sheet (and off–balance sheet) items. Such attributes include cash dividend payments, systematic risk (beta), franchise value, industry factors, and others.[6]

Suppose a bank has mostly fixed-rate assets. If interest rates increase, the market value of the bank's assets will decline. If those assets are marked-to-market values, the bank's liquidity and published net worth will be adversely affected. Bank regulators, who are concerned with safety and soundness, will exercise prompt corrective action and consider closing a bank when it is illiquid and when its published net worth shrinks to unacceptable levels.[7] Federal bank regulators evaluate banks' interest rate risk management practices and procedures to mitigate such problems.

Income Risk and Interest Rate Sensitivity

Income risk refers to the risk of losing income when movements in borrowing and lending rates are not perfectly synchronized. In banking jargon, it is a "gap" problem that arises when there is a mismatch, in terms of time and interest rates, between repricing both assets and liabilities. The OCC calls this *repricing risk.*

Assets and liabilities (both on– and off–balance sheet) may be classified as *rate-sensitive* or *non-rate-sensitive*, depending on their maturity and how often they are repriced. *Repricing* refers to the time when the interest rate on an instrument is adjusted. Some banks, such as Bank-

---

[6] Some of these issues are discussed in connection with market value accounting.

[7] The Comptroller of the Currency (OCC) also considers the market value of portfolio equity in assessing soundness. The *market value of portfolio equity* refers to the net market value, in the current interest rate environment, of an institution's existing assets, liabilities, and off–balance sheet instruments. For additional information, see *An Overview of Interest Rate Risk,* OCC staff paper (Washington, DC: Comptroller of the Currency, December 1989).

America Corporation, categorize certain assets in terms of their expected repricing periods based on historical experience rather than by their contractual repricing. Noncontractual repricing applies to certain consumer loans, deposits, and nonaccrual assets.[8] Assets and liabilities with one year or less to maturity are considered rate sensitive. Some assets with maturities up to five years or longer may also be rate sensitive.

The terms *fixed-rate loans* and *variable-rate loans* confuse the issue of rate sensitivity. The maturity and frequency of repricing assets determine rate sensitivity. For example, fixed-rate overnight loans mature and are repriced daily; therefore, they are rate-sensitive assets. In contrast, a variable-rate 25-year mortgage loan that resets the interest rates once every three years is a non-rate-sensitive asset.[9] Following are selected examples of both non-rate-sensitive and rate-sensitive assets and liabilities.

Non-Rate-Sensitive

Assets	Liabilities/Equity
Long-term fixed-rate business loans	Time deposits (long-term)
Long-term securities (e.g., bonds)	Fixed-rate notes and debentures
Mortgages (fixed-rate)	Equity capital

Rate-Sensitive

Assets	Liabilities/Equity
Floating-rate loans	Variable and short-term federal funds purchased
Federal funds sold	
Short-term securities	Other short-term, variable-rate nondeposit sources of funds

Basis Risk

Basis risk is due to differences between yield curves and markets. For example, suppose a two-year floating-rate loan is funded by a two-year fixed-rate CD with a spread of 100 basis points. The interest rate on the loan is reset every 90 days. If interest rates decline, the spread on the loan will diminish.

---

[8] BankAmerica Corporation, *Third Quarter: An Analytical Review and Form 10Q,* 1991, p. 36.

[9] Although mortgage loans with such terms are not issued today, some were issued in the early 1980s and are still on the books of the lenders.

Options Risk

Options risk occurs when a customer has the right level or timing of cash flows of an asset, liability, or off–balance sheet instrument. The refinancing of loans when interest rates decline is one example of this type of risk.

Yield Curve Risk

Yield curve risk occurs when the slope of the yield curve changes. For example, consider a structured note that is repriced every quarter. The repricing is based on the spread between three-month Treasury bills and five-year Treasury bonds. If the shape of the yield curve changes, the earnings stream and value of the note will change.

Trading Risk

Trading risk should not be confused with interest rate risk and income risk. *Trading risk* arises from mismanaged trading positions. The failure of the 233-year-old Barings PLC in 1995 is a glaring example of trading risk.[10] In that case, a single trader who speculated in futures and options caused the loss of about $1 billion and the failure of the bank. Speculating should not be confused with hedging, which is explained later in this chapter. The basic problem with Barings was that it lacked adequate internal controls to deal with this risk. Given the speed at which such transactions can be made, real-time controls are needed to measure and monitor trading risk, interest rate risk, and income risk.[11]

THE EFFECTS OF INTEREST RATE RISK ON INCOME AND VALUE

Gap and Net Interest Income

The *dollar gap* is the difference between rate-sensitive assets (RSA) and rate-sensitive liabilities (RSL) expressed in dollars:

$$\text{Gap} = \text{RSA} - \text{RSL} \tag{6-1}$$

---

[10] Marcus W. Brauchli and Nicholas Bray, "Barings PLC Officials May Have Been Aware of Traders Position," *The Wall Street Journal*, March 6, 1995, pp. A1, A7.

[11] For additional discussion, see FDIC, *Assessment of Interest Rate Risk*, FIL-60-90, August 26, 1994.

The dollar gap is widely used as a measure of interest rate sensitivity. When RSA exceeds RSL, a bank is said to be positively gapped; when RSA is less than RSL, a bank is negatively gapped. The dollar amount of the gap times the change (Δ represents change) in interest rates (r) gives the change in net interest income. *Net interest income (NII)* is interest income minus interest expense.

$$\Delta NII = Gap \times \Delta r \qquad\qquad\qquad (6\text{--}2)$$

For example, if a bank has a negative gap of $100 million and interest rates increase by 50 basis points (+0.005), NII will decline by $500,000. Notice that the negative gap is preceded by a minus (–) sign.

$$\Delta NII = Gap \qquad\qquad \times \Delta r$$
$$-\$500,000 = -\$100,000,000 \times 0.005$$

If interest rates had declined by 20 basis points (–0.002), NII would have increased by $200,000:

$$\Delta NII = Gap \qquad\qquad \times \Delta r$$
$$\$200,000 = \$100,000,000 \times -0.002$$

The use of gaps in this fashion assumes that no options are embedded in a bank's assets and liabilities. For example, adjustable-rate mortgages (ARMs) may have a 2 percent interest rate cap. In other words, interest rates on ARMs cannot increase more than 2 percentage points per year. In addition, there may be a lifetime cap—say, 6 percentage points—on mortgages. In 1994, market rates of interest increased 250 basis points. Therefore, banks that held low-yielding ARMs experienced losses in income and in the value of their portfolios.

Interest rate spreads.   Some financial managers think about managing assets and liabilities in terms of interest rate spreads. To illustrate the effects of interest rate risk on interest rate spreads, we will examine a small bank (with assets of $100 million or less) and a large bank (with assets of $1 billion or more). The proportions of their RSAs and RSLs are shown below. As a general rule, large banks tend to have relatively more rate-sensitive assets and liabilities than small banks. In this example, large banks have 60 percent RSA and small banks have 20 percent RSA. On the liability side of the balance sheet, large banks have 50 percent RSL and small banks have 40 percent RSL.

Assets		*Liabilities*	
Small-bank RSA	20%	Small-bank RSL	0%
Non-RSA	80%	Non-RSL	60%
	100%		100%
Large bank RSA	60%	Large-bank RSL	50%
Non-RSA	40%	Non-RSL	50%
	100%		100%

Using the following returns that can be earned on assets and costs of funds, the net interest spread is 3.8 percentage points for the small bank.

	Return on Assets	*Cost of Funds*
Rate-sensitive	12%	14%
Non-rate-sensitive	17%	11%

The net interest spread was calculated by multiplying the above interest rates by the proportions of assets and liabilities for each bank. For example, the average return earned on the assets of the small bank is 16 percent:

RSA: $0.20 \times 0.12 = 0.024$

Non-RSA: $0.80 \times 0.17 = \underline{0.136}$

$\quad\quad\quad\quad\quad\quad$ 0.160, or 16%

Similarly, the average cost of funds for the small bank is 12.2 percent:

RSL: $0.40 \times 0.14 = 0.056$

Non-RSL: $0.60 \times 0.11 = \underline{0.066}$

$\quad\quad\quad\quad\quad\quad$ 0.122, or 12.2%

The net interest spread is $16.0\% - 12.2\% = 3.8\%$.

If short-term interest rates increase 200 basis points (2 percent), the net interest spread on the small bank will decline to 3.4 percentage points, resulting in a loss of 40 basis points.

We can get the same result by using a modified version of equation 6–2. Equation 6–3 indicates that the change in the net interest spread is equal to the gap (expressed in percentage terms) times the change in interest rates:

$$\Delta \text{ Net Interest Spread} = \text{Gap\%} \times \Delta r \quad\quad\quad\quad (6\text{–}3)$$

$$-0.004 = -0.20 \times 0.02$$

The small bank has become negatively gapped as rates increased. Therefore, the smaller spread occurred because the proportion of the small bank's liabilities subject to the new, higher costs is greater than the proportion of its assets on which the higher rates can be charged.

The net interest spread for the large bank is 1.5%.

Average return

RSA: $0.60 \times 0.12 = 0.072$

Non-RSA: $0.40 \times 0.17 = \underline{0.068}$

$\qquad\qquad\qquad\qquad$ 0.140, or 14.0%

Average cost

RSL: $0.50 \times 0.14 = 0.070$

Non-RSA: $0.50 \times 0.11 = \underline{0.055}$

$\qquad\qquad\qquad\qquad$ 0.125, or 12.5%

Net interest spread $\qquad$ 0.015, or 1.5%

Because the large bank is positively gapped—rate-sensitive assets exceed rate-sensitive liabilities—it will benefit from the increase in interest rates. The net interest spread will increase to 1.7 percentage points, a gain of 20 basis points. Using equation 6–3, we get the same result:

$$\Delta \text{ Net Interest Spread} = \text{Gap\%} \times \Delta r$$
$$0.002 = 0.10 \quad \times 0.02$$

Effects on value.   The previous examples demonstrate that a bank's interest rate gap can affect its net interest income and net interest spread. If we assume the value of a bank is positively related to its net interest income, we can illustrate graphically the effects of interest rate changes on bank values. The top panel of Figure 6–2 shows the effects of interest rate changes on a bank that is positively gapped; that is, RSA > RSL (the symbol > means "greater than" and < means "less than"). If interest rates increase, the returns on assets will increase by more than the costs of the liabilities, thereby increasing the net interest income. As net interest income increases, the value of the bank rises. If interest rates decline, the costs of the liabilities will exceed the returns on the rate-

FIGURE 6–2
The Effects of Interest Rates on Bank Values

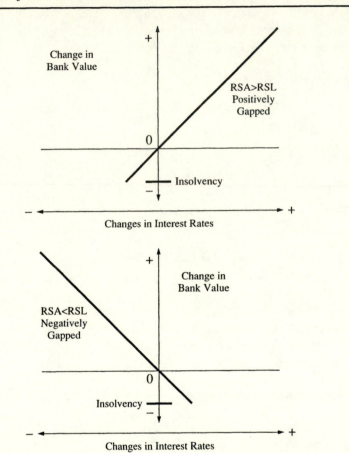

sensitive assets, and the net interest income will diminish. The value of the bank can decline and become insolvent.

The bottom panel of Figure 6–2 illustrates the effects of changes in interest rates on a negatively gapped bank. Rate sensitive assets are less than rate-sensitive liabilities (RSA < RSL). If interest rates increase, the value of the negatively gapped bank will decline because its costs will exceed its returns, resulting in lower net interest income. However, if interest rates decline, the costs will decline by more than the returns, thereby increasing the bank's net interest income and value.

Managing Interest Rate Spreads

Interest rate risk affects net interest income and the value of banks. For banks that are positively gapped, an increase in interest rates results in higher incomes and values. For banks that are negatively gapped, the reverse is true. This suggests that if banks gap correctly, they can increase their incomes and values.

Figure 6–3 shows one possible path of short-term interest rates over a business cycle. It also shows selected strategies to enhance income and values. During the recovery phase of a business cycle, short-term interest rates are expected to increase as business concerns require funds to

FIGURE 6–3
Spread Management Strategies

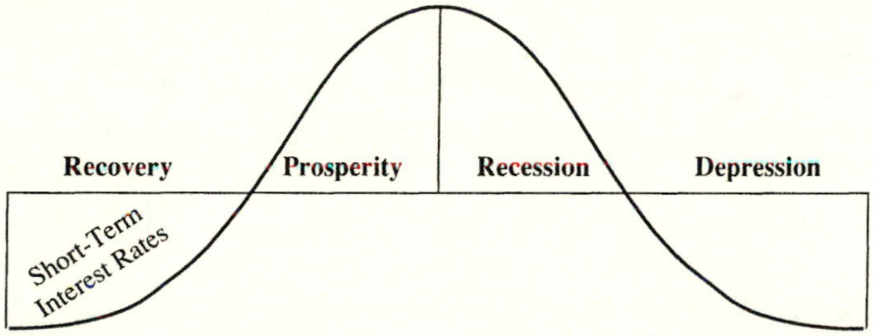

Phases of Business Cycle	Recovery	Prosperity	Recession	Depression
Strategies	*Short-Term Interest Rates*			
Assets:	• Increase rate-sensitive assets	• Encourage fixed-rate loans to lock in high yields	• Encourage fixed-rate loans	• Sell fixed-rate loans and investments to supplement income
	• Avoid fixed-rate loans			• Increase rate-sensitive assets in anticipation of higher rates when the recovery comes
Liabilities:	• Encourage fixed-cost sources of funds	• Encourage fixed-rate loans to lock in high yields	• Obtain short-term sources of funds	• Borrow long-term at fixed rate
		• Avoid high-cost fixed-rate sources		

Source: Based on Eugene A. Bonte and Gregg a Dieguez, "Spread Management: How to Maintain Profitability," *Savings and Loan News*, November 1979, pp. 54–59.

rebuild inventories and borrow for capital expansion. The rate of increase in interest rates tapers off during the prosperity phase of the business cycle. Interest rates peak and then decline. During the recession, borrowers reduce their inventories, repay loans, and delay new capital expenditures. Rates decline further during the final phase of the business cycle, and then the process begins again. Although this is a simplified version of what actually happens to interest rates over the course of a business cycle, it provides a framework for examining spread management strategies.

During the recovery phase of the business cycle, banks should increase their rate-sensitive assets and attempt to lock in longer-term, fixed-cost sources of funds. Stated otherwise, they should be positively gapped. The positive gap should be largest during this recovery phase of the cycle, diminishing as the business cycle matures. At the peak of the cycle, banks should lock in high-yield, fixed-rate loans and obtain short-term, variable-rate sources of funds; that is, they should be negatively gapped. The gap should be largest during the recession and then diminish as the cycle approaches the trough. Then the process starts again.

This section demonstrated how banks may increase their net interest income and value by taking advantage of expected changes in the direction of interest rates. These strategies work *if* interest rates behave as expected and the loans are repaid on schedule. The key word is *if*. Changes in interest rates appear to be random. Most of the monthly changes are small—less than 100 basis points when expressed in terms of annual rates. However, in the early 1980s, some monthly changes ranged from 200 to 500 basis points.

In the late 1970s, few forecasters, if any, expected Treasury bill rates to soar from 5 percent to more than 17 percent. The high levels of interest rates and the large changes contributed to the failure of banks and thrifts that were not gapped correctly. Typically, these institutions invested long term at fixed rates and borrowed short term at variable rates. These failures suggest that large positive and negative gaps are risky—and they *are* risky. Managing a financial institution means managing risk: interest rate risk, credit risk, liquidity risk, and other risks.

TECHNIQUES FOR MANAGING INTEREST RATE RISK: STRENGTHS AND WEAKNESSES

This section examines three ALM techniques: gap analysis, duration analysis, and simulation. Each technique is used to deal with interest rate risk, and each has strengths and weaknesses.

Gap Analysis

As noted previously, a bank is positively gapped when rate-sensitive assets exceed rate-sensitive liabilities. The net interest income (NII) of banks that are positively gapped increases when interest rates increase and decreases when they decline. This is so because the bank is "asset sensitive;" that is, interest income from RSAs increases more than do interest expenses from RSLs. A bank is negatively gapped when rate-sensitive assets are less than rate-sensitive liabilities. Such a bank is "liability sensitive." NII of a negatively gapped bank increases when interest rates decline. If the gap is zero (RSA = RSL), there is no interest rate sensitivity, and NII is unaffected by changes in interest rates. The extent to which banks have positive, negative, or zero gaps depends on their operating strategy, the interest rate outlook, and other factors.

Periodic gap analysis reports.   Banks use gap analysis reports to measure the interest rate sensitivity of RSA and RSL for different periods. For this reason, the gap is sometimes referred to as a *periodic gap*, in contrast to a *duration gap,* which is explained later. The periods are also called *maturity buckets.* Some banks use maturity buckets based on the maturity and repricing data for loans, leases, and deposits that are reported in the call report forms submitted to bank regulators. These periods are 0 to 3 months, 3 to 12 months, 1 to 5 years, and over 5 years. However, any periods may be used. Chase Manhattan, for example, groups its assets, liabilities, and off–balance sheet items into three groups: known maturities, judgmental maturities, and market-driven maturities.[12] Known maturities are contractually defined for fixed-rate loans, CDs, and so on. Judgmental maturities are based on past experience for credit cards, passbooks, demand deposits, and nonperforming loans. Market-driven maturities apply to all option-type instruments, including mortgages that may be prepaid if interest rates fall. Other banks use different periods depending on their operating strategy. Table 6–1 shows the interest rate sensitivity analysis for a large bank. The bank uses 0 to 30 days, 31 to 90 days, 91 to 180 days, and 181 to 365 days. Non-rate-sensitive assets and liabilities and maturities of over one year are grouped together in the final period shown. The data reveal that the bank has a negative interest rate sensitivity gap under 180 days and is positively gapped beyond that period.

---

[12] "How Chase Manhattan Bank Manages Its Interest Rate Risk," *Financial Management Collection* 3, no. 3 (Fall 1988), pp. 12–13.

TABLE 6-1
Interest Rate Sensitivity Analysis ($ Millions)

December 31,	0-30 Days	31-90 Days	91-180 Days	181-365 Days	Non-Rate-Sensitive and Over One Year	Total
Variable-rate commercial and real estate loans	$6,104	$11	$40	$14	—	$6,169
Fixed-rate commercial and real estate loans, including ARMs	856	811	1,112	2,314	$5,510	10,603
Consumer loans	1,165	326	470	878	4,639	7,478
Total loans	8,125	1,148	1,622	3,206	10,149	24,250
Securities	767	229	104	214	2,921	4,235
Federal funds sold and other earning assets	180					180
Total earning assets	9,072	1,377	1,726	3,420	13,070	28,665
Cash property and other assets					3,960	3,960
Less: Allowance for loan losses					(411)	(411)
Total assets	$9,072	$1,377	$1,726	$3,420	$16,619	$32,214
Demand deposits					$3,763	$3,763
NOW accounts					3,642	3,642
Money market accounts	$4,788					4,788
Savings deposits					1,907	1,907
Certificates of deposit under $100,000	2,781	$1,992	$2,528	$1,840	$1,582	10,723
Other time deposits	1,472	806	848	537	240	3,903
Total deposits	9,041	2,798	3,376	2,377	11,134	28,726

Federal funds purchased and other short-term borrowings	1,120				1,120
Long-term debt	151			344	495
Other liabilities				300	300
Shareholders' equity				1,573	1,573
Total liabilities and shareholders' equity	$10,312	$2,798	$3,376	$2,377	$13,351	$32,214
Interest rate sensitivity gap	$(1,240)	$(1,421)	$(1,650)	$1,043	$3,268	
Cumulative interest rate sensitivity gap	(1,240)	(2,661)	(4,311)	(3,268)	—	
Cumulative gap as percentage of earning assets at December 31, 199x*	(4.3)%	(9.3)%	(15.0)%	(11.4)%	—	
Cumulative gap as percentage of earning assets at December 31, 199x	(2.8)	(7.9)	(13.3)	(8.8)	—	

* If NOW accounts and savings deposits had been included in the 0–30 day category, the cumulative gap as a percentage of earning assets would have been a negative 23.7 percent for this category on December 31.

Source: Annual Report.

The *cumulative gap,* which is the sum of the individual gaps up to one year, is negative. Moreover, the negative $3,268 million cumulative gap is equal to the positive gap for the over-one-year period. The strategy is to offset the negative cumulative gap under one year with a positive gap beyond that period and non-rate-sensitive assets and liabilities. Thus, the bank was positioned to benefit from a decline in interest rates.

Effect of gap on net interest income.   Bank managers may use the cumulative gap to estimate the impact of changes in interest rates on net interest income. The change in NII is equal to the cumulative gap times the change in interest rates. This is similar to equation 6–2, but we use the cumulative gap here. Barnett's cumulative gap for one year and under is negative $3,268 million (see Table 6–1), and we assume maturities of more than one year are non-rate-sensitive. If interest rates decline by, say, 200 basis points, NII could increase $65.36 million:

$$\Delta\text{NII} = \text{Cumulative Gap} \times \Delta r \qquad\qquad (6\text{--}4)$$
$$\$65.36 = \$3,268 \qquad\quad \times 0.0200$$

This equation may also be used to test the sensitivity of different-size gaps or to determine what size gaps are necessary to produce a target change in NII. This type of analysis is best done with simulations, which are discussed later in this chapter.

Assumptions and limitations of gap analysis.   The use of gap analysis is based on the following assumptions which may or may not be valid depending on how a bank calculates its gap. One assumption is that the gap depends on contractual repayment schedules. If interest rates decline, early repayments of loans by borrowers refinancing at lower rates will affect NII. In addition, certain assets and liabilities have optionlike features that borrowers and lenders may exercise as interest rates change. These include drawdowns of lines of credit and deposit redemptions to name a few. Early refinancing and the exercise of options affect the bank's cash flow. The cash flow does not distinguish between principal and interest payments. Another assumption is that all of the loan payments will be made on schedule. Some borrowers may make early payments, while others will default on their loans. Finally, gap analysis is based on the assumption of a parallel shift in the yield curve; that is, both short-term and long-term interest rates change by the same amount. If changes in the yield curve are not parallel, a basis risk exists.

Gap analysis has some widely recognized limitations.[13] One limitation is that it does not incorporate future growth or changes in the mix of assets and liabilities. Another is that gap analysis does not take the time value of money or initial net worth into account. In addition, the periods used in the analysis are arbitrary, and repricing is assumed to occur at the mid-point of the period. Choosing different periods yields different results. It assumes the timing and amount of assets and liabilities maturing in a given period are fixed and does not allow for drawdowns on credit, pre-payments, or defaults. Finally, gap analysis does not provide a single reliable index of interest rate risk. With respect to the last two criticisms, the critical measure of interest rate risk is the cumulative gap rather than the individual periods, and interest rate risk is multidimensional, involving both income and investment risk.

Gap analysis is used widely despite the limitations of the assumptions, and the criticisms. One reason for the popularity of gap analysis is that it was the first method developed to deal with interest rate risk. Equally important, it works reasonably well under some circumstances. Third the data are readily available from the call reports submitted to bank regulators. Fourth, gap analysis does not require the use of a computer to determine the gaps. Fifth, it costs less than buying asset/liability management and/or simulation software. Finally, it is easier to understand than the theory and structure of duration analysis and simulations. Nevertheless, both duration analysis and simulations are widely used to report interest rate sensitivity gaps.

One critic of gap analysis states that the maturity gap is a better measure of a bank's liquidity than its interest rate risk.[14] In the event of massive withdrawals of deposits, the rate of withdrawal is limited by the maturity of the deposits being withdrawn. Similarly, maturity limits the rate at which assets can be liquidated to meet the withdrawals. This critic goes on to argue that a better measure of interest rate risk is needed.

Next, we examine duration analysis. While duration is a better measure of interest rate risk than periodic gaps, it too has limitations.

---

[13] James E. McNulty, "Measuring Interest Rate Risk: What Do We Know?", *Journal of Retail Banking*, Spring–Summer 1986, pp. 49–58; George Kaufman, "Measuring and Managing Interest Rate Risk: A Primer," *Economic Perspectives*, Federal Reserve Bank of Chicago, January–February, 1984, pp. 16–29; Alden Toevs, "Gap Management: Managing Interest Rate Risk in Banks and Thrifts," *Economic Review*, Federal Reserve Bank of San Francisco, Spring 1983; Canada Deposit Insurance Corporation, Interest Rate Risk Management (n.d.).

[14] Sherrill Shaffer, "Interest Rate Risk: What's a Bank to Do?", *Business Review*, Federal Reserve Bank of Philadelphia, May–June 1991, pp. 17–27.

Duration Analysis

The concept of duration originated in 1938 when Frederick R. Macaulay wanted an alternative to the term to maturity for measuring the average length of time an option-free (noncallable) bond investment is outstanding.[15] Duration is an index number that measures the interest rate sensitivity of any series of cash flows. The cash flows may be from individual bonds, stocks, mortgages, or loans or from portfolios of securities and loans. Duration takes into account both the timing and magnitude of the cash flows. In recent years, duration has received considerable attention from both academics and practitioners as a means of reducing interest rate risk.[16] In this section, we discuss how duration may be determined and used. Then we examine how the assumptions for duration analysis differ from those for gap analysis.

Equally important, Section 305 of the Federal Deposit Insurance Corporation Act of 1991 (FDICIA) required federal banking regulators to revise the risk-based capital guidelines to take account of interest rate risk. Interest rate risk is calculated by a modified duration that measures the change in a bank's net economic value (i.e., its equity) associated with a specific change in interest rates.[17]

Duration defined.   *Duration* is the weighted average *time* (expressed in years) to maturity to receive all cash flows from a financial instrument such as a bond or mortgage-backed security. To illustrate, assume a bond has a $1,000 face value, the coupon interest rate is 12 percent, and the term to maturity is 20 years. If the current market rate of interest is 12 percent, the duration of the bond is 7.97 years, which is about 12 years less than the 20-year term to maturity. In other words, the price of this bond will behave like a zero-coupon bond with 7.97 years to maturity. Except for zero-coupon bonds, duration is always shorter than the term to maturity. Nevertheless, long-term bonds have longer durations

---

[15] Frederick R. Macaulay, *The Movements of Interest Rates, Bond Yields and Stock Prices in the United States Since 1856* (New York: National Bureau of Economic Research, 1938).

[16] Several representative works on duration are Gerald O. Bierwag, George G. Kaufman, and Alden L. Toevs, eds., *Innovations in Portfolio Management: Duration Analysis and Immunization* (Greenwich, CT: JAI Press, 1983); Gerald O. Bierwag, *Duration Analysis: Managing Interest Rate Risk* (Cambridge, MA: Ballinger, 1987); Alden L. Toevs and William C. Haney, *Measuring and Managing Interest Rate Risk: A Guide to Asset/Liability Models Used in Banks and Thrifts* (New York: Morgan Stanley, 1984).

[17] For a detailed explanation, see 12 CFR Parts 3 et. al.

than short-term bonds. Thus, when considering price changes, the concept of duration is used instead of maturity. It follows that bonds with long durations (e.g., 10 years) will experience greater price changes than bonds with short durations (e.g., 2 years).

Measuring interest rate sensitivity. Bank managers can change their interest rate risk and improve their investment performance by using a duration strategy instead of a term-to-maturity strategy. For example, suppose the prices of long-term bonds are expected to increase (interest rates will decline). The current yield is 8 percent, and it is expected to decline to 7.20 percent. Bankers that want to profit from this information will buy long-term bonds; however, they do not intend to hold the bonds for long periods. They have a choice of a 12 percent coupon bond or a 6 percent coupon bond, each with 20 years to maturity. Bankers using a term-to-maturity strategy might favor the 12 percent bond because it pays twice as much interest as the 6 percent bond. On the other hand, they might choose the 6 percent bond because bonds with low coupon rates have greater price volatility than those with high coupon rates.

Bankers using the duration strategy would choose the 6 percent bond. The 6 percent bond (with a current yield of 8 percent) has a duration of 10.92 years, while the 12 percent bond has a duration of 9.57 years.[18] Thus, the lower-coupon bond, having a longer duration, will have greater price volatility than the high-coupon bond.

The percentage change in bond prices that will occur with a change in market yields can be approximated by the following equation:

$$\text{Percentage Change in Bond Price} = -D/(1 + i/n) \times \Delta i \qquad (6\text{--}5)$$

where

$D = \text{Duration}$[19]
$\Delta i = \text{Change in yield in percentage points}$
$i = \text{Yield}$
$n = \text{Number of interest payments per year}$

To illustrate the use of this equation, we will use a 6 percent coupon bond with a duration of 10.92 years and the 12 percent coupon bond with a dura-

---

[18] The duration of 10.92 differs from the amount shown in Table 6–1 because of different market yields.

[19] This version of duration is commonly called *modified duration*.

tion of 9.57 years. Interest is paid semiannually. Recall that market yields were expected to decline from 8.00 to 7.20 percent, a change of –0.80 percentage points. The percentage changes in the prices of these bonds are

$$6\% \text{ coupon bond} = -D/(1 + i/n) \times \Delta i$$
$$= -10.92/(1.04) \times -0.80$$
$$= 8.48\%$$

$$12\% \text{ coupon bond} = -D/(1 + i/n) \times \Delta i$$
$$= -9.57(1.04) \times -0.80$$
$$= 7.96\%$$

The actual price changes, based on bond value tables, are 8.9 percent and 7.8 percent, respectively. Thus, duration is only a linear approximation that works best when the yield changes are less than 100 *basis points* (1 percentage point = 0.01 = 100 basis points). The reason it works best for small yield changes is convexity. *Convexity* refers to the nonlinear relationship between changes in bond prices and yields.[20] For very small changes in yields, the percentage price change is about equal to the change in yields. For larger changes in yields, however, percentage price changes are not equal. The extent to which the percentage price changes are not equal gives rise to an error in pricing. Bonds with call features cause additional pricing errors due to convexity. One may compensate for convexity, which results in a better approximation of price changes.

Immunization.   The previous section demonstrated that duration can be used when trading securities. It can also be used to lock in a yield for a certain planning horizon or holding period. A *holding period* is the length of time an investor plans to hold a bond. Lawrence Fisher and Roman Weil developed an investment strategy that protects investors from changes in interest rates by matching the duration of the bonds with the length of their holding period. They said their strategy "immunized" bond portfolios.[21] Similarly, one can immunize assets and liabilities.[22]

---

[20] For information on convexity, see *Understanding Duration and Convexity* (Chicago: Chicago Board of Trade, 1990); Frank J. Fabozzi and T. Dessa Fabozzi, *Bond Markets, Analysis and Strategies* (Englewood Cliffs, NJ: Prentice Hall, 1989).

[21] Lawrence Fisher and Roman Weil, "Coping with the Risk of Investment Rate Fluctuations: Return to Bondholders from Naive and Optimal Strategies," *Journal of Business,* October 1971, pp. 408–31.

[22] Gerald O. Bierwag, George G. Kaufman, Robert Schwitzer, and Alden L. Toevs, "The Art of Risk Management," *Journal of Portfolio Management,* Spring 1981, pp. 27–36.

Immunization means obtaining a realized yield that will not be less than the yield to maturity for that holding period at the time the investments were made.

The basic idea of immunization centers on the fact that changes in interest rates have two effects on outstanding bonds, and they work in opposite directions. If interest rates increase, bond prices decline and reinvestment rates for coupon interest increase. The *reinvestment rate* is the market rate of interest. Stated otherwise, the coupon interest can be "reinvested" at the market rate of interest. Conversely, if interest rates decline, bond prices increase and reinvestment rates for coupon interest decrease.

To illustrate immunization, assume an investor wants to receive $10,000 ten years from now, and that the funds can be invested today in bond A or bond B.[23] As the following table shows, bonds A and B have different coupons, prices, and maturities. The current yield is assumed to be 8 percent; for simplicity, we ignore taxes.

	Bond A	*Bond B*
Coupon	8%	6 1/2%
Yield	8%	8%
Term to maturity	10 years	17 years
Price	$1,000	$861.92
Duration	7.07 years	10.00 years
Number of bonds purchased at the current price	4.564	5.295

To receive $10,000 in 10 years, the investor must invest $4,564 at 8 percent (compounded semiannually because interest is paid twice per year) for ten years.[24] The $4,564 will buy 4.564 units of bond A ($4,564/$1,000 = 4.564) and 5.295 units of bond B ($4,564/$861.92 = 5.295).

The investor has the choice of using a term-to-maturity strategy (buying a bond with 10 years to maturity) by investing in bond A or using a duration strategy (buying a bond with a 10-year duration) by investing in bond B. If market rates of interest remain unchanged for the next 10 years,

---

[23] This example is based on one that appears in Alfred Weinberger, Henry Nothof, and Kenneth Scott, *Duration Tables for Bond and Mortgage Portfolio Management* (Boston: Financial Publishing Company, 1980).

[24] The $4,564 invested today at 8 percent, compounded semiannually, will provide $10,000 at the end of 10 years:

$$(1 + .08/2)^{10 \times 2} = (1.04)^{20} = 2.1911$$
$$\$10,000/2.1911 = \$4,564$$

which is unlikely, both strategies will produce the desired results if all funds are reinvested at 8 percent and the bonds are sold at the end of 10 years.

No Change in 8% Market Yield

Term Strategy

Buy 4.564 units of bond A

$1,000 (bond price in 10 years) × 4.564	= $ 4,564
$40/6 months (value of reinvested coupons)	= 5,436
Total	$10,000

Duration Strategy

Buy 5.295 units of bond B

$920.87 (bond price in 10 years) × 5.295	= $ 4,876
$32.50/6 months (value of reinvested coupons)	= 5,124
Total	$10,000

A more likely case is that interest rates will change. Suppose market interest rates change from 8 to 7 percent immediately after the bond is purchased and remain at 7 percent for the entire period. In this case, the term strategy results in a loss of $274, whereas the duration strategy results in a small profit ($17). The increase in the price of bond B (the duration strategy) offsets the lower earnings resulting from the interest payments being reinvested at a lower rate (7 percent).

Market Yield Goes from 8% to 7% and Remains

Term Strategy

$1,000 (bond price in 10 years) × 4.564 units	= $4,564
Value of reinvested coupons @ 7%	= 5,162
Total	$9,726
Loss	–$ 274

Duration Strategy

$972.62 (bond price in 10 years) × 5.295 units	= $ 5,150
Value of reinvested coupons @7%	= 4,867
Total	$10,017
Profit	$ 17

Now let's see what happens when market rates of interest increase. Suppose the market rate of interest increases from 8 to 9 percent immediately after the bond is purchased and remains at 9 percent for the next 10 years. The term strategy produces a $291 profit, whereas the duration strategy produces a $17 profit. A careful examination of the bond prices at the end of 10 years and the value of the reinvested coupons explains the performance of each strategy. The duration strategy comes closer to achieving the desired results than the term strategy.

Market Yield Goes from 8% to 9% and Remains

Term Strategy

$1,000 (bond price in 10 years) × 4.564 units	= $ 4,564
Value of reinvested coupons	= 5,727
Total	$10,291
Profit	$ 291

Duration Strategy

$872.14 (bond price in 10 years) × 5.295 units	= $ 4,618
Value of reinvested coupons	= 5,399
Total	$10,017
Profit	$ 17

Rebalancing.   The previous examples were simplified because only one change in market rates of interest occurred during the investment period, and the term structure of interest rates (yield curve) was flat. In reality, changes occur daily, and the term structure of interest rates is rarely flat. Therefore, investments have to be *rebalanced*. Rebalancing is also necessary to deal with the problem of duration drift. *Duration drift* occurs with the passage of time, and a bond's duration gets shorter as the bond approaches maturity.

The more frequent the rebalancing, the more likely one is to achieve one's target returns. Semiannual rebalancing produces superior results to annual rebalancing. However, rebalancing too frequently may create more problems than it solves. One authority suggests that rebalancing should not only be based on the passage of time but also be triggered by certain interest rate movements and by events such as changes in cash flow due to prepayments and withdrawals.[25] Transaction costs also must be considered.

---

[25] Martin L. Leibowitz, "Duration and Immunization: Matched-Funding Techniques," in *Handbook of Financial Markets and Institutions,* 6th ed., ed. Edward I. Altman (New York: John Wiley & Sons, 1987), Chapter 25; Martin L. Leibowitz, ed., *Pros and Cons of Immunization: Proceedings of a Seminar on the Roles and Limits of Bond Immunization* (New York: Salomon Brothers, 1980).

Duration gap.   Duration can be used to measure the interest rate sensitivity of any series of cash flows, such as from bonds and mortgages. In addition, duration can be used to measure a bank's interest rate sensitivity gap, which is called a *duration gap*. The basic idea of duration/immunization is to manage the gap between the durations of assets and liabilities to meet the goals of the bank. Suppose the duration of the bank's assets is 360 days and the duration of its liabilities is 90 days, resulting in a gap of 270 days. The longer duration of the assets means that a given change in interest rates will change the present value of the assets more than it will alter the present value of the liabilities. The changed values of the assets and liabilities affect the net economic value of the bank's equity.

The following simplified example illustrates the change in equity.[26] Suppose a bank makes a single-payment loan with a face of $1,000 to be repaid in 360 days at an interest rate of 10 percent. Ten percent is the bank's opportunity cost. The present value of that loan (the dollar amount the bank will extend to the borrower at the beginning of the year) is $909.09 ($1,000/1.10 = $909.09). To fund the loan, the bank borrows $909.09 at 8 percent every 90 days. The total cost to the bank for funding the loan for one year is $981.82 ($909.09 × 1.08 = $981.82). The present value of the liability is $892.56 ($981.82/1.10 = $892.56). Equity is the difference between the value of the bank's assets and the value of its liabilities. Thus, the net economic value of the bank's equity is $16.53:

Present value of assets and liabilities

Assets	$909.09
Liabilities	−892.56
Equity	$ 16.53

If an unexpected 200-basis-point increase in interest rates occurs in 90 days, the present value of the assets will decline to $892.86 ($1,000/1.12 = $892.86). The dollar amount of the liabilities will increase to $995.42 due to the higher funding costs.[27] The present value of the $995.42 is $888.77

---

[26] Michael T. Belongia and G. J. Santoni, "Hedging Interest Rate Risk with Financial Futures: Some Basic Principles," *Review,* Federal Reserve Bank of St. Louis, October 1984, pp. 15-25; also see George G. Kaufman, "Measuring and Managing Interest Rate Risk: A Primer," *Economic Perspectives,* Federal Reserve Bank of Chicago, January–February 1984, pp. 16–29; and Toevs and Haney, *Measuring and Managing Interest Rate Risk.*

[27] At the end of 90 days, the liability is $926.75 ($909.09 × $(1.08)^{0.25}$). Then interest rates increase 200 basis points, and at the end of the year, the liability is $995.42 ($926.75 × $(1.10)^{0.75}$).

($995.42/1.12 = $888.77). Accordingly, the net economic value of the equity is $4.09 ($892.86 – $888.77 = $4.09). The 200-basis-point increase in interest rates resulted in a decline of $12.44 in the net economic value of the bank's equity—a 75.26 percent reduction!

Present value of assets and liabilities

Assets	$892.86
Liabilities	–887.77
Equity	$ 4.09

The volatility of the equity is due to the mismatch between the durations of the assets and liabilities. If the durations of the assets and liabilities were the same, a 200-basis-point increase in interest rates would have caused the net economic value of the equity to fall by $0.30, only a 1.8 percent decline. Stated otherwise, *interest rate risk can be eliminated or immunized by setting the duration gap equal to zero.* Nevertheless, the elimination of interest rate risk is not always the best policy. Some banks prefer to manage their gaps to take advantage of expected changes in interest rates rather than eliminating all interest rate risk.

Another advantage of using duration is that it can help gauge the effect of interest rate risk on net economic value, which bank regulators use as a measure of interest rate risk. Net economic value of a bank's equity, determined by the difference between the durations of its assets and liabilities, should not be confused with the stock market value of the bank. The stock market value of the bank takes factors other than duration of assets and liabilities into account. These factors include the payment of cash dividends, expectations about earnings, franchise value, and other considerations.

Next, the duration gap is a single number that takes into account both the timing and the magnitude of cash flows. Thus it avoids the problems associated with arbitrary maturity buckets.

Finally, investment managers may use derivative securities, such as futures contracts and swaps, to alter their duration gaps.[28]

Duration has some disadvantages. These include the fact that all cash flows must be known, which may not be the case. Duration provides a linear approximation of risk, but the risk may not be linear (e.g., convexity).

---

[28] Gerald O. Bierwag and George G. Kaufman, "Duration Gaps with Futures and Swaps for Managing Interest Rate Risk at Depository Institutions," unpublished paper, September 23, 1991.

Finally, duration drift is another problem. This requires periodic rebalancing of the portfolio.

Simulations

Simulations are computer-generated scenarios about the future that permit banks to analyze interest rate risk and business strategies in a dynamic framework. Given such information, banks may evaluate the desirability of various courses of action. The scenarios are based on a number of assumptions, such as

- Expected changes and levels of interest rates and the shapes of yield curves.
- Pricing strategies for assets and liabilities.
- The growth, volume, and mix of assets and liabilities.
- Hedging strategies.

The data used for modeling the scenarios may include both historical data and "what if" projections.

The output of simulations can take a variety of forms, depending on the user's needs. Simulations can provide current and expected periodic gaps, duration gaps, balance sheet and income statements, performance measures, budgets, and financial reports. They can provide information about "macro hedges" (the entire balance sheet) or "micro hedges" (specific assets/liabilities). The information can be presented in tabular or graphic form. Simulations can be simple or state-of-the-art. You can get whatever you want, if you are willing to pay for it. The price of simulators ranges from a few thousand dollars to hundreds of thousands of dollars, depending on the degree of sophistication and service or information provided.

The principal advantage of simulations for interest rate risk management is that they are dynamic or forward looking. The accuracy of the simulations depends on the structure of the model and the validity of the assumptions. If the structure or assumptions are wrong, inconsistent, or inappropriate for the bank using them, the output may result in inferior decisions by bank managers. Some simulation models use historical data and econometric techniques to estimate the parameters of structural equations used in the model. If the historical patterns are no longer valid, the equations will be misspecified, and the simulations will give misleading results. Similarly, suppose a simulation forecasts quarterly net income while interest rates are allowed to change more often. Changes in interest rates during the quarter may hide risks that are not revealed in the projected gap or net income at the end of the period. If managers were aware of the interim risks, they might choose different courses of action. This type of risk of using simulations and gap analysis is illustrated in Figure 6–4. It shows a bank's 0–90 day maturity bucket. Rate-sensitive assets are a six-month, floating-rate loan. Rate-sensitive liabilities are an 8 percent CD with 90 days to maturity. The gap is zero. During the 90-day period, market interest rates decline sharply, resulting in interest rate risk that the gap analysis did not reveal. Despite these shortcomings, the advantages of simulations outweigh the disadvantages. No interest rate risk management tool is perfect. So *caveat emptor.*

FIGURE 6–4
Measurement Error

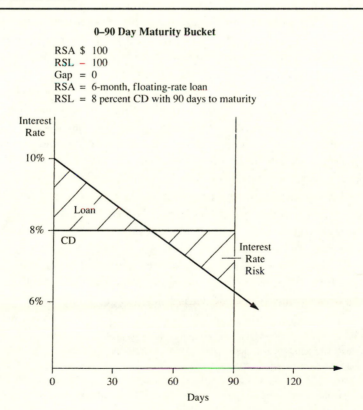

0–90 Day Maturity Bucket

RSA $ 100
RSL – 100
Gap = 0
RSA = 6-month, floating-rate loan
RSL = 8 percent CD with 90 days to maturity

HEDGING

According to Professor Merton Miller, 1990 Nobel Laureate in Economics, "A speculator is someone who is not hedging."[29] Hedging is a technique used to transfer risk. The technical definition of *hedging* is "the initiation of a position in the futures market that is intended as a temporary substitute for the sale or purchase of the actual commodity. . . ."[30] Hedging entails buying or selling derivative (and other) securities to transfer risk. *Financial derivatives* are instruments that derive their value from the performance of underlying assets, interest or currency exchange rates, or indices. Put and call options, mortgage-backed securities, swaps, caps, collars, and floors are examples of derivative securities. Derivatives may be used to mitigate the unwanted portion of interest rate risk.

The Basics of Hedging

The traditional function of the futures market is to shift the risk of price changes in commodities from those who do not want it (hedgers) to those who want it for a price (speculators). In addition to the traditional function, the futures market is used by profit-maximizing firms to enhance their incomes. In addition, buying and selling futures contracts act as temporary substitutes for cash market transactions. Futures contracts may also be used to alter the effective maturity (lengthen or shorten) of a fixed-income portfolio and to create "synthetic" financial instruments. Finally, futures contracts are more liquid than cash securities, and transaction costs are relatively low in the futures market.[31]

Interest rate futures are quoted in terms of prices rather than interest rates or yields. If market rates of interest increase, the price of interest rate futures contracts declines, and vice versa. To hedge against falling prices (rising rates), you would sell short interest rate futures contracts. A *short sale* is the sale of futures contracts (cash, commodity, or security) without taking the offsetting action of buying contracts. A speculator who sells short sells futures contracts at a high price in anticipation of buying them back at a lower price. A hedger who sells short accepts price movements

---

[29] Keith Schap, *Commodity Marketing: A Lenders' and Producers' Guide to Better Risk Management* (Chicago: Chicago Board of Trade and the American Bankers Association, 1993), p. 1.

[30] *Commodity Trading Manual* (Chicago: Chicago Board of Trade, 1985), p. 351.

[31] For further discussion of the role of the futures market, see Anatoli Kuprianov, "Short-Term Interest Rate Futures," *The CME Financial Strategy Paper*, Chicago Mercantile Exchange, 1987.

Think about This!

Derivatives and Risk

Is someone betting your bank's future in the futures or derivatives market?
   Does the compensation package for your derivatives specialists create
perverse values and encourage them to "bet the bank"?
   How much is at risk if you don't hedge?
   Did you know that the OCC considers a lack of an adequate risk control
function relative to the level of derivatives activity conducted by a bank to
be an unsafe and unsound banking practice?

---

in either direction. The difference between the high selling price and the
lower purchase price is profit. If the price goes up instead of down, a loss
results.

   To hedge against higher prices (falling rates) you would buy (go long)
interest rate futures contracts. The terms *cash market* and *spot market*
refer to commodities for immediate (same- or next-business-day) delivery. A *cash market position* refers to the physical commodity (security) as
distinguished from the futures commodity. The cash price is the price
now. A *futures position* refers to transactions in the futures market.

Minimum Variance Hedge

The following examples demonstrate how risk-avoiding hedgers use
interest rate futures to match unwanted dollar changes in assets or liabilities with offsetting dollar changes in a futures position. A fully hedged
position is where a change (Δ) in cash market position (C) is offset with an
equal but opposite change in the futures position (F). For example, a $1
million price decline in a bond portfolio (cash market position) is offset by
a $1 million price increase in the value of the futures market position. The
result is no loss or gain. The risk of price change has been eliminated.

$$\Delta \text{ Cash Price} = \Delta \text{ Futures Price} \tag{6–6}$$

$$\Delta C = \Delta F$$

   Because changes in the price of the cash commodity and the price of
futures contracts are not the same, it is necessary to determine the number

of futures contracts required to compensate for the difference in price sensitivity. The sensitivity, measured by a *hedge ratio (HR),* is determined by dividing the percentage change in the cash instrument by the percentage change in the futures instrument:

$$HR = \%\Delta C/\%\Delta F \qquad\qquad (6\text{–}7)$$

Suppose a 12 percent change in the cash price is associated with a 6 percent change in the futures price. The hedge ratio is 2 (12%/6% = 2). A hedge ratio of 2 means the cash instrument is twice as volatile as the futures contract. To obtain price equivalency, multiply the change in the futures price by the hedge ratio:

$$\Delta \text{ Cash Price} = \Delta \text{ Futures Price} \times \text{Hedge Ratio} \qquad (6\text{–}8)$$

$$\Delta C = \Delta F \times HR$$

$$12\% = 6\% \times 2$$

Hedging Strategies

A variety of hedging strategies may be used to reduce interest rate risk. Long and short hedges are the two basic types of hedges explained here. The following examples have been simplified for purposes of illustration. A list of selected references is provided at the end of this chapter for those who want to know more about the futures market before committing their funds.

Long hedge.   A long hedge is also called an *anticipatory hedge* because the hedger anticipates buying a cash commodity. It involves the purchase (going long) of futures contracts *now* in anticipation of buying a cash commodity at a *later* date. The long hedge locks in the purchase price of the cash commodity. In the case of financial futures, a long hedge protects against falling interest rates (higher prices) by fixing interest rates on future investments.

When buying a futures contract, the customer does not pay the market price or the face value. Instead, the customer makes a deposit, called *margin*, to ensure performance of the contract. For example, the *initial margin* required by the Chicago Board of Trade (CBOT) on a T-bond futures contract with a face value of $100,000, is $2,700 at the time of this writing. Prices of futures contracts change daily, and margin/commodity accounts are *marked to market*. This means gains and losses in accounts are collected daily. The minimum *maintenance margin* for T-bond futures is $2,000. Accounts falling below that amount will be required to put up additional margin. This is also the amount the CBOT requires for hedging (*hedge margin*). Margin requirements differ for other futures contracts, and they are subject to change. Moreover, brokerage firms may have different margin requirements. The point here is that buying $100,000 T-bond futures contracts requires only the deposit of the initial margin requirement plus commission. Additional margin deposits may be required during the life of the contract.

The following example illustrates a long hedge. Next month, a bank plans to buy $2 million of high-yielding Treasury bonds. To lock in the high yields now, the bank buys 29 December T-bond futures contracts at $104-00.

Over the next few weeks, interest rates decrease. The bonds that the bank planned to buy at par (100-00) are now selling at 110-00. Buying the bonds at the higher price would cost an additional $200,000. This amount represents an opportunity cost if the purchase had not been hedged. However, by using a long hedge, the bank can sell the T-bond futures contract at a profit. The price of the T-bonds futures contracts increased from 104-00 to 111-000, resulting in a gain of $203,000. The bank also realized a $3,000 profit on the transaction.

Cash Market	*Futures Market*
Now	
Plans to buy $2 million T-bonds @ 100-00	Buys 29 December T-bond contracts @ 104-00
Total: $2,000,000	Total: $3,016,000
Later	
Buys T-bonds @ 110-00	Sells 29 December T-bond contracts @ 111-00
Total: $2,200,000	Total: $3,219,000
Net Change	
–$200,000	+$203,000
Difference +$3,000	

Short hedge.   A short hedge is the second basic type of hedge we will examine. In the following examples, it is used to lock in the prices of assets or liabilities when interest rates are expected to increase. A bank holds $1 million face value long-term Treasury bonds priced at 106-08

(106 and 8/32nds) with a cash market value of $1,062,500. The forecast is for interest rates to increase sharply. The bank is concerned about the value of the bonds and wants to lock in the price. To protect against falling prices, the bank uses a short hedge. The bank sells short 13 T-bond futures contracts at 84-00. The bank does not intend to deliver the bonds it owns to offset the short position in the futures market.

Subsequently, interest rates increase, and the prices of both the bonds and futures decline. The market value of the bonds declines $100,000. Because the bank was short the futures contracts, it covered (bought) the contracts at a lower price than it sold them and made $117,000 on that transaction. The bank not only offset the $100,000 decline in the value of the bonds but also made a profit of $17,000.

Cash Market	Futures Market
Now	
Holds $1 million face value T-bonds @ 106-08	Sells 13 June T-bond contracts @ 84-00
Total: $1,062,500	Total: $1,092,000
Later	
Holds $1 million face value T-bonds @ 96-08	Buys 13 June T-bond contracts @ 75-00
Total: $962,500	Total: $975,000
Net Change	
–$100,000	+ $117,000
Difference +$17,000	

Puts and Calls

Combinations of *puts* (options to sell) and *calls* (options to buy) can be substituted for futures contracts, thereby creating *synthetic positions*. Stated otherwise, hedging can be done with futures, options, or combinations of the two. Following is a listing of synthetic positions.

To Construct a Synthetic Position	Use the Following
Futures	Cash
Long future	Long call and short put
Short future	Short call and long put
Long put	Long call and short future
Short put	Short call and long future
Long call	Long put and long future
Short call	Short put and short future

Effects of Hedging on NII and Value

Transferring risk is not free; there is a cost for trading derivative securities and hedging. Let's consider the general effects of hedging on net interest income and the value of a bank. We begin by making the following simplifying assumptions: (1) All earning assets and liabilities are interest rate sensitive and are repriced at the same time; (2) all bank earning assets and liabilities are fully hedged, or the bank is unhedged; (3) the effect of investment risk on the value of the firm is neutral; and (4) in the long term, net interest income and the value of the bank are positively related to each other. In addition, we will discuss only a few of the many financial tools available for hedging. The practical reason for this limitation is the large number of combinations that can be generated. Another consideration is that the number of financial tools for managing short-term (overnight to six months) interest rate risk exposure is larger than the number available for managing long-term (five years or longer) risks. For short-term risks, options and exchange-traded financial futures may be the tool of choice. For long-term risks, long-term debt or swaps may be appropriate.[32]

The top panel of Figure 6–5 shows changes in bank value on the vertical axis and changes in interest rates on the horizontal axis. This is similar to Figure 6–2, which was explained previously. It shows that if an unhedged bank has a positive gap (RSA > RSL), its value will increase if interest rates increase and decline if interest rates decline. If the latter occurs, the bank will become insolvent at some point. Some bankers believe the optimal gap is zero or slightly positive. We think otherwise. The optimal positive or negative size of the gap is dynamic, and it depends on the interest rate outlook and the degree of risk a bank is willing to assume.

Banks can avoid the large losses by using symmetric or asymmetric hedges. A *symmetric hedge* is a gap that is hedged so that RSA is equal to RSL to minimize interest rate risk. This type of hedge provides a constant spread between returns on assets and interest costs, leaving NII unchanged. However, the value of the bank increases because the risk is reduced. Specifically, a symmetric hedge is any strategy that reduces both the positive and negative impacts of interest rate changes. This concept is illustrated graphically in the top panel of Figure 6–5. In this case, a swap is used to form a symmetric hedge. When interest rates change, the bank's

---

[32] "How Chase Manhattan Bank Manages Its Interest Rate Risk," (1988).

FIGURE 6–5
The Effects of Hedging Interest Rate Changes on Bank Values

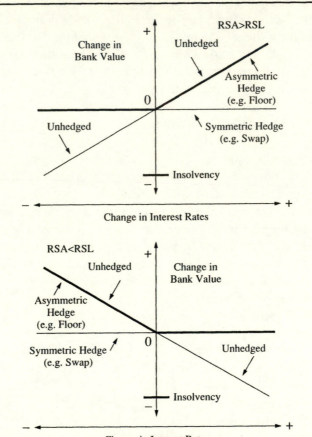

value increases to the extent that risk is reduced. However, interest rate swaps may contain both interest rate risk and counterparty risk, and they too may require hedging with swap futures, strips of Eurodollar futures, or some other means.

Alternatively, banks can use an *asymmetric hedge,* where RSA and RSL are unequal. This type of hedge provides a variable spread between returns on assets and interest costs, resulting in increases or decreases in NII and in the value of the bank. Specifically, an asymmetric hedge is any strategy that preserves the positive impact of the changes in interest rates to some extent while reducing the negative impact of such changes. As shown in the top panel of Figure 6–5, the cost of a floor used to form an asymmetric hedge is represented by the area between the unhedged position and the asymmetric hedge. This cost reduces the positive effects of increases in interest rates. However, if interest rates decline, the loss is limited to the cost of the cap. Thus, the advantage of an asymmetric hedge over the unhedged position is that the value of the bank will increase when interest rates rise, but will decrease only by the amount of the option premium if rates fall.

The lower panel of Figure 6–5 shows the value of a bank that is negatively gapped (RSA < RSL). In this case, the value of the bank increases when interest rates decline. The costs and benefits of hedging are the same as in the previous examples.

Although not shown in the top panel, a bank could have a long net futures position to increase the interest rate sensitivity of its assets. However, there is a downside risk to being long futures contracts, because they can decline in value. Thus, except for the cost of the contract, the value would be similar to that of an unhedged bank. Expanding on this concept, the effects of net futures positions on interest rate sensitivity are shown below. A net long position means the bank owns more futures contracts than it has sold. A net short position means the opposite.

	Short Position	Long Position
Assets	Decreases rate sensitivity	Increases rate sensitivity
Liabilities	Increases rate sensitivity	Decreases rate sensitivity

We can add a third dimension, time, to Figure 6–5. The time dimension is important because the degree of interest rate risk varies with the maturity of the exposure. Suppose a bank has liquidity concerns in the short term and wants to hedge its positive gap in the intermediate and long term. Using a time dimension, the bank may use a symmetric hedge to meet its liquidity needs for the first six months and then use various asymmetric hedges to cover its longer-term gapped positions.

To Hedge or Not to Hedge?

Figure 6–6 is a schematic that may be used to evaluate the costs and benefits of hedging. The first step is to identify the risk. The next step is to determine if the risk is insignificant, significant, or intolerable. If the risk is insignificant, do nothing. If the risk is significant or intolerable, follow the lines and answer the questions with a *yes* or *no* to determine which type of hedge to use.

FIGURE 6–6
Cost-Benefit Schematic

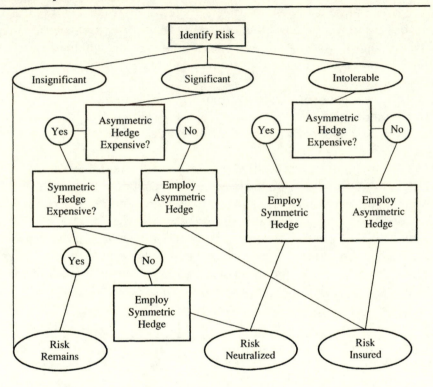

SWAPS

An *interest rate swap* is a contract between two counterparties who agree to exchange fixed- and floating-interest-rate payments based on a notional amount of principal. The *notional principal* is the amount on which the interest payments are calculated (e.g., $10 million). The notional principal does not change hands. Similarly, there are *currency swaps* involving the simultaneous purchase and sale of a foreign currency for two different value dates. Only interest rate swaps are considered here.

Suppose bank A has $10 million of assets with floating interest rates and the same amount of liabilities with fixed rates. Bank B has $10 million of assets with fixed interest rates and the same amount of liabilities with floating rates. Both banks want to hedge their portfolios against adverse changes in interest rates by using an interest rate swap; that is, bank A wants to lock in the spread on its floating-rate loans, and bank B wants to lock in the spread on its fixed-rate loans. Therefore, bank A will make fixed-rate interest payments based on the $10 million notional amount to bank B; and bank A will receive floating-rate interest payments from bank B. Now bank A's floating-rate assets are funded by floating-rate debt, and Bank B's fixed-rate assets are funded by fixed-rate debt. Thus, each bank has hedged $10 million notional principal from adverse changes in interest rates.

Uses of Swaps

The previous example illustrated one use of interest rate swaps: to hedge interest rate risk. Swaps may also be used to reduce financing costs, enhance yields, and engage in arbitrage. The simple swap that was illustrated is called a *plain vanilla swap*. However, there are many variations of swaps. For example, some swaps amortize the principal over time, while others increase the principal over time. There are also *swaptions*— options to enter into swaps—and *leveraged swaps,* whose interest rate payments may change over time. Stated otherwise, swaps can be customized to meet the needs of the counterparties. This adds a significant degree of complexity to them.

Risks of Swaps

Swaps are not risk free. First, there is counterparty (credit) risk, the risk that the counterparty will default on interest payments. Second, there is an opportunity cost. Suppose rates decline and the bank was receiving fixed rates. Then the value of the swap is above the current rate and has positive economic value. In the event of default, the bank would lose both the increased value of the swap and the interest rate payments. Finally, in some swaps (e.g., leveraged swaps), the effects of interest rate changes are exacerbated. That's good if it works in your favor, but it could be a disaster if it works against you. Procter & Gamble Company lost $157 million, part of which was attributed to swaps.[33]

---

[33] Steven Lipin, "Bankers Trust Sued on Derivatives," *The Wall Street Journal,* September 13, 1994, p. C1; Bruce Knecht, "Derivatives Are Going Through a Crucial Test," *The Wall Street Journal,* October 28, 1994.

CONCLUSION

Interest rates are a major determinant of bank incomes and values. Depending on a bank's asset/liability management policies and practices, a large change in interest rates can result in increased income and bank value, or it can lead to disaster. The latter need not be the case. Derivative securities may be used to insulate the bank from adverse interest rate changes and at the same time allow it to profit from favorable interest rate changes. According to the Federal Reserve Bank of Dallas, "derivatives are complex tools that banks and corporations can use—indeed should use—to better manage risk exposure."[34] The article goes on to summarize the recommendations of the Group of Thirty, an organization consisting of central banks, international banks, securities firms, and academia. The Group of Thirty recommends:

- The use of derivatives in a manner consistent with the bank's overall risk management and capital policies.
- Mark-to-market of derivatives positions daily for risk management purposes.
- Quantifying market risk against limits under adverse market conditions.
- Assessing credit risk frequently.
- Reducing credit risk by broadening the use of multiproduct master agreements with closeout netting provisions.
- Establishing independent credit risk management functions responsible for reviewing and monitoring risk exposures.
- Ensuring that only well-trained professionals are involved in derivatives.
- Establishing a computerized, timely risk management reporting system.
- Adopting accounting and disclosure practices for international harmonization and for greater transparency.

The Office of the Comptroller of the Currency's *Risk Management of Financial Derivatives* (October 1994) includes some other factors that

---

[34] Thomas F. Siems, "Financial Derivatives: Are New Regulations Warranted?", *Financial Industry Studies*, Federal Reserve Bank of Dallas, August 1994 (introduction).

contribute to the effective supervision of market risk. These include but are not limited to

- Appropriate board and management supervision.
- Applicable written policies and procedure controls.
- A meaningful process for establishing market risk limits.
- Reliable market valuation systems.
- Accurate and validated risk management processes.
- Timely and effective risk reporting, monitoring, and exception approval processes.

SELECTED REFERENCES

Burghardt, Galen; Morton Lane; and John Papa. *The Treasury Bond Basis: An In-Depth Analysis for Hedgers, Speculators, and Arbitrageurs.* Chicago: Probus Publishing, 1989.

Canada Deposit Insurance Corporation. *Standards of Sound Business and Financial Practice: Interest Rate Risk Management.* 1993.

CBOT Financial Instruments Guide. Chicago: Chicago Board of Trade, 1987.

Commodity Trading Manual. Chicago: Chicago Board of Trade, 1989.

Comptroller of the Currency. *Risk Management of Financial Derivatives: Comptroller's Handbook.* Washington, DC: OCC, October 1994.

The Delivery Process in Brief: Treasury Bond and Treasury Note Futures. Chicago: Chicago Board of Trade, 1989.

Fabozzi, Frank J., and T. Dessa Fabozzi. *Bond Markets, Analysis, and Strategies.* Englewood Cliffs, NJ: Prentice Hall, 1989.

Fabozzi, Frank J., and Irving M. Pollack, eds. *Handbook of Fixed Income Securities,* 2d ed. Homewood, IL: Dow Jones-Irwin, 1986.

Gup, Benton E., and Robert Brooks. *Interest Rate Risk Management: The Banker's Guide to Using Futures, Options, Swaps and Other Derivative Securities.* Chicago: Probus Publishing, 1993.

Interest Rate Futures for Institutional Investors. Chicago: Chicago Board of Trade, 1987.

Kolb, Robert W. *Understanding Futures Markets.* Glenview, IL: Scott, Foresman, 1985.

Peck, A. E., ed. *Selected Writings on Futures Markets: Explorations in Financial Futures Markets,* Book V. Chicago: Chicago Board of Trade, 1985.

Rothstein, Nancy H., and James M. Little, eds. *The Handbook of Financial Futures*. New York: McGraw-Hill, 1984.

Schap, Keith. *Commodity Marketing: A Lenders' and Producers' Guide to Better Risk Management*. Chicago: Chicago Board of Trade and American Bankers Association, 1993.

Stoll, Hans R., and Robert E. Whaley. *Futures and Options: Theory and Applications*. Cincinnati: Southwestern Publishing, 1992.

Treasury Futures for Institutional Investors. Chicago: Chicago Board of Trade, 1990.

Both the Chicago Board of Trade and the Chicago Mercantile Exchange hold seminars and have literature dealing with the topics covered here. Their addresses are

Chicago Board of Trade
Lasalle at Jackson
Chicago, IL 60604
Phone: 1-800-THE-CBOT

Chicago Mercantile Exchange
30 South Wacker Drive
Chicago, IL 60606
Phone: 312-930-1000

Chapter Seven

Managing Derivatives Risk[1]

Consider the following headline-making losses reported during the last few years:

"Crippling losses of 2.5 billion pounds are expected to be announced by Lloyds of London . . ."

"Operating profits at Credit Lyonnais slid 30 percent to 9.2 billion French francs for 1994. The result came before provisions and write-offs which dragged the group to a deficit of 12.1 billion French francs for the year . . ."

"Helmut Kohl, the German chancellor, appealed to banks to limit the damage to small businesses from the financial problems at Jurgen Schneider AG, the German property group . . ."

What did these losses have in common? All involved "traditional" financial risks—nothing exotic and nothing complex. The Lloyds losses were the result of catastrophic natural disasters that, given the scope of its business, should not have been entirely unexpected. Credit Lyonnais' problems were caused by the poor quality of its loan portfolio. The troubles at Schneider resulted from property speculation and, it appears, fraudulent misrepresentations on the part of one individual. Furthermore, none of these losses involved derivatives.

These examples illustrate the point that derivatives are not the only source of risk. Indeed, risk is a constant in virtually all areas of business, and derivatives are just one of many such risks. In fact, it is probably more correct to say that derivatives are not actually a separate risk category at all; they are merely one of the tools available for the management of risk.

Given this assertion, it obviously makes no sense to consider derivatives risk in isolation. Any risk management system that focuses only on

---

[1] This chapter is adapted from a paper by Gay Evans, Bankers Trust International PLC, presented at the Federal Reserve Bank of Chicago's Conference on Bank Structure and Competition, Chicago, May 1995.

derivatives is doomed to fail. Instead, banks require a comprehensive risk management system that encompasses the full spectrum of risks they encounter. A derivatives risk management system should be considered a single module forming part of the whole. Therefore, I would like to first focus on risk management in general before turning to the specific implications for derivatives.

WHAT IS RISK MANAGEMENT?

The Conventional View

Conventional replies to the question of what constitutes risk management tend to focus on the after-the-fact or ex post side of the equation, such as containing existing losses of "firefighting." However, risk management should also be applied ex ante and should incorporate adequate preventative measures. In a similar way, risk management is traditionally seen as a process designed to avoid risk. However, as we have already seen, risk is ever present in all areas of a business. Furthermore, because of the fundamental link between risk and return, total avoidance of risk may not necessarily be in the best interests of the bank.

The Enlightened View

Instead, risk management should be thought of as a portfolio allocation process in which the bank makes a conscious decision about which risks to take and which not to take. This decision should be based on the anticipated reward for taking a risk and the bank's capability to bear and manage that risk. Viewed in this way, risk management becomes just one more part of senior management's strategic resource allocation process.

Having established a working definition for risk management, the next question is: What is required of an effective risk management system?

Requirements of a Risk Management System

Consistent with strategy.   The primary requirement of any system is that it be consistent with the company's strategy. This means the system must allow management to make conscious decisions with regard to the firm's risk-return profile. Ideally, this process should provoke management into thinking about its profitability targets, its appetite for risk, the associated worst-case loss, and the provision of sufficient capital to cover this worst-case scenario.

Because the risk management system plays a central role in planning and measuring performance, it is important to recognize that it can also have significant implications for employee incentives. Risk management tends to be effective only if the organization develops incentives for employees to follow risk guidelines. An example would be adjusting trading profits for risk to determine trader compensation.

Comprehensive information.   A risk management system must also provide management with comprehensive and meaningful information about all of the bank's risks. This means the system should be broad enough to look at the whole portfolio of risks and sophisticated enough to allow for the ways in which those different risks interact. For example, the system should be able to allow for the correlation between different markets and asset classes when aggregating individual risks. This is essential for senior management to understand the effect diversification and concentration can have on the total level of risk.

Consistent measurement.   Third, it is important that the system use a scale of measurement that is intuitive and that allows comparisons across all of the risk categories. For example, the measure chosen to quantify risk should enable users to compare risk positions in areas as diverse as leveraged buyouts in Australia and currency trading in Latin America.

The risk measure should also accurately reflect the size of the inherent risk, which in many cases is very different than the notional value or principal amount. For example, a $10 million position in US Treasuries and a $10 million position in interest rate swaps have the same notional value but different risk profiles. One measure that would allow comparison of the risk of these two positions would be the maximum potential loss under some assumed worst-case scenario. For example, the Treasury position may have a maximum potential loss of $2 million while the interest rate swap may have a maximum potential loss of only $500,000. This measure makes the relative riskiness of each position immediately apparent.

Readily actionable.   A good risk management system should be readily translatable into actions. For example, the system should be equipped to immediately identify when risk limits have been exceeded and provide exact instructions as to how to modify the position. Likewise, the risk management framework should include plans to contain any losses that might occur. Setting up these containment strategies in advance not only makes the bank better prepared to deal with losses but also makes senior management more aware of the level and type of risk it is taking on.

Timeliness versus precision.   Finally, all risk management systems face an unavoidable trade-off between timeliness and precision. A successful system is likely to strike a careful balance between the two.

A FRAMEWORK FOR RISK MANAGEMENT

This section gives an overview of how a risk management system might be implemented in practice.

Step 1: Establish Risk Categories

The first step is to establish suitable categories in which to segment the total risk. The categories include interest rate risk, currency risk, equity, and commodity risk. The important point is that the risk should be analyzed and managed by risk type rather than by product type. This approach relies on the concept that all products can be thought of as some combination of a number of *core* financial risks. Not only is this a more meaningful approach; it also makes the task more manageable. For example, even though the number of financial transactions may be nearly infinite, the number of common financial risks of which each transaction consists is finite. Furthermore, even though the transaction mix may change quite frequently, the core categories of risk are constant.

A key operational issue is granularity, that is, how specific and detailed the segmentation should be. The answer to this question will depend on the profile of the business in question. In general, if the risk management system is to be comprehensive, the categorization must be finite enough for each and every trader to be able to manage his or her own position. At the same time, however, the data must be capable of being aggregated to provide senior management with an easily digestible overview of the risk position. It is important that this framework for categorizing risks be as simple as possible so that it makes intuitive sense to the users of the risk analysis.

Step 2: Unbundle Products

Having established risk categories, the next step is to unbundle each transaction in the portfolio into its constituent risks. This process involves analyzing each transaction's sensitivity to changes in the variables that underlie each risk category. Some of the more basic transactions will affect only one risk category, while at the other extreme, less plain vanilla structures will be sensitive to many of the risk variables.

As an example, consider a convertible bond. As Figure 7–1 shows, adding such a bond to the portfolio would create exposures in the interest rate, equity, and credit risk categories because the price of the bond is dependent on changes in interest rates, the equity market, and the credit rating of the issues. In this way, a large portfolio of financial transactions can be broken down into a finite number of core risk categories. The next step is to quantify the exposure to risk that exists in each category.

Step 3: Quantify Risk Exposures

Maximum potential loss. Quantifying *risk* exposures is partly science and partly art. The scientific part uses statistical analysis of historical data to estimate the maximum potential loss given a predetermined probability threshold and holding period. For example, the result of such an analysis might be that there is a less than, say, 1 percent chance that one would lose $10 million or more through movements in German four-year interest rates over the next year. This is a highly precise and useful mea-

FIGURE 7–1
Unbundling Risk

Risks	Basic Products	Convertible Bond	Complex Structures
Interest Rate		X	X
Currency	X		X
Equity		X	X
Commodity			X
Credit		X	X
etc.			X

sure of the bank's risk relative to four-year German rates, and it can be easily aggregated using portfolio mathematics.

Liquidity risk and stress testing. However, historical data are not always accurate predictors of the future, and this is why the quantification of risk contains an element of judgment. Examples of such judgment include allowance for liquidity risk and inclusion of stress testing. Liquidity risk is the possibility that you will not be able to close out a position within an acceptable period of time and at a reasonable bid-offer spread. This risk can add significantly to the overall exposure, especially in new and innovative markets. *Stress testing* attempts to evaluate the institution's losses should the normal order and correlation of the markets break down—for example, if all markets move down at the same time. The importance of stress testing was highlighted by the losses in the fixed-income markets in 1994, the largest uniform down movement in years.

Step 4: Risk Adjusted Capital

The role of capital is to protect the institution from risk and to give the shareholders a cushion against losses. *Risk-adjusted capital* is a measure of how much capital should be set aside for this protection to be adequate given the analysis of each underlying risk. Therefore, the calculation of risk-adjusted capital provides a valuable yardstick with which to measure the capital adequacy of the institution as a whole and of each individual business line.

Risk-adjusted capital can also be used in other ways. For example, resource allocation and performance appraisal can now be based on a more consistent, risk-adjusted measure of profitability. Likewise, the budgeting processes can be made more equitable by charging capital on a basis that more accurately reflects the real usage of that capital.

The risk capital framework can also be used for control purposes in setting individual trading limits. For example, it is widely accepted that a position in equities is far riskier than a position in gilts with the same notional value, but it is not always apparent how *much* riskier. Risk-adjusted capital provides a mechanism for quantifying this difference and therefore allows an institution to set trading limits that incorporate absolute and relative levels of risk. This provides better protection for the shareholders.

ARE DERIVATIVES ANY DIFFERENT?

We will now focus on the implications of risk management for derivatives and the aspects of derivatives that make them different from other risk categories.

At a basic level, the management of derivatives risk is little different from the management of any other risk. All derivatives can be unbundled into component categories of risk using the same process we just described. Each component can then be quantified and controlled in the same manner as any other asset class.

However, derivatives have an added dimension when it comes to the management of risk. Derivatives are highly flexible instruments that can be used to take very specific and, if necessary, complex views of future events. This makes them ideal for taking an existing risk profile and transforming it into a different, desired risk profile. Because of this ability to transform the risks, derivatives have an active role to play in the risk management process itself.

A better understanding of the role of derivatives in risk management can be gained by looking at how they are used at a macro level. Derivatives attempt to place risk in the hands of those users that attach the lowest price to that risk. The role of the intermediary in the derivatives market can be compared to that of a bank in more traditional financial markets. A bank takes in funds through deposits, transforms the nature of those funds, and then distributes them through loans. In a similar way, a derivatives intermediary accepts risks at a price from a market counterpart. The intermediary then passes on part or all of that risk by paying another counterpart, or another intermediary, to accept it. Through this process of bartering risks, the derivatives market forms a capillary system for risk transfer. Risks will continue to be bought and sold until they arrive in the hands of the institution that is best equipped to handle them.

The reason for focusing on the total risk system may now become clearer. At a macro level, the derivatives market does not create risk, nor does it neutralize risk. All it does is act as a transfer mechanism for risk.

Although in principle risk management for derivatives differs little from management of any other class of asset, several aspects of derivatives provide a unique challenge.

Price information.   The first challenge is the absence, in some situations, of a reliable external source of price information. Many derivatives transactions are individually tailored financial contracts for which no liquid market exists. However, even though there is no observable market price for the derivatives transaction, there will always be a market price for the underlying asset. Therefore, it will always be possible to reconstruct the derivatives price from the price of its constituent risks. However, this pricing process will require that some assumptions be made, and the risk management system will be only as robust or conservative as the pricing assumptions that underlie it.

Nonlinearity. Derivatives also differ in that their value often varies in a nonlinear manner; for example, the value of an option is nonlinear with respect to the underlying asset. If this nonlinearity is not fully incorporated into the risk management system, the system will fail to accurately anticipate changes in value.

Leverage. A third difference is that some derivatives make it easier for users to take leveraged positions. This means small movements in the market can result in dramatic changes in the portfolio's value. If the risk management system is to be effective, the risk limits must fully incorporate the leverage of the position.

CONCLUSION

Risk management is not nirvana—it does not provide the answer to all problems—although it is a good start in solving many of them. Risk management also does not mean never losing money. It will not help to predict which way the market is going to move; however, it should prevent surprises. Risk management does mean quantifying each risk with respect to the institution's appetite for that type of risk and reducing it if that appetite is exceeded.

Finally, good risk management is not a computer system. It is a philosophy that centers on the fundamental trade-off between risk and return, is driven by senior management, and leads to a way of thinking about risk that is applicable to all businesses and is intuitive to both managers and traders.

Chapter Eight

Credit Policies and Practices

WHAT IS CREDIT?

The Canada Deposit Insurance Corporation (CDIC) defines *credit* as "the provision of, or a commitment to provide funds, or substitutes for funds (both on– and off–balance sheet), on a secured or unsecured basis, to a debtor who is obligated to repay, on demand or at a fixed or determinable future time, the amount borrowed together with fees and/or interest thereon."[1] Thus, credit is a broader term than *lending* because credit contains commitments and certain off–balance sheet items as well as loans. Credit *risk* is the risk of financial loss resulting from the failure of the debtor to honor its financial and contractual obligations to the lender. In this chapter, we examine lending policies and practices.

CREDIT POLICIES

Credit policies vary from country to country and from bank to bank. In this section and elsewhere in this chapter, information from the CDIC and the Office of the Comptroller of the Currency (OCC) is presented. The CDIC developed its *Standards of Sound Business and Financial Practices: Credit Risk Management* in cooperation with member banks to manage and control their exposure to credit risk. There is considerable overlap between CDIC and OCC policies with respect to lending, but some differences exist as well. For example, the CDIC states that credit policies must contain a credit risk philosophy. The philosophy is a statement of principles and objectives that outline the institution's willingness to assume credit risk. It will vary with the nature of each institution's business, including other risks assumed, its ability to absorb losses, and the minimum expected return that is acceptable for a given level of risk.

---

[1] *Standards of Sound Business and Financial Practices: Credit Risk Management* (Ottawa: Canada Deposit Insurance Corporation, 1993), p. 3.

The *Comptroller's Handbook for National Bank Examiners* describes what the OCC believes to be essential elements of a bank's formal written policy statements. The board writes the statements, and management is expected to implement, administer, and amplify them. We will focus on lending to illustrate the OCC's elements of sound policies. Lending generates most of a bank's income and is where most, but not all, major frauds have occurred.

Loans must be made with the following objectives in mind.

1. Loans must be made on a sound and collectible basis.
2. Funds must be invested profitably for the benefit of shareholders and the protection of depositors.
3. The bank should serve the legitimate credit needs of the community in which it is located.

The handbook gives the following overview of lending policies that apply to banks in general:

> The lending policy should contain a general outline of the scope and allocation of the bank's credit facilities and the manner in which loans are made, serviced, and collected. The policy should be broad in nature and not overly restrictive. The formulation and enforcement of inflexible rules not only stifles initiative, but also may, in fact, hamper probability and prevent the bank from serving the community's changing needs. A good lending policy will provide for the presentation, to the board or a committee thereof, of loans that officers believe are worthy of consideration but which are not within the purview of written guidelines. Flexibility must exist to allow for fast reaction and early adaptation to changing conditions in the bank's earning asset mix and within its service area.
>
> In developing the lending policy, consideration must be given to the individual bank's available financial resources, personnel, facilities and future growth potential. Such guidelines must be void of any discriminatory practices. A determination of who will receive credit, and of what type and at what price, must be made. Other internal factors to be considered include who will grant the credit, in what amount, and what organizational structure will be used to ensure compliance with the bank's guidelines and procedures. As authority is spread throughout the organization, the bank must have efficient systems for monitoring adherence to established guidelines. That can best be accomplished by an internal review and reporting system which adequately informs the directorate and senior management of how policies are carried out and provides them with information sufficient to evaluate the performance of lower echelon officers and the condition of the loan portfolio.[2]

---

[2] *Comptroller's Handbook for National Bank Examiners* (Washington, DC: Comptroller of the Currency, September 1977), Section 205.1.

The handbook also lists components that form the basis of sound lending policies for banks. Not every component is applicable for every bank.

• *Geographic limits:* A bank should have geographic limits for its lending activities that reflect its trade area. The policy should state the restrictions and exceptions. New banks located in Iowa, for example, should not finance Texas real estate developments.

• *Distribution by category:* Limitations should be placed on the aggregate distribution of total loans in various categories of loans such as commercial, real estate, consumer, agriculture, and so on. However, some flexibility is required to meet the changing needs of the bank and the community it serves.

• *Types of loans:* Guidelines should be established in making specific types of loans (e.g., energy, out-of-area real estate development loans), depending on the expertise of the lending officers and other factors. Particular attention should be paid to loans secured by collateral that requires more than the normal policing and types of loans where there have been abnormal losses.

• *Maximum maturities:* Loans should be structured with realistic repayment plans, taking into account the value of collateral. Making a 15-year loan on equipment that has an economic life of 5 years is asking for trouble.

• *Loan pricing:* Loan pricing must reflect all relevant costs (cost of funds, overhead, compensating balances, fees, etc.) and provide for a reasonable return. The rates established on loans should take risk into account, thereby attracting certain types of borrowers and discouraging others.

• *Maximum ratio of loan amount to appraised value and acquisition costs:* Many bank fraud cases involve loans in excess of appraised values and appraised values in excess of real values. Guidelines must be established concerning appraisal procedures and the amounts that will be loaned relative to appraised values.

• *Maximum ratio of loan amount to market value and pledged securities:* Banks may go beyond the restrictions on these loans imposed by Regulation U and establish additional policies for other types of marketable securities that are acceptable as collateral for loans.

• *Financial information:* Obtaining current, complete, and accurate information concerning a borrower's credit standing is essential before granting credit and during the term of the loan. The loan policy should explain the types of information required from businesses and individual borrowers, such as audited quarterly financial statements.

• *Limits and guidelines on purchasing loans:* Loan sales and participations are a common ingredient in bank fraud. Accordingly, policy should be established concerning the aggregate limits of such loans and contingent liabilities, as well as the manner in which they are evaluated, handled, and serviced.

• *Limitations on aggregate outstanding loans:* Policy should limit the amount of loans outstanding relative to other balance sheet items.

• *Concentrations of credit:* Diversification is considered an essential element of sound lending policy to balance out expected returns and risk. The problem with loan concentration is that when the repayment of those loans depends on one or more key factors that go bad, the entire concentrated part of the portfolio is affected.

• *Lending limits:* Lending limits should be established and enforced for all loan officers, or groups of officers, based on their lending experience. The policy should also cover the loan approval process, especially for large loans.

• *Collections and charge-offs:* The policy should define delinquent loans and explain how to deal with them, including appropriate reports to the board.

Three examples of loan policies containing these and other elements of sound lending are presented in Appendixes A, B, and C at the end of the book. As a general rule, the length of a loan policy is directly related to the size of the bank at which it is used; that is, small banks have short policy statements, and large banks have large policy statements. Those shown at the end of the book are for small and medium-size banks.

Lending Authority

Loan policy statements vary widely. Nevertheless, it is useful to examine differences in procedures for loan approval at a small, medium-size, and large bank. The procedures are presented only for purposes of illustration. We do not endorse them as appropriate for other banks.

First City Bank (FCB) has $29 million in assets; the main office and two branches serve a city of 70,000 people. As Figure 8–1 shows, FCB divides loans into four categories: secured, unsecured and overdrafts, loans to insiders, and loans to employees. FCB has four loan officers. Their lending authority ranges from $1,500 for unsecured loans, to $7,500 for secured loans for the most inexperienced loan officer, to $25,000 for unsecured loans, to $50,000 for secured loans for the most experienced

FIGURE 8–1
First City Bank ($29 Million in Assets)

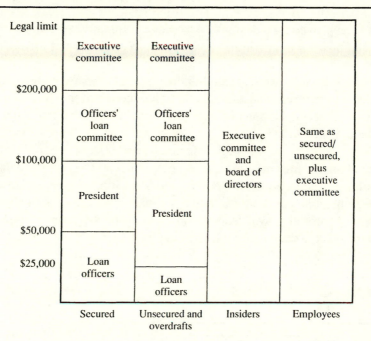

	Secured	Unsecured and overdrafts	Insiders	Employees
Legal limit	Executive committee	Executive committee	Executive committee and board of directors	Same as secured/ unsecured, plus executive committee
$200,000	Officers' loan committee	Officers' loan committee		
$100,000	President	President		
$50,000	Loan officers			
$25,000		Loan officers		

one. The president has the authority to approve unsecured and secured loans up to $100,000. Secured and unsecured loans above $100,000 must be approved by the officers' loan committee, which consists of the chairperson, president, and vice president of the bank. This committee can approve loans up to $200,000. Loans above that amount must be approved by the executive committee. The executive committee and the board of directors must approve all loans to insiders. The executive committee must also approve all loans to employees.

Southwest Bank has $150 million in assets and is part of a holding company. Southwest places heavy emphasis on commercial lending as opposed to loans to individuals. The bank has 10 loan officers. New officers' limits are $25,000 and are reviewed annually by the board of directors. With favorable reviews, lending limits might be raised to $100,000 within two years. Southwest's two most experienced officers have limits of $150,000. The president and chairperson can approve secured and unsecured loans and loans to employees up to $250,000. Loans above that amount must be approved by the loan committee (executive officers and loan officers) and reviewed by the board's loan committee (bank chairperson, president, vice president, and three rotating directors). Overdrafts must be approved by a designated employee with advice from a loan officer. The board's loan committee must approve all loans to insiders (see Figure 8–2).

Western Bankshares is a $4.8 billion holding company whose banks are divided into five regional areas. Each region has a regional loan committee that includes regional bank officers and directors. The lending authority in this bank is shown in Figure 8–3. Individual lending authorities range from zero for trainees to $500,000 secured/$350,000 unsecured for each regional president. The regional loan committee may approve loans up to $2 million. Loans between $2 million and $5 million require approval from the regional loan committee and two regional presidents; loans above that amount require approval from the holding company loan committee. In Western Bank, a customer's total lending relationship is considered when a

FIGURE 8–2
Southwest Bank ($150 Million in Assets)

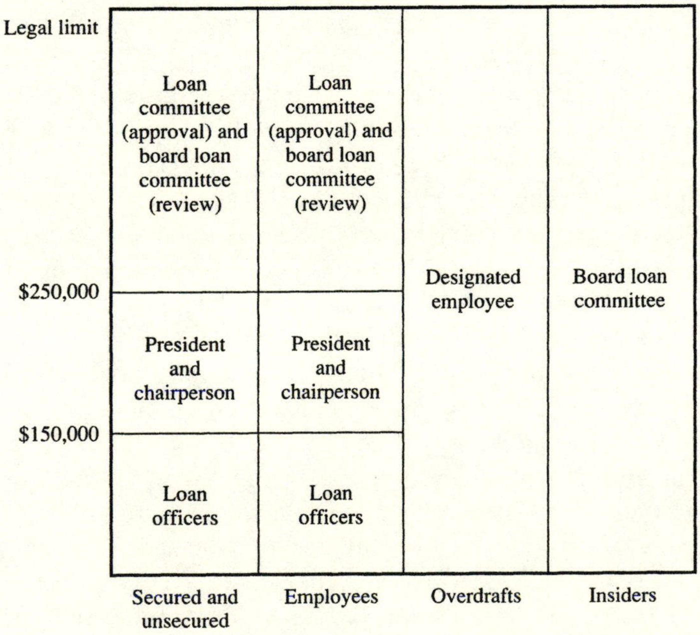

	Secured and unsecured	Employees	Overdrafts	Insiders
Legal limit	Loan committee (approval) and board loan committee (review)	Loan committee (approval) and board loan committee (review)	Designated employee	Board loan committee
$250,000	President and chairperson	President and chairperson		
$150,000	Loan officers	Loan officers		

request for a new loan is made. If a customer had an outstanding loan for $100,000 and requested an additional $10,000, the request would be considered a $110,000 loan in the approval process. Loans to insiders must be approved by the board of directors and employee loans by an officers' executive committee. This committee includes a regional president and senior vice presidents.

In reviewing the approval processes for the three banks, it is clear that large loans for all of the banks are approved by higher authorities within the bank. Since most bank failures are the result of credit risk, the board must establish ways to monitor that risk. One method involves loan reviews.

Loan Review

The primary purpose of a loan review is to audit the lending function of the bank on a regular basis. Loan reviews should be used to determine if a

FIGURE 8–3
Western Bankshares ($4.8 Billion in Assets)

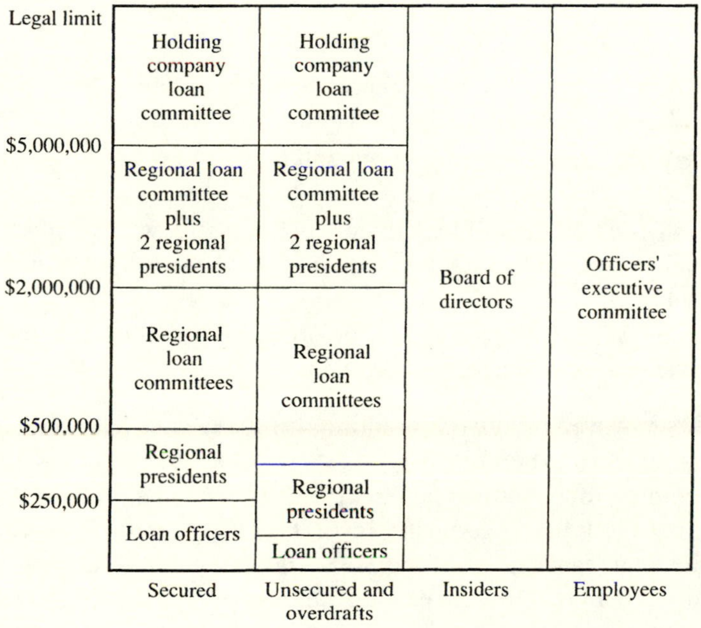

Legal limit	Secured	Unsecured and overdrafts	Insiders	Employees
	Holding company loan committee	Holding company loan committee		
$5,000,000				
	Regional loan committee plus 2 regional presidents	Regional loan committee plus 2 regional presidents	Board of directors	Officers' executive committee
$2,000,000	Regional loan committees	Regional loan committees		
$500,000	Regional presidents			
$250,000		Regional presidents		
	Loan officers	Loan officers		

bank's lending policies are being followed by its loan officers and credit analysts and if there are potential loan losses or problem loans that have not been recognized. Early detection of potential problems permits the bank to take corrective actions before they become major problems.

According to the CDIC, the common objectives of loan reviews include

- Ensuring that the lender is aware of the borrower's current financial condition.
- Ensuring that there is adequate collateral for the loan and that it is enforceable given the borrower's current condition.
- Ensuring that credits are in compliance with loan covenants.
- Providing early identification of problem credits.
- Providing early identification of the quality of the loan portfolio.

The loan reviewers may be internal or external, depending on the size of the bank. Large banks are better able to afford an internal review system than small ones. Some of the factors that must be considered in establishing an internal review are

1. *Structure of the loan review function.* Will loan review be centralized in the main bank or decentralized at the branches? Will each branch have its own loan review staff, or will there be only one loan review department?
2. *Reporting.* Who will be in charge of the loan review, and to whom will this person report? Do potential conflicts of interest exist?
3. *Staffing.* How many employees will loan review need to support its function?
4. *Functions.* What will loan review do? Exactly what should reviewers look for—documentation, credit analysis, external problems, or fraud?
5. *Scope.* Will all loans above or below a certain dollar amount be reviewed, or will a sample be taken?

Here is how a $3 billion bank holding company does its loan review. Its organization is based on functional lines of which the main divisions are the corporate group, general banking, and investments. Loan review was operated at the holding company level, and it reported to the corporate group division manager, who reported to the vice chair of the board. It had a staff of 10 loan review officers and support personnel. The loan review officers were experienced in all areas of lending and knowledgeable in documentation. The loan review department reviewed, on an annual basis, all loans over $50,000 and sampled loans below that benchmark for consumer loans. On each loan reviewed, reports were written stating whether it showed any signs of repayment problems or documentation problems. Problem loans were reviewed three or four times each year until the problems were resolved.

External reviews have certain advantages for small banks (those with assets of $50 million or less). According to a recent study, the costs of a permanent loan review staff may be too high for almost 60 percent of small banks.[3] Because of their small size, one advantage of an external review is an independent assessment of the loan review function. Another is the ability to control the costs of the review. Finally, the directors of new banks may have little experience in the area of loan review; external reviews provide that experience. Along this line, a large number of failures have occurred among new (de novo) banks and savings and loan associations. The directors of de novos need all the help they can get at a reasonable price.

The Least Directors Should Do

The CDIC states that at the minimum, directors should

- Review and approve credit risk management policies recommended by management.
- Review the credit risk management program at least once per year.
- Select and appoint qualified and competent managers to administer the credit function.
- Ensure that an internal/audit function reviews the credit operations for compliance with policies.
- Review credits to or guaranteed by officers, including polices related thereto.
- Review credits to corporations controlled by the institution, their officers and directors, and policies related thereto.
- Ratify credits that exceed the level of authority delegated to management, and be aware that they are not within the purview of existing guidelines.

---

[3] Fred H. Hays, Daniel L. Enterline, and Probir Roy, "Community Bank Directors: Should Your Bank Have an External Review?", *Journal of Commercial Bank Lending,* April 1989, pp. 21–29.

- Review significant credit exposures.
- Review trends in portfolio quality and the adequacy of provision for loan losses.
- Outline the content and frequency of management reports to the board dealing with credit risk management.

LENDING IS ABOUT RISK

Lending is how banks make most of their money—and how they lose it, too. Lending is a risky business. Banks can reduce their credit risk by using one or more of the following methods.

• *Avoid* making high-risk loans. In other words, raise credit standards to reject loans that are considered too risky or unsuitable. Bank loan policies should specify the degree of risk the bank is willing to take. A loan to finance a gold mining operation may be considered beyond the bank's risk threshold. The bank may also reject loans that it considers unsuitable. A suburban bank in a large city considers agricultural loans unsuitable because it has no expertise in that area. Similarly, a farm bank in Iowa should not make speculative real estate loans in Florida.

• *Reduce* risk by evaluating the creditworthiness of prospective borrowers and obtaining collateral and guarantees. More will be said about collateral and guarantees shortly.

• *Monitor* the behavior of borrowers to ensure compliance with the loan agreement.

• *Diversify* the loan portfolio. *Diversification* means holding a portfolio of a large number of loans from borrowers whose returns (i.e., profitability) are not closely related. For example, General Motors, Ford, and Chrysler are in the same line of business, and their returns may be closely related; but the returns of General Motors, McDonald's, and AT&T should not be related.

In addition, a portfolio cannot be diversified if it is concentrated in a few large loans. There is no magic number of loans. Nevertheless, a large number of small loans is preferred to a small number of large loans. The reason is obvious: Charging off of a few large loans could wipe out the bank's capital—and the bank.

• *Limit exposure* by restricting the size of loans to a single borrower. National banks are limited to 15 percent of the bank's unimpaired capital and surplus for loans that are not fully secured, and an additional 10 percent for loans that are fully secured.[4] Loan limits are also placed on insiders.

SEVEN WAYS TO MAKE LOANS

Banks make loans in seven ways. There is no significance to the order in which the following methods are presented.

1. Customer Requests

Customers request commercial and industrial loans. Unfortunately, many commercial loan customers are denied credit because they do not know what type of loan (e.g., term loan, line of credit) they need or how to go about asking for a loan. In addition to providing information about the borrower and its business, a loan request must specify how the borrowed funds will be used, how they will be repaid, the collateral, and other relevant information.

Most commercial loans are unique in that a loan to buy a specialized piece of equipment differs significantly from a loan to buy an inventory of manufacturers' overruns of women's dresses. Because such loans are unique, specialized knowledge is required to deal with them, and that adds value to the lending process. The extent to which the loans are unique and risky is reflected in the interest rates and fees charged by the bank. However, competitive pressures keep margins on commercial lending thin.

In contrast to loans that are unique, many consumer loans are so similar that they are handled and priced like a commodity. For example, credit card applications are scanned and evaluated by computers using credit scoring models to accept or reject applicants. Each cardholder pays the same annual fee and interest rate. There is no interest rate adjustment for risk for cardholders. If the credit card applicant is considered too risky, he or she does not get a card. Similarly, residential real estate tends to be treated like a commodity.

2. Solicit Loans

Banks actively solicit loans in both local and distant markets. Loan officers visit prospective customers to offer loans and other services provided

---

[4] For details, see 12 U.S.C. Sec. 84, and 1994 proposed modifications by the OCC.

by the bank. In the case of consumer loans, the solicitation may be done by mail, phone, or other means.

3. Buy Loans

Loans and parts of loans can be bought and sold. *Participations* are parts of loans that one bank sells to another. Suppose a large bank is making a $100 million loan to a chemical company and does not want to retain the entire loan in its portfolio. It can sell participations of, say, $5 or more to other banks. The sale of participations "downstream" to smaller banks allows them to share in loans they could not originate. Similarly, small banks can sell participations "upstream" to larger banks.

Banks can also buy and sell securitized loans. *Securitization* is the process of packaging and selling otherwise unmarketable loans. Typically these are real estate loans that have been packaged in large volume and sold as mortgage pools, some of which are guaranteed by the government. Some credit card loans and commercial loans have also been securitized. Securitization increases the liquidity of the seller's portfolio and provides a broader market for such loans.

4. Commitments

Commitments are agreements between the bank and a borrower to make loans under certain conditions. For example, the bank agrees to make a loan of $100,000 provided no material adverse change occurs in the borrower's financial condition between the time the commitment is granted and the time it is acted on.

5. Refinancing

When interest rates decline, borrowers frequently refinance their loans at lower rates. Refinancing is done at the borrower's option and occurs only when it is to the borrower's advantage.

6. Loan Brokers

Loan brokers sell loans to banks and other lenders. They are individuals or firms that act as agents between the borrower and the lender. For example, a loan broker may contact a real estate developer to find financing for a particular development.

7. Overdrafts

Overdrafts are unintentional loans made by banks to customers who do not have sufficient balances to cover their checks. *Daylight overdrafts* occur when customers wire transfer funds early in the day in anticipation of making a deposit later in the day to cover a withdrawal. The bank incurs a credit risk between the disbursement and receipt of funds.

TYPES OF LOANS

Commercial and industrial loans, real estate loans, and consumer loans account for almost 90 percent of total bank loans. In addition, banks make security loans, which are repurchase agreements with brokers and dealers, and loans to carry securities. They also make loans to finance agriculture, state and local governments, and foreign governments. Banks can make loans for any legal purpose. In this section, we examine the three principal categories of loans.

Commercial and Industrial Loans

Commercial and industrial (C&I) loans are made to businesses to finance their day-to-day operations (e.g., inventories, receivables), to finance their longer-term needs (e.g., plant and equipment), and for other business purposes. The maturity of these loans ranges from one day (called *overnight loans*) to 10 years or longer.

Different types of C&I loans are used to finance different types of assets, because one loan is not suitable for all needs. For example, suppose a retail store wants to borrow $150,000 to upgrade its cash register system and increase its inventory for the Christmas season. The store should use a line of credit to finance the inventory and a term loan to finance the equipment. These and other types of C&I loans are explained next.

Line of credit.   A line of credit is an agreement between a customer and the bank that the bank will entertain requests from that customer for a loan up to a predetermined amount. The line is established when the bank and the customer agree in writing on the terms under which the loan will be granted. If the customer does not meet the terms, the bank will not grant the loan. For example, a material adverse change in the customer's financial condition may have occurred between the time the agreement was signed and the time the loan was requested; therefore, the request will be denied.

Lines of credit are generally made for periods of one year or less. They are usually used to finance seasonal increases in working capital, such as inventory. When the inventory is sold and the receivables collected, the loan is repaid.

Revolving loan. Revolving loans are similar to lines of credit in that they are also used to finance borrowers' temporary and seasonal needs. Under a revolving loan agreement, the bank is obligated to make loans up to the amount of the commitment if the borrower is in compliance with the terms of the agreement. The loan agreement usually specifies the minimum amount of increments that may be borrowed, such as $50,000 up to $5 million. Revolvers, as they are called, frequently have a maturity of two years or longer. Revolvers that are automatically renewed for longer periods of time are called *evergreen facilities*.

Term loan. A term loan is usually a single loan for a stated period of time, or a series of loans to be made on specified dates. Term loans are used for a specific purpose, such as acquiring machinery, renovating a building, refinancing debt, and so on. They should not be used to finance day-to-day operations. Most term loans have an original maturity of five years or more. The maturity of the loan should not exceed the economic life of the asset being financed and being used as collateral.

Bridge loan. Bridge loans are used to "bridge the gap" in a borrower's financing until some specific event occurs. For example, the borrower wants to acquire a new building, but needs funds to finance the transaction until the old building can be sold. The bridge loan provides the funding and is repaid when the old building is sold.

Asset-based lending. In the broadest sense of the word, all loans secured by assets could be classified as asset-based lending. However, the term usually applies to loans secured by accounts receivable, inventory, machinery and equipment, and real estate. In asset-based lending, greater weight is given to the value of the collateral when evaluating the loan request. Equally important, asset-based lenders monitor their loans more closely than do other commercial lenders. The higher degree of monitoring helps to ensure the value of the collateral. If the borrower defaults, liquidation of the collateral is more likely to occur with asset-based lending than with other types of commercial loans.

Real Estate Loans

Real estate loans account for the largest dollar volume of loans made by commercial banks. The term *mortgage* is used in connection with real estate lending. In general terms, it is an agreement that the property will be sold if the debt is not paid as agreed on. The proceeds of the sale of the property are used to reimburse the lender. This gives the lender a security interest in the property if it is properly recorded.

Residential mortgage loans. There are two basic types of one-to-four family residential mortgage loans: conventional and government backed. *Conventional mortgage loans* are not backed by the government. *Government backed mortgage loans* are not insured by the Federal Housing Administration (FHA) or guaranteed by the Veterans Administration (VA).

Fixed-rate mortgages. The predominant form of mortgage loan has a fixed interest rate, is fully amortized, and has level payments. This means the interest rate does not change and the debt is gradually extinguished through equal periodic payments on the principal balance. Some mortgage loans are partially amortized, fixed-rate mortgages. In this case, only a portion of the debt is extinguished by level periodic payments, and the unamortized amount is paid in a lump sum—the *balloon payment*—or refinanced when the loan matures.

Adjustable-rate mortgages. The interest rate on adjustable-rate mortgages (ARMs) can change periodically, resulting in changes in periodic mortgage payments. Many different types of ARMs are available to meet the varied needs of home buyers. For example, *graduated payment mortgages* allow young home buyers to make low initial payments; the payments increase over time as the buyers' incomes increase. *Reverse annuity mortgages* are designed for senior citizens who own their homes free and clear and want to increase their incomes by borrowing against their home equity.

ARMs have *caps,* which limit how much payments can change at each adjustment period or over the life of the loan. For example, the interest rate may change no more than 2 percentage points annually or more than 6 percentage points over the life of the loan.

The idea behind ARMs is to allow lenders to maintain a positive spread between returns on their mortgage loans and their cost of borrowed funds. However, ARMs tend to be riskier than fixed-rate mortgage loans. They have higher default rates than fixed-rate loans because they are frequently used by borrowers who are stretching their funds to the maximum.

Home equity loans.   These loans are commonly used as a substitute for consumer credit because interest on home equity loans is tax deductible, but interest on consumer credit is not. A home equity loan is a second mortgage on the borrower's home. Second mortgages have maturities of three years or longer and are subordinated to first mortgage loans.

Manufactured housing.   *Manufactured housing* is the term that the government and manufacturers prefer to use for mobile homes. The Department of Housing and Urban Development (HUD) insures approved lenders against losses on manufactured home loans, and land and parks for such homes, for loans made in accordance with their rules and regulations.

In addition to the residential loans mentioned here, banks make loans for multifamily residential real estate projects.

Commercial real estate loans.   Commercial real estate loans include financing for land, construction, and development and for commercial properties such as shopping centers, office buildings, and real estate. Frequently commercial real estate loans are linked to commercial loans. For example, a firm wants to construct a new building and fill it with machinery. The bank will make a construction loan on the building and a term loan on the machinery. Before the construction loan is made, the borrower secures "permanent" financing from an insurance company or another long-term lender. Construction loans are considered "interim" financing. When construction is completed, the construction loan is repaid.

Mortgage-backed securities.   As noted earlier, securitization is the packaging of small, otherwise unmarketable loans (e.g., home mortgages, credit card loans) into large amounts that may be *enhanced* (insured or guaranteed) by a government or private agency. Credit agencies such as Standard and Poor's rate some securitized loans just as they do stocks and bonds. Securitization involves the issuance of securities that represent claims against a pool of assets, such as mortgages that are held in trust. The originator sells the loans to a trust, which then issues securities through an investment banker (underwriter) to investors. Some banks act as originators and trustees of the loans, collecting loan payments, dealing with delinquencies, and so on.

   Stripped mortgage-backed securities.   Stripped securities are created by separating interest and principal payments on the mortgages underlying the mortgage-backed security. They can be stripped into *interest-only (IO)* and *principal-only (PO)* components. Stripped securities offer investors a wide choice of maturities, cash flows, and risks. The IO portion represents a claim only on the interest payments from the underlying mortgages. As the mortgages are prepaid or amortized, they are no longer available for interest payments. Therefore, IOs are subject to *prepayment risk,* the risk that the mortgage will be paid off before maturity.

   POs are priced at deep discounts, and they accrete to their par value over time. The accretion comes from the scheduled amortization of the mortgages and prepayments that are redeemed at par. Because POs are purchased at discounts and redeemed at par, investors' returns increase with early repayment of mortgage loans. Thus, PO values rise when interest rates decline and mortgages are prepaid. The opposite is true for IOs; their value rises when interest rates increase and falls sharply when rates decline.

   Because of these pricing characteristics, IOs and POs are packaged into *tranches* (French for *slice*) that make them more attractive to investors.

   Benefits.   One benefit of securitized loans is that they permits lenders to increase the liquidity of their assets. Another is that they allow investors to diversify their portfolios by buying securitized loans that may not be available in their market. Finally, the sale of loans increases the risk-based capital-to-asset ratio by reducing the amount of risky assets.

Consumer Lending

Consumer lending is the heart of retail banking. *Retail banking* refers to banking services provided to individuals and small businesses. Consumer loans differ from other types of loans in several respects. First, except for automobile and mobile (manufactured) home loans, most consumer loans are for relatively small dollar amounts that are not secured by collateral. Many consumer loans are *open-end* (no maturity) lines of credit whereby consumers may increase their loans or pay off the loans over an indefinite period. Credit card loans are one example of open-end loans. Loans with definite maturities, such as car loans, are called *closed-end* loans. Finally, consumer lending is more heavily regulated than commercial lending. The following laws were designed to protect consumers:

- Truth in Lending Act (1968), Federal Reserve Regulation Z
- Fair Credit Reporting Act (1970)
- Fair Credit Billing Act (1974)
- Equal Credit Opportunity Act (1974)
- Home Mortgage Disclosure Act (1975)
- Consumer Leasing Act (1976)
- Fair Debt Collection Practices Act (1977)
- Right to Financial Privacy Act (1978)
- Electronic Funds Transfer Act (1978)

Because the market for consumer loans is highly competitive, there is competition on interest rates, amounts lent, fees, and noncredit services. This is common with credit cards that have no annual fee, give frequent-flyer miles for each dollar charged, give cash refunds or extended warranties, and so on.

Consumer loans are highly profitable for most banks. As Table 8–1 shows, the interest rates charged on such loans varies widely, depending on the maturity, collateral, and risk.

TABLE 8–1
Average Interest Rates at Commercial Banks, 1993

48-month new car	8.09%
24-month personal	13.47
120-month mobile home	11.87
Credit card	16.83
Contract mortgage rate on new homes	7.02
Prime rate	6.00

Source: *Federal Reserve Bulletin*, November 1994, Tables A39, A37, A25.

The default risk associated with consumer installment credit tends to increase with the size of the loan and with longer-term maturities, and is inversely related to the value of the collateral relative to the loan size. Defaults also increase during recessions, when unemployment is high. The highest delinquency rates in 1992 were 4.02 percent for mobile home loans, and 2.93 percent for credit card loans.[5] The lowest rate, 1.89 percent, was for home equity loans and second mortgages.

Leasing.   Leasing is an alternative to borrowing. Many lenders extend both operating (short-term) and capital (long-term) leases. Leasing automobiles is an alternative to making automobile loans.

EVALUATING A LOAN REQUEST

The Crucial Role of Information

Information plays a crucial role throughout the process of lending. Initially, there is *asymmetric information*. One party has substantially more information than the other. The prospective borrower knows more about his or her condition than the bank knows. It may be in the borrower's best interest to reveal only the minimum amount of information necessary to obtain a loan. For example, the borrower may not reveal that the value of certain assets is overstated or that sales projections are inflated. However, the bank wants to obtain as much information as possible to properly evaluate the loan request. Panel (*a*) of Figure 8–4 illustrates the process of making a loan. The bank receives information about the borrower at each stage in the process. Accordingly, the loan can be rejected at each stage if the information about the borrower reveals that he or she does not meet the bank's standards for granting loans or that the loan itself violates guidelines.

The process begins when a prospective borrower ask for a loan. If the borrower and the loan request are acceptable, the loan request is evaluated in terms of the borrower's ability to repay the loan and the six Cs of credit, which are described shortly. If the analysis indicates that the borrower cannot repay the loan or fails the other criteria, the loan request is rejected. If the borrower passes all of the criteria, the loan request goes to the next phase, which is preparing the loan document. The loan document contains

---

[5] *Statistical Abstract of the United States, 1993,* Table 818.

FIGURE 8–4
Making and Monitoring a Loan

(a) Evaluating a loan request

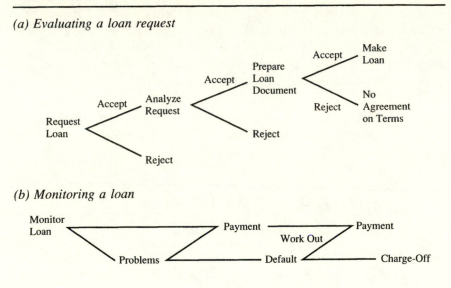

(b) Monitoring a loan

all of the terms and conditions under which the loan will be made. Interest rates and fees, the means of repayment, collateral, and other details are covered in the loan document. The prospective borrower may accept or reject the terms and conditions. If everyone is in agreement, the loan is made.

The importance of information about the borrower does not end here. The bank must monitor the loan until it is repaid or charged off as a loss. Panel (*b*) of Figure 8-4 illustrates the lending process after the loan has been made. The ideal situation is for the borrower to repay the loan on schedule. Unfortunately, not all loans are repaid on schedule. During the process of monitoring, the bank may observe early warning signals that problems with the loan are developing. For example, the borrower is late with payments and is spending more time on vacation than at work. If the problems can be resolved, the loan payments will be made on schedule. If not, the loan goes into default. At this point, the bank and the borrower must try to work out a solution to the problem. The best solution will result in the resumption of payments. The worst solution will be a charge-off of the loan. A charge-off means the loan is a loss and is no longer of sufficient value to remain as an asset on the bank's financial statements.

Citicorp has a credit-monitoring policy that has trip wires built into it.[6] It monitors loans biweekly and monthly. The trip wires include (1) client creditworthiness, (2) industry risks, (3) regional risks, and (4) consumer banking risks by product and country, and other risks that pertain mainly to very large banks. A substantial change in any of these trip wires is sufficient to warrant further investigation. Any bank can establish a similar system to monitor outstanding loans and the major factors that contribute to their successful repayment or default.

The Six Cs of Credit

Analyzing a loan request involves evaluating the six Cs of credit:

1. Character (personal characteristics of the borrower)
2. Capacity (success of the business)
3. Capital (financial condition)
4. Collateral (pledged assets)
5. Conditions (economic conditions)
6. Compliance (laws and regulations)

Character.   Banks must "know their customers" before extending credit, and knowing their character is the place to begin. *Character* refers to a combination of qualities that distinguish one person or group from another. To some extent, the words *character* and *reputation* overlap in meaning. These terms include the borrower's honesty, responsibility, integrity, and consistency and help to determine the borrower's willingness to repay the loan.

Character is the most important of the six Cs. Good character is a necessary but not sufficient condition on which to base a loan.

Capacity.   *Capacity* refers to the success of the borrower's business as reflected in its financial condition and its ability to meet its financial obligations. In the case of small businesses, it depends on the borrower's managerial experience, knowledge, and past accomplishments in running a successful business.

Capacity also refers to the legal capacity to borrow funds. That is, the person borrowing must have the legal authority to do so from the corporation or partnership she or he represents.

---

[6] James R. Kraus, "Ready for the Next Recession," *American Banker,* November 8, 1994, p. 4. Not all of the risk factors Citibank considers are listed here.

Capital.   Part of evaluating capacity involves the analysis of financial statements and pro forma statements. In this regard, audited, year-end statements should be used for the analysis. Year-end statements may contain adjustments that differ substantially from data presented in interim statements. For small businesses, consolidated financial statements from the principals of the firm should be prepared on the same year-end date. The financial analysis should focus on the firm's profitability, liquidity, and ability to repay the loan.

Collateral.   As discussed previously, *collateral* refers to assets pledged for security in a credit transaction. Guarantees by third parties, including government, may also be considered in the category of collateral. The quality of a guaranty is only as good as the quality of the guarantor. The US government has the highest-quality guarantees. More will be said about collateral shortly.

Conditions.   *Conditions* refers to factors that are external to the firm but may affect its ability to repay debts. Changes in import restrictions, changes in energy prices, and advances in technology are a few examples of such conditions.

Compliance.   Compliance with laws, regulations, and court decisions is an increasingly important consideration in lending. Consider the Comprehensive Environmental Resource Conservation and Liability Act (CERCLA) of 1980, which is commonly called the *Environmental Superfund Act*. The purpose of this act was to provide liability, compensation, and cleanup of the environment when hazardous substances are released into it. In some cases, banks may be responsible for cleaning up environmental damage caused by their borrowers. Thus, banks must be aware of environmental problems before and after granting loans.

With respect to consumer lending, consider the following issue. If a creditor routinely aggregates the incomes of married joint applicants when determining their creditworthiness but does not do so for two unmarried joint applicants, would the practice constitute marital discrimination under the Equal Credit Opportunity Act and Regulation B?[7] The answer is yes. In the case of joint credit, both obligors are required to sign a promissory note for the loan. As a result, they are jointly liable for the

---

[7] *Discrimination in Lending,* OCC Bulletin 94-52, September 23, 1994.

debt, and the creditor's rights are the same in the event of default whether the applicants are married or single. If the creditor offers joint credit, it generally may not take the applicants' marital status into account in credit evaluations.

Finally, insured banks and thrifts are required by the Community Reinvestment Act of 1977 (CRA) to meet local credit needs, including those of low- and moderate-income neighborhoods. The Financial Institutions Reform, Recovery, and Enforcement Act of 1989 (FIRREA) mandates the public disclosure of an evaluation and rating of each institution that undergoes a CRA exam. Such ratings are published by the FDIC in its news releases.

COLLATERAL

Sound banking practices require that certain types of loans be backed by collateral. *Collateral* refers to assets pledged against the performance of an obligation. If the borrower defaults on a loan, for example, the bank takes the collateral and sells it. Collateral reduces the risk to the bank when it makes a loan. However, collateral does not reduce the risk of the loan per se, which is determined by the borrower's ability to repay and other factors. While collateral reduces the bank's risk, it increases costs. The higher costs are due to the need for documentation and the costs of monitoring the collateral. Nevertheless, without collateral, some borrowers could not obtain loans. Borrowers that do not want to lose their collateral have an incentive to repay loans. Thus, collateral benefits both borrowers and lenders.

Characteristics of Good Collateral

Almost anything that is lawful may be used as collateral. However, some things are better collateral than others. The following five factors determine the suitability of items for use as collateral. The suitability depends in varying degrees on standardization, durability, identifiability, and stability of market value.

Standardization. Standardization leaves no ambiguity between the borrower and the lender as to the nature of the asset being used as collateral. Certain types of farm commodities, such as soybeans and wheat, are standardized. The standardization facilitates their use in trade and as collateral.

Durability.   Crushed rock makes better collateral than perishable flowers.

Identifiability.   Houses and automobiles are easy to identify. Retail inventories or goods in production are not easily identified.

Marketability.   *Marketability* means the collateral can be sold. It should not be confused with *liquidity*, which means that the collateral can be sold on short notice with little or no loss from current value. A house is marketable—it may take a year to sell it—but it is not liquid. Treasury bills, however, are liquid.

Stability of value.   Lenders prefer collateral that does not change (decline) in value. For example, the prices of exchange-traded stocks are more volatile than the price of real estate. However, stocks are more liquid than real estate.

Denial of Loans

Even if a prospective borrower meets the qualifications for obtaining a loan, the loan may be denied on other grounds. For example, the loan policy states that no more than 15 percent of the loans will be concentrated in a particular industry, but the loan that is being considered would increase the concentration ratio to 19 percent. The board must decide whether to change the loan policy or make an exception.

In the early 1990s, there was widespread talk of a credit crunch in the United States.[8] A *credit crunch* occurs when banks deny credit to creditworthy customers. Some argue that the credit crunch was due to bank regulators putting pressure on lenders for higher credit standards. The higher standards were a response to the large number of bank failures in recent years, which were attributed to lax credit standards. Others argue that the credit crunch occurred because bank loans to business lag the economic cycle. Whatever the reason, creditworthy customers were denied credit.

---

[8] Edward J. Green and Soo Nam Oh, "Can a 'Credit Crunch' Be Efficient?", *Quarterly Review,* Federal Reserve Bank of Minneapolis, Fall 1991, pp. 3–17.

THE WORST CASES

Charge-Off

Four things can happen to a loan: (1) It can be repaid on schedule; (2) it can be renewed or extended; (3) the bank can sell the loan to someone else; or (4) the loan can go into default, and the bank may sustain losses. The worst case occurs when a loan is considered a loss; that occurs when it is deemed uncollectible and when it is of insufficient quality to remain an asset on the bank's balance sheet. At that time, it is removed (*charged off*) from the bank's balance sheet. If enough loans are charged off, loan losses may undermine the bank's capital and cause the bank to fail.

Even if a loan is charged off, the lender may be able to recoup part of the loss. For example, a bank lent money to one of five partners in a condominium. The loan was secured by the property. The borrower defaulted on the loan, and the loan was charged off. Five years later, when the condominium was sold, the bank recovered part of its customer's share of the proceeds.

Impact on Capital

It does not take a large dollar volume of bad loans to eliminate the capital. To illustrate, assume a bank has $125 million in total assets, $100 million

---

Think about This!

Charging Off a Bad Loan Does Not Affect Earnings!

Bankers do not make bad loans intentionally. However, they do make some loans that become bad, and they know that some of the loans will become losses. To prepare for this eventuality, they charge anticipated losses to the provision for loan loss (PLL), which is an expense item on the income statement. In addition to the charge to the PLL, the bank increases the allowance for loan losses (ALL) on the asset side of the balance sheet and a reserve account in the equity portion of the balance sheet. On the balance sheet, total loans less the ALL equals net loans. Thus, the expected loss affects earnings when the charge is made to the PLL on the income statement. When a loan is charged off, the ALL and the equity account are reduced, but earnings are not affected.

in loans, and $10 million in total capital. The capital/asset ratio is 8 percent ($10/$125 = 8%), which is the minimum required by bank regulators. If the bank charges off 5 percent of its loans ($5 million), the capital/asset ratio will fall to 4.2 percent ($5/$120 = 4.2%). The bank will be subjected to regulatory "prompt corrective action." This means it must raise additional capital or fail. A few large charge-offs can spell the end of a bank.

Lender Liability

Lender liability refers to lawsuits against banks in connection with credit. In some cases, banks are sued because they denied credit to a prospective borrower. Oral statements by lenders, such as "No problem, you'll get the loan," can be the basis for a lawsuit based on *detrimental reliance*. The borrower, to his or her detriment, relied on oral statements to purchase inventory or incurred expenses; then the loan was denied. In other cases, banks are sued because they extended credit. A firm went bankrupt and sued the bank for extending credit. The firm argued that the bank should have known better than to lend that much money, which the firm could not manage properly. Lender liability also includes environment lawsuits in which bank borrowers polluted the environment and the banks were held responsible for the cleanup when they repossessed the assets.

Because of concerns about lender liability, some banks are reluctant to enforce the covenants of loans or to use discretion under the terms of the agreement. One consequence is that lenders may avoid loans where such controls are important. Another consequence is higher interest rates or fees to compensate the lenders for their increased risk of being sued.

Part of the credit risk management policy should deal with ways to avoid lender liability.[9] Effective written communications between the lender and the borrower are important in avoiding lender liability lawsuits. Effective written communications are those in which the terms and conditions (modifications and waivers) of an agreement are clearly understood and agreed on by all parties, as evidenced by their signatures. Documentation of modifications, negotiations, and discussions with the borrower are important too. The lender must also act in good faith and

---

[9] For additional information, see Marcy J. Bergman, "Lawsuits Arising from Lender Liability," *American Banker,* December 14, 1989, pp. 4, 12; Douglas V. Austin, "Mitigating Lender Liability Claims Through Improved Procedures and Disclosure Statements," *Journal of Commercial Lending,* February 1993, pp. 18–29.

avoid excessive control over and interference with the borrower's business or making threats to the borrower if the loan is not paid on time. Even if lenders do everything right, however, customers may still sue.

CONCLUSION

Boards of directors are ultimately responsible for the credit risk management programs of their institutions. Credit risk management programs involve the prudent management of all aspects of credit, including risk/reward trade-offs, quality, concentrations, currency, types of credit facilities, and more. Directors must establish such programs and ensure compliance through periodic reports from management, auditors, and bank examiners.

Lending is a complex process that begins when someone asks for a loan and usually ends when the loan is repaid or charged off. This chapter explained the crucial role of information; presented some key elements of lending, such as the six Cs of credit; and described the role of collateral. All of these tools are used to reduce the risk of making loans.

Chapter Nine

Dealing with Fraud and Insider Abuse

Fraud is a major problem for banks. The FBI reported losses from completed fraud investigation in 1992 at $1.6 billion, compared to $280 million in losses in 1983. Equally important, fraud was a contributing factor in the failure of financial institutions. In 1990–1991, the FDIC found wrongdoing in 90 percent of failed banks. In 1992, the Resolution Trust Corporation (ATC) found that criminal conduct contributed to the failure of 33 percent of RTC controlled thrifts. While it was true that fraud existed in a lot of banks and thrifts that failed, it was the proximate cause of failure in fewer than 10 percent of the failures.

During the 1988–1992 period, 2,600 defendants were convicted of fraud against financial institutions. Of that total, 1,700 persons were sentenced to prison, some for terms up to 40 years!

FRAUD AND INSIDER ABUSE

Fraud Defined

The term *fraud,* as used here, means violations of federal and state statutes pertaining to fraud at financial institutions. The principal federal fraud statutes pertaining to banks are listed in Table 9–1, and laws dealing with money laundering are listed in Table 9–2. A careful examination of the statutes and laws reveals that some frauds are not obvious crimes in the same sense that murder is a crime. Consider the following examples:

- A bank officer accepts a substantial gift from a lifelong friend to whom she has just made a loan.
- A loan applicant does not report a large debt.
- A loan applicant misrepresents her wealth in order to secure a loan.

- A bank officer does not file a currency transaction report (CTR) when a well-known and valued customer makes a cash deposit of $25,000.

Although these transactions seem innocuous, they violate federal criminal statutes.

TABLE 9–1
Selected Federal Fraud Statutes

---

18 U.S.C. Section 215. Prohibits kickbacks and bribes. It is unlawful for any officer, director, employee, agent, or other insider of a financial institution to solicit, accept, or give anything of value in connection with a transaction or the business of the institution.

18 U.S.C. 656; 961. Theft, embezzlement, or misapplication of funds by an insider with the intent to injure or defraud the bank.

18 U.S.C. 1344. Financial institution fraud; schemes or artifices to defraud a federally insured institution to take money, funds, credit, assets, securities, or other property by misrepresentation.

18 U.S.C. 1001. General false statements statute: knowingly and willfully falsifying or concealing a material fact or making a false statement, etc.

18 U.S.C. 1005. Making false entries in bank documents, including material omissions, with the intent to injure or defraud a commercial bank, a regulatory agency's examiners, or other individuals or companies.

18 U.S.C. 1014. Making false oral or written statements, such as on loan applications, an agreement with the financial institution, or other documents for the purpose of influencing federally insured institutions.

18 U.S.C. 1341 and 1343. Mail and wire fraud, respectively: a scheme or artifice to defraud that makes use of either the US mail or electronic transmissions.

18 U.S.C. 2 and 371. The general federal aiding and abetting statute and general federal conspiracy statute, often applicable when two or more persons are involved in the commission of an offense.

18 U.S.C. 1961. Racketeer-influenced corrupt organizations (RICOs).

TABLE 9–2
Money-Laundering Statutes

---

31 U.S.C. Bank Secrecy Act

26 U.S.C. Section 60501, Internal Revenue Code, Money Laundering Control Act of 1986

Money Laundering Prosecution Improvement Act of 1988

Anti-Drug Abuse Act of 1988

Crime Control Act of 1990

Federal Deposit Insurance Corporation Improvement Act of 1991, Section 206

Annunzio-Wylie Anti-Money Laundering Act of 1992

Insider Abuse

Insider abuse means wrongful actions committed by officers, directors, and insiders who intend to enrich themselves without regard for the safety and soundness of the institutions they control. Insider abuse frequently leads to criminal misconduct. *Criminal misconduct* refers strictly to criminal acts committed by such insiders against the institutions they control. Insider abuse is not necessarily illegal, but the line between abuse and criminal misconduct is very thin. Banks whose ownership is closely held and that are controlled by a dominant individual are probably more susceptible to insider abuse than other banks.

Self-dealing is a common form of insider abuse. It refers to insiders putting their own self-interest above the interest of the bank. One form of self-dealing occurs when insiders use their authority to grant loans to themselves, or to a related business, at preferential terms or use lower credit standards with the intent to make a profit in that business. For example, banking regulators sued National Bank of Georgia, Calhoun National Bank, and T. Bertram (Bert) Lance, an insider, for engaging in certain unsafe and unsound banking practices that violated federal securities laws. Lance was the former Carter administration budget director. The complaint alleged that loans and overdrafts were extended to Lance, his relatives, and friends on preferential terms without regard for their creditworthiness. The extensions of credits caused liquidity problems at Calhoun National Bank. To solve the problems, Calhoun transferred the troubled loans to other banks, but concealed the transfers by making misleading entries in its books. The loans were not reflected on Calhoun's financial statements, and no adjustments were made to the provision for loan losses. As a result, earnings and assets were overstated, and the bank failed to disclose its true state to bank regulators and investors. The National Bank of Georgia also extended credit to Lance, his relatives, and friends on preferential terms so that they could pay off loans and overdrafts to Calhoun bank. The National Bank of Georgia also failed to reserve properly for loan losses. The problems at both banks were corrected.[1]

Unwarranted fringe benefits are another type of insider abuse. Vernon Savings and Loan Association (Texas) was owned and controlled by Donald

---

[1] US House, *Fraud and Abuse by Insiders, Borrowers, and Appraisers in the California Thrift Industry,* hearings before the Commerce, Consumer, and Monetary Affairs Subcommittee of the Committee on Government Operations, 100 Cong., 1st. Sess., June 13, 1987, p. 455; US House, *Combating Fraud, Abuse and Misconduct in the Nation's Financial Institutions: Current Federal Efforts Are Inadequate,* 72 Report by the Committee on Government Operations, House Report 100-1088, October 13, 1988, pp. 95–96.

R. Dixon and his wife, Dana. When Vernon was placed in receivership in 1987, 96 percent of its loans were delinquent. Among the S&L's assets were

- A fleet of seven aircraft, including a seven-person helicopter (so the chairman could avoid crosstown traffic), a Lear jet, a Cessna Citation, a Beechcraft King Air, and others.
- A $2 million beach house in Camino del Mar, California, plus $800,000 in operating expenses. Vernon sold the house at a loss to a friend of Dixon's and financed it 100 percent.
- $5.5 million in artwork at Vernon.
- A $10 million, 100-foot yacht, used for political fund-raisers.
- A $22,000, two-week vacation to Europe that Dana Dixon called "Gastronomique Fantastique." She described the trip as a "flying house party" of "pure unadulterated pleasure."[2]

Paying high cash dividends when the bank is insolvent occurred at Manhattan Beach Savings and Loan Association (California). It was owned by Peter Sajovich. About one year before it was to be closed, Sajovich "contributed" to it a company that he owned called National Home Equity Corporation (NHEC). The contribution was made on the condition that the S&L would recapitalize NHEC with an infusion of $4.5 million in cash, which exceeded the S&L's capital. The day before the contribution was made to the S&L, Sajovich received a check for $3 million from NHEC. Of that amount, $2.525 million was a "dividend" representing the entire net worth, and the remaining $485,000 was a non-interest-bearing loan, resulting in a negative net worth for NHEC. NHEC went bankrupt, and the S&L failed.[3]

Other forms of insider abuse include putting friends and relatives on the payroll and directing the bank's business to friends and relatives.

SMALL BANKS ARE THE PRIMARY TARGETS

In the last half of the 1980s, 75 percent of the significant criminal referrals (reports of suspected crimes filed with bank regulators) occurred in banks with assets of $750 million or less. Why?

---

[2] William M. Adler and Michael Binstein, "The Speaker and the Sleazy Banker," *Bankers Monthly,* March 1988, p. 81; Federal Home Loan Bank Board, "FHLBB Places Texas Thrift into Management Consignment Program," FHLBB *News,* March 20, 1987.

[3] US House, *Fraud and Abuse by Insiders,* pp. 188–89.

One answer is that there are more small banks than large banks. About 10,800 banks exist in the United States, of which 7,800 have assets of $100 million or less.

Another reason for the failures of small banks concerns the quality of their boards of directors. The Office of the Comptroller of the Currency (OCC) found that deficiencies on boards of directors contributed to insider abuse and fraud, to bank failures, and to problem banks. The boards of such banks frequently lacked oversight responsibilities and controls, were overly aggressive, or some combination of the two. In contrast, none of the continuously healthy banks the OCC examined had such deficiencies on their boards. In general, small banks have more difficulty attracting quality directors than larger banks.

A third reason is that it is less costly for fraudsters to acquire a small bank than a large one. This is the case for problem banks with weak capital and other deficiencies. Such banks are usually the result of inept management, self-serving management, or both. Information about the financial condition of any bank is readily available in *Polks Bank Directory,* in Uniform Bank Performance Reports, and from data sold by Sheshunoff and other vendors.

A fourth reason is that small banks tend to have relatively few stockholders. It is easier for fraudsters to install a friendly board of directors in a small, closely held bank than in a large bank with actively traded stock that investors and analysts watch closely. This is not to say that directors and stockholders of large banks cannot be duped. United American Bank of Knoxville, Tennessee (UAB), had $838 million in assets when it failed. A congressional investigation characterized UAB as having a weak board that provided no independent or critical review of management's actions.

Finally, small banks lack sufficient capital to absorb large losses resulting from fraud. For example, a bank with $50 million in total assets may have $4 million in capital. It does not take many fraudulent loans or much insider abuse to create losses that wipe out the bank's capital and force regulators to close the bank.

COMMON SCHEMES

The five most common types of schemes that result in major frauds that have contributed to failures of financial institutions are as follows:

• *Nominee loans.* These are loans obtained by one person on behalf of another undisclosed person. The nominee may have no involvement in the loan transaction other than obtaining the funds and then passing them on to persons who do not want their identities known.

• *Double pledging of collateral.* Here the same collateral is used at two or more financial institutions to obtain loans. The lenders may not be aware of the double use, and the total value of the loans exceeds the value of the collateral.

• *Reciprocal loan arrangements.* These are loans made between insiders in different financial institutions who lend funds or sell loans to each other. The purpose of such "daisy chain" arrangements is to conceal loans from bank examiners.

• *Land flips.* A land flip is the transfer of land between related parties to fraudulently inflate the value of the underlying property. The land with the inflated values is used as collateral for loans, which frequently exceed the value of the underlying property.

• *Linked financing.* In this scheme, large amounts of funds are deposited in a financial institution, using brokered deposits or some other means, with the understanding that the institution will make loans conditioned on the deposit. The loans may be used to finance land flips or some other kind of deal that may or may not be legitimate.

Schemes such as linked financing and land flips are not necessarily illegal per se. However, they may occur in connection with willful misapplication of funds, false statements, intentional overvaluation of property, and other illegal activities.

INSIDERS VERSUS OUTSIDERS

Bank frauds fall into two broad groups based on whether insiders or outsiders committed them. Although insiders and outsiders may work together to defraud banks, the characteristics of each group differ substantially.

Insiders

According to California Savings and Loan Commissioner William Crawford, "The best way to rob a bank is to own one." Agha Hasan Abedi and Sheik Zayed, the owners of the Bank of Commerce and Commerce International (BCCI), are recent examples of dominant figures running an international bank for their own purposes, some of which are illegal by our standards. These owners had help from unethical attorneys, appraisers, consultants, and front people. For example, BCCI used seven Arab front people for the illegal takeover of Washington's First American Bankshares Inc. BCCI also used Clark Clifford, a well-known political figure, as a power broker to further its causes.

The "typical" insider who commits fraud in US banks is a pillar of the community who contributes to charities, is a civic leader, and a crook. The profile is a "male officer, director, or majority stockholder of a commercial bank, who either commits his crimes alone or in association with a few close associates or bank employees. He is often an outgoing, flamboyant businessman who runs his bank as if it were a sole proprietorship, such as a real estate office or automobile dealership. He spends, borrows, and lends money freely, often single-handedly exercising control over the bank. The criminal schemes he uses may be simple or complex, depending upon his own ingenuity, but they usually involve a continuing series of related transactions that extend over a substantial period of time."[4]

Outsiders

The profile for outsiders who commit fraud is different. Outsiders include national and international networks of persons who act individually and collectively to defraud banks. There are organized Asian and West African crime organizations that prey on banks. More will be said about these shortly.

Frauds committed by outsiders can be divided into two categories: large frauds and relatively small frauds. One important distinction between the two categories is that large frauds usually involve large loans at problem banks that are easy targets. Moreover, large frauds involving loans usually evolve over a longer time span. The new loans give the illusion of improving the bank's financial picture as the fees are booked. However, when the loans turn sour, the bank may fail. It takes time for the failure to occur.

Some large frauds are quick hits. Fraudulent CDs are one example. Fraudulent $8 million CDs purportedly issued by the Central Bank, NA, of Denver were in circulation in May 1993. The fraudulent certificates were used as collateral for loans or for loan payments.

---

[4] US House, *Federal Response to Criminal Misconduct and Insider Abuse in the Nation's Financial Institutions*, 57th Report by the Committee on Government Operations, House Report Number 98-1137, 98th Cong., 2d. Sess., October 4, 1984, p. 26.

Small frauds occur in any bank, regardless of its financial condition. Equally important, small frauds may occur very quickly. West African flimflams are one example. A West African fraudster opens an account with legitimate funds. He or she withdraws most of the funds shortly thereafter to make sure the account is open, then deposits a large fraudulent check (e.g., $5,000). Before the check can clear the system, the crook withdraws the funds and moves on to a new bank. Credit card frauds are another example of quick outside fraud. In 1993, credit card fraud in the United States amounted to $1 billion. The largest losses were reported by telephone companies, followed by automobile rental companies, and then banks.

MONEY LAUNDERING

Money laundering is widespread, as evidenced by recent front-page stories. The *American Banker* (December 21, 1993, p. 1) reported that a Swiss bank confessed to laundering drug money and forfeited $2.3 million to the United States. *The Wall Street Journal* (January 26, 1994, p. 1) reported that the mayor of a small southern town was indicted for money laundering.

Money laundering is the conversion of the monetary proceeds of a criminal activity into funds that have an apparently legal source, without revealing the true nature, source, or ownership of those proceeds.[5] It occurs in connection with criminal activities such as illegal drug trafficking, fraud, extortion, and tax evasion.

Illegal drug sales are a cash-and-carry business, and they generate a lot of cash. In 1991, estimated annual revenues from the sale of illegal drugs were about $300 billion worldwide and $100 billion in the United States.[6] In $20 bills, that amount of cash weighs about 26 million pounds! In one money-laundering operation in New York, a tractor trailer was required to

---

[5] US Senate, *Current Trends in Money Laundering,* report prepared for the Permanent Subcommittee on Investigations of the Committee on Governmental Affairs, 102nd Cong., 2d. Sess., December 1992, S. 102–123, p. 1; FinCen, *An Assessment of Narcotics Related Money Laundering* (redacted version), July 1992, p. 3.

[6] US Senate, *Drug Money Laundering Control Efforts,* hearing before the Subcommittee on Consumer and Regulatory Affairs of the Committee on Banking, Housing, and Urban Affairs, 101 Cong., 1st. Sess., November 1, 1989, S. Hrg. 101–492, pp. 6, 38. The estimate of drug revenues was made in 1991 by the Financial Action Task Force (FATF) of the "Group of Seven" industrial countries (US, UK, Canada, France, Germany, Italy, and Japan). The FATF was created to deal with illegal international narcotics trade.

haul $19 million in small bills. Moving bulk cash offshore is inconvenient. Customs officials have seized cash hidden in drums of textile dye ($1 million), in microwave ovens ($2 million), and in cryogenic containers that were supposed to be carrying bull semen ($6.4 million). Thus, it is easy to understand why drug traffickers are always looking for new and efficient ways to launder money.

Organized Crime

International organized crime groups engage in a wide range of illegal activities that generate funds to be laundered. Asian organized crime groups, for example, engage in heroin trafficking, counterfeit credit cards, alien smuggling, loan sharking, kidnapping, and murder, to name a few of their activities. They are the quintessential crime groups, engaging in every type of crime. Most ethnic Chinese crime groups operate out of Hong Kong. The Sun Yee Triad has more than 25,000 members and operates worldwide. The Wo Group has more than 20,000 members and has a major base of operations in San Francisco. Collectively, the Chinese groups have more than 100,000 members.

The total number of Japanese organized crime group (Yakuza or Boryokudan) members is estimated to be 88,600, but the number in the United States and Canada is not known. Nevertheless, an alleged Yakuza associate was involved in the purchase of Pebble Beach Country Club in California for $841 million in 1990. Because of questions involving the purchasers' previous criminal activities, it was sold for $500 million in 1992 to another group of Japanese investors.[7] In addition, Yakuza associates allegedly own casinos in Las Vegas.

Although the Italian La Cosa Nostra gets a lot of publicity on television, it is estimated to have only 2,000 active members in the United States, an insignificant number compared to the Asian crime groups. The latter do not have an international monopoly on money laundering or other crimes. Latin American and West African crime groups are active participants in money laundering and other crimes as well. The Latin American crime groups are most closely associated with laundering drug money. The West African groups are associated with laundering relatively small amounts of money resulting from credit card and commer-

---

[7] US Senate, *Asian Organized Crime: The New International Criminal*, hearings before the Permanent Subcommittee on Investigations of the Committee on Governmental Affairs, S. Hrg. 102–940, June 18 and August 4, 1992, pp. 52–53, 97.

cial scams. Each scam is relatively small, but collectively they add up to very large sums.

Money-Laundering Jargon

Money laundering is a business specialty of the illegal drug industry. It is also used by other industries and individuals. Money laundering, like any business activity, has its own jargon. Some of the terms law enforcement authorities and drug traffickers use include

- *Commingling*—Obscuring the illegal funds by commingling (mixing) them with the proceeds of a legitimate business (front companies) so that the all of the funds appear to be income from the legitimate business.
- *Complicity*—Money laundering facilitated by a financial institution's employees or owners. It is not limited to one bank. Various domestic and foreign banks may jointly be involved in laundering money.
- *Front company*—The illegal funds are represented as income (commingled) of front companies such as legitimate real estate agencies and pizzerias. Front companies may also be dummy corporations, such as jewelry stores and precious metal dealers, established for the express purpose of money laundering. *Shell companies* are similar to front companies, but they are usually chartered offshore to hide their identities, and they exist on paper only. They can be used to transfer funds in what appears to be a legitimate transaction.
- *Integration*—The provision of apparent legitimacy to the illegally gained wealth.
- *Layering*—Separating illegal proceeds from their source by creating multiple layers of financial transactions designed to block the audit trail and hide the source of the funds.
- *Placement*—The physical disposal of illegally obtained bulk cash proceeds.
- *Structuring/smurfing*—Structuring is the process of converting bulk cash into small amounts to evade the $10,000 CTR reporting requirement. For example, $40,000 in cash can be structured into eight deposits of $5,000 each. The individuals who "place" or carry out the multiple small transactions are called "smurfs."[8]

---

[8] US Senate, *Current Trends in Money Laundering,* hearing before the Permanent Subcommittee on Investigations of the Committee on Governmental Affairs, 102nd Cong., 2d. Sess., February 27, 1992, S. Hrg. 102–579, pp. 215–16, 437–44.

The Process of Money Laundering

The process of laundering money involves three steps: (1) placement, (2) layering, and (3) integration. These steps may occur simultaneously, or they may overlap one another. The first step, placement, may involve structuring and/or smurfing to place bulk cash in a traditional or nontraditional financial institution. This step is labor intensive and may involve hundreds of smurfs. Alternatively, the trafficker may get an exemption from a financial institution to engage in transactions in excess of $10,000. In either case, the deposited funds can be wire transferred or sent by some other means to another location. Detection of the laundering process becomes difficult once it moves beyond the placement stage.

During the second step, layering, the funds are commonly placed in monetary instruments (cashier's checks, money orders, letters of credit, stocks, bonds, etc.) and wire transfers. Launderers prefer wire transfers because they are fast and have no limits on the amounts that can be transferred. Multiple wire transfers occur through numerous institutions, front companies, and shell companies to deter detection. In addition to these techniques, illicit funds are used to purchase assets such as real estate, cars, boats, or aircraft that can be used to further the launderers' activities.

The third step, integration, occurs when the laundered funds are put back into the economy in such a way that they appear to be legitimate. For example, the funds may be used to buy real estate, establish businesses, or acquire other assets. Then the funds are recycled back into a criminal activity. One integration technique is overstating the value of exports and imports. For example, if imports to the United States are overvalued on the invoice, the difference between the actual value and the amount listed on the invoice is paid from the proceeds from illegal activities. The over-valuation of exports provides justification to receive funds from abroad.

Know Your Customers!

Federal legislation has made money laundering a criminal activity. To allow detection of criminal activity, financial institutions and businesses must report money-laundering and other suspicious transactions to federal authorities. Individuals convicted of money laundering are subject to legal sanctions.

Bank Secrecy Act. The Bank Records and Foreign Transaction Reporting Act, together with other provisions, are commonly known as the Bank Secrecy Act of 1970 (BSA). BSA was the first federal legislation targeting money laundering and other white-collar crimes, including tax evasion. It is called the Bank Secrecy Act because it helps provide information to law enforcement agencies about the secret use of foreign accounts by US customers by creating a "paper trail." While BSA aided in the tracking of money-laundering activities, it did not make money laundering per se illegal. Nevertheless, some money launderers were prosecuted for violating the BSA and the Racketeer-Influenced and Corrupt Organizations (RIC0) statutes.

The two principal parts of the BSA are (1) the requirement that financial institutions keep certain basic records for five years and (2) the requirement that financial institutions file currency transaction reports (CTRs) for domestic currency transactions (deposit, withdrawal, or exchange) in excess of $10,000 and currency or monetary instruments reports (CMIRs, Custom Form 4790) for international currency transactions over $5,000. The Treasury Department, which implements part of the act, defines financial institutions to include banks (commercial banks, savings and loan associations, and credit unions), federally regulated securities brokers, currency exchange houses, funds transmitters, check-cashing businesses, and persons subject to supervision by state or federal bank supervisory authorities. The act was amended in 1985 to include casinos in the definition of financial institutions.

Banks can grant exemptions from filing CTRs to certain legitimate firms that regularly engage in currency transactions with banks that exceed $10,000. The Treasury and the IRS handbook *Currency and Foreign Transactions Reporting Act Exemptions* explain the requirements for special exemptions and unilateral exemptions.[9] Special exemptions require prior approval from the Treasury or the IRS. Bowling alleys, car washes, dry cleaners, and other lines of business fall into this category. However, banks can unilaterally grant exemptions to certain retail businesses, bars, restaurants, hotels, and other businesses listed in the handbook. The exemptions are for a specific time period and for established dollar amounts. The handbook also explains reporting and recordkeeping requirements.

In July 1980, the Treasury closed a loophole in the law that provided for exemptions for cash transactions between domestic and foreign banks. In August 1980, the Bank of Boston exempted a deposit of almost

---

[9] For details, see US Department of the Treasury, Office of Financial Enforcement and Internal Revenue Service, *Currency and Foreign Transactions Reporting Act Exemptions*, 1988.

Think about This!

How Well Do You Know Your Customers?

A bank made a one-year, $80,000 first mortgage loan to a Panamanian cor-
poration. The loan was collateralized with a $1.1 million home owned by
the corporation. After the loan was made, a government investigation
revealed that the Panamanian corporation was owned by an illegal drug
trafficker. The government seized the property, claiming that there was
probable cause to believe the house was purchased with the proceeds from
the sale of illegal drugs. The government also claimed that the bank's president, who made the loan, should have known that the owner of the property
was a drug trafficker.

Under federal law, property that has been acquired with laundered
money is subject to seizure and forfeiture, even when it is collateral for a
bank loan. If the bank were an "innocent" lienholder, the court could "par-
don" the property. In this case, the court ruled that the bank was willfully
blind to the facts it should have taken into account. These facts were that
the Panamanian corporation was a shell corporation whose sole asset was
the property, which was vacant and up for sale. The bank did not know the
purpose of the loan or how it was to be repaid. It did not do a title search on
the property. The loan proceeds were transferred to Switzerland, and some
of the proceeds were used to buy expensive gifts for the bank president's
family. The bank lost $800,000 plus attorney's fees.

Source: Based on Cliff E. Cook, "Complying with the Spirit of BSA: 'Know Your Customer,
Policies and Suspicious Transaction Reporting'"; appears in US Senate, *Current Trends in
Money Laundering,* hearing before the Permanent Subcommittee on Investigations of the
Committee on Governmental Affairs, 102nd Cong., 2nd Sess., S. Hrg. 102–579, February 27,
1992, pp. 328–29.

$1.5 million that it handled as an international bank transfer, and it did
not file the required CTR.[10] The transaction was one of a series of
deposits from front businesses that were laundering funds for an organized drug distribution network. In this connection, the bank accepted
large cash deposits from a reputed mobster with underworld connections.
The bank had no direct knowledge of the source of the funds, but it did

---

[10] For details on this case, see Robert E. Powis, *The Money Launderers* (Chicago, Probus Publishing Company, 1992), Chapter 1.

not question their origin. The Bank of Boston pleaded guilty and was fined $500,000. A more important outcome of this case was that the concept of "knowledge" of criminal activity was expanded from "actual knowledge" to include "willful blindness," "deliberate ignorance," and "conscious avoidance."

Internal Revenue Service. The Internal Revenue Service (IRS) also has responsibilities under the Bank Secrecy Act. The BSA (USC, Title 31), the Internal Revenue Code, Section 60501 (Title 26), and the money-laundering criminal statutes require any person engaged in trade or business who receives more than $10,000 in a single transaction or a related series of transactions must file Form 8300, "Report of Cash Payments over $10,000 Received in a Trade or Business." Not everyone complies willingly. Recently lawyers were required to divulge the names of their clients who paid them more than $10,000 in cash.[11] Less sophisticated businesses may not be aware of the filing requirements. However, ignorance of the law is no excuse, and the IRS is actively pursuing nonfilers and other violators.

Money Laundering Control Act of 1986. Under this act, banks must "know their customers." This means that a bank must make reasonable efforts to determine who the borrower is, the credit history, the purpose of the loan, and other relevant information.

Banks must have appropriate procedures to detect and forestall money-laundering activities. Institutions that have failed to comply with laws have been fined and put on probation. For example, in 1990, the Bank of Credit and Commerce International (BCCI) was fined $14.8 million.[12] In July 1993, Dollar Savings and Trust Company of Youngstown, Ohio, agreed to pay a $1,182,639 civil penalty for failing to file CTRs as required by the BSA. Individual firms can be fined too. In April 1993, Essex Imports Inc., of Deerfield Beach, Florida, agreed to pay a civil penalty of $50,000 for structuring currency transactions at financial institutions to evade BSA

---

[11] "Lawyers Lose," *The Wall Street Journal,* March 2, 1994, p. 1; *US House, Effectiveness of the U.S. Department of the Treasury Programs to Address Money Laundering and Related Federal Tax Evasion,* hearings before the Subcommittee on Oversight of the Committee on Ways and Means, 102 Cong., 2nd Sess., Serial 102–21, June 23 and 30, 1992, pp. 18–28, 82.

[12] US House, *Money Laundering Legislation,* hearing before the Subcommittee on Financial Institutions Supervision, Regulation and Insurance of the Committee on Banking, Finance and Urban Affairs, 101 Cong., 2nd Sess., March 8, 1990, Serial No. 101–88, pp. 1, 50.

reporting requirements.[13] Although such fines send a strong signal to bankers and others, they are insignificant compared to the huge profits that can be made by money laundering.

Annunzio-Wylie-Anti-Money Laundering Act. The Housing Community Development Act of 1992, referred to as the Annunzio-Wylie Anti-Money Laundering Act, permits the secretary of the Treasury to require any financial institution (including employees, officers, and directors) to file reports on suspicious transactions (Suspicious Transaction Report [STR]) relevant to possible violations of laws or regulations. Banks are prohibited from notifying the person who is the subject of the report. To protect banks, the act limits their liability when filing such reports. In addition, all businesses must keep customer identification records for currency transactions between $3,000 and $10,000 and report suspicious transactions, regardless of their size. The suspicious transaction does not have to be linked to the drug trade.

Banks may not have "flagrant organizational indifference" to their obligations under BSA or to report suspicious transactions. All employees, officers, and directors must comply. Under the doctrine of "collective knowledge," information known by employees, acting within the scope of their employment, can be attributed to the organization. Thus, a bank could face a criminal charge if an employee suspects but does not report a transaction that may involve money laundering.

The Annunzio-Wylie Act strengthens the anti–money laundering efforts by giving federal bank regulators more latitude in investigating money laundering and allowing them to close or seize a bank, savings and loan association, or credit union under certain circumstances, or to terminate its insured status. In deciding whether an institution should be seized, they must consider whether employees, officers, and directors were involved in the illegal activity, the bank's policies concerning money laundering, and other factors.

The OCC's Red Flags

The Office of the Comptroller of the Currency (OCC) has published a list of red flags, or warning signs, that bankers should look for in connection

---

[13] FinCen *Trends,* Fall 1993, p. 6.

with money laundering.[14] Existence of the red flags does not mean that money laundering is occurring, but it may be one explanation for unusual activities.

1. *Activities that are not consistent with the customer's business.* One example is a retail business that deposits large volumes of checks but fails to withdraw sufficient cash to run the business. Another example is large deposits of cash, checks, and US food stamps (frequently used to buy narcotics), and wire transfers that are not consistent with the nature of that business.

2. *Unusual characteristics.* Unusual characteristics include accounts outside the bank's normal service area. The accounts may have foreign addresses in Colombia, Luxembourg, or other countries. Request for loans from a foreign company and loans collateralized by certificates of deposit may raise questions too.

3. *Attempts to avoid reporting requirements.* Attempts to avoid reporting may include asking for an exemption from CTR reporting, and then asking for frequent increases in exemption limits. The customer may make frequent deposits of cash just below the reporting threshold. The deposits may be made at the bank or at automatic teller machines.

4. *Unusual funds transfer activities.* Receiving or sending large volumes of funds to or from foreign countries is a leading indicator.

5. *Customers who provide insufficient or suspicious information.* This includes businesses that are reluctant to provide information about the purpose of the business, prior banking relationships, and the like. It also includes customers who have no references or identification and refuse to provide the information necessary to open an account. Banks are not required to accept unsuitable customers.

6. *Bank employees.* Sudden changes in the lifestyles of certain bank employees may not be due to winning the Florida lottery. Also, employees who are reluctant to take vacations may have sinister reasons for not doing so.

7. *Changes in bank transactions.* Significant changes in currency shipment patterns between corespondent banks or increases in the amount of cash handled without a corresponding increase in CTRs are reasons to be suspicious.

---

[14] Office of the Comptroller of the Currency, *Money Laundering: A Banker's Guide to Avoiding Problems,* June 1993.

WHAT CAN BE DONE TO DETER AND DETECT FRAUD?

The Role of Directors

Deterrence and detection of bank fraud go hand in hand. Deterrence begins with a bank's board of directors. The board has the ultimate responsibility for the bank's success or failure. Financially sound banks with active boards of directors who employ strong internal controls and audits have the best chance of deterring large frauds.

The legal duties of directors are dictated by laws and regulations. Under common law, directors are expected to carry out their functions with a duty of care and a duty of loyalty. Carrying out the duty of care is easier said than done when a dominant individual takes over a small or medium-size bank and controls the board of directors. Under such circumstances the chances of deterring fraud from within the bank are reduced.

Bank Security Personnel

Experienced bank security personnel can help deter and detect both large- and small-scale frauds. For example, communications between security officers of various banks alerted tellers to Nigerian flimflam operations being conducted in several southern states. The result of those communications was the arrest of the perpetrators.

Security personnel can provide background information about selected borrowers as well as verify other aspects of loan requests. This should be done before the loan is approved.

Audits

Bank audits are the next line of defense in deterring and detecting fraud. The mere knowledge that extensive audits are conducted may deter some prospective fraudsters.

Detecting fraud is a different matter. The auditors' primary concern is to attest to the correctness of management's assertions about its financial statements. Nevertheless, the US Supreme Court, in *U.S.* v. *Arthur Young & Co.*, emphasized that "The independent public accountant . . . owes ultimate allegiance to the corporation's creditors and stockholders, as well as to the investing public."[15] The public expects auditors to detect fraud or

---

[15] *U.S.* v. *Arthur Young & Co.*, 465 US 805 (1984).

other irregularities and do something about it, such as reporting bank fraud to regulators of law enforcement agencies.

Independent auditors are an important part of the process of disclosure to regulators, shareholders, and creditors. In this regard, the record of auditors in uncovering and reporting large frauds is poor. Ernst & Winney (E&W), Jake Butcher's UAB Knoxville's (Tennessee) auditor, released an unqualified audit report about 10 days before the bank failed. According to the FDIC, the financial statements were materially false and misleading. The frauds in this bank had been going on for years, during which time E&W was the auditor. Peat, Marwick Mitchell & Company gave an unqualified report for Penn Square Bank (Oklahoma) before it failed due to fraud. Arthur Young & Company gave Lincoln Savings and Loan Association (California), the nation's largest thrift failure, a clean bill of health for each of the two years prior to its failure. Jack Atchison, who was in charge of the Arthur Young audit of Lincoln, switched sides and became a high-paid official at Lincoln.

Lincoln Savings and Loan Association sued M. Danny Wall, who was then director of the Office of Thrift Supervision. Judge Stanley Sporkin, in his opinion on that case, had the following to say about auditors:

> What is hoped the accounting profession will learn from this case is that an accountant must not blindly apply accounting conventions without reviewing the transaction to determine whether it makes any economic sense without first finding that the transaction is realistic and has economic substance that would justify the booking of the transaction that occurred. Moreover, they should be particularly skeptical of any transaction where the audit trail is woefully lacking and the audit entity has failed to comply with the record keeping requirements established by a federal regulatory body.[16]

Stated otherwise, the auditors did not do their job properly.

Auditors stand the best chance of discovering large frauds by insiders where the scheme occurs over a long period of time. Auditors cannot be expected to discover small frauds committed by outsiders that occur within a period of days or a few weeks. Unfortunately, fraud by its very nature is covert and is difficult to discover. Even when fraud is discovered it may be impossible for auditors to follow its trail in different and unrelated institutions throughout the country. Unless the auditors are specifi-

---

[16] *Lincoln Savings and Loan Association v. W. Danny Wall, Director, Office of Thrift Supervision,* Consolidated Civil Action Nos. 89-1318 and 89-1323, United States District Court for the District of Columbia, Judge Stanley Sporkin, Memorandum Opinion, August 22, 1990, pp. 27–28, 40–41.

cally trying to uncover frauds, the likelihood of their discovering large, complex frauds by accident is slim.

Because a slim chance is better than none, the FDIC publishes "red flags" to indicate that something may be going on that deserves auditors' attention. Red flags include changes in ownership, out-of-territory lending, marked changes in the lifestyles of employees, financing the sale of insiders' assets to third parties, poor or incomplete documentation, loans that are unusual considering the size of the bank, and others.

Examiners

Examiners have a different role than auditors. Federal and state examiners investigate financial institutions for safety and soundness and for compliance with existing laws and regulations. In some states, such as Alabama, bank examiners also review the adequacy of audits.

Detection of fraud is an infrequent by-product of the on-site examination process, but it does occur. For example, a trainee examiner working in the First National Bank of Jacksonville, Alabama, discovered that 25 fictitious loans used the same address. The bank failed.

Even when the examiners suspect something wrong, their ability to investigate further is frustrated by due process, shortages of personnel, political pressure, and other factors. Equally important, examiners were slow to act decisively to eliminate known or suspected problems until it was too late. UAB Knoxville, Penn Square, Franklin National Bank, and Empire Savings and Loan are some examples.

In addition to conducting on-site examinations, federal bank regulators are experimenting with computer models that analyze financial statements to detect certain types of fraud and predict failures. Unfortunately, it is relatively easy to paint a rosy picture on the financial statements. Empire Savings and Loan of Mesquite, Texas, appeared to be profitable until the time it failed. One way to do this is to make loans that cover fees, charges, and interest payments for the first few years. Another way is to sell bad loans to other banks (daisy chains).

Equally important is the assumption that history will repeat itself, that the same types of frauds will be committed again and have a similar impact on financial statements. Thus, frauds involving foreign exchange computer transactions, money laundering, or misapplication of funds in trust accounts would not be detected by models based on the real estate frauds of the late 1980s and early 1990s.

Criminal Referral Reports

The final method for detecting fraud is the submission of criminal referral reports by bank officers, employees, or regulators who suspect that something is wrong. For the first 10 months in fiscal year 1992, 27,266 criminal referrals were made to the FBI. Of that total, 6.7 percent were estimated to be major frauds.

FDIC Red Flags

In an effort to detect bank fraud and insider abuse at an early stage, the Federal Deposit Insurance Corporation has published a list of red flags, or warning signs in its *Manual of Examination Policies (Appendix A)* for use by its bank examiners. The following red flags were taken verbatim from the FDIC's manual. They are listed for specific areas that represent potential problems. Keep in mind that red flags are indicators of possible cause for concern. The manual is careful to point out that generic terms widely used in law, such as *fraud,* have a central meaning that must be applied to constantly changing factual circumstances. It goes on to say that many violations of laws and regulations are subject to legal interpretation.[17] This is why the presence of red flags does not mean that fraud or insider abuse is present.

The subject areas covered by the red flags include

- Linked financing and brokered transactions.
- Loan participations.
- Secured lending (real estate and other types of collateral).
- Insider transactions.
- Credit card and electronic funds transfers.
- Wire transfers.
- Offshore transactions.
- Third-party obligations.
- Lending to buy tax shelter investments.
- Money laundering.
- Corporate culture ethics.
- Miscellaneous.

---

[17] U.S. House, Hearings, Part 2, 1384. This section covers administrative actions by the FDIC.

The red flags for linked financing and brokered deposits are presented in the following section. The red flags for the other subject areas are presented in Appendix D at the end of the book.

LINKED FINANCING AND BROKERED TRANSACTIONS

The FDIC's red flags for linked financing and brokered transactions include:

1. Out-of-territory lending.
2. Loan production used as a basis for officer bonuses.
3. Evidence of unsolicited attempts to buy or recapitalize the bank coupled with evidence of a request for large loans at or about the same time by persons previously unknown to the bank. Promises of large dollar deposits may also be involved.
4. A promise of large dollar deposits in consideration for favorable treatment on loan requests. (Deposits are not pledged as collateral for the loans.)
5. Brokered deposit transactions in which the broker's fees are paid from the proceeds of related loans.
6. Serious consideration by a bank of a loan request where the bank would have to obtain brokered deposits to be able to fund the loan.
7. Solicitations by persons who purportedly have access to millions of dollars from confidential sources that are readily available for loans and/or deposits in US financial institutions. Rates and terms quoted are usually more favorable than funds available through normal sources. A substantial fee may be requested in advance, or the solicitor may suggest that the fee be paid at closing but demand compensation for expenses, often exceeding $50,000.
8. Prepayment of interest on deposit accounts where such deposit accounts are used as collateral for loans.

Some additional red flags that apply to white-collar crime in general that are also applicable to banks are:

- Employees exceeding their scope of responsibilities.
- Failure to rescreen employees.
- Marked changes in the lifestyles of employees.

- Open-ended contracts with suppliers.
- Outside business interests of employees.
- Personal financial pressures of employees.
- Poor money management by employees.
- Unexplained rising costs or declining revenues.
- Unusual reductions in or loss of a regular customer's business.[18]

CONCLUSION

To paraphrase Willie Sutton, the well-known bank robber, "People rob banks because that's where the money is." Today bank robbers are insiders and outsiders who use various scams to defraud financial institutions of billions of dollars. The best defenses against major frauds are active boards of directors and financially sound banks. These defenses include internal controls, security personnel, and audits.

Bank examiners can help deter frauds. They must pay particular attention to the effectiveness of directors, such as strong internal controls, and to early signs of financial weakness in banks. To date, bank examiners have been lax in this area. A General Accounting Office (GAO) study reported that regulators reviewed internal controls for only 1 of the 58 banks and thrifts that were examined for the report. The GAO also reported that the reliability of 47 of the 58 exams was undermined by inadequate samples, reliance on incomplete or out-of-date data, and other problems. Potential problems in either area must be dealt with swiftly; otherwise, banks will be ripe for major internal frauds.

---

[18] Joseph T. Wells, "Red Flags: The Key to Reducing White-Collar Crime," *Corporate Accounting,* Spring 1987, pp. 51–53; Robert J. Lindquist and James E. Baskerville, "To Catch a Thief," *World,* July–August 1985, pp. 32–35.

Chapter Ten

A Director's View
of Internal Controls
and Auditing

Having and using strong internal controls is one of the best deterrents to fraud and insider abuse at financial institutions. The spectacular failure in 1995 of the 233-year-old Barings Bank, PLC, which experienced close to $1 billion in losses from trading futures and options, was due in part to a lack of internal controls.[1] This chapter examines internal controls, audits, examinations, and security officers in connection with detecting and deterring frauds and insider abuse.

INTERNAL CONTROLS

What Are Internal Controls?

The term *internal controls* means different things to different people. In general it is defined as "a process, effected by an entity's board of directors, management and other personnel, designed to provide reasonable assurance regarding the achievement of the following categories:

- Effectiveness and efficiency of operations.
- Reliability of financial reporting.
- Compliance with applicable laws and regulations."[2]

---

[1] Nicholas Bray and Michael R. Seist, "Barings Was Warned Controls Were Lax but Didn't Make Reforms in Singapore," *The Wall Street Journal,* March 2, 1995, pp. A3, A10; "Barings PLC Officials May Have Been Aware of Trader's Position," *The Wall Street Journal,* March 6, 1995, pp. A1, A7.

[2] *Internal Control—Integrated Framework,* Executive Summary, Committee of Sponsoring Organizations of the Treadway Commission, September 1992, p. 1.

The process of internal controls consists of five interrelated components:

1. The control environment—the corporate culture, including integrity, ethical values, operating style, and so on.
2. Risk assessment—the identification of external and internal risks relevant to the firm's objectives.
3. Control activities—policies and procedures that ensure the achievement of management's objectives.
4. Information and communications—internal and external communications necessary to control the business and provide external reporting.
5. Monitoring—the ongoing assessment of the quality of performance.

Reasons for Using Internal Controls

The General Accounting Office found that "Pervasive internal control weaknesses are a major cause of bank failures."[3] Therefore, it follows that a substantial amount of fraud can be prevented using strong internal controls, as the following case illustrates.[4]

According to Bob Serino, deputy chief counsel of the operations section of the OCC, this situation was the best example of the worst controls he knew of. The installment loan department of a community bank in Colorado was under the control of one individual. The loan officer's responsibilities included accepting applications, making credit decisions, and granting extensions and renewals. The bank's directors were pleased with the loan officer's performance. The installment loan portfolio increased in size and generated needed income. The portfolio had a low level of loan losses, and the volume of past-due accounts was manageable. New customers were brought into the bank.

Over a three-year period, OCC examiners and external auditors criticized the bank for poor internal controls in all departments. Recognizing that smaller banks have a limited number of personnel and have logistical problems in segregating duties, the importance of close supervision and review was continually stressed for areas where proper controls could not be realistically applied. Management reporting systems were weak. The board of directors was not receiving the accurate information it needed to

---

[3] US General Accounting Office, *Failed Banks*, GAO/AFMD-91-43, p. 7.

[4] This case was written by Sara L. Strait, national bank examiner.

fully exercise its duties and responsibilities. The reports the board reviewed were often erroneous. Problems in the management information systems were repeatedly brought to the board's attention, but they persisted.

As a result of the identified deficiencies, the scope of the examinations and audits was expanded. Additional reporting errors were disclosed. Consistent reprimands for internal control deficiencies and reporting errors contributed to the dismissal of the installment loan officer.

Then the problem multiplied. The quality of the installment loan portfolio deteriorated, and the volume of past-due loans increased. Loans were found to be undercollateralized, and the volume of extensions was extremely high. It was then discovered that the installment loan officer had made fraudulent loans and embezzled the proceeds. Loans were made under fictitious names, either unsecured or secured with the same collateral held for legitimate loans. With complete control of the installment loan department, it was not difficult for the installment loan officer to extend payments on fraudulent loans, maintaining a current status. New loans were created to pay maturing loans. A legal lending limit violation was concealed to prevent scrutiny of the loan portfolio. Management reports were generated manually and were easily manipulated to reflect a high-quality loan portfolio.

Research by external auditors and an enlightened board of directors disclosed that the defalcation amounted to more than $1 million. The bank's capital could not sustain such a large a loss, and shortly thereafter the bank failed.

Devising and maintaining internal controls are management's responsibility. Internal controls can be defined as the plan of organization, methods, and measures used to safeguard assets, ensure the accuracy and reliability of data, ensure compliance with policies and applicable laws and regulations, and promote management efficiency.[5] Stated otherwise, internal controls are procedures for prevention and detection within the context of accounting and administrative systems. They are intended to

---

[5] This discussion drew on the following sources: Committee on Auditing Procedure, American Institute of Certified Public Accountants, *Internal Control* (New York: AICPA, 1949), p. 6; US General Accounting Office, *Bank Failures, Independent Audits Needed to Strengthen Internal Control and Bank Management*, GAO/AFMD-89-25, May 1989, p. 15; Jack C. Robertson and Frederick G. Davis, *Auditing*, 3rd ed. (Plano, TX: Business Publications, 1982), pp. 204–06; American Institute of Certified Public Accountants', Statement on Auditing Standards Number 55, "Consideration of the Internal Control Structure in a Financial Statement Audit"; Comptroller of the Currency, *Comptroller's Handbook for National Bank Examiners*, Section 001.1.

prevent individuals from taking unscrupulous actions, such as altering financial records, and they help detect errors and irregularities. Errors are unintentional mistakes or omissions. Irregularities are *intentional* mistakes or omissions and include fraudulent financial reporting. A loan that does not conform to an institution's loan policy may be an error. Making a fictitious loan is an irregularity. The mere knowledge of the existence of strong internal controls may be sufficient to deter some fraudulent acts. According to the comptroller of the currency, good internal controls exist when no one person is in a position to make significant errors or perpetrate significant irregularities without timely detection. Internal controls also allow managers and auditors to verify the accuracy of the accounting for transactions. Thus, internal controls are an essential element of good management. However, even the best control systems will not work if they are not used properly. Someone, or a group of individuals, who is intent on circumventing controls can probably do so.

There are additional reasons for using internal controls. First, the Foreign Corrupt Practices Act of 1977 has accounting provisions that apply to all publicly held companies that have securities registered with the Securities and Exchange Commission.[6] The act requires such firms to keep reasonably detailed financial records reflecting their financial activities and disposition of assets. The act also requires them to devise and maintain a system of internal controls sufficient to provide reasonable assurances that transactions are executed in accordance with management's authorization; that transactions are recorded to permit the preparation of financial statements in conformity with generally accepted accounting standards, and to maintain accountability for assets; and that access to assets is permitted only with management's authorization.

Second, the board of directors of a financial institution has a fiduciary responsibility to its depositors and shareholders to provide an adequate internal control structure and to ensure that the controls are operating effectively.

Finally, strong internal controls serve as a buffer against adverse economic conditions, and they can help deter insider abuse and fraud. According to a US General Accounting Office (GAO) study, weaknesses in internal controls were a significant factor in bank failures.[7] The study cov-

---

[6] The Foreign Corrupt Practices Act amends the Securities Exchange Act of 1934, 15 U.S.C. 78q(b1); The affected companies must have $3 million or more in assets and have 500 or more shareholders.

[7] US General Accounting Office, *Bank Failures*, pp. 3, 25, 39.

ered external factors over which management had no control, such as adverse economic conditions and restrictions on branch banking. These factors affected all banks in Texas and other parts of the country. Controls must change to adapt to changing business environmental and external factors. Some changes in the business environment that may weaken existing controls are the acquisition of new types of businesses where the existing accounting systems are left in place, the introduction of new products or technologies that may affect reserves for loan losses, and rapid growth that overburdens individuals responsible for control procedures.[8] The GAO found that severe internal control weaknesses were pervasive in all of the banks that failed, and were present to a lesser extent at healthy banks.

In a separate study of failed thrifts, the GAO found internal control deficiencies, violations of laws and regulations, and unsafe practices at all of the institutions.[9] According to GAO director Frederick D. Wolf,

> Some within the financial institutions industry have expressed the view that the unprecedented problems and resultant failures are largely due to economic downturns in certain regions. However, both of our reviews lead to a different conclusion. Well-managed institutions with strong internal controls appeared able to remain viable despite downturns in local economies. Conversely, existing problems at poorly run institutions were exacerbated by adverse economic conditions, often leading to failure.[10]

The key points here are that well-managed institutions survived and that strong internal controls are one aspect of good management. Conversely, lack of strong internal controls raises questions about the quality of management.

Establishing Internal Controls

In the past, accounting controls were considered separate from administrative controls. In April 1988, the American Institute of Certified Public Accountants (AICPA) considered the two together and described them as

---

[8] Kenneth A. Merchant, *Fraudulent and Questionable Financial Reporting: A Corporate Perspective* (Morristown, NJ: Financial Executives Research Foundation, 1987), p. 14.

[9] US General Accounting Office, *Thrift Failures: Costly Failures Resulted from Regulatory Violations and Unsafe Practices*, GAO/AFMD-89-62, June 1989, p. 62.

[10] US General Accounting Office, *Failed Financial Institutions: Reasons, Costs, Remedies and Unresolved Issues*, statement of Frederick D. Wolf before the Committee on Banking, Finance, and Urban Affairs, House of Representatives, GAO/T-AFMD-89-1, January 13, 1989, p. 11.

the "internal control structure." The AICPA defines *internal control struc-ture* as "the policies and procedures established to provide reasonable assurance that specific entity objectives will be achieved." The AICPA Statement on Auditing Standard No. 55, *Consideration of the Internal Control Structure in a Financial Statement Audit,* describes the three ele-ments of an internal control structure. The first element, *control environ-ment,* concerns the environment within which the controls are used. The effectiveness of controls depends on the collective effect of various fac-tors, including management philosophy, organizational structure, the role of the board of directors and its committees, the communication of author-ity and responsibility, management control methods, the internal audit function, personnel policies and procedures, and environmental factors. The second element, *accounting system,* deals with the methods and records used to report transactions and maintain accountability for assets and liabilities. The final element, *control procedures,* concerns the poli-cies and control procedures established to ensure that management's objectives are carried out.

Auditing Standard No. 55 provides guidance for independent auditors who must evaluate the internal control structure of an organization and for planning and performing an audit. Federal and state bank examiners have somewhat different but overlapping concerns in evaluating a bank's inter-nal controls.

The *Comptroller's Handbook for National Bank Examiners* explains the comptroller of the currency's view of internal controls and provides detailed "Internal Control Questionnaires" for areas of concern to national bank examiners.[11] The OCC states that while procedures are an important element of internal controls, actual practices must be taken into account. In addition, the procedures must be performed by competent individuals. Equally important is independent performance. This refers to the effective segregation of duties or "positions," such as cashier. For example, a cashier is the sole check signer, and an assistant prepares the monthly rec-oncilement. Although both individuals may be competent, the assistant is under the direct supervision of the cashier. Therefore, the assistant's duties should be viewed as if they were performed by the cashier.

The Internal Control Questionnaires are a starting point for examiners to evaluate a bank's control procedures. The questionnaires are general in

---

[11] The *Comptroller's Handbook for National Bank Examiners* is distributed to national banks. The publication is looseleaf and is updated periodically.

nature because the OCC recognizes that what applies to one bank may not apply to another. Accordingly, the questionnaires provide some insights as to what the OCC considers good controls, as well as problem areas that might undermine the controls. Table 10–1 lists selected items from the Internal Control Questionnaire for Commercial Loans and is used to illustrate typical questions.

TABLE 10–1
Selected Items from the OCC's Internal Control Questionnaire for Commercial Loans

The question numbers are those that appear in the *Comptroller's Handbook for National Bank Examiners,* August 1982.

1. Has the board of directors, consistent with its duties and responsibilities, adopted written commercial loan policies that:
   a) Establish procedures for reviewing commercial loan applications?
   b) Define qualified borrowers?
   c) Establish minimum standards for documentation?
3. Is the preparation and posting of subsidiary commercial loan records performed or reviewed by persons who do not also:
   a) Issue official checks or drafts singly?
   b) Handle cash?
7. Are documents supporting recorded credit adjustments checked or tested subsequently by persons who do not also handle cash?
13. Are any independent interest computations made and compared or tested to initial interest records by persons who do not also:
   a) Issue official checks or drafts singly?
   b) Handle cash?
14. Are multicopy, prenumbered records maintained that:
   a) Detail the complete description of collateral pledged?
   b) Are typed or completed in ink?
   c) Are signed by the customer?
   d) Are designed so that a copy goes to the customer?
23. Has the bank instituted a system which:
   a) Insures that security agreements are filed?
   b) Insures that collateral mortgages are properly recorded?
   c) Insures that title searches and property appraisals are performed in connection with collateral mortgages?
   d) Insures that insurance coverage (including loss payee clause) is in effect on property covered by collateral mortgages?
34. Are collection notices handled by someone not connected with loan processing?

Source: *Comptroller's Handbook for National Bank Examiners,* August 1982.

AUDITING

Closing the Expectation Gap

The Securities and Exchange Commission (SEC) is the principal federal agency involved in accounting and auditing standards for publicly traded companies. It establishes rules and regulations for public disclosure and independent audits. The SEC has adopted the generally accepted accounting principles (GAAP) promulgated by the Financial Accounting Standards Board and the generally accepted auditing standards (GAAS) implemented by the AICPA as the standards for meeting its disclosure requirements. Federal banking regulators also impose reporting requirements for the institutions they regulate. Independent audits are an important part of the disclosure process. "Full, fair, and accurate disclosure of financial results is a cornerstone of our system of public securities markets. . . . The public accountant's audit is an important element in the financial reporting process because the audit subjects financial statements, which are management's responsibility, to scrutiny on behalf of shareholders and creditors to whom management is responsible."[12]

Against this background, our primary concerns are with bank fraud and the ongoing operations of banks. We know that the existence and effective operation of internal controls reduces the chance for fraud and enhances the ability of a bank to survive. Nevertheless, fraud exists and banks fail for a variety of reasons. Therefore, the issues are (1) to what extent can auditors detect fraud, and (2) if they do discover fraud, what should they do about it? Also, to what extent do auditors detect and report financial difficulties that may affect the survival of a bank? One difficulty in examining these issues involves the so-called "expectation gap," which is the difference between the public's and the accounting profession's expectations of auditors. The public expects auditors to be able to detect fraud or irregularities and do something about it, such as reporting fraud to bank regulators or law enforcement officials. The public expects auditors to have some insight concerning the ability of banks to survive. The public confidence in auditors was shaken in the mid-1970s for reasons that will be explained shortly. This lack of confidence was

---

[12] US General Accounting Office, *CPA Audit Quality: Status of Actions Taken to Improve Auditing and Financial Reporting of Public Companies*, GAO/AFMD-89-38, March 1989, pp. 8–9.

expressed in the following accountant's report, which appeared in *Forbes* (March 15, 1977):

To the directors and stockholders:

We have examined the Consolidated Balance Sheet of the company and Consolidated subsidiaries as of December 31, 1976 and 1975. In our opinion, these financial statements present fairly the financial position of the companies, in conformity with generally accepted accounting principles consistently applied.

On the other hand, there is a growing body of opinion that holds that our opinion is not worth a damn.

As part of an effort to alter this opinion, Congress introduced legislation (House Bill 5439) in 1986 requiring auditors to detect and report material fraud directly to the SEC. The accounting profession has a different set of expectations. What is an audit and the auditor's point of view?

According to the American Accounting Association, "Auditing is a systematic process of objectively obtaining and evaluating evidence regarding assertions about economic actions and events to ascertain the degree of correspondence between those assertions and established criteria and communicating the results to interested users."[13] This comprehensive definition suggests that auditors seek to determine if management's full and fair disclosures about the bank's financial condition are represented fairly within the context of generally accepted accounting standards. To make this determination, auditors take into the account audit objectives for various components of the financial statements. Selected objectives for auditing a bank's assets are presented to illustrate one aspect of the audit process.[14] These audit objectives are:

1. Existence or occurrence: Determine if the assets presented in the balance sheet exist.

2. Completeness: Determine if the quantities of particular assets, such as securities, include all items on hand, held by others, or in transit. In addition, determine if all amounts that should be recorded are in fact recorded.

3. Rights and obligations: Determine if the bank has legal title to the assets, excluding collateral owned by others or pledged on loans.

4. Valuation or allocations: Determine that assets are properly valued at cost, market value, or fair value.

---

[13] Robertson and Davis, *Auditing*, p. 4. The text also presents other, narrower definitions of auditing.

[14] *Audits of Banks* (New York: American Institute of Certified Public Accountants, 1983), pp. 35–36.

5. Presentation and disclosure: Determine that the assets are properly categorized on the balance sheet and that their basis for valuation, pledging, or assignment is adequately disclosed in the financial statements.

All of this is done to determine if management is fair in its assertions about its assets. Different audit objectives are applied to other parts of the financial statements to determine "fairness." Unfortunately, fraud is, by its very nature, covert and difficult for auditors and investigators to uncover. This is especially so when a complex fraud involves numerous seemingly unrelated banks and firms. Thus, the discovery of fraud is an infrequent by-product of the audit process. Therefore, it is not surprising that auditors' track records in discovering fraud are poor. Moreover, if they did discover fraud, they did not disclose it to the public or regulatory authorities. A long history of controversy surrounds auditors' reporting responsibilities.[15] They are guided by conflicting demands (the Code of Professional Ethics, Statements of Auditing Standards, laws, and so on), and pulled by the interests of various stakeholder groups—shareholders, creditors, the SEC, bank regulators, and others. Each of these groups expects the auditors to act for them, and consequently auditors have compartmentalized their responsibilities. Their primary reporting responsibility is to the client for illegal acts, to the SEC for filings, to the IRS for tax returns, and to shareholders and creditors for their opinions on financial statements taken as a whole.

In the early 1970s, several large companies were exposed for making illegal or questionable payments to foreign officials as bribes to get contracts and for other purposes. In a 1976 program of voluntary disclosure to the SEC, some 250 companies admitted to such payments. In 1977, Congress enacted the Foreign Corrupt Practices Act, which requires SEC registrants to maintain the accounting standards explained previously. The following year, the Commission on Auditors' Responsibilities (the Cohen Commission) recommended that auditors have a duty to search for fraud. In 1987, the National Commission on Fraudulent Financial Reporting (the Treadway Commission) made 49 recommendations to detect and deter fraudulent financial reporting.[16] The Treadway Commission examined 119 enforcement actions against public companies or individuals and 42

---

[15] R. K. Mautz and Hussein A. Sharaf, *The Philosophy of Auditing* (Sarasota, FL: American Accounting Association, monograph no. 6, 1961).

[16] *Report of the National Commission on Fraudulent Financial Reporting,* National Commission on Fraudulent Financial Reporting, October 1987; US General Accounting Office, *CPA Audit Quality: Status of Actions,* pp. 11, 13.

enforcement actions against public accountants or their firms brought by the SEC from 1981 to 1986. Its study revealed that fraudulent financial reporting was usually the result of environmental, institutional, or individual forces or opportunities. A frequent incentive for engaging in fraudulent reporting was to improve a company's financial appearance or to postpone dealing with financial difficulties.

In 1988, the AICPA's Auditing Standards Board issued new Statements of Auditing Standards (SASs) that addressed some of the issues raised here, but did not resolve them to everyone's satisfaction. Traditionally, auditing standards recognized the auditor-client relationship, and the auditor's primary reporting responsibility for illegal acts was to the client. This reporting relationship is changing, as demonstrated in the following auditing standards. Although auditors reported to their clients, the U.S. Supreme Court, in *United States* v. *Arthur Young & Co.*, emphasized that "The independent public accountant . . . owes ultimate allegiance to the corporation's creditors and stockholders, as well as to the investing public."[17]

SAS No. 53, *The Auditor's Responsibility to Detect and Report Errors and Irregularities.*   This standard states that auditors should exercise due care in auditing and the proper degree of professional skepticism to "achieve reasonable assurance that material errors or irregularities will be detected."[18] If irregularities are detected, the auditor must assess the risk that they will have a direct and material effect on the determination of financial statement amounts. If such a condition exists, the auditor should insist that the statements be revised and, if they are not, give a qualified or adverse opinion and disclose the reasons for doing so. The auditor should communicate the findings to the audit committee or the board of directors. Under certain conditions, a duty may exist to make disclosures to parties other than the client. Those conditions are:

- When the organization reports an auditor change to the SEC on Form 8-K.
- To a successor auditor when inquiries are made in accordance with SAS No. 7, *Communications Between Predecessor and Successor Auditors.*

---

[17] *United States* v. *Arthur Young & Co.*, 465 U.S. 805, 8-7-818 (1984).

[18] Statement on Auditing Standards No. 53, *The Auditor's Responsibility to Detect and Report Errors and Irregularities,* AICPA, April 1988, p. 3.

- In response to a subpoena.
- To a funding agency or government agency requiring audits of organizations receiving its financial support.

SAS No. 53 goes on to say that because of ethical and legal considerations, the auditor may wish to get legal counsel before discussing the results with parties outside other than the client. It also states that the subsequent discovery of material misstatement in financial statements does not, in and of itself, mean the audit was inadequate.

SAS No. 54, *Illegal Acts by Clients.* This standard defines illegal acts as violations of laws or government regulations. Illegal acts by clients are acts attributable to the entity whose financial statements are under audit or acts by management or employees on behalf of the client. They do not include personal misconduct by the entity's personnel that is unrelated to their business activities.

The final determination of legality is normally beyond the scope of an auditor's professional competence. Keeping this in mind, auditors should consider laws and regulations from the perspective of their known relation to the audit objectives and report and/or disclose irregularities accordingly. The Financial Institutions Reform, Recovery and Enforcement Act of 1989 (Title XII) requires the FDIC (or other federal insurance corporations) to designate the applicable laws and regulations relating to safety and soundness that managements of financial institutions must consider. It also requires independent public accountants to review and report on management's assertions concerning its internal controls and compliance with applicable laws and regulations.

If the illegal act does not have a direct and material impact on the financial statements and the audit was conducted in accordance with generally accepted auditing standards, there is no assurance that the illegal act will be detected or that any contingent liability that may result from that act will be disclosed. However, as in SAS No. 53, the auditor may have a duty to notify outside parties of the illegal acts.

SAS No. 58, *Reports on Audited Financial Statements.* This standard clarifies the auditor's role with respect to new statements in the auditor's reports. The statements say the financial reports are the responsibility of the entity's management, and the auditor's responsibility is to express an opinion on those statements. The auditor's report goes on to elaborate on the procedures performed and on auditor assurance.

SAS No. 59, *The Auditor's Consideration of an Entity's Ability to Continue as a Going Concern.* This standard deals with the potential failure of a firm. The auditor has the responsibility in all audits to evaluate whether substantial doubt exists as to the entity's ability to continue as a going concern for the next year. If there is substantial doubt, the auditor should consider the adequacy of disclosure and include an explanatory paragraph in the audit report to reflect that conclusion. If the firm's disclosures are not adequate in this regard, the auditor may give a qualified or adverse opinion. One member of the Auditing Standards Board dissented on voting on this SAS. He argued that without new auditing procedures to fulfill this new responsibility, the result is a widening, rather than a narrowing, of the expectation gap.

SAS No. 60, *Communications of Internal Control Structure Related to Matters Noted in an Audit.* This standard concerns significant deficiencies or "reportable conditions" in the design or operation of the internal control structure. Auditors who find conditions that could adversely affect the organization's ability to produce reliable financial disclosures are required to report them to the audit committee or its equivalent.

SAS No. 61, *Communications with Audit Committees.* This standard requires auditors to ensure that the audit committee or its equivalent receives information regarding the audit that may assist it in overseeing the financial reporting and disclosure process for which management is responsible. The statement does not require such communications with management.

Auditors' ability to detect and report banks' financial difficulties in the recent past leaves a lot to be desired. The GAO studied the most recent audit reports performed by certified public accountants (CPAs) on 11 failed S&Ls.[19] The study found that in six cases, the CPAs failed to ade-

---

[19] US Government Accounting Office, *CPA Audit Quality: Failures of CPA Audits to Identify and Report Significant Savings and Loan Problems,* GAO/AFMD-89-45, February 1989; US General Accounting Office, *The Need to Improve Auditing in the Savings and Loan Industry,* statement of Frederick D. Wolf before the Committee on Banking, Finance and Urban Affairs, House of Representatives, GAO/T-AFMD-89-2, February 21, 1989.

quately audit and/or report the S&Ls' financial or internal control problems in accordance with professional standards. The latest audit reports for the 11 S&Ls showed a combined net worth of about $44 million before failure. At the time the S&Ls failed, which ranged from 5 to 17 months after the audit reports, they had a combined *negative* net worth of about $1.5 billion. No doubt some failures occurred after the audits were done. Nevertheless, that does not explain the following examples of CPA audits and disclosures:

• Lack of sufficient evidence in working papers that the CPA firm performed an analysis of the collectibility of acquisition, development, and construction (ADC) loans because the loans were new and the CPA firm assumed them to be collectible. In its defense, the *AICPA Audit and Accounting Guide for Savings and Loan Associations* contained little discussion of the risks associated with land and ADC loans.

• Lack of sufficient evidence in working papers that the CPA firm identified and evaluated the effect of restructured loans. Federal examiners found that the S&L did not report that it had restructured about $625 million in loans during the period covered by the audit. In that same audit, the CPAs did not evaluate the collectibility of $30 million past-due loans guaranteed by two principal shareholders.

• A CPA firm did not properly disclose in its audit report that an S&L incorrectly reported $12 in expected recoveries from lawsuits that were pending. The S&L used the expected recoveries to offset reported losses. Accounting principles prohibit the reporting recoveries from lawsuits until the cases are resolved. Also, the CPA firm did not disclose its own findings that the S&L's losses would probably be greater than reported.

• A CPA firm failed to disclose that an S&L had several hundred million dollars of loans secured by property in a limited geographic area. Most of the loans were made to principal shareholders of the S&L.

• Two CPA firms reported that their clients had no material weaknesses in internal controls despite the fact that the S&Ls were under formal regulatory enforcement actions for severe internal control weaknesses.

The expectation gap is narrower than it was before; but we still have a long way to go before it will be closed. High-profile cases and lawsuits against accounting firms keep the issue alive. For example, *Business Week* (September 27, 1992, p. 32) reported that following the collapse of Silverado Banking, a Colorado-based savings and loan, Washington-based

Coopers & Lybrand agreed to pay the FDIC $20 million for its failure to detect Silverado's weak financial position.

In August 1992, the lead article in *The Wall Street Journal* was about a $338 million judgment awarded against Price Waterhouse for allegedly failing to detect a weak loan portfolio in a Phoenix bank.[20]

In March 1994, Deloitte & Touche (D&T) agreed to pay $312 million to the government in settlement of claims based on alleged accounting and auditing failures at banks and S&Ls it had audited.[21] Specifically, D&T failed to account for hedges in accordance with GAAP in its audit of Franklin Savings and Loan Association of Ottawa, Kansas; it failed to mark to market trading accounts in accordance with GAAP in its audit of Colombia Savings and Loan Association of Beverly Hills, California, and additional failures at other thrifts in New Jersey and Colorado.

Some issues will never be resolved. For example, the author of a recent article stated that "companies search for accounting methods that best suit the game plan. This results in a patchwork of accounting methodology that adheres to particular, and often conflicting, viewpoints while objectivity falls by the wayside."[22]

Another factor that inhibits the gap from closing is that auditors are not trained criminal investigators. Auditing methodology is directed toward objectivity and away from criminal investigation.[23] To illustrate one difference, consider the concepts of materiality and evidence. Auditors must determine if a "reasonable assurance" exists that important information about financial transactions is fairly presented. They set the desired level of assurance to fit the existing circumstance and acquire the information or evidence to achieve the desired level of assurance. Under the rules of law, matter offered in evidence in a case must be relevant to the issues and either tend to establish or disprove them. What is relevant and material, admissible, and inadmissible is clearly delineated, and there is little room for "reasonable assurance."

---

[20] Lee Berton and Stephen J. Adler, "How Audit of a Bank Cost Price Waterhouse $338 Million Judgment," *The Wall Street Journal,* August 14, 1992, p. A1.

[21] "Deloitte & Touche Settles with OTS, RTC & FDIC," joint release, FDIC, RTC, and OTS, March 14, 1994.

[22] James R. Davis, "Ambiguity, Ethics, and the Bottom Line," *Business Horizons,* May–June 1989, p. 67.

[23] David L. Nich and Robert D. Miller, "White-Collar Crime," *The Internal Auditor,* December 1984, pp. 24–27.

Internal Auditors

The previous discussion centered on independent audits. However, the first line of defense against unsafe and unsound banking practices is the internal auditors. The objective of the internal audit function is to assist the audit committee and management by providing them with a continuous objective evaluation of the accuracy, adequacy, and effectiveness of various aspects of ongoing operations. These include internal controls, audit trails, operational procedures, compliance, and so on. To perform these tasks on a daily basis, the internal auditors must be qualified, and, to the extent possible, they should be independent from the bank's lending and operation functions.

A Bank Administration Institute report, *Bank Audit and Security* (1990), stated that today's internal auditors are less concerned with financial statement presentations. Their focus is on

1. Identifying the bank's exposures.
2. Determining if systems are in place to protect the bank from losses.
3. Determining if systems are in place to provide real-time correct financial data.

The Institute of Internal Auditors (IIA) is a professional association dedicated to the professional development of internal auditors. The IIA conducts seminars and conferences on control, deterrence, and investigation of fraud and publishes the *Internal Auditor,* which contains articles dealing with fraud, internal controls, and other subjects.[24] The IIA bookstore provides books, videos, software, and other items for professional development of internal auditors.

Finally, a 1995 report from the Financial Executives Institute states, "As traditional command-and-control management systems are being replaced by modern quality-based management systems, internal audit's traditional policing role is becoming progressively more inappropriate and new roles are emerging to replace it."[25] In the case of Canada Resources, internal auditors identified more control concerns than the corporate auditors had found previously. At American Standard, internal auditors helped to spread new systems to the firm's administrative areas around the world.

---

[24] The Institute of Internal Auditors, 249 Maitland Ave., Altamonte Springs, FL 32701, phone 407-830-7600.

[25] James A. F. Stone and Frank M. Werner, *Internal Audit and Innovation* (Morristown, NJ: Financial Executives Research Foundation Executive Report, 1995), pp. 9–10.

The Role of Bank Examiners

Some readers may confuse bank examiners with auditors. Bank examiners are not auditors. Bank examiners perform two types of examinations, one for safety and soundness and the other for compliance. Safety and soundness examinations are based on the CAMEL and BOPEC systems. CAMEL is the Uniform Interagency Bank Rating System acronym for *c*apital adequacy, *a*sset quality, *m*anagement, *e*arnings, and *l*iquidity. BOPEC (*b*ank, *o*ther subsidiaries, *p*arent company, *e*arnings, and *c*apital) is used to rate bank holding companies. In some states, such as Alabama, bank examiners review the adequacy of the audits. Compliance examinations determine whether banks are complying with existing laws and regulations, such as the Truth in Lending Act (Federal Reserve Regulation Z).

Bank examiners report their findings to the bank and may share their information with other regulatory and government agencies. When they find problems, they may take a series of actions to attempt to correct them. The extreme action is the closing of the bank.

Detection of fraud is an infrequent by-product of bank examinations. For example, a trainee examiner working in the First National Bank of Jacksonville, Alabama, discovered that three people who had loans with the bank used the same address. Further examination revealed more than 25 fictitious loans using the same address. The bank failed.

One reason detection of fraud is an infrequent by-product may be that bank examiners are not doing their jobs properly. A study by the General Accounting Office (GAO) revealed that OCC examiners "did not comprehensively evaluate internal controls that were critical to the safe and sound operation of the banks they examined."[26] The study further reported that insufficient work was performed to assess loan quality and reserves. The Office of Thrift Supervision (OTS) had similar problems. Another GAO study stated that the "OTS did not review enough loans to accurately assess the safety and soundness of individual thrifts."[27] Furthermore, the loans that were selected for examination were not representative of the thrift's portfolio. The OTS also failed to examine internal controls, and the conclusions of their exams were inconsistent. Finally, GAO studies of Federal Reserve and the FDIC examinations were criti-

---

[26] US General Accounting Office, *Bank Examination Quality* (OCC), GAO/AFMD-93-14, February 1993, p. 2.

[27] US General Accounting Office, *Thrift Examination Quality* (OTS) GAO/AFMD-93-11, February 1993, p. 3.

cal as well.[28] The Federal Reserve was also criticized because it did not assess the risks associated with bank loans to nonbank affiliates within holding companies. There were no formal programs to assess state examinations.[29] Don't count on auditors to detect fraud or insider abuse!

Security Personnel

Security officers are responsible for developing and implementing systems intended to reduce robberies and other crimes. Their duties include[30]

- Physical security
- Personnel security
- Investigations
- Computer security
- Communications security
- Crisis management

Security personnel can help to deter and detect both large- and small-scale frauds. Communications between security officers of various banks resulted in tellers being alerted to Nigerian "flim-flam" operations being conducted in several states and the arrest of the perpetrators.

Security personnel can provide background information about borrowers as well as verifying other aspects of the loan request before loan approval.

CONCLUSION

The bottom line with respect to internal controls is simple: Strong banks have strong internal controls, and weak banks lack them. Thus, internal controls are an essential element of good management.

While banks must have independent audits to determine if management's assertions about their financial statements are "fair," a GAO study suggests that some auditors did not detect or report financial difficulties of financial institutions that failed shortly after being audited.

The obvious conclusion is that directors must take an active role in ensuring that their banks have proper internal controls and that the external audits accurately reflect the condition of their banks.

---

[28] US General Accounting Office, *Bank Examination Quality*, (FDIC) GAO/AFMD-93-12, February 1993; US General Accounting Office, *Bank Examination Quality* (FRB), GAO/AFMD-93-13, February 1993.

[29] US General Accounting Office, *Bank and Thrift Regulation* (FRB), GAO/AFMD-93-15, February 1993.

[30] *Security in Financial Institutions: The Role of the Security Officer* (Rolling Meadows, IL: Bank Administration Institute, 1990).

Chapter Eleven

Mergers and Acquisitions

LARGE NUMBERS OF MERGERS

Friendly mergers, acquisitions, hostile takeovers, proxy fights, leveraged buyouts, and corporate restructuring are part of the day-to-day landscape in which businesses operate. According to the Department of Commerce, 620 mergers and acquisitions of financial institutions took place in the United States in 1992, including 166 commercial banks.[1] These were large mergers that involved a 40 percent stake in a target, or an investment of at least $100 million or more.

Financial Institutions	Number
Commercial banks	166
Savings and loans	144
Securities and commodities brokers	74
Insurance	106
Credit insurance	42
Real estate, mortgage bankers, and brokers	88
Total	620

Because more than 70 percent of the banks in the United States have assets of less than $100 million, the Department of Commerce figures significantly understate the number of bank mergers. The total number of bank mergers reported by the FDIC was 501 in 1992.[2] If all of the Department of Commerce data understate mergers by two-thirds, the total number of mergers of financial institutions is about 1,871! Why are so many mergers occurring? Before we attempt to answer that question, let's define a few terms.

---

[1] US Department of Commerce, *Statistical Abstract of the United States, 1994,* Tables 855, 856.

Merger: The combination of two or more economic entities in which only one survives and retains its identity.

Acquisition: The purchase of the controlling interest of an economic entity.

Consolidation: The combination of two or more economic entities combine to form a new entity, whereupon the original entities cease to exist.

CREATING SHAREHOLDER VALUE

There are as many reasons for bank mergers as there are mergers. In general terms, mergers are a means to achieve rapid asset growth, expand into different markets, and add new products and services. As a result, managers can gain greater power and rewards.[3] The real issue is not the psychology behind mergers but whether they indeed create shareholder value.

A recent study presented six commonly accepted rules for determining whether a merger will create value for an acquirer and its shareholders.[4] We use their rules to discuss some aspects of creating value.

Rule 1: Pure Conglomerate Mergers May Not Create New Shareholder Value

A conglomerate merger involves the combination of essentially unrelated firms. Investors can achieve the same combination in their portfolios by buying shares in each of the companies.

To create value, synergy must exist in the combination of firms that is not present in either company on a stand-alone basis. For example, Mellon Bank Corporation acquired Dreyfus Corporation, the sixth largest mutual fund, in an effort to change from a corporate lender to a fee-generating

---

[2] *FDIC Historical Statistics on Banking: 1934–1992,* Table CB-2.

[3] For a detailed explanation of why firms merge, see Alexandra M. Post, *Anatomy of a Merger* (Englewood Cliffs, NJ: Prentice Hall, 1994), Chapter 8. This book also provides a comprehensive survey of the merger literature.

[4] Bob Case, Dhiren Shah, and Andrew de Pass, "Mergers and Acquisitions," *The WG&L Handbook of Financial Strategy and Policy* (Cincinnati, OH: Warren, Gorham & Lamont, 1995).

financial service organization. Mellon Bank's *1993 Annual Report* stated that it is "The Bank of the Future—a diversified financial services institution with a bank as its core." Mellon sees synergies from combining the products of the two firms and cross-selling them.[5] Customers will be able to set up checking accounts, mutual funds, and 401(k) tax-free savings plans and get investment advice in a single visit. This process should also save costs.

Mellon's stock plunged 7.6 percent on the announcement of the Dreyfus acquisition in December 1993.[6] One year later, the bank's earnings plummeted 70 percent.[7] Part of the loss was due to the acquisition of Dreyfus and the accounting method (pooling of interest) used. Losses in Dreyfus were passed on to Mellon. Another part of the loss was attributed to Mellon's acquisition of The Boston Company, which subsequently suffered losses in its securities lending portfolio.[8]

The conventional wisdom is that merged firms are more efficient than the individual firms. However, a study by Tanya Azarchs, Standard & Poor's bank analyst, found just the opposite.[9] According to Azarchs, in-market mergers had an efficiency ratio (noninterest expenses divided by total revenues of the organization, excluding nonrecurring items) of 59 percent, out-of-market mergers had a ratio of 60 percent, and non-merged banks had a ratio of 59.8 percent. She concluded that mergers may be beneficial for diversification, but not for efficiency. Similarly, a study by Joel Houston and Michael Ryngaert found no significant cost savings from bank mergers. Stephen A. Rhodes, Board of Governors of the Federal Reserve System, revealed substantial cuts in costs and some improvement

---

[5] Gabriella Stern and Sara Calian, "Mellon Is Out to Prove the Value of Its Big-Ticket Buy," *The Wall Street Journal,* December 10, 1993, p. B4.

[6] Gordon Matthews and Karen Talley, "Mellon to Acquire Dreyfus, Joining Ranks of Fund Giants," *American Banker,* December 7, 1993, pp. 1, 16; Yvette D. Kantrow, "Mellon Looking Less and Less Like a Bank," *American Banker,* December 7, 1993, pp. 1, 15.

[7] Howard Kapiloff, "Mellon's Earnings Plunge 70 percent: Hits on Securities Lending Cited," *American Banker,* January 17, 1995, p. 4; "Mellon Reports Fourth Quarter and Full Year 1994 Results," Mellon News Release, January 13, 1995.

[8] Securities lending is the process of lending securities in a trust or custody client's portfolio to broker-dealers and investing the cash collateral in debt securities. The brokers pay for the use of the securities, and Mellon invested the funds in debt securities. When interest rates increased, the value of the debt securities declined. Mellon took a $130 million after-tax charge on the loss.

[9] Daniel Kaplan, "Mergers Can't Be Counted on to Boost Efficiency, S&P Says," *American Banker,* January 6, 1995, p. 20.

in the efficiency of merged banks relative to peers.[10] The bottom line appears to be that bank mergers do not result in greater efficiencies.

Rule 2: Countercyclical Acquisitions May Not Create Value

Mergers that eliminate unsystematic (non-market-related) risk may not improve the investment profile of the acquirer. Everyone knows that interest rates go up and down. It follows that acquiring businesses that are interest rate sensitive may not reduce risk. The mortgage banking business was growing and profitable when interest rates were declining during the 1980s and early 1990s. When interest rates increased in 1994, growth opportunities and profits shrank. Accordingly, in early 1995, Barclays Bank PLC and AmSouth Bancorporation wanted to sell their mortgage banking affiliates.[11] They had large numbers of adjustable-rate mortgages in their portfolios. Unfortunately, the ARMs carried low rates and had interest rate caps of 2 percentage points, while interest rates increased 250 basis points in 1994. It was not a good time to hold such loans.

Rule 3: The Stock Market Does Not Reward Growth Due Exclusively to Acquisitions

Investors know that acquiring firms pay significant premiums to the target firms. The amount paid reduces the target's contributions to cash flow and earnings. The likelihood of paying small premiums to acquire large numbers of firms that will contribute positively to earnings is slim.

Rule 4: Related Diversification Can Create Value

The most successful mergers involve situations where the assets, skills, or knowledge of one company can be applied to the problems or opportunities

---

[10] Joel F. Houston and Michael D. Ryngaert, "The Overall Gains from Large Bank Mergers," *Journal of Banking and Finance,* December 1994, pp. 1155–76; Stephen A. Rhodes, "The Efficiency Effects of Bank Mergers: Rationale for a Case Study Approach and Preliminary Findings," *Proceedings of the 29th Annual Conference on Bank Structure and Competition,* Federal Reserve Bank of Chicago, May 1993, pp. 337–99.

[11] James H. Saft, "Barclays Seeing a Buyer for U.S. Mortgage Unit," *American Banker,* January 10, 1995, pp. 1, 12; AmSouth Bancorporation, news release, January 17, 1995.

of the other company. For example, a bank with a strong deposit base but limited growth opportunities could benefit from association with banks that have growth opportunities. Consider First National Jasper Corporation (Alabama). In the early 1980s, the one-bank holding company's principal asset, First National Bank of Jasper, was extremely profitable, was well capitalized, and had the dominant market share, but it had nowhere to grow; it was a cash cow in rural Alabama.[12] To take advantage of its under-utilized resources, a de novo bank was formed in Birmingham, Alabama, that provided growth opportunities in a major metropolitan area. Subse-quently, de novo banks were opened in other Alabama cities. Opening de novo banks is analogous to acquisitions. This combination of a cash cow plus de novo banks in growth areas proved to be very successful.

Rule 5: Mergers Can Be Used to Reach a Critical Size Where Size Is a Factor

A small bank may not be able to afford a trust department, but a large holding company consisting of banks of various sizes can afford a trust department, an international department, discounts on quantity purchases, and so on. In 1995, AmSouth Bancorporation announced that it was sell-ing its mortgage banking operation, including its servicing portfolio and out-of-market mortgage origination offices. One reason for the sale was that the firm had not achieved the level of business it needed to benefit from the economies of scale. As mentioned previously, higher interest rates reduced the attractiveness of mortgage banking.

Rule 6: Acquisitions Can Be Used to Defer Taxes

Case, Shah, and de Pass focused on deferring taxes on cash dividends.[13] Firms distribute cash dividends to shareholders, who must pay income tax on them. Alternatively, a firm can retain the funds and use them to make acquisitions that may add to shareholder value. This tax strategy defers dividends, and the taxes that must be paid on them, until the time the firm pays higher dividends. Of course, if the merger does not pay off, the

---

[12] Barbara Rudolph, "People Like to Do Business with Folks they Know," *Forbes*, October 26, 1981, pp. 142–46; various annual reports of First National Jasper Corporation. The name was changed in 1985 to Prospectus for First Commercial Bankshares, Inc.

[13] Case, Shah, and de Pass, "Mergers and Acquisitions."

> **Think about This!**
>
> *When Is a Sale a Sale?*
>
> According to the Supreme Court of Delaware, once a board of directors indicates its intention to sell the corporation to an acquirer, it is obligated to the shareholders to auction and sell to the highest bidder. The "auction duty" is triggered when the firm to be acquired is for sale for cash or debt, but it may not be triggered if a stock-for stock swap takes place. A sale implies a change of control of the voting stock. However, it is not clear whether control changes when one owns 25, 40, or 50 percent of the stock. Equally important, a "strategic merger" or a "strategic alliance" may not constitute a sale. These are issues for the court to decide.

shareholders lose both the dividends they would have received and shareholder value.

Other tax benefits can result from mergers. For example, inheritance taxes can be avoided by selling private firms. The seller's heirs may be able to profit by selling their shares through a trust with a favorable tax status that avoids high inheritance taxes. Stock-for-stock exchanges avoid taxes altogether. In the case of leveraged buyouts, the interest payments on the debt are tax deductible. Moreover, tax loss carryovers and capturing the accelerated depreciation of existing assets is also possible with mergers and acquisitions.

MERGER TERMS

The terms of mergers include cash, cash plus common stock, common stock plus preferred stock, and debt securities. These terms have various implications for the sellers.

Taxes

The composition of the merger terms affects income taxes for investors in the acquired company and for the acquiring company. An exchange made for voting stock of the acquiring company is generally considered a *tax-free exchange*. The voting stock is usually common stock or convertible preferred stock. Convertible preferred offers investors a higher dividend yield than common stock, but it must be noncallable for at least five years to qualify in a tax-free exchange.

In contrast, exchanges for cash or nonvoting securities, such as bonds, are taxable for the stockholders of the acquired firm. Because some sellers want cash and are willing to pay the tax and others do not, companies may offer sellers a choice of merger terms.

Depreciation is another consideration. If the exchange is taxable, as previously described, depreciation of the acquired firm's assets is based on the price paid for the firm. Suppose a firm is acquired for $20 million, but its assets have a book value of $17 million. The acquiring firm will use $20 million as the depreciation basis. On the other hand, if the exchange is nontaxable, the assets will have a depreciation basis of $17 million, the same basis used by the selling firm. Some acquiring firms favor taxable exchanges because they provide greater depreciation, increased cash flow, and lower taxable income.

Liability

An acquiring company can buy stock or assets of the acquired company. We just looked at the tax implications of the exchange; liability is another element to consider. If the acquired company is dissolved, liabilities and other claims against it must be satisfied before shareholders can receive dividends or assets. In contrast, the purchase of physical assets does not carry with it the liabilities of the acquired company.

Market Value Exchange Ratio

The value of the terms of a proposed merger to the shareholders of the firm to be acquired can be measured by the *market value exchange ratio,* which is calculated as follows:

$$\text{Market Value Exchange Ratio} = \frac{\substack{\text{Market Value of Benefits} \\ \text{Offered to Seller}}}{\text{Market Value of Seller's Stock}} \quad (11\text{--}1)$$

The ratio compares what the shareholders are being offered with what they have. If the ratio is greater than 1, they are being offered more than they have. If the ratio is less than 1, they will be worse off if they accept the merger terms. As a rule, acquiring firms pay a premium to shareholders to make the acquisition attractive.

To illustrate the use of the market value exchange ratio, consider the following situation. The acquiring company is offering the prospective seller a choice between the following exchanges for each share of common stock: (1) $2 cash and 0.4 shares of common stock valued at $50 per share or (2) 0.375 shares of common stock valued at $50 per share of preferred stock valued at $30 per share. The seller's stock currently sells for $20 per share. (For simplicity, we will ignore the tax effects of the exchange, as well as cash dividends.) The ratio focuses on the immediate value of the exchange. Using the market value exchange ratio, we can determine that the seller is better off with the second offer, which gives the larger premium:

$$\text{Offer 1: } \frac{\$2 + 0.4\,(\$50)}{\$20} = 1.1$$

$$\text{Offer 2: } \frac{0.375\,(\$50) + 0.25\,(\$30)}{\$20} = 1.3$$

Price/Book Value Ratio

In the distant past, when banks had short-term assets and short-term liabilities, book value or net worth (assets − liabilities = net worth) was a meaningful figure on which to base value. The price/book value ratio became the accepted standard for valuing a bank, and it is still used today. For example, BankAmerica bought Continental Bank for 124.96 percent of its book value (the price/earnings ratio was 6.71), and Boatman's Bancshares bought Worthern Banking for 199.62 percent of its book value (the P/E was 14.03).[14]

Over the years, banks changed from being exclusively short-term borrowers and lenders to longer-term borrowing and lending, which means the book value is not the same as the market value. Banks broadened their banking powers, made acquisitions, and engaged in off balance sheet activities. The net result of all of these activities is that book value does not measure the true value of a bank. Even when adjustments are made for

---

[14] "Top 150 Bank and Thrift Deal Announced in 1994," *American Banker M&A Roundup*, January 23, 1995, p. 4A.

intangible assets, credit loss reserves, market value of investments, and off–balance sheet activities, the book value is a misleading number. There-fore, we focus on price/earnings ratios, which are not perfect measures but are better than book value when a bank has positive earnings. However, the price/earnings ratio is not meaningful when the bank has losses.

Price/Earnings Ratio

Price/earnings (P/E) ratios are one of the most widely used methods of determining the value of common stock. Perhaps the major reason for its popularity is that it is easy to calculate and convenient to use. We deter-mine it by dividing the market price of the stock by its earnings per share. Newspapers and some investment services use a firm's most recent annual earnings to calculate the P/E ratios used in their publications. A better approach, however, is to use a firm's expected earnings, if such figures are available. If a stock is selling at $60 per share and its earnings are $3, the P/E ratio is 20. Stated otherwise, investors are paying 20 times earnings to buy shares of that company. It is easier to think about 20 times earnings than about equations and discounting. Nevertheless, the P/E ratio embod-ies some of the theoretical considerations of the dividend valuation model, although generally they are not made explicit. The P/E ratio may be related to the dividend valuation model as follows:[15]

$$\text{P/E} = \frac{1-b}{k_e - g} \tag{11–2}$$

where

b = Proportion of earnings retained by the firm after cash dividends have been paid

k_e = Rate of return required by equity investor

g = Growth rate of dividends

---

[15] An alternative form that is more similar to the dividend valuation model is as follows:

$$P_o = \frac{D_1}{k_e - g}$$

$$\frac{P_o}{E_1} = \frac{D_1/E_1}{k_e - g}$$

Here $D_1/E_1 = 1 - b$.

If b is 0.50, k is 0.20, and g is 0.10, the P/E ratio is 5, determined as follows:

$$P/E = \frac{1 - 0.50}{0.20 - 0.10}$$

$$= 5$$

If the growth rate were 15 percent, the P/E ratio would be 10. Similarly, a growth rate of dividends of 18 percent would produce a P/E ratio of 25. In general, a high P/E ratio implies that investors expect substantial growth.

If a firm retains all of its earnings $(1 - b = 0)$, equation 11–2 cannot be used. However, it may be expected that the firm will pay dividends at some time in the future. When the retention rate (b) is 100 percent over a finite period in the future, an adaptation of equation 6–8 can be used to determine the theoretical P/E ratio.

As noted earlier, the P/E ratio is used in mergers to determine the value of common stock. A more important reason for considering P/E ratios in mergers involves assessing the merger's effect on the combined earnings of the merged firms. To illustrate, we'll examine the financial data presented in Tables 11–1 and 11–2.

Table 11–1 shows that an acquiring firm's stock earns $5 per share and has a P/E ratio of 12, which means the market price of the stock is $60 per share. Three situations are shown for the firm to be acquired (the seller): a higher P/E ratio, the same P/E ratio, and a lower P/E ratio than the acquiring firm (the buyer). As shown, if the seller's P/E ratio is 16, the total

TABLE 11–1
Selected Financial Data before Merger

	Acquiring Firm (Buyer)	Firm to Be Acquired (Seller)		
		Higher P/E	Same P/E	Lower P/E
Earnings	$1,000,000	$600,000	$600,000	$600,000
Number of shares	200,000	300,000	300,000	300,000
EPS	$5	$2	$2	$2
P/E ratio	12	16	12	8
Market value per share	$60	$32	$24	$16
Total equity	$12 million	$9.6 million	$7.2 million	$4.8 million

TABLE 11–2
Selected Financial Data after Merger

	Higher P/E (16)	Same P/E (12)	Lower P/E (8)
Cost at market value	$9,600,000	$7,200,000	$4,800,000
Additional to buyer's capital shares*			
Market value of seller's stock/buyer's price per share	$9,600,000/$60 = 160,000 shares	$7,200,000/$60 = 120,000 shares	$4,800,000/$60 = 80,000 shares
Combines earnings	$1,600,000	$1,600,000	$1,600,000
Number of shares after merger	360,000	320,000	280,000
EPS of combined company*	$4.44	$5.00	$5.71
Initial P/E ratio of combined company	$60/$4.44 = 13.5	$60/$5.00 = 12.0	$60/$5.71 = 10.5

* The market value exchange ratio is 1.0:

$$\frac{\text{Market Value Offered Seller}}{\text{Market Value of Seller's Stock}} = \frac{\$60/\text{share} \times 160{,}000 \text{ shares}}{\$9{,}600{,}000} = \frac{\$9{,}600{,}000}{\$9{,}600{,}000} = 1.0$$

equity of the seller's firm is $9.6 million; if the seller's P/E ratio is 12, the equity is worth $7.2 million; and if the P/E ratio is 8, total equity is worth $4.8 million.

Now let's assume the buyer plans to pay the seller the full price of the equity by exchanging shares of common stock (here the market value exchange ratio is 1). As Table 11–2 shows, if the seller has a higher P/E ratio than the buyer, the buyer will have to give the seller 160,000 shares of stock. This is determined by dividing the total value of the seller's equity by the market price of the buyer's stock ($9.6 million/$60 = 160,000).

Notice that the combined earnings of both companies ($1,000,000 + $600,000 = $1,600,000) and the increased number of total shares outstanding (200,000 + 160,000 = 360,000) result in lower earnings per share (EPS) for the buyer. Before the merger the buyer's EPS was $5 (Table 11–1), but after the merger the combined EPS is $4.44. If the stock price of the merged company is $60 per share, the initial P/E ratio of the combined companies will be higher, at 13.5, than the buyer's original P/E ratio of 12. When the seller and the buyer have the same P/E ratio, earnings per share will stay the same and the initial P/E ratio after the merger will also remain as before. If the seller's P/E ratio is lower than the buyer's, the combined earnings per share will increase to $5.71 and the initial combined P/E ratio will be lower, at 10.5. The initial effect after a merger of the buyer's and seller's price/earnings ratios on the combined companies' earnings per share is summarized in Table 11–3.

The word *initial* is important here, because the initial earnings are only a starting point for the combined companies. The important thing is how the combined companies will perform in the long run. Table 11–3 illustrates this point. Without the merger, expected earnings will increase over the years. With the merger, in spite of an initial dilution in earnings, the combined earnings potential is greater over the long run than without the merger.

TABLE 11–3
The Initial Effect of P/E Ratios on Earnings per Share of the Combined Companies

Buyer's P/E	Seller's P/E	Earnings per Share of Buyer
Buyer >	Seller	Increased
Buyer =	Seller	Same
Buyer <	Seller	Decreased

Soft Issues

So far, we have mentioned only financial considerations. Soft issues are important too. These include differences in corporate culture, strategies, and personnel issues after the merger is completed. Many mergers result in large numbers of layoffs and early retirements in an effort to reduce noninterest expense. Moreover, new compensation schemes (incentive plans) are introduced. The net effect of these actions may be higher noninterest expenses. Finally, the early retirements force some of the most productive employees to leave. Some go to competing institutions. In some cases, one wonders if the acquiring bank isn't killing the goose that laid the golden egg.

OFFENSIVE AND DEFENSIVE MERGER TACTICS

As suggested at the beginning of the chapter, not all mergers are friendly. In fact, some are hostile, and that is why a variety of offensive and defensive merger tactics have been developed to make it easier to take over a firm or to avoid being taken over. Several of the principal tactics in each category are presented here.

The Offense

The use of a tender offer is the offensive tool most widely used when the target company is likely to oppose the acquisition. In a tender offer, the acquiring company offers to buy from shareholders of the target company a certain number of shares for cash or some combination of cash and securities.

The method's major advantage is speed; the offer can be made by announcements in major newspapers, and unprepared target companies have little time to respond. This is what T. Boone Pickens of Mesa Petroleum did when he tried to take over giant Gulf Oil. After obtaining 10 percent of Gulf's stock on the open market, he made a tender offer at $65 per share for 21 percent of the company's outstanding shares. Gulf's management was not prepared for the assault. Other firms joined in the melee with bids as high as $87 per share. Socal (Standard Oil of California) was the winner at $80 per share. Don't feel sorry for Pickens; he made a $760 million profit on his $1 billion investment in Gulf shares.[16]

---

[16] "Why Gulf Lost Its Fight for Life," *Business Week*, March 19, 1984, pp. 76–84.

Buying shares of the target company's stock before making a formal offer, as T. Boone Pickens did when he acquired 10 percent of Gulf's stock on the open market, is another common offensive strategy. Rupert Murdoch, an Australian entrepreneur, made such pre-offer purchases during an attempt to take over Warner Communications, Inc. He acquired 7 percent of the company's outstanding shares for $100 million before announcing his intention to buy 49.9 percent of the shares. Warner was able to buy Murdoch's stock for $180 million, giving him an $80 million gross profit for not getting the company he wanted.

Sometimes stockholders solicit bidders to acquire their bank's stock. Consider Compass Bancshares Inc. of Alabama.[17] Harry Brock, who retired from Compass as chairman and chief executive officer, tried to persuade other shareholders and directors to sell the bank to First Union Corporation of North Carolina. If the merger went through, Brock stood to gain about $24 million. However, Brock's successor at Compass, D. Paul Jones, Jr., didn't want to lose his $842,121-per-year job and fought against the acquisition. Equally important, many bank employees and stockholders didn't want to sell, at least not at that time and not under Brock's terms. Brock promised a proxy fight to gain control of a sufficient number of shares to force the merger. He lost the fight.

The Defense

It is sometimes said that the best defense is a good offense. One offensive tactic to defend against takeovers involves changing corporate charters and bylaws to make unwanted takeovers difficult. Such changes focus on keeping purchasers of large blocks of stock from exercising too much voting power. The following list cites several common changes:

- Staggering the terms of the corporate directors so that only a few are elected in any year.
- Abolishing cumulative voting.
- Requiring that a supermajority (such as 80 percent) of shareholders approve mergers, sales of certain assets, and some other transactions.

---

[17] Rick Brooks and Nikhill Deogun, "Civil War: Battle for Alabama Bank Is Personal, Nasty—and Heating Up," *The Wall Street Journal,* February 8, 1995, pp. S1, S3; Kenneth Cline, "Compass Founder, in Proxy Fight, Discloses Takeover Bid by First Union," *American Banker,* February 16, 1991, pp. 1, 5.; Patrick Rupinski, "Brock Seeks Shareholder Allies," *Birmingham Post-Herald,* January 31, 1995, p. C1.

- Enacting provisions protecting existing officers and directors from removal from office. (These are known as *golden parachutes*.)
- Finding white knights. (White knights are merger partners of the target company's own choosing.)
- Repurchasing shares to reduce the number outstanding and retain as much control as possible.
- Arranging defensive mergers.
- Negotiating contracts with labor unions, banks, and so on to force renegotiation of contracts or accelerated payment of debts in the event of a substantial change in management or ownership.

ACCOUNTING FOR MERGERS

The method used to account for mergers affects the value of assets and earnings of the merged firms. The purchase method and the pooling of interests method are considered here.

Purchase Method

According to Accounting Principles Board (APB) Opinion 16, the *purchase method* treats a business combination as the acquisition of one company by another. The buyer records the cost of the acquired assets at their fair market value. If the fair market value of the assets exceeds the value shown on the seller's books, the difference is recorded as goodwill. The buyer accounts for the increase in the assets' total value by increasing the value of the equity account. The following example will clarify the point.

Table 11–4 shows entries from the balance sheets of a buyer and a seller before and after a merger. According to the terms of the merger, the buyer exchanged stock valued at $3 million, a $2 million premium over the value of the equity shown on the seller's balance sheet. Accounting rules require that a $2 million increase on the right side of the balance sheet be matched by an equivalent increase on the left side. The $2 million on the left side is allocated as follows. The fair market value of the seller's assets is $11 million, although the amount shown on the books is $10 million. Therefore, there is a $1 million increase in the value of the assets. The remaining $1 million is recorded as goodwill. After the merger, the combined balance sheet shows net tangible assets of $41 million ($30 million + $11 million = $41 million) and goodwill of $1 million, for a total of $42 million. Because the liabilities assumed by the buyer do not change, the value of the equity account increases by $2 million to make the balance sheet balance. Accordingly, the value of the equity after the merger is $8 million ($5 million + $1 million on the seller's books + $2 million premium paid over book value for the seller's stock = $8 million). The total value of the liabilities and equity is $42 million.

The allocation of the premium paid over the book value of the stock between net tangible assets and goodwill has important tax implications. The increased value of the net tangible assets is depreciable for both income tax purposes and reporting to shareholders. The increase in goodwill is not deductible for income tax purposes, but can be amortized for reporting to shareholders. It follows that the increased depreciation resulting from the increased value of the assets results in lower taxable income but increased cash flow.

TABLE 11–4
*Accounting for Mergers (Millions of Dollars)**

	Balance Sheet Entries before Merger		Balance Sheet Entries after Merger	
	Buyer	*Seller*	*Purchase Method*	*Pooling of Interests Method*
Net tangible assets	$30	$10	$41	$40
Goodwill	0	0	1	0
Total	$30	$10	$42	$40
Liabilities	$25	$9	$34	$34
Equity	5	1	8	6
Total	$30	$10	$42	$40

* Merger terms:

1. The buyer exchanged stock valued at $3 million, a $2 million premium over the book value of the seller's equity.

2. The fair market value of the seller's net tangible assets was $11 million, a $1 million increase over book value.

3. The difference between the premium paid for the equity ($2 million) and the increase in value of the seller's assets ($1 million) is goodwill ($1 million) under the purchase method.

Pooling of Interests Method

According to APB Opinion 16, the pooling of interests method treats a business combination as the uniting of equity interests of two or more companies through the exchange of stock. Both ownership interests continue, the former basis of accounting is retained, and the merger is recorded by combining the balance sheets of the two companies. As Table 11–4 shows, if the merger described earlier had been accounted for on a pooling of interests basis, the combined balance sheet would show $40 million in total assets ($30 million + $10 million = $40 million). The premium for the stock that was exchanged is not shown; hence, there is no goodwill.

Again, the value of the tangible assets is less when the pooling of interests method is used than when the purchase method is used: $40 million under pooling and $41 million under the purchase method. Thus, reported earnings are higher under the pooling method because less depreciation can be deducted.

Income

Another difference between the two methods of accounting for mergers concerns reporting income. Under the purchase method, income is recorded from the date of the merger; that is, income that was earned before the merger is not recorded on the combined books. Under the pooling method, income for both companies for all prior periods is combined and restated as income of the combined corporation. Thus, under the pooling method, the acquiring company can restate its historical earnings to include the earnings of the newly acquired company.

Restrictions

Accountants have specified conditions under which pooling of interests can be used. Following are several major restrictions:

1. The merger must have been accomplished through the exchange of stock and not primarily through the use of cash, other assets, or liabilities.
2. The stock exchanged in the merger must have the same powers as the majority of the acquiring company's outstanding voting common stock.

3. The combining companies must have been autonomous for at least two years before the merger was initiated.

4. Each of the companies must be independent of other combining companies.

5. The combined corporation must not plan to dispose of its assets within two years after the combination occurs, except for transactions that would occur in the ordinary course of business.

6. No agreements can be made that will negate the exchange of equity that occurred. In other words, no preferential loans to prior stockholders are allowed.

CONCLUSION

To merge or not to merge is not the real issue. The real issue is: Will the merger or acquisition create shareholder value? This chapter presented six general rules dealing with this issue. A review of the rules suggests that not all mergers create value. Moreover, the value of acquired firms changes over time. For example, the acquisition of mortgage banking affiliates was profitable when interest rates were declining but unprofitable when rates increased.

The chapter also examined merger terms and the income tax implications of mergers, with particular attention to price/earnings ratios. Finally, the chapter explained both offensive and defensive merger tactics.

Appendix A

Loan Policy for Lakeside Bank

Chapter Eight addressed the issue of loan policies. Appendixes A, B, and C examine the loan policies of three banks, illustrating different approaches to loan policies. They are not being proposed as the "ideal" loan policies, because each bank's needs are different.

Lakeside Bank shall have a standing Executive Committee elected by the Board, which will also serve as the Directors Loan Committee. It shall consist of the Chairman of the Board, President, and Senior Loan Officer as permanent members, and not less than two other Directors to serve at the pleasure of the Board.

The Executive Committee shall review and approve all loans $15,000.00 and over, and approve all loans over $500,000.00 prior to the loan being made. In case of emergency, loans over $500,000.00 may be approved by the President, Executive Vice President, and one member of the Executive Committee. These emergency loans must be ratified by the entire Committee at their next meeting. The Committee shall keep minutes of its meetings and report its actions in writing at each regular meeting of the Board. Non-salaried Directors shall be paid a fee as set by the Board.

There shall be an Officers Loan Committee which shall consist of the President and Vice Presidents in charge of Commercial and Installment Loans. This Committee shall meet daily to review all loans made the preceding day and approve or disapprove all applications requiring their approval as set out in the loan policy.

I. **GENERAL POLICY**   It is the general policy of the Board that all loans should have a plan of liquidation at the time they are granted. This is considered to be the keystone of sound credit administration, and all loan and discount committees and lending officers are requested to observe this basic principle when approving loans. It is recognized that there will be exceptions to this policy on rare occasions. The Board believes these exceptions should be held to conditions where loans are fully collateralized by cash surrender value of life insurance policies, savings accounts, certificates of deposit, and government bonds with adequate margin. The lending officer should state the plan of liquidation in writing on the note or make it a part of the credit file. This is a requirement on all loans made, whether submitted to the Committee for approval or not.

All new loans to customers having a total indebtedness in excess of $15,000.00 must be supported by a completed loan memorandum. This memorandum should contain the name, date, amount, and rate of the loan. Also it should tell the purpose, repayment plan, and source of those funds. If there is no arrangement made other than a set maturity, it is assumed the loan will be paid off on that date. This memorandum should be made a part of the credit file, and any subsequent changes to the original terms should be reflected as a change in the original memo.

II. **TRADE AREA**   This Board believes that sound local loans are one of the most satisfactory and profitable means of employing the bank's funds. Therefore, it is the intent of the Board that with few exceptions the bank's lending area be limited to Lake County and the adjoining counties covering the northern part of the state. It is recognized that there will be occasions when exceptions to this policy are desirable. These exceptions should be rare. Also, reasons for exception to the policy should be clearly set forth in the minutes of the appropriate committee meeting. This policy does not prohibit participation with other banks of substantial and recognized standing when we have funds available for lending that cannot be readily invested in our local trade area.

III. **DESIRED LOANS**   It will be the policy of the Board of Directors of this bank not to be content with accepting and consummating all sound loans *offered* to the bank. The bank will be aggressive in seeking desirable loans of the type described hereinafter.

Loans of the following types will be considered desirable provided each loan meets the test of a sound, prudent loan:

(a)   Loans to business concerns on a short-term basis, against a satisfactory balance sheet and earnings statement, usually for not more than 180 days.

(b)   Loans to business concerns secured by a chattel mortgage on marketable business equipment, such loans to be amortized over a period of not more than 60 months, or 72 months, when approved by the Officer's Loan and Discount Committee. The amortization terms are to be such that the residual value of the business equipment will at all times be equal to or greater than the unpaid balance of the loan. Proof of insurance and a UCC-1 filed with the Secretary of State are required.

(c) Loans to business concerns secured by accounts receivable and inventory. Because accounts receivable may be proceeds of inventory, a security interest in both is necessary and should be perfected by filing a UCC-1. It is also recommended that regular aging reports be requested and verified periodically.

It is recognized that there will be exceptions where it is not practical for our customer to make an assignment of his or her accounts receivable on a notification basis. It is accepted by the Board that such loans will be limited to a few of the bank's best customers. Also, the loan will have additional proper collateral, as herein provided, or a satisfactory balance sheet and earnings statement, in which case the loan should be approved additionally by the Officers Loan and Discount Committee. The Board regards accounts receivable financing as somewhat more hazardous than the normal type of lending conducted by the bank. All committees and lending officers are required to give such loans careful scrutiny and greater than average surveillance at all times, with strict requirements as to liquidation or substitution of additional collateral of other accounts receivable at any time the accounts receivable are not liquidated in accordance with terms.

In addition, proper precautions and due diligence are to be exercised to avoid the co-mingling of funds on such accounts. In no instance shall accounts receivable be accepted when they are more than 60 days beyond date of invoice.

(d) (1) Loans secured by negotiable US Government Bonds or State, County, or Municipal Bonds properly supported by credit information. Such loans to be not more than 90 percent of the market value of the bonds.

(2) Loans secured by securities listed on a recognized exchange or over-the-counter market; such loans to be not more than 80 percent of the market value of the collateral and to comply in all respects with Regulation U of the Federal Reserve System. The bank will *not* make loans to carry securities where Regulation U margin requirements apply. All stock certificates or registered bonds must have the proper stock power attached.

(3) Although loans secured by the listed market securities depend on the collateral, it also is prudent to obtain a personal financial statement of the borrower and to know his or her credit background. This information should be part of the credit file on the loan and be presented to the appropriate committee at the time of loan approval.

(4) Loans with securities as collateral should be checked at each renewal as to value and marginal requirements and each officer notified when the margin becomes lower than previously stated on a loan for which he or she is responsible.

(5) The customer should be notified at the time of borrowing of his or her responsibility to provide additional collateral and that the occasion might arise when the bank would be required to sell collateral to protect its loan.

(6) All security loans should have a definite repayment program agreed to by the customer. Such repayment should be from sources other than the sale of securities to eliminate tax problems and to avoid misunderstandings with the customer.

NOTE: It is recognized by the Board that there will be situations where individual circumstances may vary. It is our desire to consider each customer's particular problem and to serve the needs of the customer. However, such variations from the foregoing securities policy must be approved by the Officers Loan and Discount Committee, and a memorandum clearly stating the reasons for deviating from the policy and the conditions under which the loan is being made must be submitted.

(e)   Loans against the cash surrender value of life insurance policies should not exceed the cash surrender value if the loan is to be considered a fully secured loan, and must be accompanied by the proper assignment form and questionnaire to the insurance company.

(f)   Loans secured by the assignment of savings accounts and certificates of deposit in this bank must have an interest rate 1 percent greater than that paid on the security. We recommend that the loan officer try to charge 3 percent more than the rate on the security.

(g)   Loans secured by the assignment of savings accounts and certificates of deposit in other lending institutions. These assignments must be acknowledged in writing by the issuing institution. Knowledge of the financial strength and abilities of the issuing institution is essential.

(h) Real estate loans, secured by first liens on improved real estate, including improved farm land, and improved business and residential properties. A loan secured by real estate shall be in the form of an obligation or obligations secured by mortgages. The amount of such loan shall not exceed 66 2/3 percent of the appraised value of the real estate offered as security when made on a nonamortized basis. No such loan shall be made for a term longer than one year, except that . . .

(1) Any such loan may be made in an amount not to exceed 80 percent of the appraised value of the real estate offered as security, and for a term of not longer than 10 years, if the loan is secured by an installment amortized mortgage. The amortized term may be for a period up to 15 years with the prior approval of the Officers Loan and Discount Committee. Real estate mortgages taken as additional collateral do not have to meet the percent of appraised value requirement.

(2) Real estate appraisals on which mortgage loans are based shall be made by appraisers approved by the Officers Loan and Discount Committee. Appraisals up to $150,000.00 in value may be made by two loan officers of this bank. Exceptions to this must be initialed by the President or Executive Vice President.

(3) Hazard insurance is required in amounts and with companies acceptable to the bank on all real estate. This also includes flood insurance where necessary.

(4) Title insurance is required on all real estate loans in excess of $15,000.00. For loans less than $15,000.00 we can accept a title opinion at the option of the loan officer.

(5) Regardless of the value of the security, real estate mortgage loans shall not be made to borrowers who do not have a satisfactory credit record, nor in cases where it appears likely that the property may have to be liquidated to satisfy the debt.

(i) Unsecured consumer installment personal loans and loans secured by appliances to persons of good character with an assured income and satisfactory credit records, when the purpose of the loan will be of ultimate benefit to the borrower; such loans to be payable in monthly installments not to exceed 36 months or in a single payment of 90 days or less, and perfected by the proper UCC-1 recording.

(j) Personal loans secured by new or used automobiles, pickup trucks, boats, motors, trailers. Terms should not exceed the following:

Current-year new cars	60 months
Previous-year new cars	42 months
One- and two-year models	36 months
Three-year models	30 months
Four- and five-year models	24 months
Older models	12 months

(1) All such loans must have current titles showing Lakeside Bank as lien holder, inspection report or bill of sale, and proof of insurance coverage showing Lakeside Bank as lien holder.

(k) Loans secured by a chattel mortgage on livestock. The herd securing any such loan shall be registered livestock and be approved by the Officers Loan and Discount Committee. Such loans shall not exceed 70 percent of the appraised value of the livestock securing the loan, and shall be for a term of not more than 12 months.

(l) Personal loans secured by second mortgages on personal homes. Such loans to be repayable in monthly installments not to exceed 120 months. These loans must have the same documentation required for first mortgages in (h) above. In addition, there should be notification to and acknowledgment by the first mortgagee of our second mortgage.

(m) Personal loans secured by new mobile homes, with adequate down payment, shall be repayable within 120 months. All mobile homes must be properly insured and our lien perfected by title or UCC-1 recording as appropriate.

(n) Loans to business concerns and/or individuals for the purpose of financing insurance premiums; policy to be assigned to bank with insurance company's acknowledgment of assignment and agreement to rebate premium directly to bank in case of cancellation. Each such loan will have a recourse endorsement by the agent guaranteeing payment. Two months' premium must be paid down so that rebate amount always exceeds amount of loan and repayment to be made in equal monthly installments of no more than 10 months.

(o) Construction mortgage loans, where the amount advanced does not exceed the permanent loan commitment and where the loan matures prior to the expiration of the permanent loan commitment. A checkoff list of needed items is available in the Collateral Department.

(p)   Officers are encouraged to put as many loans as possible on variable interest rates.

IV. **UNDESIRABLE LOANS**   Loans of the following type are considered undesirable loans for this bank and ordinarily will be declined unless specifically approved by the Officers Loan and Discount Committee for reasons which appear to justify an exception to the bank's general policy:

(a)   Accommodation loans will not be made to poor credit risks on the strength of a good endorser. If the loan will not "stand on its own feet," the loan should be made to the endorser and the endorser should make a loan to the person whom he or she wishes to accommodate.

(b)   Capital loans to a business enterprise where the loan cannot be repaid within a reasonable period, except by borrowing elsewhere or by liquidating the business.

(c)   Loans to a new enterprise if the repayment of the loan is solely dependent upon the profitable operation of the enterprise.

(d)   Loans to persons whose integrity or honesty is questionable.

(e)   Real estate mortgage loan secured by property located outside the bank's recognized trade area.

(f)   Loans secured by an assignment against undistributed estate.

(g)   Loans secured by stock in a closed corporation which has no ready market. This type of stock may be taken as additional collateral for loans.

(h)   Loans for the purpose of enabling the borrower to speculate on the futures market of securities or commodities, unless the loan is properly collateralized and liquidation not dependent on a rise in the market.

(i)   Loans for the purpose of financing speculative transactions.

V. **LOANS TO EMPLOYEES, DIRECTORS, OFFICERS, AND RELATIVES OF LENDING OFFICER**

(a)   Lending Officers will not make loans to their personal relatives, but should refer them to another Lending Officer to avoid any conflict of interest.

(b)   All loans to Directors, whose total debt exceeds $25,000, must have prior approval of the entire Board of Directors.

(c) Officers indebtedness to any bank or other financial institution will be reported to the President in writing within ten days of the indebtedness. The President shall report this to the Board at its next regular meeting. Each Officer shall submit a financial statement and a list of his or her indebtedness by February 20th of each calendar year to the President, who, in turn, shall submit this information to the Executive Committee.

(d) Officer and employee loan policy attached hereto as Addendum "A".

VI. FINANCIAL INFORMATION

(a) A financial statement not over fifteen months old is required for the following.

(1) All unsecured loans over $2,500.00

(2) All secured loans over $15,000.00 unless fully secured by cash surrender value of life insurance, savings accounts, certificates of deposit, or listed marketable stocks with a 20 percent margin.

(b) Prior-year operating statements are required on all business loans requiring a financial statement. In some cases the tax return is acceptable.

(c) Business financial statement submitted by CPAs should be a review or audit report.

(d) Unsecured loans to business firms involving $100,000.00 or more should have a certified public accountant's unqualified audit report as to the financial condition of the company within the current 12-month period. Where individuals are involved and if required, the loan officer shall verify assets and liabilities and submit a written summary of action taken with respect to his or her recommendations.

(e) A current credit application is required for any loan to an individual when a personal financial statement is not required. A report from a consumer reporting agency is required for the following:

(1) Individual debtors and co-signers.

(2) Endorsers and guarantors.

(3) Principal Officers of a closely held corporate borrower.

(4) Owners or partners of an unincorporated business.

(f) A current trade report should be obtained on loans to businesses. In addition, loans to contractors should also be supported by direct checks of suppliers on a periodic basis.

VII. INTEREST RATES

(a) It is the policy of the Board of Directors that a loan should be turned down rather than made at an unprofitable interest rate.

(b) We wish to compete for all good loans; but do not believe that unprofitable interest rate loans should be made, regardless of competition.

(c) It is the desire of the Board of Directors that there should be a uniformity of interest rates based on the quality of credit risk, and it is the belief of the Board that where the risk is greater, the interest rate should be commensurate with the risk. In addition, consideration should be given to deposit relations and other factors contributing to total yield.

VIII. **PAST-DUE POLICY**   Officers will receive a list of all past-due installment loans and all past-due commercial loans every seven days. All lending officers will meet periodically to review past-due loans. A list of all commercial loans with appropriate comments which have been past due since the 25th of the preceding month will be presented to the Board of Directors and all lending officers monthly.

IX. **COLLECTION POLICY**   The basic policy of the Board of Directors is that bank officers use all means available to them for the collection of indebtedness properly due the bank, including all legal action available by law. It is recognized that on some past-due loans, there will be mitigating circumstances which require careful consideration as to collection tactics that will be employed. In some cases, the President is charged with the responsibility of reviewing all facts with the bank's general counsel, and a course of action determined. Should the circumstances indicate the need for further consideration, a special meeting of the Executive Committee shall be called and a decision made as to proper action. The controlling action should, in all cases, be to take every step open to us to collect money due or to protect the bank from any loss.

X. **CHARGE-OFF POLICY**   The board recognizes that the lending of money is a business and necessarily includes some risks. The management is willing to undertake such reasonable risks. Some losses are to be expected, and it is the intention of the Board that adequate reserves for losses be maintained at all times. It will be a policy of this bank to charge off known losses at the end of each calendar quarter. These charge-offs shall be approved by the Executive Committee and reported to the Board at its next regular meeting. Also, it is the firm intention of the Board to administrate the lending operations so that it will not be necessary for the examining authorities to recommend actions for charge-offs.

XI. OVERDRAFT POLICY

(a) It is the policy of the Board of Directors that employees' overdrafts will not be tolerated. See separate overdraft policy in personnel manual.

(b) Overdrafts by bank customers will be honored where an associated account exists which covers the overdraft, and on which the bank has the legal right of offset. See FIRA of 1978 for overdrafts on Directors.

(c) Overdrafts where there are no associated accounts on which the bank has the legal right of offset will not be honored except in specific circumstances where officers feel it is important to do so. Customers' accounts which repeatedly have overdrafts and returned checks will be reviewed for the purpose of closing the account.

XII. **LOAN AUTHORITY**   Loan Limits: The Executive Committee may approve loans up to the limits authorized by Lakeside Holding Company Loan Administration Policy. Loan limits will be delegated to the various lending officers based on the officer's lending experience. A loan limit will be set up for each of the following types of loans:

(a) Fully secured by one of the following:
(1) Savings Accounts.
(2) Certificate of Deposit.
(3) Cash Surrender Value of Life Insurance.
(b) Fully secured by marketable collateral such as: chattel mortgages, various types of assignment, etc.
(c) Unsecured.

XIII. **LAKESIDE HOLDING COMPANY LOAN POLICY**   The loan policy adopted by the Holding Company Board and amended from time to time is considered as additional loan policy for the bank. The policies set out by the Holding Company Board are hereby considered as a part of this loan policy.

XIV. **COMPLIANCE**   The Board insists that all laws and regulations of all governmental authorities be strictly adhered to by all officers and employees. Compliance with the following is a must requirement:

(a) Regulation Z —Truth in Lending and Fair Credit Billing Act.
(b) Regulation B—Equal Credit Opportunity Act.

(c)   Regulation C—Home Mortgage Disclosure Act.
(d)   Regulation U.
(e)   Regulation X—Real Estate Settlement Procedures Act.
(f)   All usury laws.
(g)   The Community Reinvestment Act.
(h)   Financial Institutions Regulatory and Interest Rate Control Act of 1978.

XV. LOANS TO FEDERAL, STATE, COUNTY, AND MUNICI-PAL OFFICE HOLDERS   All lending officers should be sensitive to any loans that are made to federal, state, county, and municipal office holders. At the same time, it is understood that there is a need in most cases to make such loans, and we want to accommodate all reasonable requests that fall within our normal loan policy from these office holders. All lending officers being aware of the present climate in which we operate should submit to the Officers Executive Committee on an annual basis a report of all loans made and then outstanding to any federal, state, county, and municipal office holders. In addition, it will be the responsibility of each lending officer to make certain that all such loans are completely documented and memoranda detailing amounts, interest rates, repayment schedules, purpose, financial data, and credit reports.

XVI. CONCENTRATIONS OF CREDIT

(a)   The Board requires that all excess funds be invested daily through the sale of Federal Funds to other banks. Sales should only be made to Holding Company, approved banks, and sales to any *one* bank should not exceed 25 percent of our stockholders' equity.

(b)   The Executive Committee is charged with the responsibility of preventing excessive concentrations of credit to any industry or related group of individuals.

XVII. LOAN REVIEW   A continuing loan review program is essential. The program should emphasize the following:

(1)   Credit evaluation and rating.
(2)   Loan officer evaluation and training.
(3)   Documentation.
(4)   Compliance with loan policy.
(5)   Compliance with all federal and state laws.

XVIII. TAX FREE LOANS   A request for tax-exempt financing should be considered on the following basis:

(a)   The borrower should meet all the lending criteria required in the granting of commercial loans.
(b)   The granting of the request should provide an economic benefit for the community (jobs) and the bank (deposits and related banking business).
(c)   The terms are not to exceed 15 years.
(d)   Rates shall float with Holding Company base rate.
(e)   The Senior Corporate Loan Officer or Senior Corporate Investment Officer should be consulted before committing to any tax-exempt funding over $100,000.00 and quoting a rate.
(f)   In the event that the Holding Company is required to restrict tax-free income, the Letter of Credit guaranty may be used to facilitate financing. For a fee our bank would issue a Letter of Credit to back the bonds, and they would be sold to someone else. All other requirements of tax-exempt loans would also apply to these guarantees.

XIX. **RELEASING COLLATERAL**   The release of collateral from any active loan requires the signature of two loan officers and a documenting memorandum in the credit and collateral file. The exception to this policy is where a specific lot release was negotiated at the inception of the loan.

XX. **EXTENSIONS POLICY**   Extensions: It is the policy of the bank to grant an extension of an installment loan payment(s) only in special or unusual situations, where it can be clearly exhibited by the customer that his or her problems are of a short-term nature. Below is a more definitive description of the bank policy.

(a)   No free extension will be granted.
(b)   No more than one extension in a 12-month period without prior approval from the head of the Installment Loan Department.
(c)   A customer with a note two or more installments past due will not be granted a 30-day extension unless the other delinquent payments are collected.

Renewals: It will be the policy to allow a customer to renew a loan that is past due when it can be documented that such renewal will help the customer and the bank is in a stronger position as a result of the renewal.

Before approving the renewal of a past-due loan, the lending officer should develop full information as to the reason for the request. The documentation in the file will be:

(a) Memorandum giving reasons for the renewal, what it did for customer and the bank.

XXI. **CHARGE-OFF POLICY**   All loans (accounts) will be charged off when it is determined they are uncollectible but not later than when the loan is 90 days past due. Delinquencies are to be determined on a contractual basis and not on a recency of payment basis. For example, payment due on 4-20-96 is 30 days delinquent 5-20-96 and would be 90 days delinquent 7-20-96, at which time the loan is to be charged off. If the 3-20-96 payment was made on 7-20-96, the account is still 90 days past due and subject to immediate charge-off, unless it can be ascertained recovery will be received within the next 45 days:

(a) From collection of a physical damage insurance policy, or
(b) From collection on sale of marketable collateral, or
(c) From other collateral such as cash value life insurance or savings accounts, or
(d) Other unspecified reason that is approved by the head of the Installment Loan Department.

A list of all loans not charged off after 90 days by reasons of the above exceptions or for any other reason should be reported to the President at the end of each quarter.

XXII. **STUDENT LOANS**   The Board encourages participation in the guaranteed student loan program. It shall be the duty of the Officers Executive Committee to set the requirements and limits for this program.

XXIII. **LETTERS OF CREDIT**   All Letters of Credit issued by this bank must be signed by the President or Executive Vice President. The loan officer should submit all credit information, collateral documentation, and final draft of the Letter to obtain approval. Collateral documentation required is the same as for a loan made under the same conditions.

All Letters of Credit involving international companies or anything other than simple domestic Letters will be issued through the Holding Company's International Department.

XXIV. **MASTERCARD AND VISA**   We encourage the issuance of these cards to build the base of receivables for this bank. The President is authorized to enter into an agreement with the Holding Company to issue cards and service these accounts for this bank.

Appendix B

Loan Policy for
Metropolitan Bank

This document contains the official loan policy of Metropolitan Bank. Its purpose is to set forth in writing the concepts by which the loan function shall be governed within the Bank.

In keeping with the general requirements of the loan policy, all loan personnel are required to apply the appropriate, existing banking regulations to carry out the loan program in a manner consistent with the directives of the Board of Directors and the Bank's executive management. This policy is supported by the Bank's Interest Rate and Maturity Manual, which contains significant information used in the lending process. Adherence to the general guidelines contained in this policy is required at all times; significant variations shall be deemed unacceptable. This policy shall apply to all members of the Bank's staff who exercise loan authority and shall remain in effect until it is amended or rescinded.

GENERAL STATEMENT

The Lending Policy of Metropolitan Bank shall at all times be flexible enough to meet the needs of our trade area. In addition, strong emphasis is given to providing good service and prompt decisions; and all loan personnel are required to apply their knowledge and skills in lending in a competent and efficient manner. It is the intent of senior management to place sufficient authority in the hands of loan officers and loan committees to effectively serve our present customer base and to assist in the securing of loan relationships from the Bank's prospective customers. Loan decisions made independently within the assigned loan limits are encouraged.

In all cases, the loan portfolio with recognition of the mix and the loan to deposit ratio required by senior management should:

1. Satisfy demand.
2. Provide a reasonable diversification.
3. Obtain a reasonable balance of maturity distribution.
4. Acknowledge the requirements of the Bank's high credit standards and indicate the generally conservative nature of its lending posture.
5. Carry proper and profitable interest rate differentials.

When considering a loan request of any nature, proper consideration shall always be given to the applicant's overall banking relationship. This approach to credit will provide assistance in pricing the loan as well as providing the opportunity to develop additional Bank business.

As a commercial bank, we are entrusted with the ability to create money through the extension of credit. We should all be aware of the fact that acceptable growth and profitability depends, to a large degree, upon a consistent and workable loan policy.

GEOGRAPHICAL LENDING AREA

It is the opinion of executive management that the primary lending area for the Bank is constituted within the corporate boundaries of Sierra, Highland, and Boulder Counties. The majority of our loans are generated within these counties and the immediate surrounding area.

Loans extended outside our immediate trade area should be restricted to national line accounts and purchased loan participations.

TYPES OF LOAN SOUGHT

Wholesale—Primarily lines of credit issued to national concerns who are not necessarily located within the Bank's immediate trade area.

Commercial—Loans made to business interests which may be secured or unsecured. The loans are balance related and extended to provide the credit requirements of the business community.

Real Estate—Loans which are made on a basis consistent with the Bank's policy which may be amended from time to time. The loans may be secured by residential or commercial real estate and may or may not be balance related.

Consumer—Personal and consumer loans made for various purposes, secured and unsecured and not necessarily balance related.

Broadly, the makeup of our loan portfolio on a percentage basis shall be:

1. Wholesale   5%
2. Commercial   40%
3. Real Estate   20%
4. Consumer   35%

Concentration in any one area of service or industry should not exceed 10 percent of the total loan portfolio. Wholesale loans shall be generally limited to "prime rate" accounts. The installments loan portfolio shall not contain a concentration in any one consumer category that would exceed 25 percent of the total installment loan portfolio, except for motor vehicles. It should be noted that outstandings on VISA are considered an installment credit within the loan policy.

Our basic maturities shall be as follows:

Single-Payment Loans—Naturally mature within 90 days. Extended maturities on single-payment loans can adversely affect the Bank's average lending rate.

Term Loans—Term loans made to businesses shall normally mature in no more than 5 years and be payable monthly. All term loans extended shall be repaid on at least a quarterly basis and be fully secured.

Real Estate Loans—Residential and commercial mortgage loans may be made with maturity and repayment schedules which will vary with the marketplace as determined by executive management. This category includes construction loans for residential or commercial purposes.

Installment Loans—Certain types of loans are exempted, such as second mortgage or real estate, 10 years, and loans on new mobile homes, 10 years.

Repayment Provision—An understanding of the repayment provision shall be reached with the borrower at the inception of the loans. If the note itself does not specify the terms of repayment, then the repayment provision should be incorporated into an appropriate credit file memorandum. In the case of rolling stock of any type, machinery, or other forms of depreciable equipment that is in use shall have a specific repayment plan. Preferably repayment will be in the form of monthly or quarterly payments which will retire the debit within the useful life of the collateral. It is highly desirable that a plan of repayment be an integral part of all loans made by the Bank's lending officers.

PERCENTAGE OF LOANS TO APPROPRIATE BALANCE SHEET ITEMS

It is the policy of Metropolitan Bank to meet the credit demands generated within its trade area. A loan to deposit ratio of sixty-five to seventy-five percent (65% to 75%) is desirable and appears to be sufficient to meet the needs of our borrowers. Other factors which will have significant bearing upon an acceptable loan to deposit ratio are liquidity, types of loans, concentration, and general economic conditions which directly relate to the Bank's performance. The upper limits of a desirable loan to deposit ratio may be changed from time to time at the discretion of executive management.

INTEREST RATE STRUCTURES

Interest on loans is the single source of bank income and traditionally represents the major portion of total earnings. The basis of this important source of income is directly influenced by the factors of supply and demand in the money market. The effects of economic conditions which weigh heavily on the strength or weakness of loan demand usually dictates the general level of interest rates throughout the country and in our immediate trade area. Therefore the setting of loan interest rates for the various types of credit extended will reflect the existing market conditions and will bear a relationship to the prime lending rate. The setting of interest rates shall be within the legal contract rate structures provided for by federal and state regulatory agencies.

The following factors should be considered when setting an interest rate on a given loan.

1. Supply and demand in the money market.
2. The cost of money within the Bank.
3. The prevailing market levels of rates for the type of loan being considered.
4. Borrower's overall relationship with the Bank.

Taking into consideration the fundamentals contained above, interest rates on loans should always represent a fair value both to the Bank and to the borrower.

GENERAL POLICIES ON COLLATERAL AND DOCUMENTATION

1. *Stocks and Bonds*—On closely held stocks, we should not normally accept the shares for collateral unless there is a known market usually represented by a repurchase letter from a responsible, prospective buyer. Normal advance should not exceed 33 1/3 percent of book value. Over-the-counter stocks with known markets should be held in the range of 60 to 65 percent. Listed stocks may be taken up to 75 percent of value depending on the market and the stocks' recent trading history. Corporate and municipal bonds may be taken with an advance equal to 80 percent of the current market value. Recent developments have indicated a severe deterioration in this category of collateral. United States government bonds may be taken as collateral with advances up to 90 percent of the current market value. Consideration should be given to maturity, interest rates, and current prices in the government bond market.

2. *Savings Accounts or Certificates of Deposit*—100 percent of the available balance may be advanced with the passbook or instrument in hand with the proper assignment and acknowledgment.

3. *Cash Value Life Insurance*—Loans may be made up to the net cash value indicated for the year prior to the loan request. Close attention should be given to the possibility of automatic premium loan provisions in lending against cash value of life insurance.

4. *Real Estate*—Advances may be made on improved residential property up to 90 percent of appraised value or cost, whichever is less. Improved commercial real estate loans may be made up to 80 percent of appraised value or cost, whichever is less. "Cost" may be waived due to the circumstances of the loan request. Accurate appraisals are desirable in all types of real estate lending.

5. *Automotive*—Loans may be advanced to 80 percent of cost for new autos and to the average loan value for used autos and small trucks with a physical appraisal of the vehicle. The Black Book shall be used as a source to determine the average loan values for used vehicles. Large trucks, buses, and specialty type vehicles shall be financed on the basis of

66 2/3 percent of cost for new purchases and 50 percent for used. The advance can be adjusted upward to consider the strong type commercial borrower and type of dealer recourse.

6. *Construction, Farm, and Other Special Types of Machinery and Equipment*—Loans may be made equal to 66 2/3 percent of cost. Special emphasis should be given to U.C.C. filing on untitled equipment.

7. *Inventory and Accounts Receivable*—Loans made purely against inventory should not exceed 50 percent of stated value with consideration being given to salability and perishability. Loans secured by accounts receivable should not exceed 80 percent of the accounts acknowledged as current within 60 days. Based upon the strength of the borrower, receivables financing may be made with or without notification of the assignment and with or without direct payment being made to the Bank through the use of a collateral account. Approval of the Senior Loan Committee required.

8. *Other Forms*—Other forms of collateral may be taken at the option of the Bank. When dealing with collateral other than the normal types of bank collateral, use your common sense and, if you are in doubt, discuss it with your department head or senior loan officer.

All loan personnel shall be expected to be familiar with the various forms of documentation used in the Bank in order to establish the debt and to secure proper lien positions in collateral taken. Loan personnel shall be expected to maintain at their desk or have immediate access to the *Comptrollers' Manual for National Banks, the Federal Reserve Bank Regulations,* and *Departmental Operating Procedures.* It is the Bank's intention to comply with all laws, regulations, and interpretations issued by regulatory authorities pertaining to the extension of credit.

In cases where written commitments are desirable, the commitment letter shall be carefully reviewed to be certain the Bank is fully protected in the matters of commitment. All written commitments must have an expiration date which normally should not exceed one (1) year. It is desirable for the senior loan officer or the members of the senior loan committee to review all letters of commitment before they are mailed from the Bank. Formal lines of credit may only be granted with the concurrence of one (1) executive officer. It shall be the Bank's policy to require audited statements when total loans of a business interest exceed $250,000.00, regardless of the basis of the credit. This requirement may be exempted based upon the type of collateral pledged and the basis of repayment. Waivers shall be granted by action of the Bank's Senior Loan Committee. When in doubt concerning documentation or matters of commitment, advice of Bank Counsel should be sought.

The requirements contained in this section of the loan policy represent normal and desirable conditions. It should be recognized by all persons exercising loan authority that *reasonable* variations will be allowed based upon the unique circumstances of a loan request. Exceptions or variations which, in the loan officer's judgment, are justified shall be detailed in an appropriate memorandum directed to the credit file of the borrower.

AUTHORIZED APPRAISERS

All collateral pledged to the Bank to secure loans shall be properly appraised in order to determine the appropriate percentage of advance against value. The Bank recognizes the sources of appraisal for commodities, stocks and bonds, automobiles, et cetera as provided for by various financial media and publishing houses. Items of collateral which do not have a readily available and dependable source of valuation shall be appraised by at least two (2) bank lending officers. When possible, those officers making the appraisal should not be involved in the process of the loan applications. A statement of value signed by those persons making the appraisal shall be placed in the appropriate collateral file.

Real estate appraisals shall be made by two (2) lending officers prior to the granting of commitment. Following the determination of a fair market value, the maximum loan amount will be calculated within the Bank's current policy. All real estate loans made by the Bank shall comply without exception to the appropriate Federal and state statutes and meet the requirements of RESPA Revised, Federal Flood Insurance, and the disclosure of real estate loan location as required by Census Tract Coding.

Annual appraisals are required on all real estate loans when the principal balance exceeds $250,000.00. This requirement specifically addresses commercial real estate loans which may, in part, be secured by machinery and equipment in addition to real estate.

The Executive Vice President or the Senior Loan Officer of the Bank shall from time to time designate those loan officers who are authorized to provide the appraisals as required above.

LOANS TO DIRECTORS AND THEIR INTERESTS

Metropolitan Bank recognizes its responsibility to provide for the normal borrowing requirements of the members of its Board of Directors and their various interests. In the extension of credit to Directors and their interests, all lending personnel shall be expected to apply the requirements placed on all other credit applicants. Compromises such as low rates, high advances, and extended maturities shall be deemed unacceptable in every case. We should normally require the submission of any information necessary to render good credit judgment on all loans granted to Directors and their interests. Loans to Directors, or influenced by a Director, which may be classed as accommodations are discouraged.

All loans within this category shall be made on an "arm's length" basis. Situations which in the loan officer's opinion deserve special consideration should be deferred to the President, Executive Vice President, or Senior Loan Officer.

INAPPROPRIATE CREDIT PRACTICES

It is the intention of the Bank to meet the credit requirements of its customers with a full range of loan services; however, our loans should be for constructive purposes. It is in this light that the following types of credit would be deemed inappropriate:

1. Loan requests which represent high-risk, speculative ventures should be avoided.
2. We should not necessarily encourage unwarranted expenditures through the extension of credit which might appropriately be deferred.
3. Loans to businesses only for the purpose of acquiring their own capital stock should be avoided.
4. Unsecured "front side" or "down payment" loans should be avoided at all times. Unsecured equity financing usually represents an extremely weak credit.
5. Loan requests should always be handled at "arm's length." All persons with loan authority shall refrain from taking applications for credit in which they have a personal interest in the transaction. Loans of this type shall be referred to a disinterested loan officer for processing.

6. Loans for purely speculative purposes with respect to the various commodity and stock markets.

7. Loans for obvious land speculation transactions in which there is not a well-defined plan of development with a source of permanent financing.

Undesirable loans such as those mentioned above can easily be avoided through the application of good lending techniques, compliance with regulations, and, of equal importance, the use of common sense.

RECOMMENDED LOAN AUTHORITY STRUCTURE

All loans shall be extended on a secured or unsecured basis with specific limits assigned in each lending category to officers who have been granted loan authority. Loan authorities are assigned on the basis of the borrower's total debt relationship, including all names in which he or she may borrow, and should not be applied on the basis of single transactions. No officer shall commit to any loan, or combination of loans, which would create a total liability in excess of his or her secured limit. The loan officer may request another with greater lending authority to join in the making of loans which exceed his or her limits. In this regard, the officers shall be required to initial all loan documentation.

Within the context of loan authority, secured loans are usually those collateralized by liquid, self-evident, and fully negotiable collateral. This type of preferred collateral is in most cases held by the Bank with proper assignments, which allows the collateral to be sold and the loan balance liquidated without action on the part of the borrower. Loans may be secured by other types of collateral as described on Page 7 and 8 of the Loan Policy. These loans are subject to proper documentation and should be made within the limits of recommended advances and maturities. All other loans will be considered unsecured for loan authority purposes. Formal lines of credit and letters of commitment which exceed a loan officer's authority may only be granted and issued by the Senior Loan Committee, the Executive Committee, or an Executive Officer. Lending limits for individual loan officers and the various committees shall be established or amended from time to time by executive management.

SPECIFIC LENDING PROCEDURES

In order to set forth, in a specific manner, procedures of the Bank for certain types of loans, operating procedures have been established by the loan departments. Necessary additions or deletions will be made based upon recommendations of executive management.

NONDISCRIMINATORY PRACTICES

The Lending Division will make credit available to all creditworthy persons without regard to race, color, religion, national origin, sex, marital status, or age; because all or part of the applicant's income derives from any public assistance program; or because the applicant has in good faith exercised any right under the Consumer Credit Protection Act.

It will continue to be the policy of the Lending Division to extend credit to present and future customers that qualify under our standards. It will also be the continued policy of the Lending Division to extend credit to our customers without discriminating against them on a prohibited basis with respect to any aspect of a credit transaction.

The Lending Division does not deny mortgage or home improvement loans to anyone for reasons of race, color, religion, sex, or national origin. The Division does not discriminate in the fixing of the amount, interest rate, duration, or other terms, such as application and collection procedures.

SYNOPSIS

While this loan policy is not all inclusive, it does give a clear indication as to the Bank's position in the lending process. It is the opinion of bank management that if you are adhering to the guidelines contained in the loan policy, you will be performing your duties within acceptable parameters.

The loan policy is subject to annual review by the Bank's executive officers, and interim additions or deletions may be made as deemed necessary.

Loan Policy for County Bank

I. *General Purpose*

The Board of Directors believes that sound loans are one of the most satisfactory and profitable means to investing the Bank's funds, and therefore desires to make all of the sound loans that its resources permit and opportunities afford. The Board of Directors intend that this loan policy help the management of the Bank in the maintenance of proper credit standards, in avoiding unnecessary risks, and in proper evaluation of new business opportunities. The Board will review this policy annually.

II. *Loans*

A. *Geographical Lending Area*

For the purpose of this policy, the lending area is the five counties surrounding Hamilton County. These counties include . . . Loans made outside this trade area should be approved by a Senior Officer of the Bank.

B. *Types of Loans*

1. *Commercial:* These loans are made to encourage the growth of business within the lending area. Loans in this category should be based on sound banking principles and not be of a speculative nature. Loans should be secured by adequate collateral which can be applied to the debt in case of default. Loans secured by accounts receivable, furniture, and inventory should be conservatively made, with close monitoring necessary, to protect the security interest of the Bank.

2. *Real Estate:* Sound real estate secured loans are encouraged by this policy. These loans should be properly amortized over a period of not more than 15 years and can be

secured by residential, commercial, or agricultural real
estate. Single-payment real estate loans may also be made.
All real estate loans should not exceed 80 percent of the
appraised value.

3. *Consumer (Personal):* Unsecured personal loans should be
made to persons of good character with an assured income
and satisfactory credit record when the purpose of such
loans will be of ultimate benefit to the borrower. Such
loans are to be not more than 20 percent of the borrower's
annual income and usually are to be payable in monthly
installments not to exceed twenty-four (24) months. Single-pay notes may be made at the discretion of the lending
officers. All unsecured loans over $10,000.00 should be
accompanied by a personal financial statement.

4. *Construction:* Construction mortgage loans are permissible
when made to a competent contractor or financially
responsible individual borrower, providing they produce a
satisfactory commitment from an investor for the long-
term financing.

5. *Agricultural:* Agricultural loans may be made to good agriculture bank customers. These loans should be secured by
crops, equipment, and/or real estate. A financial statement
should also be required from the customer.

6. *Livestock:* Land and equipment should be used to secure
livestock loans and/or hogs if the amount of the loans
exceeds seventy-five percent (75%) of the cost or current
value of the livestock.

7. *Stocks and Bonds:* Loans secured by US Government
Bonds may be made at not more than 90 percent of the
market value of the bonds. Unlisted securities should not
be in excess of 70 percent of the market value and all loans
secured by stock shall conform to Regulation U as set forth
by the Board of Governors of the Federal Reserve System.

8. *Cash Value of Life Insurance:* Loans may be made against
cash value of life insurance, but these loans should not
exceed the cash value of the policy.

9. *Certificate and Savings Account:* Loans may be made to
owners of accounts at institutions that are federally
insured, and the loans should not exceed $100,000.
Acknowledgment should be received from the institution

where the deposit is held. Loans secured by CDs and savings from our bank should be actively solicited.

10. *Automobile:* Loans secured by new autos may be for not more than 80 percent of manufacturer's suggested retail price. On loans secured by used vehicles, the amount loaned shall not be more than the average loan value as set out in a current NADA book. Care should be exercised by bank employees to require proper documentation for vehicles and that the vehicles are properly insured to protect the security interest of the Bank.

11. a. *Dealer:* Loans to individuals for the purchase of automobiles, mobile homes, equipment, or furniture where the loan is originated by the dealer/seller shall be made provided they are on a full recourse basis. The dealer shall maintain a reserve of not less than 5 percent.

    b. Floor plan loans may be made if proper agreements with the dealer are in place and the loans are properly secured and documentation is complete.

12. *Commodity:* Commodity loans should be secured by warehouse receipts in bonded warehouses. The property securing these loans should be protected by insurance or other satisfactory means.

C. *Undesirable Types of Loans:*

1. Capital loans to a business enterprise where the loan cannot be repaid within a reasonable period except by borrowing elsewhere or liquidating the business.

2. Loans to a new enterprise, if the repayment of the loan is dependent solely upon the profitable operation of the enterprise.

3. Loans to persons whose integrity or honesty is questionable.

4. Real estate mortgage loans secured by property located outside the Bank's recognized trade area, unless approved by a Senior Officer.

5. Loans secured by an assignment against an undistributed estate.

6. Loans secured by stock in a closed corporation which has no ready market and where the value cannot be determined by a financial statement.

7. Loans for the purpose of enabling the borrowers to speculate on future market of securities or commodities.

8. Great care should be exercised in making loans to individuals who lack credit experience even with a satisfactory co-signer.

9. Loans to persons who have had loans previously charged off at the Bank.

10. Loans to individuals who have taken bankruptcy.

11. Loans secured by a second or third mortgage on the said property that total more than 80 percent of the fair market value of the property as determined by the Bank's appraisers.

12. Loans on real estate or property when the repayment of the loan is based upon the selling of the property.

D. *Procedures for Loans:*

1. All loan officers of the Bank shall have the authority to make loans in amounts indicated by their respective names, without prior approval of the Loan Committee, provided such loans are in accordance with all other sections of the Loan Policy. Loans to any person, firm, or corporation in excess of the limits indicated shall be prior approved by the Loan Committee. A loan, in this instance, means the total indebtedness of the borrower.

Secured—may include unsecured

_____	$50,000	$25,000
_____	50,000	20,000
_____	25,000	5,000
_____	20,000	5,000
_____	4,000	2,000

E. *Interest Rates:*

Interest rates shall be in accordance with the Schedule of rates adopted by Senior Management. These rates shall be within the range of rates as approved by law.

III. *Documentation:*

All secured loans shall be supported by the necessary technical documentation. Proceeds of such loans generally should not be dispersed until supporting documents are on file. The responsibility of acquiring technical documents shall be that of the loan officer originating the loan.

IV. *Officer and Employee Loans:*

Loans to officers and employees of this Bank may be made so long as such loans conform to this policy and to generally accepted lending principles; however, employee loans will be approved in advance by the Loan Committee. All loans to officers must be reported to the Board of Directors at its next meeting. Lines of credit for Executive Officer loans will be approved annually by the Board of Directors. The lines of credit for Executive Officers are listed with customers' lines of credit.

V. *Insurance:*

On all loans where it is appropriate, the bank requires credit life insurance, accident and health insurance, or accident insurance to protect the bank. A copy of the policy should be on file at the bank.

VI. A. *Lines of Credit and Commitments:* Lines of credit and commitments will be established for our creditworthy customers. Current fiscal year financial statements will be maintained on all lines of credit. The customer should not be notified that the commitment/line exists until approval of the Board of Directors has been obtained.

A list of all approved commitments and lines of credit should be maintained.

A list of all lines of credit and commitments will be furnished to each loan officer.

On an annual basis the Board of Directors will review all lines of credit, and at that time they will be either confirmed or discontinued. A line shall not be made beyond one year from the date of approval.

Any advance of funds under expired lines or commitments requires the same approval as new loans. Absence of proper approval constitutes an unauthorized advance of funds.

Two types of lines of credit will be used. Under one line the customer is advised that the line exists, and under the other line the customer is not advised. Both are defined as follows:

1. *Line of Credit*—A revocable agreement in which the borrower is informed that funds will be made available up to a stated amount and under mutually satisfactory terms and conditions subject to periodic review. Revocation of the line is rare and normally occurs when serious declines in credit conditions are evident.

2. *Internal Guidance Line*—This agreement is similar to a line of credit, but the customer is not advised. It is established for internal bank purposes and provides financing for recurrent requests without referring each one to a credit committee. Normally, such an agreement would be advised to the borrower, but in some cases, the Bank may not wish to do so.

Advances under established lines of credit/commitments do not require prior approval by any committee even though the advance may exceed the officer's loan limit. However, the officer must determine that all requirements of the line/commitment have been met and that the advance does not exceed or result in the borrower's total liability exceeding the approval limit.

B. *Letters of Credit:* Letters of credit are analyzed using the same policy and procedures as loans. In other words, the same authority is required to approve a letter of credit as is required to approve a loan. Officers Loan Committee and/or Executive Loan Committee limits, as outlined in this policy, also apply to letters of credit.

VII. *Lending Activities:*

All lending activities of the Bank will be under the general supervision of the President, who will follow the policies as set forth in the loan policy. All loan officers shall seek advice and counsel of the President when in doubt as to credit decisions or questions involving the interpretation or application of loan policies.

VIII. *Loan Review:*

All loans shall be reviewed by the loan officers on a weekly basis. A loan review officer will review the documentation on loans of $25,000 or more.

IX. *Miscellaneous Guidelines:*

A. *Maximum Limit to One Borrower:* Special care must be made to see that no one borrower shall be loaned more than twenty percent (20%) of the capital, surplus, and undivided profits. Where loans exceed ten percent (10%) of such capital, such excess shall be secured by good collateral. To consider the aggregate debt of one customer, all direct, indirect, overdrafts, and uncollected funds should be taken into consideration.

B. *Nonaccrual of Interest:* It is the policy of the bank that only interest which is collectible will be taken into income. This policy will be governed by FDIC regulations and our loan policy, Section XI (D), regarding Collections and Charge-offs. It will be the responsibility of the Senior Loan Officer to see that this policy is followed.

Loans are to be transferred to nonaccrual status if:

1. They are not maintained on a cash basis because of deterioration in the financial position of the borrower.
2. Payment in full of interest or principal is not expected.
3. Principal or interest has been in default for a period of 90 days or more unless the obligation is both well secured and in the process of collection.

A nonaccrual asset may be restored to an accrual status when none of its principal or interest is due and unpaid or when it otherwise becomes well secured and in the process of collection.

NOTE: Loans to individuals for household, family, and other personal expenditures are usually loans of smaller amounts and should be charged off, per this loan policy, rather than being placed in nonaccrual.

C. *Capitalization of Interest:* Crediting income to the bank books for any interest added to the unpaid balance of any loan is prohibited. An exception (only in rare circumstances) may be made with the approval of the CEO. Additional tangible collateral should be secured if necessary.

D. *Collection Policy:* It is the responsibility of the lending officer to monitor all of his or her loans. When a loan becomes delinquent, the officer should coordinate all efforts to bring the loan(s) current with every method that possibly can be used to collect the loan, at the earliest time (15–30 days) possible. Contact with the customer should be made and information in the files updated as to current address, telephone number, employment, etc. The customers should be informed that unless the account is paid current, the collateral may be repossessed. Every effort should be made to work with the customer; however, the primary objective is collection of the account.

Charging Off Loans: Installment loans more than 180 days past due and single-pay loans more than 90 days past due shall be charged off unless specifically excepted by the Loan Committee. Potential problem loans (60 days past due) should be noted by the loan officer from the weekly past-due report and appropriate action taken to avoid losses. A record correspondence, legal action, and communication with the borrower should be maintained in the loan file. The bank should charge off loans whose collectibility is sufficiently questionable that the Bank can no longer justify showing the loan as an asset on the balance sheet. To determine if a loan should be charged off, all possible sources of repayment should be analyzed. Possible sources of repayment include the potential of cash flow, the value of the Bank's collateral, and the strength of co-makers or guarantors. When these sources do not add up to a reasonable probability that the loan can be collected, it is charged off.

The fact that a loan has been charged off does not in any way diminish the borrower's obligations to the Bank. The borrower still owes the same amount of money as before the charge-off. Charged-off loans are off–balance sheet assets and require an active collection and management program

E. *Rebooking Charge-offs:* The rebooking of charged-off loans should be done only if the financial position of the borrower has changed significantly.

F. *Charged-off Recovery:* It will be the responsibility of the lending officer to review his or her charge-offs and monitor them for possible recovery.

G. *Bad Debt Reserve:* The Bank's goal is to have a minimum of 1 percent of total loans in the Reserve for Loan Losses. The Reserve for Loan Loss account will be reviewed monthly by the Board of Directors. Management will make recommendations to the Board based on prior loan loss experience, knowledge of local economic conditions, a Watch List (that is updated monthly), comparison of peer group, and knowledge of the loan portfolio.

H. *Other Real Estate:* Other real estate should be booked at a current appraised value. Any overage of the appraised value should be charged off at that time. To comply with State Banking Department regulations, assets should be written down to $1.00 within a sixty (60) month period. Continuous effort to dispose of this real estate should be made.

I. *Participations:* As a general rule, the Bank avoids involvement in loan participations, but from time to time the Bank will purchase participations in loans from other banks. When this is done, the Bank exercises all the precautions used to originate a loan. A complete credit analysis is done, and the same documents are required as would be required by a loan. The collateral will be analyzed and the lien status will be researched to ensure that it is acceptable. A credit file will be maintained for each purchased participation; these credit files will be identical to the credit files the Bank maintains on its loan customers.

J. *Appraisals:* All loans secured by real estate will be supported by appraisals. For those loans in excess of $10,000, an appraisal signed by two lending officers will be required. For those loans in excess of $25,000, two officers other than the lending officer of record shall sign the appraisal. Outside appraisals performed by a qualified appraiser independent of the Bank and the borrower will be required for all loans in excess of $100,000.00, or to coincide with FDIC regulations.

K. *Extensions of Loan Payments (Installment Loans):* Occasionally a customer may find it difficult to pay an installment as originally scheduled on the contract. In deserving cases, payments may be deferred for a specified period of time in accordance with the guidelines set forth below. If the customer has a legitimate reason for wanting a revision of the contract, the officer should determine that the following factors are favorable prior to granting the request:

1. Customer desire and ability to pay.
2. Condition of the collateral.
3. Past payment history.
4. Customer's equity in the collateral.
5. Actual value of the collateral.
6. Income source for making the next payment.

Not more than two extensions of the loan per year should be granted to the borrower. Lending officers shall have the authority to approve more than two extensions if determined to be in the best interest of the Bank to do so. Each extension would extend the date of one monthly payment for 30 days. Due dates on remaining installments should not be affected, and all extensions must bring the loan current. If the extension fails to do so, then a payment(s) must be collected at the time of extension. All extensions on past-due loans must be approved by the lending officer.

The customer should be charged an extension fee equal to the amount of interest that would have accrued that month under the Rule of 78s. The extension fee should be collected at the time an extension is granted.

L. *Renewals:* Loan officers are expected to see that all notes are paid in full or renewed no later than the maturity date of the note. At the time of renewal, all interest accrued to date must be collected from the customer in good funds. Checks in payment of interest or principal should not place an account in an overdrawn status. All renewals will follow the same approval process as new notes. Continuous short-term borrowing is discouraged. A repayment program should be established. Unsecured consumer purpose loans are to be reduced at each renewal in the amount sufficient to pay the loan in full within 30 months of the original date of the loan.

Unsecured business purpose loans are to be reduced at each renewal in an amount sufficient to pay the loan in full within 36 months of the original date of the loan. Loans secured by items such as vehicles, equipment, real estate, or similar collateral should not be made or renewed for longer than one year (six months is more desirable) without a reduction or being placed on an amortization schedule that conforms to our loan policy.

These restrictions do not apply to notes granted under an approved line of credit.

M. *Concentrations of Credit:* A concentration of credit consists of direct, indirect, or contingent liabilities exceeding 25 percent of the Bank's capital structure. This includes the aggregate of all types of loans, overdrafts, cash items, securities purchased outright or under resale agreements, sale of federal funds, leases, acceptances, letters of credit, loan endorsed, guaranteed, or subject to repurchase agreements, and any other actual or contingent liability. Concentrations involve one borrower, an affiliated group of borrowers, or borrowers engaged in or dependent on one industry.

All concentrations are dependent on a key factor. If weaknesses develop in that factor, all loans making up the concentration will be adversely affected. For example, loans which are concentrated in one borrower are, to a large degree, predicated on the financial capacity and character of that individual or entity. Concentrations within or dependent on a particular industry are subject to risk factors of external economic conditions and market acceptance which might equally affect all members of the group. For these reasons, a listing of the following types of concentrations will be prepared by management on a annual basis and presented to the Board of Directors for their review.

1. Loans and other obligations of one borrower or an affiliated group of borrowers.

2. Loans dependent upon one industry group.

The Board of Directors will determine at the time of the review whether to allow the concentration to remain or if measures should be implemented to reduce the concentration to a more desirable level. It is recognized that in certain instances, concentrations may be necessary for the Bank to service the legitimate needs of the trade area.

N. *Overdrafts:* It is the Bank's policy not to permit overdraft accounts. Under certain circumstances, because of technical problems or for customer relations, it may be necessary to make an exception to this policy.

Overdrafts are to be strongly discouraged, and accounts with excessive overdraft activity are to be given close scrutiny as to why the account should not be closed. In every case where an overdraft is allowed, it must have the approval of a lending officer who may make such approval only to the extent of his or her unsecured lending authority or any special overdraft authority that may have been granted by the Board. Any amounts in excess of this authority must be referred to (1) the branch manager, (2) a senior loan officer, and (3) the President, for approval.

Overdrafts for insiders, employees, and executive officers must be approved by the branch manager or senior officer. Charges for overdrafts will not be waived unless there is good and sufficient reason, which will be put in writing.

X. *Monitoring Financial Statements:*

The bank should maintain a current financial file on loans as needed when the amount of the loan should require it. All unsecured loans over $10,000,00 and all secured loans over $50,000,00 should be supported by financial information, unless specifically exempted by the President. The file should be kept current with annual statements. Residential mortgage loans are exempt.

XI. *Reports to the Board:*

It shall be the duty of the President of the Bank to submit the following reports to the Board each month:

A. All new loans over $25,000.00.

B. Accrual loans over $10,000.00, past due over 60 days or more.

C. Installment loans over $10,000.00, past due over 90 days or more.

D. Indebtedness totaling $100,000.00 or more.

E. Proposed charged-off loans for the month.

F. Statement of whether any federal funds have been borrowed.

G. Percentage of ratio of loans to deposits and total assets.

XII. *Nondiscrimination and Compliance:*

It shall be the Bank's intention to comply with the various acts and regulations of the US Government that are applicable to loans which the bank may make.

XIII. *Executive Committee:*

The Executive Committee should be composed of six (6) members, four (4) to be loan officers, one of whom will be the President and two (2) outside Directors. This committee will have a lending authority up to $600M. If one (1) member votes "no," the loan request must be referred to the full Board of Directors.

XIV. *Loan Committee:*

The Loan Committee shall consist of four lending officers (two senior and two others) up to $100M. Over $100M and up to $200M will require the President and two other lending officers.

XV. *Environmental Considerations:*

A. Each loan officer should thoroughly review present and past ownership of all real estate which will secure loans at County Bank. This may include review of public records to determine past ownership and use of properties.

B. Each loan officer should be aware of proposed use of properties to be mortgaged to the Bank. Any activities that might be considered environmentally dangerous should be reviewed and discussed thoroughly.

C. The Bank will thoroughly review the necessary documents before foreclosing on real estate properties to determine if foreclosure warrants environmental risk to the Bank.

D. It is not the Bank's policy to participate in the management of property. However, should this happen, we realize we may not be exempt under CERCLA regulations regarding environmental cleanup.

E. A loan officer will be assigned to the environmental risk program.

F. An environmental review item should be added to real estate loan checklist sheets. By checking this block, the loan officer is verifying he or she has reviewed the environmental risk on this loan. It is not the Bank's intention to assume any environmental risk on real estate transactions.

G. All loan officers and collection personnel will be advised of this policy, and it will be reviewed annually.

H. Potential problem sites (in our area) would include industrial sites, dry cleaners, print shops, gasoline stations, and auto repair shops

XVI. *Policy Exceptions:*

All officers are expected to follow the spirit and intent of these policies. At the same time, however, the policy will not fit every situation, and there will be valid reasons to deviate from the policy. When it is in the Bank's best interest, policy exceptions are permitted. When the total credit relationship is $200,000 or less, the exception can be approved by the Officers Loan Committee. When the total credit relationship is more than $200,000 and not more than $600,000, the exception can be approved by the Executive Committee. If the exception involves a credit relationship of more than $600,000, then the Board of Directors must approve the exception.

Each time an exception is made, a memo will be written to the credit file specifying what the exception was and why it was in the Bank's best interest that the exception be granted.

XVII. *Changes to Policy and Amendments to This Manual:*

The authority to change policy rests solely with the Board of Directors. As a practical matter, any officer can suggest loan policy changes. These suggestions are then discussed with the President, and if the President agrees that a policy change is needed, he or she makes appropriate recommendations to the Board of Directors. The policy change goes into effect as soon as it has been approved.

Amendment 1: Real Estate Loans

The amendment establishes limits and standards for extensions of credit secured by liens or interests in real estate, or are made for the purpose of financing construction of a building or other improvements, consistent with the Bank's lending practices. The following considerations are set forth to establish these limits and standards:

1. It shall be understood that any consideration not specifically addressed by this amendment will be governed by the Bank's current loan policy. Most particularly, documentation, approval and reporting standards, portfolio diversification, and administration are to be governed by current loan policy.

2. The loan-to-value (LTV) limits are established by this amendment:

Raw land	65%
Land development	75%
Construction of commercial, multifamily, and other nonresidential	80%
Construction of single-family residence	85%
Purchase of existing commercial, multifamily, and other nonresidential	85%
Owner-occupied residence	90%

Stated LTVs will be observed along with prudent underwriting standards reflecting relevant credit factors, including capacity to service the debt, creditworthiness and character of the borrower, value of the mortgaged property as reflected by an appropriate appraisal or evaluation, equity, secondary sources of repayment, additional collateral, or other enhancements. Pricing shall be structured by management and provided to lending personnel on a regularly scheduled basis. The Bank's management shall monitor conditions in its real estate market so that it can react quickly to changes in conditions that are relevant to its lending decisions. Factors to consider are population and employment trends, zoning requirements, vacancy rates, construction and absorption rates, rental rates, sales prices, and valuation trends.

Exceptions: In addition to the current loan policy regarding exceptions, real estate loans exceeding the LTVs established by this amendment will be identified in the Bank's records, and reported at least quarterly to the Bank's Board of Directors. The aggregate amount of *all* loans in excess of LTVs shall not exceed 100 percent of total capital. Within this total, loans for all commercial, agricultural, multifamily, or other non 1–4 family residential properties should not exceed 30 percent of total capital. Approval of all exceptions shall be supported by written justification that sets forth relevant credit factors supporting the decision and maintained in the loan file.

Appendix D

FDIC Red Flags for Fraud and Insider Abuse[1]

This appendix contains the warning signs, or red flags, published in the FDIC's *Manual of Examination Policies* (1-90). The manual is used by bank examiners to detect potential fraud and insider abuse. The subject areas for which red flags are presented here include

- Corporate culture/ethics.
- Insider transactions.
- Loan participations.
- Real estate lending.
- Secured lending.
- Third-party obligations.
- Lending to buy tax shelter investments.
- Linked financing/brokered deposits.
- Credit cards and ATM transactions.
- Advance fee schemes.
- Offshore transactions.
- Wire transfers.
- Money laundering.
- Securities trading activities.
- Miscellaneous.

A caveat is in order. The presence of one of more red-flags does not mean that insider abuse is occurring or that fraud is being committed. It does mean that further investigation is required. It also suggests that the institution's policies may require changes and/or that exceptions to its policies must be well documented.

---

[1] FDIC, *Manual of Examination Policies*, Division of Bank Supervision, "Bank Fraud and Insider Abuse" (1-90), pp., 8.3-1–8.3-23.

Corporate Culture

1. Absence of code of ethics.
2. Absence of a clear policy restricting or requiring disclosure of conflicts of interest.
3. Absence of a policy restricting gifts and gratuities.
4. Lack of oversight by the institution's board of directors, particularly outside directors.
5. Absence of planning, training, hiring, and organizational policies.
6. Absence of clearly defined authorities and lack of definition of the responsibilities that go along with the authorities.
7. Lack of independence of management in acting on recommended corrections.
8. CEO controls internal and outside auditors.
9. Lax control and review of expense accounts.

Insider Transactions

1. Insider lending personal funds to customers or borrowing from customers.
2. Insider involvement in silent trusts or partnerships and/or shell corporations.
3. Insider appears to receive special favors from institution customers or shows unusual favoritism toward certain institution customers.
4. Insider purchases assets from the institution, directly or indirectly, and there is no evidence of independent appraisal of the assets.
5. Insider has apparent reciprocal lending arrangements with insiders of other institutions, and his or her institution has correspondent relationship with those institutions.
6. Insider is involved in a business that arranges its financing through the institution.
7. Insider "perks" include use of expensive institution-owned automobiles, boats, airplanes, housing, and so on, where the institution's earnings do not appear to support such extravagance.
8. Insider is heavily indebted and debt service appears to require most, if not all, of the insider's salary.
9. Insider's financial statements show large or unusual fluctuations. Net worth cannot be reconciled from disclosed sources of income.

10. Insider is financing large purchases (home, auto, etc.) through private, nonbanking sources that may have a business relationship with the institution.

11. Insider's financial statements reflect heavy concentration of high-risk investments and speculative ventures.

12. Insider sells personal assets to third party and the institution provides financing without the benefit of independent appraisal.

13. Insiders and their interests frequently appear on transactions suspense items listings or on computer-generated past-due loan lists, but do not appear on the "updated" version presented to the board of directors or to examiners.

14. Insider "unofficially" guarantees loans and/or loan participations.

15. Insider is responsible for clearing up audit exceptions on loan balance confirmations.

16. Insider "forgets" to process credit entry for official bank checks causing the account to be out of balance because checks are sometimes paid (debited) before the credit is posted, sometimes several days later.

17. Insider conducts a cash turnover over $10,000 but "forgets" to have the institution file a currency transaction report or asks an employee to "structure" the transaction to avoid filing the report.

18. Insider's stock in the institution is pledged to secure loans obtained from sources other than financial institutions. If true, what is the purpose of the loan, and are the payments current?

19. Insider conducts personal business from institution using equipment, supplies, employees, and so on, and/or spends most of his or her time outside of the institution on business unrelated to the institution.

20. Insider has substance abuse problems or is known to associate with people who have these problems.

21. Insider is known to associate with "high rollers."

22. Insider suggests that the institution change servicers or vendors even though there appears to be no problem with the current servicers or vendors.

23. Insider abruptly suggests changes in outsider auditors or legal counsel.

24. Insider loans increase dramatically at about the same time the institution is recapitalized.

25. Insider's major assets are parcels of real estate that appear to increase in value at a rate that is not consistent with market conditions.

26. Insider sells his or her stock to an employee stock option plan, sometimes arranging for the ESOP to obtain a loan to purchase the stock.

27. Insider's interests have a direct business relationship with the institution, and compensation for services is not commensurate with the level of services provided.

28. Insider agrees to buy fixed assets from the institution with the understanding that the institution will repurchase them at some future date.

29. Insider receives incentive pay or "bonuses" based on volume of loans generated.

30. Insider buys a home from a builder whose development project is financed by the institution.

31. Insider is involved in "churning" the institution's securities portfolio.

32. Insider arranges sale of EDP equipment at book value in connection with the conversion to a new data processing servicer. Also check "side" deals.

33. Insider authorizes ORE-related expenses, such as landscaping, remodeling, and so on, when such expenses do not appear to be justified (may be making improvements or repairs to personal residence).

34. Insider makes frequent trips at the institution's expense to areas where the institution has no business relationships.

35. Insider will not allow employees to talk to examiners.

36. Insider keeps an unusual number of customer files in his or her desk.

37. Insider is making payments on other borrowers' loans.

38. Insider receives commissions on credit life insurance premiums and those commissions are not properly adjusted in cases where the insurance company gives rebates to borrowers for prepayment of the loan or gives refunds to borrowers for premium overcharges.

39. Insider sells some of his or her personal stock of the institution to borrowers (as a condition for approving a loan) and buys more stock from the institution at about the same time the institution is under pressure to increase capital.

40. Insider purchases investment securities for his personal portfolio through the institution but "forgets" to reimburse the institution until a few days or weeks later, and then only if the investment has increased in value. In spite of the increase in value, the insider pays only the original purchase price to the institution.

41. Insider's accounts at the institution are frequently overdrawn. Deposits to cover overdrafts come from loans or some undisclosed source.

42. Insider maintains total control over the institution and does not allow other officers and employees to make independent decisions.

43. Insider has past-due loans at other financial institutions.

44. Insider maintains signed, blank notes in personal or customer loan files.

45. Insider is rumored to have financial problems due to divorce, business failure, gambling losses, or other problems.

46. Insider maintains several personal accounts outside of his or her own institution.

47. Insider frequently takes loan papers out of the institution for customer signatures; personally handles the disbursement of the loan proceeds; routinely cashes checks for customer loan proceeds; and insists on personally handling certain past-due accounts as a "special favor" to certain customers.

48. Insider insists that different audit firms audit different divisions or departments. (Hopes there will be no comparison of findings among firms.)

49. Insider insists that different departments be audited at different times. (This makes it easier to hide fraudulent interdepartmental transactions.)

Loan Participations

1. Excessive participations of loans between closely related institutions, correspondent institutions, and branches or departments of the lending institution.

2. Absence of any formal participation agreement.

3. Poor or incomplete loan documentation.

4. Investing in out-of-territory participations.

5. Reliance on third-party guaranties.

6. Large paydown or payoff of previously classified loans.

7. Some indication that there may be informal repurchase agreements on some participations.

8. Lack of independent credit analysis.

9. Volume of loan participations is high in relation to the size of the institution's own loan portfolio.

10. Evidence of overlapping of loan participations. For example, the sale of a loan participation equal or greater than, and at or about the same times as, a participation that has matured or is about to mature.

11. Disputes between participating institutions over documentation, payments, or any other aspect of the loan participation transaction.

12. Formal participation agreements are missing; therefore, responsibilities and rights of all participating institutions may be unclear.

13. Participations between affiliated institutions may be "placed" without the purchasing institution having the benefit of reviewing normal credit information, particularly where there is dominant ownership and a "rubber stamp" board of directors.

14. Payments that are not distributed to each participant according to the participation agreement may indicate preferential treatment; or, where the participants are affiliated, may indicate an attempt to disguise the delinquent status of the loans in the weaker institution.

15. Informal guarantees by insiders may be one method of disguising insider transactions.

16. There is some indication that the credit information contained in the selling institution's files is not the same as the credit information in the purchasing institution's files.

17. Reciprocal arrangements in the sale or purchase of participations. For example, institution A sells a 100 percent participation in a loan to an insider of the selling institution to institution B, which in turn sells a 100 percent participation in a loan to one of its insiders to institution A.

18. There are a number of outstanding items in correspondent accounts just prior to or during an examination or audit relating to participations purchased or sold.

19. There is some indication that payments on participations purchased are being made by the selling institution without reimbursement from the borrower.

Real Estate Lending

1. An unusually large number of loans in the same development are exactly equal to the institution's loan-to-value (LTV) ratio for real estate mortgages.

2. The institution has an unusually high percentage of "no doc" loans. (A "no doc" loan is one in which extensive documentation of income, credit history, deposits, etc. is not required because of the size of the down

payment, usually 25 percent or more. Theoretically, the value of the collateral is to protect the lender.)

3. Borrower has never owned a home before and does not appear to have the financial ability to support the size of the down payment made.

4. Property securing a loan has changed ownership frequently in a short period of time. Related entities may be involved.

5. Insured value of improvements is considerably less than appraised value.

6. Appraiser is a heavy borrower at the institution.

7. Appraisal fee is based on a percentage of the appraised value.

8. Borrower furnishes his or her own appraisal, which is a photocopy of an appraisal signed by a reputable appraiser.

9. Use of "comparables" that are not comparable.

10. Appraisal is based on an estimated future value.

11. All comparables are new houses in the same development that were built by the same builder and appraised by the same appraiser.

12. An unusual number of "purchases" are from out of the area or out of state.

13. Credit history, employment, and so on, are not independently verified by the lender.

14. A large number of applicants have income from sources that cannot be verified, such as self-employment income.

15. Applicant makes $90,000 per year and wants to purchase only a $90,000 home.

16. Applicant is 45 years old, but the credit history dates back only five years.

17. The institution's normal procedure is to accept photocopies of important documents rather than to make its own copies of the originals.

18. If copies of income tax returns are provided, columns are uneven and/or do not balance.

19. Appraiser is from out of the area and not likely to be familiar with local property values.

20. A close relationship exists among builder, broker, appraiser, and lender.

21. Construction draws are made without visual inspections.

22. All "comparables" are from properties appraised by the same appraiser.

23. Generally, housing sales are slow, but this development seems unusually active in sales.

24. There seems to be an unusual number of foreclosures on 90 to 95 percent of loans with private mortgage insurance on homes in the same development built by the same builder. (Sometimes it is cheaper for the builder to arrange for a straw buyer to get the 95 percent loan and default than it is to market the home if the market is sluggish.)

25. Applications received through the same broker have numerous similarities.

26. Sales contracts have numerous crossed-out and changed figures for sales price and down payment.

27. Appraiser for project owns property in the same project.

28. Lending officer buys a home in a project financed by the institution.

29. Assessed value for tax purposes is not in line with appraised value.

30. The project is reportedly fully occupied, but the parking lot always appears to be nearly empty.

31. The parking lot is full, but the project appears to be empty. Nobody is around in the parking lot, pool, or other areas.

32. After a long period of inactivity, sales suddenly become brisk.

33. A sales contract is drawn up to fit the lender's LTV requirements. The buyer wants an $80,000 home but has no down payment. The lender lends only 80 percent of the appraised value or selling price. A contract is drawn up to show a selling price of $100,000 instead of the actual selling price of $80,000.

34. Builder claims a large number of presold units not yet under construction, while many finished units remain unsold.

35. Place of employment of prospective borrower/purchaser is 100 miles from location of property while comparable housing is readily available within 10 miles of place of employment.

36. Applicant's stated income is not commensurate with his/her stated employment and or years of experience.

37. Applicant's financial statement shows numerous assets that are self-evaluated and cannot be readily verified through independent sources.

38. Applicant claims to own partial interest in many assets but not 100 percent of any asset, making verification difficult.

39. Appraised value of property is contingent on the curing of some property defect, such as drainage problems.

40. Applicant's financial statement reflects expensive jewelry and artwork, but no insurance coverage is carried.

41. Applicant's tax return shows substantial interest deductions, but financial statement shows little debt. For example, the borrower's tax return shows substantial mortgage interest deductions, but the self-prepared financial statement show no mortgage or a very small mortgage.

42. Appraised value of a condominium complex is arrived at by using the asking price for one of the more desirable units and multiplying that figure by the total number of units.

43. Loans are unusual considering the size of the institution and the level of expertise of its lending officers.

44. There is a heavy concentration of loans to a single project or to individuals related to the project.

45. There is a heavy concentration of loans to local borrowers with the same or similar real estate collateral that is located outside the institution's trade area.

46. There are many loans in the names of trustees, holding companies, and/or offshore companies, but the names of the individuals involved are not disclosed in the institution's files.

47. A loan is approved contingent on an appraised value of at least a certain amount and the appraised value is exactly that amount.

48. Independent reviews of outside appraisals are never conducted.

49. The institution routinely accepts mortgages or other loans through a broker, but makes no attempt to determine the financial condition of the broker or to obtain any references or other background information.

50. Borrower claims substantial income, but his or her only credit experience has been with finance companies.

51. Borrower claims to own substantial assets, reportedly has an excellent credit history and above-average income, but is being charged many points and a higher than average interest rate which is indicative of high-risk loans.

52. The institution allows borrowers to assign mortgages as collateral without routinely performing the same analysis of the mortgage and mortgagor as it would perform if the institution were the mortgagee.

53. Asset swaps—sale of other real estate or other distressed assets to a broker at an inflated price in return for favorable terms and conditions on a new loan to a borrower introduced to the institution by the broker. The new loan is usually secured by property of questionable value, and the borrower is in weak financial condition. Borrower and collateral are often outside the institution's trade area.

Secured Lending

1. Lack of independent appraisals of collateral.
2. Significant out-of-territory lending.
3. Loans with unusual terms or conditions.
4. Poor or incomplete documentation used to intentionally conceal material facts.
5. Loans that are unusual considering the size of the institution and the level of expertise of its lending officers.
6. Heavy concentration of loans secured by same or similar types of collateral.
7. Financing of 100 percent of the value of any collateral that is subject to rapid depreciation or wide fluctuation in market value.
8. Appraisals that appear to be made to cover the borrower's loan request rather than reflect the true value of the collateral.
9. Appraisal fee based on amount of loan or on appraised value of collateral may encourage inflated appraisals.
10. Review of records indicates numerous related-party purchases and sales of the collateral that could be used to inflate the collateral price far beyond actual market value.
11. Loans in the names of trustees, holding companies, and offshore companies may disguise the identities of the actual owners.
12. Assigned notes and mortgages are accepted as collateral without verifying all underlying documentation and conducting normal credit analyses on the obligors.

Third-Party Obligations

1. Documentation on guaranties is incomplete.
2. Loans are secured by obligations of offshore institutions.
3. Lack of credit information on third-party guaranty.
4. Financial statements reflect concentrations of closely held companies or businesses that lack audited financial statements to support their value.
5. A guaranty signed in blank may be used indiscriminately by some dishonest individuals to cover weak loans. Guaranties signed in blank may also be legally unenforceable if contested.
6. Guaranties that are separate from the notes may contain restrictions that could render them worthless unless the restrictions are closely followed.

7. Third-party obligor is not informed of assignment of obligation to institution, which may allow payments to be diverted to some use other than payment of the loan.

8. Guaranties or letters of credit to guarantee payment from insurance companies are accepted without evaluation of the financial soundness of the guarantor and its ability to honor the guaranties or letters of credit if necessary.

9. Guaranties or letters of credit from insurance companies are not directly verified with the issuer.

10. The institution's audit procedures do not include a request for acknowledgment of guaranties by guarantors.

11. Corporate guaranties are used, but there is no information in the institution's files to support the authority of the corporation to make the guaranties or to indicate that they are still in force.

12. The institution purchases substandard consumer contracts from a third party, relying on recourse to the seller without doing proper analysis of the seller's financial condition.

13. The institution purchases substandard consumer contracts for automobile loans, home improvement loans, and other loans, while relying on some type of insurance to delinquencies, skips, and so on, without verifying the financial condition of the insurer.

Lending to Buy Tax Shelter Investments

1. Block loans to individuals to buy tax shelters arranged by a tax shelter promoter.

2. Shelters that promise tax deductions that would not appear to withstand the scrutiny of the IRS.

3. Specific use of invested funds cannot be ascertained.

4. Loan payments are to be made by a servicing company.

5. Investments reflect no economic purpose except to generate tax write-offs.

6. Financial "no cash" deals where transactions are structured to avoid any actual cash flow. For example, a long-term CD is matched against a loan payable for the proceeds of the CD at its maturity. Interest accumulates on the CD in an amount equal to or greater than the compound interest owed on the corresponding loan. The depositor/borrower never provides or receives any cash but still gets the tax write-off.

Linked Financing/Brokered Deposits

1. Short-term, volatile deposits are used to fund long-term loans of questionable credit quality.

2. A generous point spread exists between the loan interest rate and the interest rate on the deposits, which is usually below prevailing market rates.

3. Out-of-territory lending to previously unknown borrowers.

4. Large dollar deposits are offered in consideration for favorable treatment on loan requests, but deposits are not pledged as collateral for the loans.

5. Brokered deposit transactions where the broker's fees are paid from the proceeds of related loans.

6. Institution is presented with a large loan request that cannot be funded without the use of brokered deposits.

7. An unsolicited offer to purchase the institution comes at about the same time brokered deposits and related loans are processed.

8. Long-term discounted CDs pledged or matched at face value and not actual book value and structured to repay the loan automatically.

Credit Cards and ATM Transactions

1. Lack of separation of duties between the card-issuing function and the issuance of personal identification number (PIN).

2. Poor control of unissued cards and PINs.

3. Poor control of returned mail.

4. Customer complaints.

5. Poor control of credit limit increases.

6. Poor control of name and address changes.

7. Frequent malfunction of payment authorization.

8. Unusual delays in receipt of cards and PINs by the customers.

9. The institution does not limit the amount of cash a customer can extract from an ATM in a given day.

10. Evidence that customer credit card purchases have been intentionally structured by a merchant to keep individual amounts below the "floor limit" to avoid the need for transaction approval.

11. Credit card merchant accounts are opened without obtaining any background information on the merchant.

12. Credit card merchant account activity reflects an increase in the number and size of chargebacks.

13. The institution's credit card merchant is depositing sales drafts made payable to a business or businesses other than the business named on the account.

14. Credit card merchant frequently requests the wire transfer of funds from the merchant account to other institutions in other parts of the country or to offshore institutions almost immediately after deposits are made.

15. Merchant is engaged in telemarketing activities and is subject to frequent consumer complaints.

16. The institution contracts with a third-party servicer to process credit card customer and merchant transactions without verifying the financial stability and reputation of the servicer.

17. The institution contracts with a third party to establish and market a secured credit card program without verifying the financial stability and reputation of the third party and without determining the institution's potential liability for participation in the program.

18. Credit card merchant account deposits appear to exceed the level of customer activity observed at the merchant's place of business.

19. Merchant has access to EDC (electronic data capture) equipment but frequently inputs credit card account numbers manually. Be especially alert if manually keyed transactions exceed 10 percent of total transactions.

20. Merchant has a sudden or unexplained increase in the level of authorization request from a particular merchant location.

Advance Fee Schemes

1. A person having no previous relationship with the institution suddenly appears and offers fantastic opportunities for the institution and/or its customers.

2. Broker claims to be part of a major financial organization, but this claim cannot be verified.

3. Broker claims to have access to huge sums of money from a secret, undiscoverable, or unverifiable source.

4. Broker becomes irritated if the institution suggests that references be checked.

5. Broker makes frequent references to terms such as "ICC for 254, 290, or 322" and frequently uses the terms *emission rate, prime bank notes, tranches, letters of commitment, bank acceptances, arbitrage, hedge contracts,* or *escrow agreements.*

6. Broker initially requests an advance for his or her services but often "reluctantly" agrees to defer the fee until settlement of the transaction.

7. As the deadline for settlement nears, the broker urgently requests an advance on his or her fee to cover expenses such as travel, documentation, or communication costs.

8. Broker states that funds will be forthcoming from some offshore bank in the Caribbean or South Pacific.

9. Attempts to verify the broker's references are unsuccessful.

10. Broker's references include telephone numbers that are answered by machines and addresses that are mail drops, hotel rooms, and the like.

11. Broker proposes a self-liquidating loan where earnings from a deposit or other investment will be such that they will pay the principal and interest on the loan with no additional funds needed from the borrower.

12. Broker conducts most negotiations by telephone or telex and appears to resist any meeting with the institution's counsel.

13. Broker repeatedly delays the settlement of a deal, citing numerous "technical' problems.

14. The deal frequently falls through at the last minute while the broker searches for another source of funds.

15. Broker asks institution to serve as a transfer bank, intermediary, or agent in the transfer of funds between a sending institution and a receiving institution.

16. Broker who originally presents the deal may be known to the institution, but other persons involved are unknown to the institution and have questionable backgrounds.

17. Broker asks for the institution's telex numbers and long, instructional telexes from the lender's agent are frequently received by the institution.

18. The receiving institution is asked to send a number of letters, contracts, or telex messages to the lender's agent or the lender's institution.

19. Broker expresses a great deal of urgency in completing the transaction so that the loan will not be lost.

20. Broker offers funds that the borrower can invest in US Treasury notes or similar investments at a 4- or 5-point spread that will help the borrower cover part of the fees, but offers only flimsy excuses as to why the lending institution does not directly invest in these instruments.

21. Broker does not allow the borrower or the institution any direct contact with the proposed lender, often citing confidentiality requirements

by the lender or some sensitive political situation in the lender's home country.

22. Broker often requests that the borrower's institution issue a standby letter of credit to the foreign lender to guarantee payment.

23. Broker is often a name dropper, but the people named are either deceased or impossible to contact for reference because of political reasons.

Offshore Transactions

1. Loans made on the strength of a borrower's financial statement when the statement reflects major investments in and income from businesses incorporated in bank secrecy haven countries such as Panama, Cayman Islands, Netherlands Antilles, Montserrat, and others.

2. Loans to companies domiciled in bank secrecy haven countries.

3. Loans secured by obligations of offshore institutions.

4. Transactions involving an offshore "shell" institution whose name may be very similar to the name of a major legitimate institution.

5. Frequent wire transfers of funds to and from bank secrecy haven countries.

6. Offers of multimillion-dollar deposits at below market rates from a confidential source to be sent from an offshore institution or somehow guaranteed by an offshore institution through a letter, telex, or other "official" communication.

7. Offshore companies are used to disguise the true identities of borrowers or guarantors.

8. No independent verification of the financial strength of the offshore institution is available from any source.

9. To make an offshore bank transaction appear legitimate, innocent third parties are brought into the scheme, unaware of its fraudulent nature.

Wire Transfers

1. Lack of separation between authority to initiate a wire transfer and authority to approve a wire transfer.

2. Indications of frequent overrides of established approval authority and other internal controls.

3. Intentional circumvention of approval authority by splitting transactions.

4. Wire transfers to and from bank secrecy haven countries.

5. Frequent or large transfers for persons who have no account relationship with the institution.

6. Large or frequent wire transfers against uncollected funds.

7. Frequent requests for immediate wire transfer of funds from a credit card merchant account to institutions in other parts of the United States, offshore institutions, or foreign institutions.

8. Frequent wire transfers from accounts with numerous cash deposits of just under $10,000 each.

9. Frequent errors in payment by authorized system officials.

10. Lack of security of wire transfer system safeguards such as a password and other details of wire transfer transactions.

11. Unconfirmed wire transfer request initiated by telephone.

12. Incoming wire transfers in which the account name and account number do not match.

13. Wire transfer or payment request that does not conform to established procedures.

14. Absence of written funds transfer agreements between the institution and its customers.

15. Large international funds transfers to or from the accounts of domestic customers in amounts and of a frequency that are not consistent with the nature of the customer's known business activities.

16. Receipt of funds in the form of multiple cashier's checks, money orders, traveler's checks, bank checks, or personal checks that are drawn on or issued by US financial institutions and made payable to the same individual or business, in US dollar amounts that are below the $10,000 Bank Secrecy Act reporting threshold and are then wired transferred to a financial institution outside the United States.

17. Funds are deposited into several accounts and then aggregated into one account, followed by the wire transfer of the those funds from that account outside of the United States when such action is not consistent with the known business of the customer.

18. Any other unusual international funds transfer requests wherein the arrangements requested appear to be inconsistent with normal funds transfer practices, for example, where the customer directs the institution to wire transfer funds to a foreign county and advises the institution to expect same-day return of funds from sources other than the beneficiaries initially named, thereby changing the source of the funds.

19. A pattern of wire transfers of similar amounts both in and out of the customer's account on the same day or next day.

20. Wire transfers by customers operating a cash business, such as, customers depositing large amounts of currency.

21. Wire transfer volume is extremely large in proportion to asset size of institution.

22. The institution's business strategy and financial statements are inconsistent with large volumes of wire transfers, particularly out of the United States.

Money Laundering

1. Increase in cash shipments that is not accompanied by a corresponding increase in number of accounts.

2. Cash on hand frequently exceeds limits established in security program and/or blanket bond coverage.

3. Large volume of cashier's checks, money orders, traveler's checks, and so on, sold for cash to noncustomers in amounts ranging from several hundred dollars to just under $10,000.

4. Large volume of wire transfers to and from offshore institutions.

5. Large volume of wire transfers for noncustomers.

6. Accounts that have a large number of small deposits and a small number of large checks with balances on the accounts remaining relatively low and constant. The accounts have many of the same characteristics as accounts used for check kiting.

7. A large volume of deposits to several different accounts with frequent transfers of major portions of the balances to a single account at the same institution or another institution.

8. Loans to offshore companies and loans secured by obligations of offshore institutions.

9. Large volume of cashier's checks, money orders and/or wire transfers deposited to an account where the nature of the accountholder's business would not appear to justify such activity.

10. Large volume of cash deposits from a business that is not normally cash intensive, such as a wholesaler.

11. Cash deposits to a correspondent account by any means other than through an armored carrier.

12. Large turnover in large bills that appear uncharacteristic for the institution's location.

13. Cash shipments that appear large relative to the dollar volume of currency transaction reports filed.

14. Dollar limits on the list of customers exempt from currency transaction reporting requirements that appear unreasonably high considering the types and locations of the businesses. No information is in the institution's file to support the limits.

15. Currency transaction reports (CTRs), when filed, are often incorrect or lack important information.

16. The list of exempted customers appears unusually long.

17. A customer expresses some urgent need to be included on the institution's list of customers exempted from currency transaction reporting requirements.

18. A customer requests information on how to avoid filing currency transaction reports on cash transactions involving amounts over $10,000.

19. Upon being informed of the currency transaction reporting requirements, the customer withdraws all or part of the transaction to avoid filing the CTR.

20. A customer frequently conducts cash transactions in amounts just under $10,000 each.

21. A customer refuses to provide information required to complete the CTR.

22. A corporate customer makes frequent large cash deposits and maintains high balances but does not avail itself of other services such as loans, letters of credit, payroll services, and so on.

23. A customer almost never comes to the institution but has numerous couriers making deposits to the account.

24. A large increase in small-denomination bills and a corresponding decrease in large-denomination bills with no corresponding CTR filings.

25. Customers who open accounts providing minimal or fictitious information or information that is difficult or expensive for the institution to verify.

26. Customers who decline to provide information that normal customers would provide to make them eligible for credit or other banking services that normal customers would regard as valuable.

27. Customers who appear to have accounts with several institutions within the same locality, especially when there is a regular consolidation of balances in the accounts and transfer of funds out of the accounts by wire transfer or other means to offshore institutions or to large domestic institutions.

28. Customers whose deposits frequently contain counterfeit bills or bills that appear musty or extremely dirty.

29. Customers who have deposit accounts at the institution but frequently purchase cashier's checks, money orders, and so on, with large amounts of cash.

30. A retail customer that deposits a large volume of checks but seldom, if ever, requests currency for its daily operations.

31. A retail business has dramatically different patterns of cash deposits than other similar businesses in the same general location.

32. An exempted customer frequently requests increases in exemption limits.

33. A substantial increase in cash deposits in any business without any apparent cause.

34. A substantial increase in cash deposits by professional customers using client accounts or in-house company accounts such as trust accounts, escrow accounts, and so on.

35. Customers who make or receive large transfers to or from countries associated with production, processing, and marketing of narcotics.

36. Size and frequency of cash deposits increase rapidly without any corresponding increase in noncash deposits.

37. Size and frequency of cash deposits are not consistent with observed activity at the customer's place of business.

38. A customer makes large and frequent cash deposits, but checks or other debits against the account are not consistent with the customer's stated line of business. For example, the customer claims to be in the retail jewelry business, but checks are mostly to individuals and/or firms not normally associated with the jewelry business.

39. A customer frequently deposits large amounts of currency that is wrapped in currency straps that have been stamped by other financial institutions.

40. A customer frequently deposits strapped currency or currency wrapped in rubber bands that is disorganized and does not balance when counted.

41. A customer is often observed entering the safety deposit box area just prior to making cash deposits of just under $10,000.

Securities Trading Activities

1. Management lacks the expertise needed to fully understand the ramifications of proposals made by brokers, and/or they perceive an unrealistic opportunity to enhance income.

2. Investments bear no reasonable relationship to the institution's size or its capital accounts.

3. Overreliance is placed on the purported safety of the securities since they involve US government issues.

4. Little or no attention is given to "interest rate risk" prior to the transaction taking place.

5. Delayed settlements over unreasonable time periods sometimes allow management to make imprudent purchases and avoid booking transactions on a timely basis.

6. The institution engages in reverse repurchase agreements with brokers, which allows institutions to erroneously deter recognition of losses.

7. Securities held for short-term trading are not appropriately identified and segregated from those that are held primarily as a source of investment income.

8. Trading account securities are not revalued periodically and are not reported consistently at market value or lower of cost or market value.

Miscellaneous

1. Lack of supervision of lending activities by officers of the institution.

2. Lack of lending policies or failure to enforce existing policies.

3. Lack of code of conduct or failure to enforce existing code.

4. A dominant figure allowed to exert influence without restraint.

5. Lack of separation of duties.

6. Lack of accountability.

7. Lack of written policies and/or internal controls.

8. Circumvention of established policies and/or controls.

9. Lack of independent members of management and/or board.

10. Entering into transactions in which the institution lacks expertise.

11. Excessive growth through low-quality loans.

12. Unwarranted concentrations.

13. Volatile sources of funding, such as short-term deposits from out-of-area brokers.

14. Too much emphasis on earnings at the expense of safety and soundness.

15. Compromising credit policies.

16. High-rate, high-risk investments.

17. Underwriting criteria that allow high-risk loans.

18. Lack of documentation or poor documentation.

19. Lack of adequate credit analysis.

20. Failure to properly obtain and evaluate credit data, collateral, and so on.

21. Failure to properly analyze and verify financial statement data.

22. Too much emphasis on character and collateral and not enough emphasis on credit.

23. Lack of balance in loan portfolio.

24. Poor loan administration after credit is granted.

25. Unresolved exceptions or frequently recurring exceptions on exception report.

26. Out-of-balance conditions.

27. Purpose of loan is not recorded.

28. Proceeds of loan are used for a purpose other than the purpose recorded.

29. Lax policies on payment of checks against uncollected funds.

30. The institution is a defendant in a number of lawsuits alleging improper handling of transactions.

Index

A

Accessibility, 56–57
Account liquidity, 12
Accountability, 239
Accounting method, 256
Accounting principles, 249
Accounting Principles Board (APB), 268, 270
Accounting systems, 240, 241
Accounts receivable, 73, 200
Acquisition, development, and construction (ADC), 249
Acquisitions, 132, 254, 261
ADC. *See* Acquisition, development, and construction
Adjustable-rate mortgages (ARMs), 145, 201–202, 257
Adverse consequences, 140
After-tax losses, 141
Aggregate outstanding loans, limitations, 190
AICPA. *See* American Institute of Certified Public Accountants
AIMR. *See* Association for Investment Management and Research
Alabama Business Corporation Act, 9
ALM. *See* Asset/liability management
American Accounting Association, 244
American Institute of Certified Public Accountants (AICPA), 240, 241, 243, 245
American Marketing Association, 43
Analysis, steps, 73–74
Analyst groups, 42
Analysts, 36
Annual meetings, 42
Annual published information, 38–41
Annual report, 38–41
Annunzio-Wylie-Anti-Money Laundering Act, 228
Anticipatory hedge, 168
APB. *See* Accounting Principles Board

ARMs. *See* Adjustable-rate mortgages
Asset class, 185
Asset liquidity, 90
Asset quality, 83, 91–92, 101, 101
Asset size, 32
    distribution, 92
Asset-based lending, 200–201
Asset/liability committee, 11–12
Asset/liability management (ALM), 29, 139–178
    policies and practices, 176
Association for Investment Management and Research (AIMR), 35
Assurance, 71
Asymmetric hedge, 172, 173
Asymmetric information, 205
Audit committee, 11, 248
Audit reports, 7, 248
Audited financial statements, 247
Auditing, 243–253
    director's view, 236–253
Auditor assurance, 248
Auditor-client relationship, 246
Auditors, 231, 232, 243, 248. *See also* External auditors
Audits, 230–232
Automatic teller machines, 25, 68
Available-for-sale equity securities, 130
Available-for-sale securities, 78

B

Balance sheets, 11, 73, 74, 83, 128, 142, 145, 164, 211, 268, 270
Balloon payment, 201
Bank, other subsidiaries, parent company, earnings, and capital (BOPEC), 73, 252
Bank Administration Institute, 251
Bank assets, 74–78

Bank capital, 126–138
Bank of Commerce and Commerce
    International (BCCI), 219, 220, 227
Bank data, 96
Bank directors, 73
    duties, 1–16
    point of view, 83–92
Bank employees, 220, 229
Bank examinations, review, 7
Bank examiners, 73, 91–92
    classifications, 91–92
    role, 252–253
Bank failures, 26, 210
Bank financial statements, 74–83
Bank firms, factors, 26–28
Bank holding company, 194
Bank incomes, 176
Bank for International Settlements (BIS), 140,
    141
Bank liabilities, 78–79
Bank loans, 199, 210
Bank marketing strategy, development, 43–72
Bank operations, 11
Bank Records and Foreign Transaction
    Reporting Act, 224
Bank regulators, 9, 126, 127, 136, 151
Bank report, 97
Bank Secrecy Act of 1970 (BSA), 224, 225,
    227, 228
Bank security personnel, 230
Bank transactions, 229
Banking, electronic age, 29
Banks
    actions, 15
    financial performance, evaluation, 73–125
    profile, 101–125
    value, 33–36
Basis risk, 143
BCCI. See Bank of Commerce and Commerce
    International
Benefits, 203
Beta, 142
Bidding strategies, 65
Bid-offer spread, 184
BIS. See Bank for International Settlements
Board of directors, 3–5, 193, 230
    independence, 3
    responsibilities, 5–10
Bond portfolios, 158, 167
Bond prices, 158
Bond yields, 158

Bonds, 142
Book value, 269
BOPEC. See Bank, other subsidiaries, parent
    company, earnings, and capital
Bridge loan, 200
Brokerage firms, 169
Brokered deposits, 234
Brokered transactions, 233, 234–235
BSA. See Bank Secrecy Act of 1970
Budgets, 164
Bureaucracy, 71
Business cycle, 149, 150
Business judgment rule, 7–8
Business operations, monitoring/assessment, 7
Business strategies, initiation, 7
Buyer motivation, 51
Buying behavior, 51

C

Call options, 166
Call reports, 97, 130
Calls, 170
CAMEL. See Capital, asset quality,
    management, earnings, and liquidity
Canada Deposit Insurance Corporation
    (CDIC), 126, 140, 187, 194, 195
Capacity, 207
Capital, 83, 89–90, 208. See also Core capital;
    Risk-adjusted capital; Sufficient capital;
    Supplementary capital
    absorption, 134
    asset quality, management earnings, and
        liquidity (CAMEL), 73, 252
        rating, 132
    distributions, 132
    growth facilitation, 132–134
    impact, 211–212
    role, 132–138
Capital adequacy, 11, 27
Capital amount, 28
Capital expansion, 150
Capital markets, 21, 138
Capital ratio, 138
Capital requirements, 126–132, 138
Caps, 166, 173, 201
Cash, 74–75
Cash commodity, 167, 168
Cash dividend payments, 142
Cash dividends, 89, 163, 217
Cash flow, 60, 62, 154, 156, 260

Cash market, 167
  position, 167
  transactions, 166
Cash securities, 166
Cash-and-carry business, 221
CBOT. *See* Chicago Board of Trade
Cease-and-desist orders, 10
CDIC. *See* Canada Deposit Insurance
  Corporation
CDs. *See* Certificates of deposit
CERCLA. *See* Comprehensive Environmental
  Resource Conservation and Liability Act
  of 1980
Certificates of deposit (CDs), 14, 151, 220,
  229. *See also* Fixed-rate CDs
Certified public accountant (CPA), 248, 249
Character, 207
Charged off, 136
Charge-offs, 190, 206, 211, 212
Chicago Board of Trade (CBOT), 168, 169,
  178
Chicago Mercantile Exchange, 178
Chinese Wall, 12
C&I loans. *See* Commercial and industrial
  loans
Civil money penalties, 10
Client creditworthiness, 207
Closed-end loans, 204
CMIRs. *See* Currency or monetary instruments
  reports
Code of Professional Ethics, 245
Collars, 166
Collateral, 188, 194, 196, 197, 201, 204–206,
  208–210
  benefits, 210
  characteristics, 209–210
  double pledging, 219
Collection, 190
Commercial banks, 31, 254. *See also* FDIC-
  insured commercial banks
Commercial and industrial (C&I) loans,
  199–201
Commercial loans, 30, 197, 199–201
Commercial real estate loans, 202
Commingling, 223
Commission on Auditors' Responsibilities, 245
Commitments, 83, 198
Committee on Banking Regulations and
  Supervisory Practices, 140
Committees, 10–13
Commodity, 197

Commodity risk, 182
Common stock, 259, 261, 265
Communications, improvement, 35–36
Community Reinvestment Act (CRA) of 1977,
  27, 33, 36, 209
  responsibilities, 30
Company performance, 36
Compensation schemes, 266
Competitive advantage, 23, 25, 30, 47. *See
  also* Sustained competitive advantage
Competitive market situations, 67
Competitive pricing, 62, 64–65
Competitive strategy, 54
Competitive-bid pricing, 64
Competitive-parity pricing, 64
Competitors, strategies, 51
Complacency, 20
Compliance, 208
  examinations, 252
Complicity, 223
Comprehensive Environmental Resource
  Conservation and Liability Act of 1980,
  208
Concentrated strategy, 54, 55
Concentration, 181
Conditions, 208
Conflicting interests, 9
Conglomerate mergers, 255–256
Construction loan, 202
Consumer banking risks, 207
Consumer credit, 202
Consumer Leasing Act (1976), 204
Consumer lending, 203–205
Consumer loans, 198, 199, 204
Consumer loyalty, 45
Consumer surveys, 53
Control procedures, 241
Conventional mortgage loans, 201
Convertible bond, 183
Convexity, 158
Core capital, 126–127
  leverage ratio, 88, 137
Core financial risks, 182
Corporate culture ethics, 233
Corporate factors, 33, 34–35
Corporate goals, statement, 39
Corporate lender, 255
Corporate restructuring, 254
Cost economies, 55
Cost leadership, 46, 47
Cost structures, 65

Cost-oriented pricing, 62–63
Cost-plus pricing, 62, 63
Countercyclical acquisitions, 257
Counterparty risk, 172
Coupon bonds, 157
Coupon rates, 157
CPA. *See* Certified public accountant
CRA. *See* Community Reinvestment Act of
    1977
Credit, six Cs, 205, 207–209, 213
Credit analysts, 194
Credit card loans, 198, 204
Credit card transfers, 233
Credit cards, 31, 151
Credit concentrations, 190
Credit crunch, 36, 210
Credit decisions, 237
Credit exposures, 196
Credit loss recoveries, 82
Credit losses, 82
    allowance, 78–79, 82, 91
    provisions, 79
Credit policies, 187–213
Credit practices, 187–213
Credit problems, 82
Credit risk, 150, 176, 183, 187, 193, 195, 199
    management, 195, 196, 212
Credit transaction, 208
Credit-monitoring policy, 207
Creditors, 230, 231
Credit-related financial instruments, 83
Credits, quality, 11–12
Creditworthiness, 196. *See also* Client
    creditworthiness
Criminal misconduct, 216
Criminal referral reports, 233
Criminal referrals, 217
Cross-elasticity. *See* Demand
CTR. *See* Currency transaction report
Cumulative gap, 154
Cumulative voting, 267
Currency or monetary instruments reports
    (CMIRs), 225
Currency risk, 182
Currency swaps, 174
Currency transaction report (CTR), 215, 223,
    225, 226, 229
Customer analysis, 49–51
    scope, 51–53
Customer expectations, 71
Customer intimacy, 31

Customer requests, 197
Customer satisfaction. *See also* Long-term
    customer satisfaction
    dimensions, 69–70
    shortfalls, diagnosis, 70–72
Customer-perceived differences, 51
Customers
    knowledge, 224–228
    needs/satisfaction, 21

D

Daisy chain arrangements, 219
Daylight overdrafts, 199
De novo bank, 132
Debt securities, 130, 259
Decision processes, 52
Decision-making process, 7, 16
    complexity, 21–22
Default, 175, 207
Default risk, 205
Delinquency rates, 205
Demand, cross-elasticity, 64
Demand-based pricing, 62, 63–64
Demographics, 51
Department of Housing and Urban
    Development (HUD), 202
Deposit accounts, 234
Deposit insurance, 134
Deposit redemptions, 154
Deposits, 78–79
Depreciation, 260, 269
Deregulation, 58
Derivatives, 30, 130, 167, 176. *See also*
    Financial derivatives
    differences, 185–186
    risk management, 179–186
    system, 180
    transaction, 186
Detrimental reliance, 212
Differential response, 56
Differentiated strategy, 54, 55
Differentiation strategies, 47
Digital money, 29
Directors, 39, 195–196. *See also* Bank
    directors; Shareholders
    role, 230
    ten commandments, 8
    view. *See* Auditing; Internal controls
Disclosure, 245
    process, 243

Distribution, 58, 189. *See also* Exclusive
    distribution; Intensive distribution;
    Selective distribution; Services
    systems, 44
Diversification, 181, 196, 257–258. *See also*
    Portfolio diversification
Dividend income, 88
Dividend payout ratio, 89
Dividend policy, 29
Dividend valuation model, 262
Dividends, 132. *See also* Cash dividends
Divisional operations, 39
Dollar deposits, 234
Dollar gap, 144
Drawdowns, 154, 155
Due from banks, 74–75
Dummy corporations, 223
Durability, 210
Duration, definition, 156–157
Duration analysis, 150, 151, 155–164
Duration gap, 162–164
Duration drift, 161
Duration strategy, 160
Duty of care, 5–7
Duty to investigate, 6
Duty of loyalty, 5, 8–10

E

Earnings per share (EPS), 265
Economic theory, 23
Economies of scale, 62
Efficiency ratio, 86, 256
Efficient-scale facilities, 46
Electronic Funds Transfer Act (1978), 204
Electronic funds transfers, 233
Empathy, 71
EPS. *See* Earnings per share
Equal attention, 44–46
Equal Credit Opportunity Act (1974), 204, 208
Equity, 182, 183, 265
    economic value, 139
    net economic value, 162, 163
Equity capital, 135, 136
Equity securities, 127
Eurodollar futures, 172
Evergreen facilities, 200
Examiners, 232. *See also* Bank examiners
Exclusive distribution, 69
Expectation gap, 243–246
Expenses, 79–82

Experience-curve pricing, 63
Exposure limits, 196–197
External auditors, 238
External data processing services, 30
External environment, 19, 26–28
External factors, 29–30

F

Failed strategies, 19–26
Failure, reasons, 20–21
Fair Credit Billing Act (1974), 204
Fair Credit Reporting Act (1970), 204
Fair Debt Collection Practices Act (1977), 204
Fair market value, 33, 268
Fair value, 244
FBI, 214
FDIC. *See* Federal Deposit Insurance
    Corporation
FDIC deposit insurance premiums, 134
FDIC insurance fund, 131
FDICIA. *See* Federal Deposit Insurance
    Corporation Act of 1991
FDIC-insured bank, 97
FDIC-insured commercial banks, 92, 128, 135,
    137
Federal Deposit Insurance Corporation (FDIC),
    6, 7, 13, 33, 130, 209, 214, 231, 232,
    247, 252, 255
    Manual of Examination Policies, 233
    Quarterly Banking Profile, 92–96
    red flags, 233–234
Federal Deposit Insurance Corporation Act of
    1991 (FDICIA), 156
Federal funds, 75
Federal Home Loan Bank Board (FHLBB), 9
Federal Housing Administration (FHA), 201
Federal insurance fund, 13
Federal Reserve, 97, 204, 252, 253
Federal Reserve Bank of Dallas, 176
Federal Reserve Bank of Kansas, 25
Federal Savings and Loan Insurance
    Corporation (FSLIC), 134
FHA. *See* Federal Housing Administration
FHLBB. *See* Federal Home Loan Bank Board
FIMS. *See* Financial Institutions Monitoring
    System
Financial Accounting Standard (FAS)
    87, 40
    96, 40
    106, 40

Financial Accounting Standard (FAS)—*Cont.*
   107, 41
   112, 40
   115, 78, 130, 138
Financial communications efforts, evaluation
   criteria, 37–41
Financial derivatives, 166
Financial data, 87
Financial information, 189
Financial institutions, 150, 214, 219, 225
Financial Institutions Monitoring System
   (FIMS), 97
Financial Institution's Reform, Recovery, and
   Enforcement Act of 1989 (FIRREA), 6,
   209, 247
Financial instruments. *See* Synthetic financial
   instruments
Financial leverage, 88, 102, 134–136
Financial performance, 83. *See also* Banks
   comparison, 92–101
Financial ratios, 86, 87, 101
Financial reports, 35, 164
Financial risks, 179. *See also* Core financial
   risks
Financial statements, 12, 101, 189, 232, 244,
   247. *See also* Audited financial statements
Financial summary, 39–40
Financial transactions, 183
FIRREA. *See* Financial Institution's Reform,
   Recovery, and Enforcement Act of 1989
Fixed-rate assets, 140, 175
Fixed-rate CDs, 143
Fixed-rate debt, 175
Fixed-rate loans, 143, 151, 202
Fixed-rate mortgage loans, 202
Fixed-rate mortgages, 201
Floating-rate assets, 175
Floating-rate debt, 175
Floating-rate loan, 143
FNMA securitized mortgage loans, 130
Focus groups, 52–53
Footnotes, 39–40
Forecasting, 18
Foreign Corrupt Practices Act of 1977, 239,
   245
Franchise value, 142, 163
Fraud, 214–235
   common schemes, 218–219
   definition, 214–215
   detection/deterrence, 230–234
Front company, 223

FSLIC. *See* Federal Savings and Loans
   Insurance Corporation
Funds, initial source, 132–133
Futures contracts, 163, 166, 168, 170. *See also*
   Interest rate futures contracts
Futures position, 167

G

GAAP. *See* Generally accepted accounting
   procedures
GAO. *See* U.S. General Accounting Office
Gap, 144–148, 171, 20. *See also* Cumulative
   gap; Dollar gap; Duration gap; Expec-
   tation gap; Maturity gap; Net interest
   income
Gap analysis, 150, 151–155. *See also* Periodic
   gap analysis reports
   assumptions/limitations, 154–155
Gap problem, 142
Generally accepted accounting procedures
   (GAAP), 243
Geographic distribution, 92
Geographic limits, 189
Geographic location, 25
Geographic market, 28
Going-rate pricing, 64
Good faith, 8
Goodwill, 126, 268, 269
Government backed mortgages, 201
Government securities, 128
Graduated payment mortgages, 201
Granularity, 182
Gross negligence, 6
Growth, 24–26, 155. *See also* Capital;
   Long-term growth
   constraints, 133
   potential, 47
Growth rate of assets, 89–90
Growth rate of equity, 89–90

H

Hedge ratio (HR), 168
Hedges. *See* Anticipatory hedge; Asymmetric
   hedge; Macro hedges; Micro hedges;
   Long hedge; Minimum variance hedge;
   Short hedge; Symmetric hedge
Hedging, 166–174
   basics, 166–167
   determination, 173
   effects. *See* Net interest income; Value

Hedging strategies, 164, 168–170
Held-for-maturity securities, 78
High-quality information, 35
High-risk loans, 196
Holding company, 5
Holding period, 158
Home equity loans, 202
Home Mortgage Disclosure Act (1975), 204
Home mortgage loans. *See* Long-term fixed-
    rate home mortgage loans
Homogeneity, 54
Hostile takeovers, 254
HR. *See* Hedge ratio
HUD. *See* Department of Housing and Urban
    Development
Hybrid debt instruments, 127

I

Identifiability, 210
IIA. *See* Institute of Internal Auditors
Immunization, 157–161
Income portfolio, 128
Income risk, 142–143
Income statements, 73, 164
Income/value, interest rate risk effects,
    144–150
Industrial loans, 197, 199–201
Industry factors, 142
Industry risks, 207
Inflation, 63
Information, role, 205–207
Initial margin, 168
Innovation, 45
Insider abuse, 214–235
    definition, 216
Insider transactions, 233
Insiders, 36
    outsiders comparison, 219–221
Installment loan portfolio, 237
Institute of Internal Auditors (IIA), 251
Integration, 223, 224
Intensive distribution, 68
Interest costs, 172
Interest expense, 79, 88
Interest income, 75, 79, 88. *See also* Net
    interest income
Interest margins. *See* Net interest margins
Interest payments, 232
Interest rate adjustment, 197
Interest rate futures contracts, 166

Interest rate payments, 175
Interest rate risk, 83, 139–178, 182
    definition, 139–140
    effects. *See* Income/value
    exposure, 171
    management, 142
        techniques, 150–165
    measurement, 157–158
Interest rate sensitivity, 11, 82, 142–143, 173
Interest rate spreads, 145–147
    management, 149–150
Interest rate swaps, 172, 174–175
Interest rates. *See* Short-term interest rates
Interest-bearing deposits, 75
Interest-only (IO) components, 203
Interests method, pooling, 270
Intermediary, 185
Internal auditors, 251
Internal Control Questionnaire, 241, 242
Internal control structure, 241, 248
Internal controls
    definition, 236–237
    director's view, 236–253
    establishment, 240–242
    usage reasons, 237–240
Internal factors, 28–29
Internal Revenue Code, 226
Internal Revenue Service (IRS), 225, 226, 245
International banking, 30
Internet, 25
Interviews, 42
Inventories, 73, 150, 199
Investment committee, 12
Investment risk, 140–142
Investments, 60, 194
IO. *See* Interest-only components
IPCs, 79
IRS. *See* Internal Revenue Service

J

Judgmental maturities, 151

K

Known maturities, 151

L

Land flips, 219
Layering, 223, 224
LBO. *See* Leveraged buyout

Leader pricing, 64
Leases to deposits, 90
Leasing, 205
Lender liability, 212–213
Lending authority, 190–193
Lending limits, 190, 191
Lending policies, 194
Lending risk, 196–197
Letters of credit, 83, 130
Leverage, 186
Leverage ratio, 131. *See also* Core capital
Leveraged buyout (LBO), 135, 181, 254
Leveraged swaps, 175
Liability, 260
Liability liquidity, 90
Limited-life preferred stock, 127
Lines of credit, 154, 197, 200. *See also*
    Open-end lines of credit
Linked financing, 219, 233, 234–235
Liquid assets, 90
Liquidity, 83, 90, 210. *See also* Account
    liquidity
  risk, 150, 184
Loan amount to appraised value and
    acquisition ratio, 189
Loan amount to market value and pledged
    securities ratio, 189
Loan brokers, 198
Loan commitments, 130
Loan committee, 12, 191, 192
Loan covenants, 194
Loan limits, 133, 197
Loan losses. *See also* Provisions for loan losses
  allowance, 127
  reserve, 127–128
Loan officers, 26, 190, 194
Loan participation, 233
Loan payments, 206
Loan policy, 28
  statements, 190
Loan portfolio, 128, 194
Loan pricing, 189
Loan production, 234
Loan repayment policies, 14
Loan request, evaluation, 205–209
Loan review, 195
  function, structure, 194
Loan reviewers, 194
Loans, 78–79. *See also* Aggregate outstanding
    loans; Unsecured loans
  denial, 210

Loans—*Cont.*
  making, 197–199
  purchase, 198
    limits/guidelines, 190
  solicitation, 197–198
  types, 189, 199–205
Loans to employees, 190
Loans to insiders, 190, 191
Long hedge, 168–170
Long-term bonds, 156
Long-term customer satisfaction fundamentals,
    69–72
Long-term debt, 127, 171. *See also*
    Subordinated long-term debt
Long-term fixed-rate home mortgage loans, 20
Long-term goals, 19
Long-term growth, 59
Long-term investments, 27
Long-term lender, 202
Long-term neutrality, 142
Long-term risks, 171
Losses, 134. *See* Loan losses
Low-cost strategies, 46
Lump sum, 201

M

Macro hedges, 164
Maintenance margin, 169
Management actions, 14
Management control, 28–30
Management decisions, 24
Management reporting systems, 237
Management shortsightedness, 20
Managerial malpractice, 21
Manufactured housing, 202
Margin, 168. *See also* Initial margin;
    Maintenance margin
  deposits, 169
Margin/commodity accounts, 168
Marked to market, 168
Market coverage, 68
Market position, 55
Market research, 59
Market risk, 176, 177
Market segmentation strategies, 54–57
Market segments, definition, 56–57
Market share, 46, 60
Market valuation systems, 177
Market value, 139, 244
  exchange ratio, 260–261

Market yields, 158
Marketability, 210
Market-driven maturities, 151
Marketing management, tasks, 43–48
Marketing mix, 65
   variables, 58
Marketing strategy, 56
   crafting, 44–48
   development, 49–51
   implementation, 58–69
Marketing variable, 56
Mass-market strategy, 54, 68
Maturity, 157, 189, 204, 205
Maturity buckets, 151, 163
Maturity gap, 155
Measurability, 56
Merger tactics, 266–268
Merger terms, 259–266
Mergers, 254–255
   accounting, 268–271
Mergers and acquisitions, 254–271
Micro hedges, 164
Minimum variance hedge, 167–168
Monetary Control Act of 1980, 75
Money laundering, 215, 221–229, 233
   jargon, 223
   process, 224
Money Laundering Control Act of 1986,
   227–228
Mortgage banking, 258
   affiliates, 271
Mortgage loan portfolios, 31
Mortgage loans. See FNMA securitized
   mortgage loans
Mortgage pools, 198
Mortgage-backed security, 156, 166, 202–203.
   See Stripped mortgage-backed securities
Multiple-coverage segmentation strategy, 55
Mutual funds, 25

N

Narrow banking, 138
National Commission on Fraudulent Financial
   Reporting, 245
National Home Equity Corporation (NHEC),
   217
Negligence, 6. See also Gross negligence
Net charge-offs, 91
Net economic value, 162, 163. See also Equity
Net income, 82

Net interest income (NII), 79, 88, 144–148,
   154
   gap effect, 154
   hedging effects, 171–173
Net interest margins (NIMs), 15, 88–89
Net loans, 90, 128
Net tangible assets, 269
Net transaction accounts, 75
New York Stock Exchange (NYSE), 2,
   134–135
NHEC. See National Home Equity Corporation
NII. See Net interest income
NIM. See Net interest margins
Nominee loans, 218–219
Nonaccrual basis, 91
Nonbank credit card issuers, 27
Nonbank firms, 20
Noncontractual repricing, 143
Nonearning assets, 15
Nonfinancial firms, 20
Noninterest expense, 256, 266
Noninterest income, 79
Non-interest-bearing loan, 217
Nonlinearity, 186
Non-merger banks, 256
Nonperforming loans, 91, 151
Non-rate-sensitive assets, 143, 151, 154
Notional principal, 174, 175
NYSE. See New York Stock Exchange

O

OCC. See Office of the Comptroller of the
   Currency
OECD. See Organization of Economic
   Cooperation and Development
Off-balance sheet, 142, 187
   activities, 83, 139
   claims, 130
   instruments, 144
   items, 140, 142, 151, 187
Office of the Comptroller of the Currency
   (OCC), 3, 9, 142, 167, 176, 187, 188,
   218, 237, 241, 242, 252
   Comptroller's Handbook for National Bank
      Examiners, 188
   red flags, 228–229
Office of Thrift Supervision (OTS), 231, 252
Officers, 39
Offshore transactions, 233
OLEMs. See Other loans especially mentioned

On-balance sheet, 142, 187
Open-end lines of credit, 204
Operating environment, 33, 34
Operational excellence, 31
Operating expense, 86
Operating income, 86
Option-free bond investment, 156
Options risk, 144
Option-type instruments, 151
Organization, self-knowledge, 19
Organization of Economic Cooperation and
    Development (OECD), 130
Organizational gaps, 71
Organized crime, 222–223
OSHA, 38
Other loans especially mentioned (OLEMs), 92
OTS. See Office of Thrift Supervision
Out-of-territory lending, 234
Outsiders, 220–221. See also Insiders
Overdrafts, 190, 199

P

Paper trail, 225
Participants, 198
Past-due accounts, 237
Past-due loans, 15, 238
P/E. See Price/earnings ratio
Pension plans. See State-funded pension
    plans
Peer group, 96, 97, 101
Percentile rankings, 96
Performance. See also Banks; Company
    performance
  appraisal, 184
  chance, 23–24
  measures, 164
  reality, 23–26
  theory, 23
Periodic gap analysis reports, 151–154
Periodic gaps, 164
Personal selling, 68
Personnel committee, 13
Personnel policies, 29
Placement, 223, 224
Plain vanilla structures, 183
Plain vanilla swap, 175
Pledging requirements, 12
PLL. See Provision for loan losses
PO. See Principal-only components
Portfolio diversification, 12

Positioning. See Target markets
  alternative bases, 57–58
  options, 58
  strategy, 57
Potential loss, 183–184
Precision, 182
Preferred stock, 89, 259. See also Limited-life
    preferred stock
Prepayments, 161
Prestige pricing, 64
Price, 58
  information, 185–186
  lining, 64
  risk, 140
Price/book value ratio, 261–262
Price/earnings (P/E) ratio, 262–265, 271
Pricing objectives, 60
Pricing policy, development, 60–62
Pricing strategies, 60, 164
Pricing strategy options, 62–65
Primary stakeholders, 32
Principal-only (PO) components, 203
Proactive strategy, 59
Problem credits, 194
Product leadership, 31
Products, unbundling, 183
Profit, 60–61. See also Short-run profits
  maximization, 60, 61
Profitability, 83, 87–89
Profitability targets, 180
Projections, 36
Promotion, 58
  mix, formulation, 67–68
  objectives, 66–67
  strategy, 65
Prompt corrective action, 131–132
Provision for loan losses (PLL), 128
Public deposits, 90
Published information, 41–42. See also Annual
    published information
Pull strategy, 67
Purchase method, 268–269
Push strategy, 67, 68
Put options, 166
Puts, 170

Q

Qualification questions, 37–38
Quantitative techniques, 18
Quarterly reports, 41

R

Racketeer-Influenced and Corrupt
    Organizations (RICO) statutes, 225
Rate-sensitive assets (RSA), 143–148, 151,
    171, 172
Rate-sensitive liabilities (RSL), 82, 144–148,
    151, 165, 171, 172
Reactive strategy, 59
Real estate loans, 199, 201–203
Rebalancing, 161, 164
Receivables, 199, 200
Reciprocal loan arrangement, 219
Refinancing, 198
Regional risks, 207
Regulation B, 208
Regulation U, 189
Regulation Z, 204, 252
Regulators, 136–138, 230, 231. *See also* Bank
    regulators
Regulatory compliance, 36
Reinvestment rate, 159
Reliability, 56, 57, 71
Repayment, 206
Repo rate, 75
Reportable conditions, 248
Reporting errors, 238
Reports of Condition and Income, 97, 130
Repos, 75
Repricing, 142. *See also* Noncontractual
    repricing
    data, 151
    risk, 142
Repurchase agreements, 75, 199
Research-based findings, 71
Reserve. *See* Loan losses
Residential mortgage loans, 201
Resolution Trust Corporation (RTC), 214
Resource allocation, 184
    process. *See* Strategic resource allocation
        process
Responsiveness, 71
Restructured loans, 82, 91, 249
Retail banking, 203
Return on assets (ROA), 22–24, 32, 87, 88,
    96, 97, 136–138, 172
Return on equity (ROE), 87, 88, 136–138
Return on investment, 61
Reverse annuity mortgages, 201
Reverse repos, 75
Revolvers, 200

Revolving loan, 200
RICO. *See* Racketeering-Influenced and
    Corrupt Organizations statutes
Right to Financial Privacy Act (1978), 204
Risk assessment, 237
Risk capital framework, 184
Risk categories, establishment, 182
Risk exposures, quantification, 183–184
Risk factors, 36
Risk management, 185, 186
    conventional view, 180
    definition, 180–182
    enlightened view, 180
    framework, 182–184
    policies, 29
    process, 177
    reporting system, 176
    steps, 182–184
    system, 179, 186. *See also* Derivatives
        requirements, 180–182
Risk profiles, 181, 185
Risk reporting, 177
Risk weights, 130
Risk-adjusted capital, 184
Risk-based assets, 88
Risk-based capital, 83
    guidelines, 27
Risk-return profile, 180
Risk-weighted assets, 126, 128–131
Risk-weighted capital requirements, 130
ROA. *See* Return on assets
ROE. *See* Return on equity
RPs, 75
RSA. *See* Rate-sensitive assets
RSL. *See* Rate-sensitive liabilities
RTC. *See* Resolution Trust Corporation

S

Sales objective, 67
SASs. *See* Statements of Auditing Standards
Savings banks, 96
Savings institutions, 92
Savings and loan associations (S&Ls), 4, 5,
    20, 96, 249
SCA. *See* Sustained competitive advantage
Scale. *See* Sufficient scale
SEC. *See* Securities and Exchange
    Commission
Secondary stakeholders, 32
Secured lending, 233

Secured loans, 190, 191
Securities, 75–78. *See also* Equity securities;
    U.S. Treasury securities
  gains/losses, 86
  portfolios, 141
Securities and Exchange Commission (SEC),
    243–246
  guidelines, 36
Securitization, 198, 202, 203
Security personnel, 253
Segment operations, 39
Segmentation, 58
  strategy. *See* Market segmentation
    strategies; Multiple-coverage segmen-
    tation strategy; Single-segment
    segmentation strategy
Selective distribution, 69
Self-dealing, 216
SERVE principle, 15–16
Service development strategies, 60
Service life cycle, 67
Services, 58
  development strategy, 58–60
  distribution, 68–69
Servicing fees, 130
Shareholder advisory committees, 2
Shareholder value, creation, 255–259
Shareholders, director accountability, 1–3
Shell companies, 223
Sheshunoff Information Services, 92, 96
Short hedge, 169–170
Short sale, 166
Short-run profits, 61
Short-term bonds, 156
Short-term interest rates, 149
Short-term risks, 171
Short-term sales promotion, 68
Short-term strategy, 61
Simulation, 150, 164–165
Single-segment segmentation strategy, 55
Situation analysis, 48–49
S&Ls. *See* Savings and loan associations
Small banks, 217–218
Smurfing, 223
Smurfs, 223, 224
Soft issues, 266
Specialization, 30
  strategies, 47–48
Spot market, 167
Stakeholders, 32–33, 36
  definition, 32–33

Standard & Poor's
  Composite Index, 24
  rate, 203
Standardization, 209–210
Start-up expenses, 133
State-funded pension plans, 27
Statement of income and expenses, 79
Statement of operations, 79–82
Statements of Auditing Standards (SASs), 245,
    246
  No. 53, 246–247
  No. 54, 247
  No. 58, 247–248
  No. 59, 248
  No. 60, 248
  No. 61, 248–250
Stochastic process, 24–26
Stockholders, 136–138, 218, 230, 231
  equity, 79
STR. *See* Suspicious Transaction Report
Strategic management, 17–42
  definition, 17–19
Strategic resource allocation process, 180
Strategies. *See also* Failed strategies;
    Successful strategies
  consistency, 180–181
Strategy selection, preconditions, 48–53
Stress testing, 184
Stripped mortgage-backed securities, 203
Structuring, 223
Subordinated long-term debt, 127
Substantiality, 56
Success, keys, 19
Successful strategies, 19–26
Sufficient capital, 31
Sufficient scale, 31
Sufficient technology, 31
Supplementary capital, 127–128
Suspicious Transaction Report (STR), 228
Sustained competitive advantage (SCA),
    30–31, 46, 48
Swaps, 163, 171, 174–175. *See also* Currency
    swaps; Interest rate swaps; Leveraged
    swaps; Plain vanilla swap
  risks, 175
  uses, 175
Swaptions, 175
Symmetric hedge, 171
Synthetic financial instruments, 166
Synthetic positions, 170
Systematic risk, 142

T

Tangibles, 71
Target markets, 71
    positioning, 57–58
Target-return pricing, 63
Tax laws, 26
Tax Recovery Act of 1986, 26
Tax shelter investments, 233
Taxes, 259–260
T-bond futures. *See* U.S. Treasury bond futures
Teachers Insurance Annuity Association-
    College Retirement Equities Fund
    (TIAA-CREF), 1–3
Technological changes, 26
Technologies, 51
Technology, 63. *See also* Sufficient technology
Term loan, 197, 200
Term strategy, 160, 161
Term-to-maturity strategy, 157, 159
Tertiary stakeholders, 33
Third-party obligations, 233
Thrifts, 214, 240
TIAA-CREF. *See* Teachers Insurance Annuity
    Association-College Retirement Equities
    Fund
Tier 1 capital, 88, 126, 128, 131
Tier 2 capital, 126–128
Timeliness, 182
Total liabilities, 90
Total loans, 91
Trading account securities, 78
Trading risk, 144
Tranches, 203
Transaction costs, 161
Treadway Commission, 245
Treasury Department. *See* U.S. Treasury
    Department
Tripwires, 131, 207
Trust audit committee, 12
Trust committee, 12
Trust department, 258
Trust services, 30
Truth in Lending Act (1968), 204

U

Uniform Bank Performance Reports (UPBRs),
    87, 92, 96–101
    user guide, 97
Unsafe practices, 13–15

Unsecured loans, 133, 190, 191
Unsound practices, 13–15
Unwarranted fringe benefits, 216
UPBRs. *See* Uniform Bank Performance
    Reports
U.S. Department of Commerce, 254, 255
U.S. General Accounting Officer (GAO), 3,
    235, 237, 239, 240, 248, 252, 253
U.S. government agencies, 130
U.S. Supreme Court, 230
U.S. Treasuries, 181
U.S. Treasury bill rates, 140, 141
U.S. Treasury bond futures (T-bond futures),
    168–170
U.S. Treasury Department, 225
U.S. Treasury securities, 27
Usage patterns, 52

V

VA. *See* Veterans Administration
Value. *See* Income/value
    hedging effects, 171–173
    stability, 210
Variable-rate loans, 143
Vault cash, 75
Veterans Administration (VA), 201
Virtual companies, 28
Volatile liability dependence, 97

W

Watchdog committee, 11
White-collar crime, 13, 225, 234
Wire transfers, 233
Withdrawals, 161, 199
Worst cases, 211–213
Worst-case scenario, 181

Y

Year-end adjustments, 74
Year-end averages, 86
Yield curve, 154
Yield curve risk, 144
Yields, 130, 157, 159. *See also* Bond yields;
    Market yields

Z

Zero-coupon bonds, 156=1A